JAMES SHIRLEY, DRAMATIST

JAMES SHIRLEY
DRAMATIST

*A BIOGRAPHICAL
AND CRITICAL STUDY*

BY

ARTHUR HUNTINGTON NASON
M.A. (BOWDOIN); PH.D. (COLUMBIA)

ASSISTANT PROFESSOR OF ENGLISH IN
NEW YORK UNIVERSITY AND INSTRUC-
TOR IN UNION THEOLOGICAL SEMINARY

Benjamin Blom
New York

First published 1915
Reissued 1967 by
Benjamin Blom, Inc. New York 10452
Library of Congress Cat. Card No. 67-23860

PRINTED IN THE U.S.A.

PREFACE

TO eliminate at least a few of the inaccuracies of fact and inference that have perverted previous accounts of Shirley's life; to remove the popular impression—fostered by many a better critic than Charles Kingsley—that Shirley is merely a contributor to the comedy of manners at its worst; to trace Shirley's development as a dramatist from the realistic to the romantic school; and to show the quality of his work not merely in the comedy of manners and of humors but notably in dramatic romance, in romantic comedy, and in romantic tragedy: such, in the fields of scholarship and appreciation, is the endeavor of this biographical and critical study of the principal dramatic poet of the reign of Charles the First.

Begun under the inspiring influence of Professor William Peterfield Trent, continued under the friendly oversight of Professor William Witherle Lawrence, and completed under the searching criticism of Professor Ashley Horace Thorndike, the work here submitted is the result of many satisfying hours of labor in the graduate school of Columbia University.

To these gentlemen preëminently, and to the other

[v]

members of the department of English and Comparative Literature at Columbia, my thanks are due; yet my debt elsewhere must not pass unacknowledged. To the officers of the libraries of Columbia University, of New York University, of Yale, of Harvard, and of the University of Pennsylvania; of the New York City, the Boston, and the Maine State libraries; of the British Museum and the Bodleian; to the officers of Merchant Taylors' School, of St. Mary Woolchurch, of St. Giles Cripplegate, and of St. Giles in the Fields; to the Oxford University Press, to the Misses Stokes and Cox, record agents, to Mr. Arthur P. Monger, photographer, and to The De Vinne Press: to all of these I return grateful thanks.

Nor must I close without a word of hearty congratulation to my friend Dr. Robert Stanley Forsythe of Adelbert College, upon the appearance of his study, *The Relations of Shirley's Plays to the Elizabethan Drama.* Although his conclusions upon certain questions of Shirleian chronology are somewhat more conservative than I could wish, I account his book not merely a most scholarly addition to our knowledge of the plays of Shirley, but also a notable contribution to the history of dramatic art.

A. H. N.

New York University,
    March 16, 1915.

CONTENTS

—

PART I: THE LIFE OF SHIRLEY

CONTENTS

CONTENTS

Part II: THE PLAYS OF SHIRLEY

CONTENTS

Chapter IX. The First Dramatic Period Concluded. From *The Humorous Courtier* to *The Ball*.

Chapter X. The Second Dramatic Period Begun. From *The Arcadia* to *The Young Admiral*.

Chapter XI. The Second Dramatic Period Continued, *The Gamester* and *The Example*.

CHAPTER XIX. CONCLUSION.

CONTENTS

ANNOTATED BIBLIOGRAPHY

LIST OF ILLUSTRATIONS

—

PART I
THE LIFE OF SHIRLEY

CHAPTER I

AMONG the dramatists of the reign of Charles the First, James Shirley stands preëminent: the last of the Elizabethans, the prophet of the Restoration. Born in the spacious times of great Elizabeth, in the very year in which Raleigh and Lord Howard of Effingham took and sacked Cadiz; school-boy, university man, and teacher in the reign of James the First; favorite dramatist of the court of Charles, friend of the king and champion of the queen; follower of the Duke of Newcastle in the Civil War; and then, through the Protectorate and the first six years of the reign of Charles the Second, schoolmaster again and miscellaneous writer: James Shirley, in the course of three score years and ten, embodied in himself as man and dramatist something of the chivalric spirit of the Elizabethans, something of the impetuous loyalty of the Cavaliers, something of the fine patience of the great poet of the Puritans, and something of that licentiousness of thought and speech characteristic of the entire seven-

[3]

teenth century though more often ascribed merely to the courtiers and dramatists of the Restoration.

As a lover of Shakspere, as a student of Lope de Vega, as a reviser of plays by Chapman and by Fletcher, as an avowed disciple of Ben Jonson, Shirley brought to his profession a taste genuinely catholic and a technique highly developed. What part he played in the dramatic activities of his time, we may learn by reading his record for a single twelvemonth. In the spring of 1633, when William Prynne, the Puritan fanatic, virulently assailed the queen and her ladies for participating in a play at court, Shirley, as "Servant to her Majesty," offered the retort discourteous in his ironical dedication to *The Bird in a Cage*. In the autumn of that year, Shirley was the author of the play presented in honor of the king's birthday— the romantic tragicomedy, *The Young Admiral*. In the same year, when Charles desired the dramatization of a favorite story, he, through his Master of the Revels, gave the plot to Shirley. On this plot, Shirley wrote *The Gamester,* which was acted at court on February 6, 1633/4. "The King," wrote Sir Henry Herbert, "sayd it was the best play he had seen for seven years." In that same February of 1633/4, seven months before the youthful Milton produced his masque of *Comus* for the Earl of Bridgewater, Shirley provided another masque, *The Triumph of*

Peace, for the Inns of Court to present before the king. For Milton's masque, Lawes composed the music, and Inigo Jones designed the scenery. For Shirley's masque, the same composer and artist were engaged; and upon its presentation, the Inns of Court expended twenty thousand pounds.

Such was Shirley's record for a single year: look now at his achievement as a whole. In the eighteen years of his career as dramatist, Shirley produced thirty-one plays that have survived. Of these, twelve are pictures of London life and manners—a connecting link between the plays of Jonson and those of Wycherley and Congreve. One, his earliest, is a mixture of the realistic and the romantic styles. The other eighteen are romantic plays—dramatic romance, romantic comedy, and romantic tragedy—plays that recall the work of Fletcher, of Webster, and of Shakspere, and that lead onward to the tragedies and heroic plays of Dryden and of Otway. Well might Milton's nephew, Edward Phillips, writing nine years after Shirley's death, declare that, in dramatic poesy, "he hath written both very much, and for the most part with that felicity that by some he is accounted little inferior to Fletcher himself." Well might he call Shirley "a just pretender to more than the meanest place among English poets."

In the present study of the life and works of Shirley, the endeavor is threefold: first, to examine the little that we know of Shirley's life, to determine, fact by fact, the value of the evidence, and, on a basis of this critical examination, to construct a chronology more accurate than has been hitherto available; second, on a basis of this revised chronology, to restudy the dramatic works of Shirley, in order to determine, if possible, the course of his development as a dramatist; and, third, from this same examination of the plays, to determine the distinctive characteristics of his dramatic works. To the second and third of these endeavors will be devoted the fourteen chapters of Part II; to the first, the five chapters of Part I.

Concerning the events of Shirley's life, which constitute our subject in Part I, the principal accounts are those of Anthony à Wood in his *Athenæ Oxonienses,* 1691–2, of Dyce in 1833, and, more recently, of Fleay, of Ward, and of Nissen. Gosse, Swinburne, Schelling, Neilson, and Schipper have likewise written upon Shirley; but their contributions have been primarily critical rather than biographical. Of the five accounts of Shirley's life, that by Wood is characterized by grave omissions, by assertions based seemingly on hearsay and now incapable of verification, and by at least one conspicuous mistake—the age of the dramatist at death; yet this record is, on many points, our sole "authority," and has been all but universally accepted. The account by Dyce is more scholarly and more complete, and yet leaves much to be desired. Of the articles by Fleay, Ward, and Nissen, each has its excellences, and each embodies, in one department or another, the results of laborious research. Each, however, if I may venture an opinion, has here and there been over-positive on matters not yet certain; each has contributed something to the correction of its predecessors; and yet even the latest, that of Nissen, not only accepts the unsupported statements of Wood without a scruple but even cites that delightfully imaginative paraphrase, Shiels's *Cibber's Lives of the Poets,* 1753, as an authority worthy of credence with the best. My task, therefore, in preparing a new account of Shirley's life, is not to add new facts, but rather to reëxamine the evidence, and to discriminate between what has been proved and what has not. I shall not everywhere reject the accepted facts of Shirley's life merely because the evidence for their truth is lacking; but I shall at least give warning in such cases that I base my statement upon tradition, and on nothing more.

My discussion of the life—as distinguished from the works—of Shirley may be best presented under five heads; and to each I shall devote a chapter. The first chapter, which I have entitled Shirley's Predramatic Period, will recount the events of his career from his birth in 1596 to the licensing of his first play in 1625; the second, Shirley's First Dramatic Period, his career thence to the licensing of *The Ball,* November 16, 1632; the third, Shirley's Second Dramatic Period, from the supposed date of the acting of his *Arcadia,* November 19, 1632, to his departure for Ireland in the spring of 1635/6; the fourth, thence to the closing of the theaters in 1642, his Third Dramatic Period; and the fifth chapter, Shirley's Post-dramatic Period, from the closing of the theaters to his death in 1666. The basis of my division into periods will be more evident when, in Part II, we examine the course of Shirley's development as a dramatist.

Concerning the parentage of James Shirley, previous biographers have offered nothing that bears examination. Indeed, of the three hypotheses they have advanced, each can be all but conclusively refuted. The first of these—that our dramatist was of the Warwickshire family of the same name—was one of two proposed by Anthony à Wood: "James Shirley," he says, "the most noted drammatick Poet of his time, . . . was descended from the Shirleys of Sussex or Warwickshire, as by his Arms (if he had right to them) painted over his picture hanging in the School-gallery at Oxon, appears."[1] The arms in the

[1] Wood, 1691–1692, II, 260; cf. 1817, III, 737.

Oxford portrait are indeed the arms of the Shirleys of Warwickshire: "Paly of six or and azure, a quarter ermine." [2] To be more explicit, they are the arms borne, in Shirley's time, by Sir George Shirley, Bart., lord of Eatington (1559–1622); by his son, Sir Henry Shirley, Bart., lord of Eatington (1588–1633/4); and then, successively, by the two sons of Sir Henry: Sir Charles Shirley, Bart. (1623–1646), and Sir Robert Shirley, Bart. (1629–1656). [3] Two circumstances, moreover, might support the supposition that the dramatist was related to these Shirleys of Eatington, or Etindon, in County Warwick. In 1632, he dedicated his comedy, *Changes, or Love in a Maze,* to "the right honorable the Lady Dorothy Shirley," wife of Sir Henry Shirley, Bart. [4] In 1639, Thomas Bancroft included four doggerel lines to one James Shirley, presumably our dramatist, in the *Two*

[2] E. P. Shirley, *Noble and Gentle Men of England,* pp. 255, 254; cf. E. P. Shirley, *Stemmata Shirleiana,* 1841, pp. 13, 78, 102, etc.

[3] *Ibid.,* p. 48.

[4] Gifford, in the Gifford and Dyce edition of the works of Shirley, II, 271, note, appears to be incorrect in several of his statements concerning Lady Dorothy Shirley and her husband. According to E. P. Shirley, *Stemmata Shirleiana,* 1841, p. 48, the Lady Dorothy Devereux, second daughter of Robert, second earl of Essex, married not Sir Robert Shirley, Bart., as Gifford says, but Sir Henry Shirley, Bart. The date of the wedding was not 1615, as Gifford says, but was August 1, 1616. Sir Robert Shirley, born 1629, was not her husband but her son. Moreover, she was not "probably a widow when these verses were addressed to her" in 1632; for Sir Robert did not die in February, 1632, as Gifford asserts, but on February 8, 1633/4.

Bookes of Epigrammes that he dedicated to Sir Henry's successor, Sir Charles Shirley, Bart. Neither these dedications, however, nor the presence of a namesake's arms in the Bodleian portrait, can establish James Shirley's claim to be included among the Warwick Shirleys. Even Wood, who first offered this hypothesis, qualified it with the words: "his Arms (if he had right to them)"; and the worthy Oxonian would scarcely have expressed this doubt without good reason. E. P. Shirley, who gave much time and labor to establishing the pedigree of the Shirley family, "Lords of Nether Etindon in the County of Warwick," found no place in the family tree for James Shirley the dramatist. In the first edition of his *Stemmata Shirleiana,* 1841, E. P. Shirley referred to "the poet, who, from the arms which he assumed, *is supposed* to have sprung from some younger branch of the house of Eatington";[5] but in his enlarged edition, 1873, he changed his wording to "perhaps *supposed himself* to have sprung";[6] and further on he wrote: "Of James Shirley the poet . . . there is no reason to believe that he belonged to the House of Ettington."[7] So thorough were the researches of E. P. Shirley, that we should account his judgment practically conclusive.

[5] E. P. Shirley, *Stemmata Shirleiana,* 1841, p. 92.
[6] *Ibid.,* 1873, p. 119.
[7] *Ibid.,* 1873, p. 339.

A second hypothesis, that James Shirley was of the Shirley (or Sherley) family of Sussex, is no more tenable than the first, and yet it is not without supporters. They have even asserted his close kinship to Henry Sherley, author of *The Martyred Soldier.* As early as 1644, a news-letter quoted in Tierney's *Arundel*[8] referred to "Master Henry Sherley, kinsman to Mr. James Sherley the playwright, and who did excell him in that faculty"; and Wood, in 1691–2, remarked: "I find one Henry Shirley, gent., author of a play called *The Martyr'd Soldier,* Lond. 1638. qu. Which Henry I take to be brother or near kinsman to James."[9] Fleay inferred, "from the fact that Henry Shirley [who was murdered in 1627] preceded James by so many years, that he was his father and not his brother as has been generally conjectured."[10] More interesting is the fact, unnoted, I believe, by previous biographers, that in the engraving of James Shirley inscribed "G. Phenik pinx: R. Gaywood fecit 1658," the arms are differenced with a crescent—a mark of cadency which, according to *Stemmata Shirleiana,*[11] was regularly borne by the Sherleys of Wiston in Sussex, Henry Sherley's fam-

[8] Tierney's *Arundel,* I, 67, note *a.* See also *Notes and Queries,* 1st Ser., XII, 26–27, July 14, 1885; and Hunter, *Chorus Vatum Anglicanorum,* III, 417–422.

[9] Wood, 1691–1692, II, 262; cf. 1817, III, 741.

[10] Fleay, in *Anglia,* VIII, 414.

[11] E. P. Shirley, *Stemmata Shirleiana,* 1841, pp. 179–224.

ily. If this engraving be, as some suppose, a modi-
fication of the Bodleian portrait, the presence of the
crescent may be indicative either of growing modesty
in the aging dramatist or of greater honesty in the
engraver; but it does not necessarily imply that Shirley was now asserting kinship with the Sussex Sherleys. The crescent, difference of the second son,[12]
was borne by the Sherleys of Wiston in Sussex because they were descended from Ralph Sherley of
Wiston, Esq. (*ob.* 1510), *second* son of Ralph Shirley
of Ettington, Esq.;[13] but the crescent might be borne
by the descendant of the second son of any other generation. Nevertheless, just as the Bodleian portrait
gives to James Shirley the arms that of right belonged
to Sir Charles Shirley, Bart., lord of Eatington, and
then to his brother and successor, Sir Robert, as
sixth in descent from John Shirley, *eldest* son of
Ralph Shirley, Esq., lord of Eatington;[14] so the engraving of 1658 gives to the dramatist the arms that
of right had belonged to Henry Sherley, gent., author
of *The Martyred Soldier,* as fifth in descent from the
second son of the same Lord of Eatington.[15]

How unfounded was James Shirley's claim to kin-

[12] Legh, *Accedens of Armory,* 1576, fols. 107a–110b; Bossewell,
Workes of Armorie, 1597, fol. 10b.

[13] E. P. Shirley, *Stemmata Shirleiana,* 1841, p. 180; 1873, p. 235.

[14] *Ibid.,* 1841, pp. 30 and 48; 1873, pp. 39 and 61.

[15] *Ibid.,* 1841, p. 180; 1873, p. 235.

ship with this Sussex branch, has been made evident
by the researches of E. P. Shirley. In the second edition of his *Stemmata Shirleiana,* he gives in detail the
genealogy of the Sherleys[16] of Wiston in Sussex. In
this he records the names of the sons and daughters
of Sir Thomas Sherley the younger, among whom
Henry Sherley, author of *The Martyred Soldier,*
was the oldest to survive to manhood. This Henry
Sherley, according to Harl. MSS. 4023, p. 122 B, was
"sine sobole occisus." If this be true, Henry Sherley
cannot have been James Shirley's father; if the list of
the children of Sir Thomas be correct, Henry Sherley cannot have been James Shirley's brother.[17] In
1855, E. P. Shirley published a long communication
concerning the identity of Henry Sherley. With regard to Henry's alleged kinship to the greater dramatist, he says: "I wish I could include the more cele-
brated poet James Shirley—the author of those noble

[16] To base any argument upon the spelling of the name, would be
unwise. It is true that the Sussex branch, according to E. P. Shirley
(*Stemmata Shirleiana,* 1841, p. 179, note), generally spelled the name
"Sherley," and that the dramatist usually spelled it "Shirley." But
in this we find no perfect uniformity. The name is spelled with an
"i" on most of his title-pages, in his will (if my transcript be accurate), and even in the engraving of 1658, "Jacobus Shirlæus." On the
other hand, the name is spelled "Sherley" in the probation register of
Merchant Taylors' School; "Shurley" in the register of christenings
of St. Giles without Cripplegate, February 26, 1624/5; "Shirly" (but
never "Sherley") on a small minority of his title-pages; and "Sherley"
in the burial record of St. Giles in the Fields, October 29, 1666.

[17] E. P. Shirley, *Stemmata Shirleiana,* 1841, pp. 207–208; 1873, pp.
269–272.

verses 'The glories of our birth and state'—also among the worthies of the family tree; but the genealogy of the Shirleys of Sussex is so well ascertained that I fear this to be impossible." [18]

A third hypothesis remains: the very natural assumption that James Shirley the dramatist, born in London and educated in a London school, was in some way related to that James Shirley of London, goldsmith, who was the financial agent of the Plymouth colony. Unfortunately for our hypothesis, however, the genealogy of this family also is well known—indeed, a matter of contemporary official record. In the Visitation of London for the years 1633, 1634, and 1635, [19] we find the pedigrees of John Sherley of London, goldsmith, and of his brother, James Sherley of London, goldsmith, second and third sons respectively of Robert Sherley of Wistonson and of London, gentleman, who was son of Rafe or Ralph Sherley of Wistonson, Cheshire. These pedigrees name the children of both John and James, and mention a James among the sons of each; but they forbid our identifying the dramatist with any James belong-

[18] *Notes and Queries,* 1st Ser., XII, 27; July 14, 1855.

[19] *Publications of the Harleian Society,* XVII: *The Visitation of London, Anno Domini 1633, 1634, and 1635. Made by Sr. Henry St. George, Kt., Richmond Herald, and Deputy and Marshal to Sr. Richard St. George, Kt., Clarencieux King of Arms. Vol. II. Edited by Joseph Jackson Howard, LL.D., F.S.A. London, 1883,* pp. 235–236.

ing to this London family. Our dramatist cannot be identical with James Sherley, goldsmith, for the will of the dramatist names a list of children that in no wise agrees with those of the goldsmith as recorded in the Visitation. Our dramatist cannot be identical with either James the son or James the nephew of the goldsmith; for neither could have been born as early as 1596. Moreover, the arms of this family as exemplified to the goldsmith's father, Robert Sherley of London, gentleman, by Sir William Segar, September 10, 1609, are not the arms used by James Shirley the dramatist, but "Gules, a chevron checky argent and sable between three fleurs-de-lis or; crest, on a torse, three arrows or, entwined with a wreath vert."[20] "These bearings," says E. P. Shirley, "if there is any use or meaning in the science of heraldry, point to a totally different origin for this London family."[21]

In short, if we are to consider only the three hypotheses proposed by previous biographers, we find no trace of Shirley's parentage. In the genealogies of the Shirleys of Warwick, of the Sherleys of Sussex, and of the Sherleys who were London goldsmiths, our dramatist receives no place.

But why confine ourselves to these hypotheses? Why not seek our dramatist (despite his arms) out-

[20] *Ibid.*, and *Stemmata Shirleiana*, 1873, p. 335.
[21] *Stemmata Shirleiana*, 1873, p. 335.

side the three lines known to heraldry? Once we admit this possibility, we come immediately to a fourth hypothesis: an hypothesis not before proposed by any scholar, and yet, in view of the evidence extant, an hypothesis both obvious and satisfying. Two clues we have. The first is Wood's statement concerning the place of Shirley's birth. "James Shirley, the most noted drammatick Poet of his time," says Wood, "did make his first entry on the stage of this transitory world, in or near, the Parish of S. Mary Woolchurch (where the Stocks market now is) within the City of London."[22] "So," adds Wood in a foot-note, "I have been informed by his Son, the Butler of Furnivals inn, in Holbourn, near London."[23] Our second clue concerns the date of Shirley's birth: a series of statements, strangely inconsistent, in the probation register of Merchant Taylors' School. In the tables of the "Schooles Probation" for December 11, 1608, March 11, 1609, and September 11, 1609, the date of Shirley's "nativitie" is set down merely as "1596 Sept." In the seven tables following, from December 11, 1609, to December 11, 1611, inclusive, the date is written "1596 Sept. 13." In the final table, March 11, 1612, the date becomes "1596 Sept. 18." As Dyce remarked in his account of Shirley,

[22] Wood, 1691–1692, II, 260; cf. 1817, III, 737.
[23] *Ibid.,* note.

an d'm
1596

15 Giles the sonne of John Wheatland was baptized the iiijth of februarie.

16 Elizabeth daughter of George Dale was baptized the viijth of marche.

1596

1 Thomas the sonne of John Dale was baptized the fourth of aprill.

2 John the sonne of John Fidler was baptized the xxiiijth of aprill.

3 Thomas the sonne of Thomas Hill was baptized the second of maie.

4 Anne the daughter of Richard Crot was baptized the xxiiijth of June.

5 Jone the daughter of Isaac Fillmore was baptized the xxvjth of June.

6 Willm the sonne of Willm Horton was baptized the fyrste of Julie.

7 Thomas the sonne of William Eltinton was baptized the xxiijth of august.

8 James the sonne of James Sharlie was baptized the seaventh of september.

9 Reinald the sonne of dudlie Chadoke was baptized the xiijth of september.

10 Thomas the sonne of William Colton was baptized the xxjth of september.

11 Marie the daughter of John Hill was baptized the second of october.

12 Nicolas the sonne of Robart Barwike was baptized the xiijth of october.

13 Martha the daughter of Willm Wilson was baptized the xxiijth of october.

14 Thomas the sonne of Anthome Crew was baptized the tenth of november.

an regni
39

15 Mildred the daughter of Robart dodson was baptized the sixteenth of Januarie.

16 Nathanael the sonne of Edward Woodward was baptized the twentieth of februarie.

an d'm
1597

1597

1 Edward the sonne of Thomas White was baptized the xxiijth of aprill.

2 William the sonne of Willm Harrison was baptized the fyrst of maie.

RECORD OF THE BAPTISM OF "JAMES THE SONNE OF JAMES SHARLIE"

From the Register of St. Mary Woolchurch, September 7, 1596

"Whether the latter date was a correction of the former, or a slip of the pen, cannot be discovered."[24]

Such are our two clues: as to the place of Shirley's birth, a statement at once definite and well substantiated; as to the date, three statements of unknown authority, incomplete or contradictory, but agreeing upon the month and year. If, from this evidence, we turn now to the parish records of St. Mary Woolchurch, we find, indeed, no record of a James Shirley born either on the thirteenth or the eighteenth of September, 1596; but we do find, in the record of baptisms for that year, the following entry:

James the sonne of James Sharlie was baptized the seventh of September.[25]

Who was this "James the sonne of James Sharlie"

[24] Dyce, in *Works*, I, iii, note. For my transcripts from this entry-book, I am indebted to the courtesy of the present officers of Merchant Taylors' School and to the accuracy of Misses Stokes & Cox, record agents, London. Concerning the original records, they report: "The volumes of this Register were rebound this year [1911], but it contains no frontispiece or title-page. The pages whence references were taken were all in good state of preservation, the writing good and clear, and all figures distinctly made. Unfortunately, several gaps occur throughout, owing to missing pages."

[25] A photograph of the page of the parish record on which appears this entry, is among my illustrations. Cf. p. 310 of the published *Transcript of the United Parishes of S. Mary Woolnoth and S. Mary Woolchurch Haw, in the City of London . . . 1886 . . .* For the references to William Sharlie and his family, see *Ibid.*, pp. lviii, 300, 301, 302, 370, 371, 372, 378, 379; to Thomas and his family, *Ibid.*, pp. 308, 347, 379; to James and his family, *Ibid.*, pp. 310, 311, 312, 313, 383, 384, and 388.

baptized in the same parish and in the very month in which our James Shirley is alleged to have been born? An analysis of the entries that contain the family name enables us to present with reasonable assurance his genealogy.

The first of the name to be mentioned in the parish records is one William Sharlye, Sharley, Shorley, or Sharlie—seemingly the grandfather of "James son of James." To him and to his wife and children apparently refer eleven entries. On November 30, 1564, was buried an unnamed "childe of William Sharlie." On April 25, 1566, was baptized "Thomas, son of William Shorley"; on January 18, 1567/8, "James, son of William Sharlie"; and on July 3, 1569, "Brigit, daughter of William Sharlie." On July 19 of the same year was buried "Brigit, daughter of William Sharlie." On November 20, 1571, was baptized "Elizabeth, daughter of William Sharlie"; and on November 13, 1573, "Elizabeth, daughter of William Sharlie," was buried. In the list of churchwardens of the parish, there appears the double entry: "1576. John Newman—William Sharlye. 1577. William Sharley—John Maskall." And finally, with honorable prefix, were buried, February 21, 1592/3, "Mr. William Sharlie," and, on March 1, 1593/4, "Mistris Sharley, Widoe."

To Thomas, the elder son of William, and to his

family, seemingly refer the entries following: On June 29, 1590, was baptized "Elizabeth, daughter of Thomas Sharlie"; and on September 2, 1594, "Elizabeth, daughter of Thomas Sharley," was buried. On January 21, 1598/9, were married "Thomas Sherle and Elizabeth Lacke."

Of more immediate interest is the record of William's second son, James, and of his family. First among his children—presumably the future dramatist—was "James, son of James Sharlie," baptized September 7, 1596. Next comes "Ellin, daughter of James Sharlie," baptized May 1, 1598. Third comes "Elizabeth, daughter of James Sharloe," baptized July 15, 1599. The fourth is "William, son of James Sharlie," baptized December 27, 1601, and presumably identical with the "William Sharlie" of unnamed parentage who was buried September 12, 1603. The fifth is "Marie, daughter of James Sharlie," baptized March 4, 1603/4, and buried September 18, 1606. Finally, on June 2, 1617, was buried "Mr. James Sharlie."

Such, for three generations, is the family into which was born "James, son of James Sharlie," baptized in St. Mary Woolchurch, September 7, 1596. Was this the James Shirley, Dramatist, who, according to the statement of his son to Wood, was born in St. Mary Woolchurch, and who, according to the register of Merchant Taylors' School, was born either on the thirteenth or the eighteenth of September, 1596—six days or eleven days, be it noted, subsequent to the date of this baptismal record? Absolute certainty in such a case we must not claim; but, in view of the agreement as to place and of the approximate agreement as to date, we may, until further evidence appears, account this explanation all but certain: that the "James, son of James Sharlie" baptized in St. Mary Woolchurch, September 7, 1596, was none other than the future dramatist.

Concerning Shirley's schooling, we have the main facts. Wood asserts that he was "educated in Grammar learning in Merchant Taylors School";[26] and the records of the school confirm this statement. The eleven tables just cited, concur in the statement that he was admitted to the school October 4, 1608. At the "probation and triall of the whole school" made by the master and three ushers December 11, 1608, Shirley stood thirteenth in the fourth form; by March he was in the ninth place; and by September, in the seventh. Promoted to the fifth form, he fell temporarily to fifteenth place; but in the tables for September 11, 1610, December 11, 1610, and March 11, 1611, he stood first in his form. In the sixth form, he stood tenth in September and December, 1611;

[26] Wood, 1691–1692, II, 260; cf. 1817, III, 737.

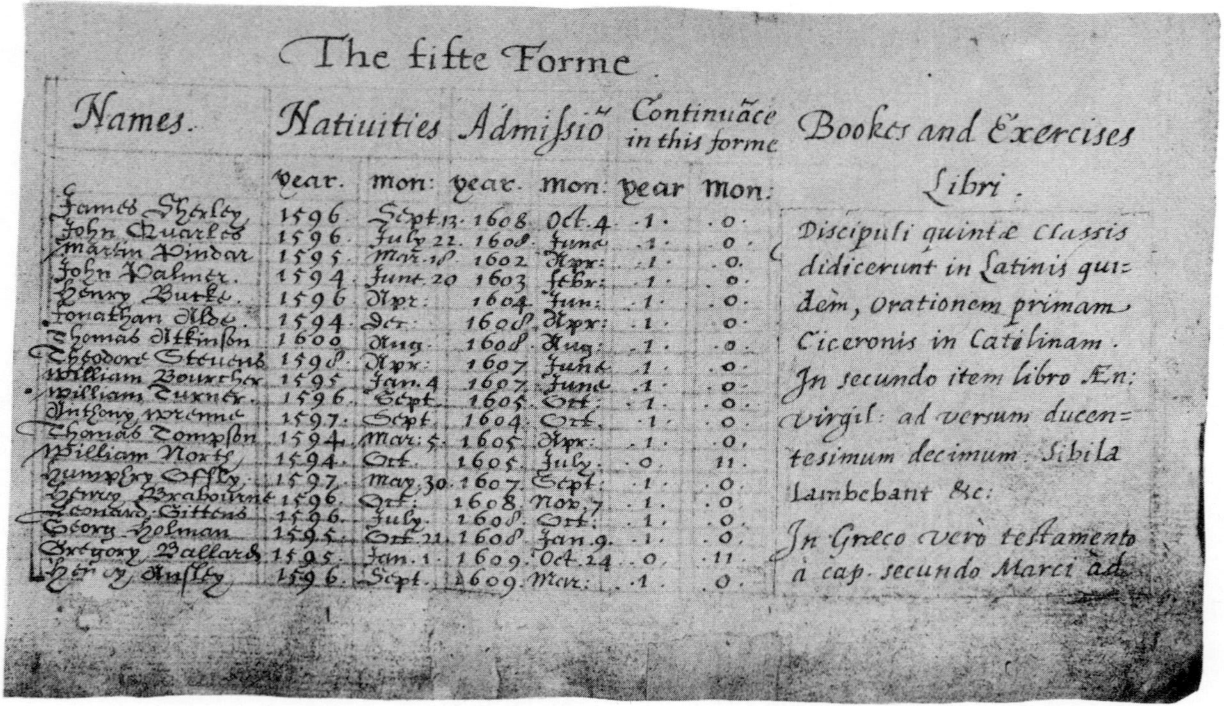

The fifte Forme.

Names.	Natiuities		Admissiō		Continuãce in this forme	
	year.	mon:	year.	mon:	year	mon:
James Shirley	1596	Sept.13	1608	Oct.4	1	0
John Quarles	1596	July 22	1608	June	1	0
Martin Windar	1595	Mar.18	1602	Apr:	1	0
John Walmer	1594	June 20	1603	Febr:	1	0
Henry Burke	1596	Apr:	1604	Jun:	1	0
Jonathan Alde	1594	Oct:	1608	Apr:	1	0
Thomas Atkinson	1600	Aug	1608	Aug:	1	0
Theodore Stevens	1598	Apr:	1607	June	1	0
William Bourcher	1595	Jan.4	1607	June	1	0
William Turner	1596	Sept	1605	Oct	1	0
Anthony Wrenne	1597	Sept	1604	Oct	1	0
Thomas Tompson	1594	Mar:5	1605	Apr:	1	0
William North	1594	Oct	1605	July	0	11
Humphry Offly	1597	May 30	1607	Sept	1	0
Henry Brabourne	1596	Oct:	1608	Nov.7	1	0
Leonard Gittens	1596	July	1608	Oct:	1	0
Georg Holman	1595	Oct 21	1608	Jan.9	1	0
Gregory Ballard	1595	Jan.1	1609	Oct.24	0	11
Henry Ansley	1596	Sept	1609	Mar:	1	0

Bookes and Exercises

Libri.

Discipuli quintæ Classis didicerunt in Latinis quidem, Orationem primam Ciceronis in Catilinam. In secundo item libro Æn: Virgil: ad versum ducentesimum decimum: Sibila lambebant &c:

In Greco verò testamento à cap. secundo Marci ad

RECORD OF JAMES SHIRLEY IN THE FIFTH
FORM OF MERCHANT TAYLORS' SCHOOL

From the Register of the School's Probation, September 11, 1610

and eighth on March 11, 1612. For the probations of September and December, 1612, the page is missing; and when the record resumes with the probation of March, 1613, the name of Shirley is not there. We may conclude with Dyce, however, that, "he left the school on the 11th of June, [1612], the annual election day, when the 'upper boys' almost invariably depart." [27]

Of James Shirley's university career—if indeed he had one—we can state little with assurance; but the account of Wood is interesting if not authoritative:

Shirley . . . was . . . educated in Grammar learning in Merchant Taylors School, and transplanted thence to S. Johns Coll., but in what condition he lived there, whether in that of a Servitour, Batler, or Commoner, I cannot yet find. At the same time Dr. Will Laud presiding that house, he had a very great affection for him, especially for the pregnant parts that were visible in him, but then having a broad or large mole upon his left cheek, which some esteemed a deformity, that worthy Doctor would often tell him that he was an unfit Person to take the sacred function upon him, and should never have his consent so to do. Afterwards leaving this University without a degree, he went to Cambridge, where I presume he took those in Arts: so that soon after entring into holy Orders, he became a minister of God's word in, or near to, S. Albans in Hertfordshire.[28]

[27] Dyce, in *Works,* I, iv.
[28] Wood, 1691–1692, II, 260; cf. 1817, III, 737.

[21]

Whether these assertions of Wood, which have been received and elaborated by Shirley's biographers to the present time, should be accepted in a critical study, is a matter open to debate. It would appear that Wood's statements may not have been based upon a first-hand knowledge; that much of the supplementary evidence is questionable or worse; and that no traces of Shirley's presence have been discovered in the records of either university. Under these circumstances, a detailed examination of the evidence is here appropriate.

To Wood's assertion that Shirley was once a student of St. John's College, Oxford, it is objected, first, that no record of his presence has survived at the university. "I never remember," wrote Bliss, the editor of Wood's *Athenæ,* to Dyce, "to have had a longer, and certainly never a more unsatisfactory search than in the present instance; for no entry whatever of James Shirley can I find, although I have looked over every book that can throw any light on such an admission, if it ever took place. . . . I have also had access to a list of the members of St. John's College, *actually in Laud's own handwriting,* and no such name occurs." [29]   Are we to accept Wood's assertions in the absence of official record?

And, secondly, what witness supports Wood in de-

[29] Dyce, in *Works,* I, v, note.

claring Shirley an Oxonian? One Shiels, who published in 1753 that charming work of fiction, *Cibber's Lives of the Poets*. Let whoever thinks of Shiels as an "authority," compare his account of Shirley[30] line for line with that of Wood. If ever there was a cheerful plagiarist, not lacking in imagination, Shiels was the man. And yet, his paraphrase of Wood has recently been cited[31] as if to corroborate Wood's statements.

But the portrait of Shirley—does not its presence in the Bodleian Gallery at Oxford prove that Shirley was once a student there? Not necessarily. Indeed, we might with equal reason argue—if we had no other clue—that the story that Shirley was once an Oxford student was invented to account for the presence of the picture.

And finally, it might even be objected that Wood himself is a witness neither reliable nor competent: that Wood—writing an *Athenæ Oxonienses*—must claim Shirley as a sometime Oxford man—even upon no better evidence than the presence of the portrait in the Bodleian Gallery—or must omit from his list of notables "the most noted dramatic poet of his time"; and that Wood, writing in 1691–2 concerning the events of 1612–18, was scarcely in a position, even had he the desire, to set forth the truth.

[30] Cibber, 1753, II, 26–32.   [31] Nissen, pp. 7–8.

The second half of this objection will bear elaboration. Was Wood in a position to know the facts concerning Shirley's alleged career at Oxford? It is possible, of course, that he had access to university records that no more exist; but his own words, we must admit, give precisely the opposite impression. He gives no dates; he "cannot yet find" whether Shirley lived at Oxford as "Servitour, Batler, or Commoner"; he is specific only with respect to the anecdote of the mole and Dr. Laud, and such an anecdote might have originated anywhere. Had Wood ever met our dramatist? Not when Shirley was in Oxford (if he ever was): for Shirley left Merchant Taylors' School in 1612; and Wood was not born until December 17, 1632.[32] Nor had Wood met our dramatist in London: for Shirley died in 1666; and Wood's first visit to London, as he himself expressly says, was made in June, 1667.[33]

And yet, notwithstanding these objections, I incline to the opinion that Wood's statements may be substantially correct. He had been born in Oxford, and had there spent nearly his entire life. Who, then, so well equipped as Wood accurately to record the traditions of the university? Wood, by his own statement, had been "informed" of Shirley's birthplace by Shir-

[32] Wood's autobiography in *The Lives of . . . Leland . . . Hearne and . . . Wood . . . Vol. II. Oxford . . . MDCCLXXII*, p. 2.
[33] *Ibid.*, p. 206.

ley's son, "the Butler of Furnivals inn, in Holbourn, near London." May he not have been "informed" by the same son, of Shirley's university career? The bare fact that Bliss could find no record of Shirley at Oxford University does not prove that such a record did not once exist. As for Shiels's testimony, it can affect the truth no more one way than the other. If Shirley made but a brief stay at the university, it is not surprising that Wood could give no positive details; but as to the mere fact of Shirley's presence, Wood would be likely to know the truth, and would scarcely dare to risk a falsehood in a case in which, after all, he had so little to gain and was so liable to detection. In the absence of official record—especially in this instance, in which the records appear to be extant—we must be cautious in accepting Wood; nevertheless, that Shirley was for a time a student at St. John's College, Oxford, is at least possible.

As for Wood's other assertion, that Shirley was ultimately a resident at Cambridge, its truth is rather more than possible. Indeed, the witnesses are even agreed upon his college and, approximately, upon the year of his degree. The year, moreover, tallies well with the date of his leaving Merchant Taylors' School.

Of the evidence for Shirley's residence at Cambridge—as of the evidence for his residence at Oxford—much is open to objection. Wood himself is especially indefinite: "Afterwards, leaving this University [Oxford] without a degree, he went to Cambridge where I presume he took those in Arts." Even Wood, be it noted, merely "presumes" that Shirley took degrees.

In elaboration and support of Wood, Dyce offers two pieces of evidence, neither of which, if isolated, will bear examination. The first of these is an alleged transcript of a title-page quoted in *Censura Literaria* "from a MS. note to Astle's copy of Wood's *Athenæ*" as follows: *"Eccho, or the Infortunate Lovers, a poem, by James Sherley, Cant. in Art. Bacc. Lond. 1618. 8vo. Primum hunc Arethusa mihi concede laborem."* [34] This transcript follows Wood in ascribing Shirley's baccalaureate degree to Cambridge, and includes a date by which Shirley might possibly have achieved the honor. But will the transcript bear examination? Do not the order and content of this title-page render it an object of suspicion? Why should the motto stand *below* the date? Why should the abbreviation "8vo." stand *amidst* the title? If the transcriber took such liberties as these, why may he not have inserted the *"Cant. in Art. Bacc."* upon his own authority—or perhaps on the authority of

[34] Dyce, in *Works,* I, vi, quoting Brydges, *Censura Literaria,* II, 381, ed. 1815. The edition of 1806 gives the passage as II, 382.

Wood? In the Stationers' Register, moreover, the entry for this book runs thus: "4 Januarij 1617 [i.e. 1617/18]. *Ecc[h]o and Narcissus the 2 vnfortunate Louers* written by Jeames Sherley."[35] In view of all these uncertainties, do Dyce and his modern followers do well to offer as proof of Shirley's university degree, this note in manuscript written no one knows by whom or when? Even were the transcript self-consistent, why should its anonymous testimony be accepted?

As a further proof that Shirley received a baccalaureate degree from Cambridge, Dyce offers a manuscript addition written upon the fly-leaf of a copy of *Lacrymæ Cantabrigienses,* 1619, in the possession of one David Laing of Edinburgh, and by him communicated to Dyce.[36] This addition consists of verses and an epitaph, signed *"Flens post posuit Jac. Shirley, Aul. Cather. in Art. Bac."* A portion of these verses Shirley elsewhere acknowledged as his own; but the value of the alleged signature as proof of Shirley's academic honors depends upon who put it in this book, and when. Without further information, its evidence is worthless.

Dyce's third witness, fortunately for Wood, is more reliable: a "memorandum in the hand-writing of the

---

[35] *Stationers' Register,* ed. Arber, III, 286.
[36] *Works,* VI, 514–515, note.

accurate Dr. Farmer"[37] in Dyce's copy of Shirley's *Poems,* 1646: "James Shirley, B. A., Cath. Hall, 1619."[38] If we grant—as perhaps we should not grant—that Dyce was correct in assuming this note to be by Farmer, we have here the testimony of the man to whose favorable mention of Shirley in *An Essay on the Learning of Shakspere,* 1767, Dyce[39] and Ward[40] attribute the revival of Shirley's reputation as a dramatist. "What was Dr. Farmer's authority for the memorandum," says Dyce, "I cannot discover."[41] Were we relying wholly on the evidence of "the accurate Dr. Farmer," this admission would be fatal; but as Dr. Farmer's testimony is but supplementary, we may content ourselves with the possibility that Farmer, as principal librarian of Cambridge University, had access to sources of information now unknown.

The best evidence that Wood spoke truly concerning Shirley's connection with Cambridge University, occurs in the thirteenth epigram in the first book of *Two Bookes of Epigrammes and Epitaphs . . . Written By Thomas Bancroft . . . 1639:*

[37] Dyce, in *Works,* I, vi.

[38] *Ibid.*

[39] *Ibid.,* I, xi.

[40] Ward, in *Dictionary of National Biography,* LII, 129, and in *English Dramatic Literature,* III, 95.

[41] Dyce, in *Works,* I, vi, note.

TO IAME[S] SHIRLEY

Iames, thou and I did spend some precious yeeres
    At Katherine-Hall; since when, we sometimes feele
In our poetick braines, (as plaine appeares)
    A whirling tricke, then caught from Katherine's
        wheele.[42]

Here at last we have passably good evidence in support of Wood; for that *two* James Shirleys of the period were possessed of "poetick braines" is scarcely possible.

If to this explicit statement of the epigrammatist, we add the fact that Shirley, later in life, was the author of a Latin grammar, we need neither the anonymous insertions in Astle's copy of Wood's *Athenæ* and Laing's copy of *Lacrymæ Cantabrigienses,* nor the "memorandum in the hand-writing of the accurate Dr. Farmer," to prove that James Shirley "did spend some precious yeeres at Katherine-Hall." True it is, that Shirley's name appears nowhere in the records of that college; but in this case, unlike that of St. John's College, Oxford, the omission is easily explained: according to a letter quoted by Dyce, "the dates in the Admission and Commons' Books at Catherine Hall go no farther back than the year 1642."[43] In view, therefore, of the testimony of

[42] Cf. Dyce, in *Works,* I, v, and note.
[43] *Ibid.,* I, v–vi, note.

Bancroft's epigram, and of the absence of all evidence to the contrary, we may conclude that Wood's assertion concerning Shirley's *residence* at Cambridge is highly probable.

Whether, as Wood "presumes," Shirley *took degrees* at Cambridge, is another question; and the fact that Shirley on no title-page extant makes use of a degree, renders this question doubly pointed. Fleay, to be sure, accepting the accuracy of the manuscript note in Astle's copy of Wood's *Athenæ,* insists that on January 4, 1617/18, the date when *Eccho and Narcissus* was entered in the Stationers' Register,[44] Shirley was already "B.A."[45] But of the title-page noted in Astle's volume, no original exists; and we have seen reason to believe that the words *"Cant. in Art. Bacc."* may be an insertion of the transcriber. Probably much more reliable is the "memorandum in the handwriting of the accurate Dr. Farmer": "James Shirley, B. A., Cath. Hall, 1619."[46] But precisely how reliable this is, we are now unable to discover. If, as we believe, the "Mr. James Sharlie" who was buried on June 2, 1617, was the father of the future dramatist, then it is not impossible that the death of the father may have prevented the graduation of the

[44] *S. R.,* ed. Arber, III, 286.
[45] Fleay, in *Anglia,* VIII, 405.
[46] Dyce, in *Works,* I, vi.

son. In short, the question whether Shirley actually received even a baccalaureate degree cannot with certainty be answered.

I conclude then, with respect to Shirley's alleged university career: (1) that, notwithstanding the absence of Shirley's name from the extant records of St. John's College, Oxford, his residence there is, in view of the testimony of Wood, a possibility; (2) that, in view of Wood's testimony and of the explicit statement of the Bancroft epigram, Shirley's residence at Catherine Hall, Cambridge, is highly probable; but (3) that until more certain evidence appears, we shall do well to avoid saying that Shirley did or did not receive degrees in arts.

The strongest evidence, however, of James Shirley's university training, is to be found not in these fugitive documents but in his subsequent career and in his works.

For the five or six years from Shirley's supposed departure from the university to his appearance as a London playwright, we know of Shirley chiefly from the account of Wood:

Soon after entring into holy Orders, he became a Minister of God's word in, or near to, S. Albans in Hertfordshire. But being then unsetled in his mind, he changed his Religion for that of Rome, left his Living, and taught a Grammar School in the said Town of S. Alban; which employment also he finding uneasie to him, he retired to the Metropolis, lived in Greys inn, and set up for a play-maker.[47]

Of the accuracy of this account, we cannot judge. Concerning his ministry, we have no evidence; concerning his conversion to the Roman Church, we have only what Dyce and other scholars have been pleased to discover in his dramatic works;[48] and concerning his term as pedagogue, we have merely the more or less unauthenticated statements contained in various histories of Hertfordshire. Of these, the most specific account is that contributed by Leach to Page's *Victoria History of the County of Hertford-shire:*

In January, 1621, another distinguished author illuminated the head mastership of St. Albans. This was James Shirley, known to fame, that is, to the *Dictionary of National Biography,* as 'the last of the Elizabethan dramatists.' . . . At St. Albans the reign of Shirley, or Sherley as he was called, was signalized by a large expenditure on school building, the roof being renewed with no less than 624 lbs. of lead, and by the entry in the account books not merely of the number but of the names of the boys who paid entrance fees. Eight names were entered in 1622–3 in a most excellent copper-plate hand. On 1 July, 1624, Shirley left St. Albans, having become a

[47] Wood, 1691–1692, II, 260–261; cf. 1817, III, 737.
[48] Dyce, in *Works,* I, vii, note, and Gifford, *Ibid.,* II, 52, note; and Ward, *English Dramatic Literature,* III, 90, note.

Romanist, and . . . was followed in January, 1625, by John Westerman . . . appointed [*Corporation Minutes*] at St. Albans 1 July, 1624.[49]

This record brings us at last to the year of Shirley's appearance as a London playwright; but before we enter upon the first period of his dramatic work, we may do well to summarize our conclusions concerning his predramatic period. That James Shirley the dramatist is to be identified with that "James the sonne of James Sharlie" who was baptized in St. Mary Woolchurch on September 7, 1596, and that he was not immediately connected with the Shirleys of Warwick, the Sherleys of Sussex, or the Sherleys who were London goldsmiths, is all but certain. That he attended Merchant Taylors' School from 1608 to 1612 is definitely established. But that he went thence to St. John's College, Oxford, and from there to Catherine Hall, Cambridge; that he was graduated B.A. from Catherine Hall, either in 1619, as Farmer holds, or some time before January 4, 1617/18, as Fleay would have it, or at some other time; that he subsequently proceeded to his M.A., took orders, held a living in or near St. Albans, turned Romanist, and so became master of the grammar school of the same town, founded by charter of Edward VI: all this—unless perhaps that he "did spend some pre-

[49] Page, *The Victoria History of the County of Hertfordshire*, II, 63.

cious yeeres at Katherine-Hall" and that he was for a time master of the St. Albans school—rests upon such vague authority that, although we may account it probable, we must not count it certain. In short, we believe that we know something of Shirley's parentage, birth, and early schooling; but of his youth and early manhood, we must be content, at present, to offer merely this: that the James Shirley who, about the year 1625, "retired to the Metropolis, lived in Greys inn, and set up for a playmaker," had somehow acquired a proper education, and could— or at least did—sign himself "James Shirley, gentleman."

CHAPTER II

SHIRLEY'S FIRST DRAMATIC PERIOD

1625–1632

IN considering the career of Shirley from the licensing of his earliest play, *Love Tricks, or The School of Complement,* February 10, 1624/5, to the licensing of *The Ball,* November 16, 1632, we may best marshal our material under three heads: first, the circumstances of Shirley's arrival in London; second, the chronology of the licensing and publication of his works; and, third, the disputed identity of one of his early plays, *The Brothers* of 1626.

Of the date when Shirley took up his residence in London we have no definite evidence. Wood says merely that, finding the teaching of St. Albans grammar-school "uneasie to him," Shirley "retired to the Metropolis, lived in Greys inn, and set up for a play-maker."[1] Whether he was in residence in London when, on February 10, 1624/5, his first play was

[1] Wood, 1691–1692, II, 261; cf. 1817, III, 737.

licensed for presentation, we cannot prove;[2] but that he was living in town when, on February 26, his eldest son was baptized at St. Giles, Cripplegate, seems probable. In the record of christenings in the Register Book belonging to the parish church of St.

[2] Nissen, in his monograph on Shirley, attempts to place the date when Shirley took up his residence in London, in the period between February 10, 1624/5, and March 27, 1625. His argument in support of this conclusion runs as follows:

"Sir Henry Herbert, the well-known Master of the Revels, licensed on February 10, 1625, the presentation of the play *Love Tricks, with Complements.* . . . That Shirley did not live in London at that time, may be inferred from a passage in the prologue to this play:

> " '. . . This play is
> The first fruits of a Muse that before this
> Never saluted audience, nor doth mean
> To swear himself a factor for the scene.'

"This means," continues Nissen, "that our author, at the time of the composition and of the first presentation of the piece, had by no means the intention of devoting himself to the profession of writing plays; he probably, therefore, at that time still resided at St. Albans. In the following month, on March 27, 1625, King James I died. Shirley composed upon the death of James a poem that must have originated soon afterwards. In it he relates that, on the news of the death of the monarch, he went to the king's palace and from there to Whitehall, where he saluted the new king, Charles. When the change of kings took place, he was, therefore, present in London. From this it follows that he transferred his home to the metropolis in the time between February 10 and March 27, 1625." (Nissen, pp. 8–9.)

In certain of Nissen's conclusions, and still less in Nissen's arguments, I find myself unable to concur. I think it probable that Shirley was in London at the time of King James's death; but my belief is not strengthened by the argument just quoted. Surely the mere fact that Shirley, in his poem *Upon the Death of King James* (*Works,* VI, 443), represents himself as doing what any London gentleman might think to do, is no proof that Shirley really did it. The poet's visit to the king's palace and to Whitehall may, of course, be actual; but I see no more necessity for accounting these lines an autobiographic

Giles without Cripplegate, there occurs, under the date of February 26, 1624/5, the following entry:

Mathias, sonne of Mr. James Shurley, gentleman.[3]

That "Mr. James Shurley, gentleman," is James Shirley the dramatist, we need not question; for, in the will of the dramatist, which I shall later quote more fully, he refers to his "eldest son, Mathias Shirley."[4] Small is the chance that there should be in London at this time, more than one James Shirley, father of a Mathias. We know, at all events, that

document than I do for accounting Shakspere's vituperative sonnets other than artificial exercises. But, granted that Shirley was "present in London" when the change of kings took place: does it follow that he had "transferred his home to the metropolis"? Was Shirley incapable of being "present in London" merely as a visitor? Why, from Shirley's poem *Upon the Death of King James,* must one infer that Shirley had "transferred his home"?

And what of Nissen's argument that Shirley could not have come to London *before* February 10, 1624/5? What has Shirley's prologue to do with it?

> ". . . This play is
> The first fruits of a Muse that before this
> Never saluted audience, nor doth mean
> To swear himself a factor for the scene."

In the first place, why should we accept these lines as a true statement of the poet's purpose? Does not many a young dramatist adopt this very pose until he finds how the critics like his work? And secondly, even if we grant that this passage correctly represents the attitude of Shirley on the day the play was licensed, does it follow that Shirley, at that time, "still resided at St. Albans"? Could not all that the prologue says be true, even though Shirley had lived in London all his life?

[3] From a transcript of the original record, made for the purposes of this monograph.

[4] Prerogative Court of Canterbury, Mico, folio 170.

James Shirley the goldsmith had no son so named.[5]
If, then, our dramatist had an eldest son baptized at
St. Giles, Cripplegate, on February 26, 1624/5, may
we not infer that, on or before that date, James Shirley had taken up his residence in London?[6]

Whatever may have been the date of Shirley's entrance into London, the years 1625 and 1626 saw the
new dramatist well on his way to an assured compe-
tence. His first play, *Love Tricks, with Complements,* was licensed by Sir Henry Herbert, Master of
the Revels, on February 10, 1624/5;[7] and his "second
birth," *The Maid's Revenge,* on February 9, 1625/6.[8]
A third play, *The Wedding,* the licensing of which
is not on record, was presented, if Fleay's hypothesis
be right, on May 31, 1626.[9] A fourth, licensed as
The Brothers, November 4, 1626,[10] has been generally identified with the play published under the same
title in 1652; but is probably to be identified neither

[5] Harleian Society: *The Visitation of London,* II, 235–236.

[6] "It is possible," writes Ward (*English Dramatic Literature,* III,
90), "that an early marriage, which there are indications of his having
contracted in or about 1623, may have added to his difficulties"—an
early marriage at the immature age of twenty-seven! If this Mathias
was Shirley's eldest son, Ward elsewhere writes (*DNB.,* LII, 126),
"an early marriage may have played its part *in the crisis of his life.*"
"Ward hält es für möglich," says Nissen (p. 8), "dass er durch eine
frühe Ehe . . . *in bedrängte Lage geraten sei"!*

[7] Malone, *Shakspere,* 1821, III, 231, note.

[8] *Ibid.*

[9] Fleay, in *English Drama,* II, 236, and in *Anglia,* VIII, 405.

[10] Malone, *Shakspere,* 1821, III, 231, note.

with *The Brothers* of 1652 nor with the play printed by Bullen, in 1883, as *Dicke of Devonshire*.[11] The identity of *The Brothers* I shall discuss at length in the latter portion of this chapter; the date of *The Wedding* I shall consider presently: first, however, it is fitting that I say a word as to the nature of the evidence by which we determine the dates when Shirley's plays were licensed for presentation.

For the dates of the licensing of Shirley's plays, our ultimate source is the office-book of Sir Henry Herbert, Master of the Revels.[12] This book, unfortunately, is not extant: we know it only through the extracts and summaries that Edmond Malone embodied in his edition of Shakspere, 1790 and 1821. As Malone did not make a complete transcript of the

[11] In *A Collection of Old English Plays* . . . *Vol. II*, . . . London. *1883*.

[12] Concerning this office-book, Malone wrote thus: "For the use of this very curious and valuable manuscript, I am indebted to Francis Ingram, of Ribbisford near Bewdley in Worcestershire, Esq., Deputy Remembrancer in the Court of Exchequer. It has lately been found in the same old chest which contained the manuscript Memoirs of Lord Herbert of Cherbury, from which Mr. Walpole about twenty years ago printed the Life of that nobleman, who was elder brother to Sir Henry Herbert." (Malone's *Shakspere,* 1821, III, 57, note.) Again Malone writes: "The office-book of Sir Henry Herbert contains an account of almost every piece exhibited at any of the theatres from August, 1623, to the commencement of the rebellion in 1641, and many curious anecdotes relative to them, some of which I shall presently have occasion to quote. This valuable manuscript, having lain for a considerable time in a damp place, is unfortunately damaged, and in a very mouldering condition: however, no material part of it appears to have perished." (*Ibid.,* 59, note.)

record, but contented himself with bringing together and tabulating the entries concerning the plays of any dramatist, his notes are liable both to error and to omission. We may accept as probably accurate the statement of Malone that he found in Herbert's office-book a record of the licensing of *Love Tricks, The Maid's Revenge,* and *The Brothers,* on the dates mentioned; but we may not infer from the fact that Malone gives no record of *The Wedding,* that therefore it was never licensed. Herbert may have entered the play, and Malone have neglected to transcribe the entry.

However this may be, no record of the licensing of *The Wedding* has been preserved. Ward, indeed, asserts that it was licensed "9 Feb. 1626"; [13] but this statement is obviously a clerical error due to a repetition of the date above—that of the licensing of *The Maid's Revenge.* The accepted date of presentation is fixed by a passage in a mock legal document embodied in Act III, scene ii: "In witness whereof, I have hereunto put my hand and seal . . . the last day of the first merry month and in the second year of the reign of King—Cupid"; [14] i.e., the thirty-first day of May, in the second year of the reign of King Charles. For this clever and plausible interpreta-

[13] Ward, in *DNB.,* LII, 130.
[14] *The Wedding,* III, ii; *Works,* I, 406.

tion, chronologists are indebted to Fleay.[15] As the play was printed in 1629, Fleay's error—if he be in error—is not large.

For nearly two years after the licensing of *The Brothers* of 1626, Shirley brought no new play before the public; then, on October 3, 1628, he obtained license for *The Witty Fair One*.[16] Thirteen months later, on November 3, 1629, *The Grateful Servant* was licensed under the title *The Faithful Servant*.[17] According to their title-pages, these two plays, like all other extant plays of Shirley's first dramatic period, with the single exception of *Changes, or Love in a Maze*,[18] were acted by the Queen's men at Drury Lane.

In the year last mentioned, 1629, *The Wedding*— acted, according to Fleay's hypothesis, three years before—was given to the press: the earliest play of Shirley to be published. Fleay asserts that it was entered for J. Grove;[19] but in the Stationers' Register I find no record. The play, dedicated to William Gowre, Esq., was introduced by commendatory verses

[15] Fleay, in *Anglia*, VIII, 405.

[16] Malone's *Shakspere*, 1821, III, 231, note.

[17] *Ibid.*

[18] "Presented at the Private House in Salisbury Court, by the Company of his Majesties Revels." (Title-page of 1632; from the copy belonging to the late Robert Hoe, Esq.)

[19] Fleay, in *English Drama*, II, 233; but with a reference to *S. R.*, 1638, April 28.

by Edmond Colles, Robert Harvey, Thomas May, John Ford the dramatist, and William Habington. Of these verses, the lines of Ford shall serve as an example:

> Of this Ingenious Comedy, The WEDDING:
> To Mr. James Shirley, the Author.

> The bonds are equal, and the marriage fit,
> Where judgment is the bride, the husband wit.
> Wit hath begot, and judgment hath brought forth,
> A noble issue of delight and worth,
> Grown in this Comedy to such a strength
> Of sweet perfection, as that not the length
> Of days, nor rage of malice, can have force
> To sue a nullity, or work divorce
> Between this well-trimmed Wedding and loud Fame,
> Which shall in every age renew thy name.[20]

The title-page of this edition reads:

The Wedding.   As it was lately Acted by her Maiesties Seruants, at the Phœnix in Drury Lane.   Written By Iames Shirley, Gent.   Horat.—Multaq; pars mei Vitabit Libitinam—London.   Printed for Iohn Groue, and are to be sold at his shop at Furniualls Inne Gate in Holborne. 1629.[20a]

A year later, on February 26, 1629/30, *The Grate-*

---

[20] *Works,* I, lxxi.
[20a] From the copy belonging to the late Robert Hoe, Esq.

ful Servant was entered upon the Stationers' Register for J. Grove.[21]   The title-page of this edition reads:

The Gratefvll Servant.   A Comedie.   As it was lately presented with good applause at the priuate House in Drury-Lane, By her Majesties Servants.   Written by Iames Shirley Gent.—Vsque ego postera Crescam laude recens.   London.   Printed by B. A. and T. F. for John Groue, and are to be sold at his shop at Furnivals-Inne gate, 1630.[22]

Prefixed to the published play were nine poems, including one by Philip Massinger, all written in lavish commendation of the comedy.   "The reason," wrote Shirley, "why my play cometh forth ushered by so many lines, was the free vote of my friends, whom I could not with civility refuse.   I dare not own their character of myself, or play; but I must join with them that have written, to do the comedians justice, amongst whom, some are held comparable with the best that are, and have been, in the world."[23]

In the following year, 1631, three more of Shirley's plays were licensed for presentation: *The Traitor,* May 4;[24] *The Duke,* May 17;[25] and *Love's Cruelty,*

---

[21] *S. R.,* IV, 195.

[22] From the copy belonging to the late Robert Hoe, Esq.

[23] *Works,* II, 5.

[24] Malone's *Shakspere,* 1821, III, 231, note.

[25] *Ibid.,* 232, note.   Fleay, in *English Drama,* II, 237, and Ward, in *DNB.,* LII, 132 but not 133, misprint this date as May 7 for May 17.

November 14.[26]   The second of these is probably
identical with the play which, when entered in the
Stationers' Register, July 29, 1639, was entitled *The
Humorous Courtier.*[27]

To the same year, 1631, belongs the publication of
Love Tricks, under the new title *The Schoole of
Complement,* entered in the Stationers' Register for
F. Constable, February 25, 1630/31.[28]   The title-
page of this edition reads:

> The Schoole of Complement.   As it vvas acted by her
> Maiesties Seruants at the Priuate house in Drury Lane.—
> Hæc placuit semel.   By J. S.   London, Printed by E. A.
> for Francis Constable, and are to be sold at his shop in
> Pauls Church-yard, at the signe of the Crane.   1631.[29]

The year 1632 was equally productive.   On January 10, 1631/2, was licensed *The Changes;*[30] on
April 20, 1632, *Hyde Park;*[31] and on November 16,
The Ball.[32]   A fourth play, *The Arcadia,* probably
belonging likewise to this year, I reserve for the following chapter.   Shirley's only publication for this

[26] Malone's *Shakspere,* 1821, III, 232, note.

[27] *S. R.,* iv, 447.   Fleay, in *Anglia,* VIII, 409, and in *English Drama,*
II, 234, misprints this date as July 20 for July 29.

[28] *S. R.,* IV, 215.   Fleay, in *Anglia,* VIII, 406, gives this date as 1630
without specifying that it is Old Style.

[29] From the copy belonging to the late Robert Hoe, Esq.

[30] Malone's *Shakspere,* 1821, III, 232, note.

[31] *Ibid.*

[32] *Ibid.*

year was *Changes, or Love in a Maze,* entered in the Stationers' Register for W. Cooke, February 9, 1631/2.[33] Its full title reads:

Changes: or, Love in a Maze. A Comedie, As it was presented at the Private House in Salisbury Court, by the Company of His Majesties Revels. Written by Iames Shirley, Gent. — — Deserta per avia dulcis Raptat Amor. London: Printed by G. P. for William Cooke, and are to be sold at his shop neere Furnivals Inne gate in Holborne, 1632.[34]

Of the four plays belonging to this year 1632, one, *The Ball,* was shortly to occasion further record. On November 18, 1632, two days after it was licensed, Sir Henry Herbert, Master of the Revels, made this entry in his office-book:

In the play of *The Ball,* written by Sherley, and acted by the Queens players, ther were divers personated so naturally, both of lords and others of the court, that I took it ill, and would have forbidden the play, but that Biston [Christopher Beeston, the manager] promiste many things which I found faulte withall should be left out, and that he would not suffer it to be done by the poett any more, who deserves to be punisht; and the first that offends in this kind, of poets or players, shall be sure of publique punishment.[35]

---

[33] *S. R.,* IV, 238.
[34] From the copy belonging to the late Robert Hoe, Esq.
[35] Malone's *Shakspere,* 1821, III, 231–232.

To this passage, we shall have occasion to recur in our critical study of the play in Chapter IX.

Having now considered the circumstances of Shirley's entrance into London, and having recorded the licensing and the publication of the works of his first dramatic period, I shall devote the remainder of this chapter to a discussion of the identity of the play licensed as *The Brothers,* November 4, 1626. This work, in Fleay's opinion,[36] cannot be identical with Shirley's *The Brothers* of 1652, published as one of *Six New Playes,* 1653;[37] but is rather to be identified with the tragicomedy called *Dicke of Devonshire,* which Bullen,[38] in 1883, ascribed to Heywood. Of Fleay's conclusions in this matter, Schelling has recently remarked: "There seems some reason for this opinion."[39] Later, however, he declares: "It is impossible to follow Fleay in the nice distinctions by which he transfers the title, *The Brothers,* to the anonymous *Dick of Devonshire,* and identifies Shirley's play before us [*The Brothers* of 1652] with *The Politic Father,* licensed for the King's men in 1641."[40] In view of this uncertainty concerning the identity of the plays in question, an examination of

---

[36] Fleay, in *English Drama,* II, 236–237, and in *Anglia,* VIII, 405–406.
[37] In this collection, the joint title-page is dated 1653; but of the individual title-pages, all but the last are dated 1652.
[38] Bullen, *Collection of Old English Plays,* II, 1–4.
[39] Schelling, *Elizabethan Drama,* I, 293.
[40] *Ibid.,* II, 288.

the evidence is here in order. To readers who enjoy such critical investigations, the problem presented will appeal as one of the most fascinating puzzles of the Shirley canon; to others, I fear, the discussion must seem a waste of time and printers' ink.

I

THE initial link in Fleay's long argument, is to show that the play known to us as *The Politician*[41] is not the play licensed as *The Politique Father,* May 26, 1641.[42] So slight is the argument in favor of their identity, that one begrudges the space necessary to its refutation; yet refuted it must be, if *The Politique Father* is to be identified instead with *The Brothers* of 1652. Dyce found *The Politique Father* licensed but, under that title, never printed, and *The Politician* printed but, under that title, never licensed; and, desiring to account for both, he jumped to the conclusion that the two were one. Under these circumstances, the burden of proof is wholly upon Dyce; but all that he offers us is this:

---

[41] *Works,* v, 89–176. The title-page of my copy reads as follows: "*The Polititian, A Tragedy. Presented at Salisbury Court by her Majesties Servants; Written by James Shirley. London. Printed for Humphrey Moseley and are to be sold at his Shop at the Princes Armes in St. Pauls Church-yard. 1655.*"

[42] Malone's *Shakspere,* 1821, III, 232, note.

[47]

Mr. Gifford observes that *The Politician* "does not appear to have been licensed by the Master of the Revels": he thinks that it was produced not later than 1639; and that it may indeed have been represented while the poet was in Ireland. I feel convinced, however, that the following entry in Sir Henry Herbert's office-book, relates to this tragedy: *"The Politique Father,* May 26, 1641": we have already seen that Shirley's dramas were not always printed with the names under which they had been licensed. *The Politician* was given to the press in 1655, as *Presented at Salisbury Court by her Majesties Servants.*[43]

Before accepting this hypothesis, we may justly ask of Dyce three things: (1) that his hypothesis shall best account for the fact that *The Politique Father,* although licensed, was, under that title, never printed; and for the fact that *The Politician,* although printed, was, under that title, never licensed; (2) that the title of the licensed play shall be appropriate to the subject-matter of the drama published; and (3) that the hypothesis proposed shall not conflict with known facts or with strong probabilities.

Tried by these tests, the hypothesis of Dyce fails of establishment. In the first place, to assert the identity of *The Politique Father* and *The Politician* is not the best way to account for the fact that no play of the former title has been published and no play of

[43] Dyce, in *Works,* I, xxxviii–xxxix.

the latter title has been licensed. Other hypotheses are quite as good. Concerning the published play we might assume, for example, that this play, although published as "Presented . . . by her Majesties Servants," was never actually licensed or presented. In 1655, both Shirley and his publisher might well have been in ignorance of what had been done with the manuscript by her Majesty's Servants during Shirley's absence in Ireland fifteen years before. Indeed they might even—for the sake of better sales—have ventured a false statement on the title-page: in 1655 such a statement would pass without detection. Better still, we might assume that the reason why we have no record of the license is not that the play was never licensed in due form, but merely that Malone, by some oversight, failed to transcribe the license-record from the now-lost office-book: this is not the only extant play of Shirley for which we lack this record. Concerning the licensed play, *The Politique Father,* we might assume either that the play was never published, or better (as we shall see) that it is to be identified not with *The Politician* but with the play published as *The Brothers* in 1652. In his letter of August 7, 1641, the Lord Chamberlain, the Earl of Essex, named as the property of the King's men three plays by Shirley: *"The doubtfull heire. The Imposture. . . . The Brothers.*"[44]   If, by August 7, 1641, the name of the play licensed as *Rosania,* June 1, 1640, had been changed by its author or by its actors to *The Doubtful Heir,* surely there was no reason why the play licensed as *The Politique Father,* May 26, 1641, should not, by August 7, 1641, become *The Brothers.*   Since these various suppositions are quite as adequate as is the hypothesis of Dyce, the mere fact that *The Politique Father* was licensed but, under that title, never printed, and that *The Politician* was printed but, under that title, never licensed, is not sufficient to prove the two identical.

In the second place, the title of the play known to us from the license-record is not appropriate to the subject-matter of the published drama.   Gotharus, the politician, proves to be neither "politique" nor a "father"; the credulous King of Norway, father of Prince Turgesius, is even less politic than his minister; and as for Count Altomarus, father of Haraldus, he is politic only in the fact that he had the foresight to die before the action of Shirley's play begins.   Moreover, in the "Small Characters of the Persons" prefixed to *The Politician,* no one of the characters is described as "politique," as might be

---

[44] The letter is reprinted in full by E. K. Chambers in *The Malone Society Collections, Parts IV & V,* pp. 364–369.

expected were *The Politician* but a new name for
The Politique Father. In short, no appropriateness
of title to material indicates that the play licensed as
The Politique Father is the play that has come down
to us as *The Politician.*

And in the third place, Dyce's hypothesis must be
accepted, if at all, in the face of the strong probability
that the plays he would identify belonged to rival
companies. From the title-page of *The Politician,*
we know that it was acted by the Queen's men: "Presented at Salisbury Court by her Majesties Servants."
From the date of the licensing of *The Politique Father,* we can be all but certain that the play was
licensed for the King's men. Malone's extracts from
the lost office book of the Master of the Revels do not
specify for what companies the plays were licensed.
The title-pages of the printed plays, however, tell us
by what company each play was acted: from these
title-pages we know that, before Shirley went to Ireland, he wrote, with but a single exception [45] (unless
The Brothers be a second), for the Queen's men at
the private house in Drury Lane; [46] that during his
absence in Ireland, his new plays were presented in

[45] The exception is *Changes, or Love in a Maze,* "presented at the
Private House in Salisbury Court by the Company of His Majesties
Revels." Note that this is not the company of the "King's men," i.e.,
"his Majesties Servants."

[46] See the full title-pages in the Bibliography.

London by the new company of Queen's men at Salisbury Court;[47] and that after his return, he wrote
without exception (unless it be this *Politique Father*)
for the King's men.[48]   In the absence, therefore, of
evidence to the contrary, we must deem it all but certain that *The Politique Father,* licensed after his
return from Dublin, was acted, like every other play
of Shirley's presented subsequent to his return, by his
Majesty's Servants.   How then stands our argument?   From the title-page of *The Politician,* we
know that it was acted by the Queen's men.   From
the date of *The Politique Father,* we deem it all but
certain that that play was licensed for the King's men.
If this be so, the hypothesis of Dyce that the two
plays are identical, is highly improbable.

But perhaps it may be objected that the title-page
of *The Politician* is incorrect: that this drama was
not, in reality, "Presented at Salisbury Court by her
Majesties Servants."   Even then, the hypothesis of
Dyce would be improbable.   We have established the
strong probability that *The Politique Father* was licensed for the King's men.   We know from the title-
page of *The Cardinal,* that that tragedy was acted by
the same company.[49]   We know further, that *The*

[47] See the full title-pages in the Bibliography.
[48] *Ibid.*
[49] *"The Cardinal, A Tragedie, As It was acted at the private House
in Black Fryers . . . ,"* i. e., by the King's men.

Politique Father, whatever its identity, antedates *The Cardinal;* for the former was licensed May 26, 1641, and the latter on November 25 of the same year.[50] But *The Cardinal* is expressly called, in its epilogue, the first tragedy that Shirley wrote for the King's men:

> . . . the Play is a Tragedy,
> The first that ever he compos'd for us.[51]

Therefore, *The Politique Father,* which antedates it, cannot be a tragedy.[52] *The Politician,* however, is a tragedy not only in its title but in fact.[53] For this second reason, therefore, *The Politique Father*—provided always that it was acted, as its date indicates, by the King's men—cannot be, as Dyce assumed, *The Politician.*

In short, the hypothesis of Dyce survives no one of the tests we have applied to it. It does not best account for the known facts concerning *The Politique Father* and *The Politician:* other hypotheses prove as good or better. It ignores the fact that the title of *The Politique Father* is in no wise appropriate to the subject-matter of *The Politician.* It conflicts with

[50] Malone's *Shakspere,* 1821, III, 232, note.
[51] *The Cardinal,* 1652, p. 70; or *Works,* V, 352.
[52] Fleay, *English Drama,* II, 246.
[53] *The Polititian, A Tragedy . . . 1655.*

the probabilities (which are all but certainties) that the two plays were one a comedy and the other a tragedy, and that they belonged to rival companies. Under these circumstances, the hypothesis of Dyce may be rejected.

II

No longer hampered by the supposition that the play published as *The Politician* in 1655 is to be identified, as Dyce assumed,[54] with the play licensed as *The Politique Father* in 1641, we are now free to proceed to our second point, namely: that the play published as *The Brothers* in 1652 is identical with *The Politique Father* of 1641 rather than with the play licensed as *The Brothers* in 1626.

This proposition is plausible from the start. We know of no instance in which a play of Shirley was renamed during presentation by the Queen's men of Salisbury Court; but we do know that *Rosania* was renamed during presentation by the King's men of Black Friars. Surely, then, we may as reasonably assume that *The Politique Father* was a play of the King's men ultimately renamed *The Brothers,* as that it was a play of the Queen's men ultimately renamed

[54] Dyce, in *Works,* I, xxxviii.

The Politician. Moreover, although, as we have noted, the title *The Politique Father* fits ill with the subjèct-matter of *The Politician,* it fits excellently with the story of *The Brothers;* for Don Ramyres[55] proves exceeding "politique" in marrying his sons to best advantage. All this proves nothing; but it goes to show that, if there be arguments to support our proposition, the field is open.

From possibility, therefore, we proceed to probability: three arguments make *probable* the change of title. In the first place, *The Brothers* of 1652 was published as one of a collection of which the joint title ran:

Six New Playes, Viz. The Brothers. Sisters. Doubtfull Heir. Imposture. Cardinall. Court Secret. The Five first were acted at the Private House in Black Fryers with great Applause. The last was never Acted. All Written by James Shirley. Never printed before. London, . . . 1653.[56]

Of these six plays, all with the possible exception of *The Brothers* were produced by Shirley in the years

[55] Fleay gives the title a different application: that the "politique father" is not Don Ramyres but Don Carlos. His interpretation, however, is based solely upon the chance comment of Francisco to Don Carlos, in Act I, scene i: "You show a provident father." Aside from the difference between "provident" and "politique," the facts of the play make Fleay's application most unlikely: Don Carlos is anything but politic. See, however, Fleay, *English Drama,* II, 246.

[56] From the title-page of the copy in the possession of the present writer.

1640–1642: for of four we know the license-date, and for the fifth we have Shirley's own statement that "it happened to receive birth when the stage was interdicted,"[57] that is, after the closing of the theaters in 1642. In view of these facts, is it probable that Shirley would include, and would place first, in this company of *New Plays,* a work that had remained unpublished for nearly a generation?

In the second place, one bit of internal evidence relates *The Brothers* of 1652 with the period of *The Politique Father,* 1641, rather than with that of *The Brothers* of 1626. When *The Brothers* of 1652 was acted, there was, presumably, some special meaning in the prologue's line:

You're all betray'd here to a Spanish plot.[58]

When *The Politique Father* was acted in 1641, no allusion could have been more timely than one to the king's Spanish plot of that year—his plot to give Spain a part of the Irish army.[59] Unless we assume that this passage is a late interpolation, we must see in it an additional argument for supposing that the play published as *The Brothers* in 1652 was acted about the year 1641—the date when *The Politique*

[57] Dedication of *The Court Secret,* in *Works,* v, 428.
[58] Prologue to *The Brothers,* in *Works,* I, 191.
[59] Fleay, in *Anglia,* VIII, 410; and in *English Drama,* II, 246.

Father was licensed—or even for concluding the two plays identical.

In the third place, the play published as *The Brothers* in 1652, is described on its individual title-page and on the joint title-page of *Six New Playes,* 1653, of which it formed a part, as "acted at the Private House in Black Fryers," [60] that is, by the King's men, for whom Shirley began writing in 1640. This circumstance all but negatives the assumption that the play published in 1652 is the play licensed under the same name in 1626; for, previous to 1640, we know of but one instance in which Shirley wrote for any company other than the Queen's men, and in that instance [61] he wrote not for the King's men at Black Friars but for the Company of his Majesty's Revels at Salisbury Court.[62] That Shirley should have written one play for the King's men while he was in the employ of the Queen's men, may not be impossible, but is at least untimely. We must conclude rather that, since the play published as *The Brothers* in

[60] From the title-pages of the copy in the possession of the present writer.

[61] *Changes, or Love in a Maze.*

[62] One play, *Love Tricks, or The School of Complement,* which antedates by a few weeks the organization of her Majesty's Servants, was originally acted by the Lady Elizabeth's men; but appears to have been transferred to the repertoire of the new company by Christopher Beeston when the Queen's men, upon their organization, succeeded to the occupancy of the Phœnix in Drury Lane. See Murray, *English Dramatic Companies,* I, 259.

1652 was "acted at the Private House in Black Fryers," it was acted not in 1626 but during the period from 1640 to 1642. This argument points not to *The Brothers* of 1626 but to *The Politique Father* of 1641.

These three arguments—that *The Brothers* of 1652 was published as the first of six "new" plays, that it contains a line best explained as an allusion to the Spanish plot of 1641, and that it was acted by the King's men, for whom, so far as we know, Shirley began writing in 1640—support the probability that the play published as *The Brothers* in 1652 is identical with the play licensed as *The Politique Father* in 1641 rather than with the play licensed as *The Brothers* in 1626. Probability, however, is not certainty. The certainty—or approximation to certainty —comes rather from two considerations still to be presented.

The first of these was advanced thirteen years ago, by Nissen.[63] In the dedication of *The Brothers* of 1652, Shirley, addressing Thomas Stanley, Esq., writes:

This composition, . . . after its birth, had in my thoughts a dedication to your name. . . . You were pleased to grace it with your fair opinion, when it was represented. . . .[64]

[63] Nissen, p. 13, note 6.
[64] Dedication to *The Brothers*, in *Works*, I, 189.

That Shirley should have written thus of *The Brothers* of 1626 is most improbable; for, as Thomas
Stanley was but one year old in 1626, he would scarcely
have been, even in Shirley's thoughts, the recipient
of a dedication, and certainly would not have graced
the drama with his fair opinion. If, however, continues Nissen, *The Brothers* of 1652 is really, as
Fleay maintains, *The Politique Father* of 1641, then
the dedication to Thomas Stanley, Esq., would be
wholly appropriate; for Stanley had entered the university in 1639.

This argument is conclusive in so far as it concerns
the relation of *The Brothers* of 1652 to *The Brothers*
of 1626; but it is not conclusive with respect to the
relation of *The Brothers* of 1652 to *The Politique
Father* of 1641. Their identity, however, appears to
be conclusively established by a bit of evidence left
us by Shirley's publisher, Humphrey Moseley. In
the library of the late Robert Hoe, Esq.,[64a] in a cata-

[64a] In the spring of 1911, while this monograph was in preparation,
the library of Mr. Hoe was placed on exhibition by the Anderson
Auction Company of New York City, preparatory to the sale that
began on April 24. Among the books exhibited was perhaps the most
nearly complete collection of the works of Shirley—especially of first
editions—that has ever been assembled in America; and to this collection, through the courtesy of the company, the writer of this monograph was given access, with opportunity for leisurely and detailed
examination. For courtesies then extended to him, he takes this
opportunity to thank the company and its representatives, especially
Mr. E. F. Hanaburgh.

logue bound with Shirley's *Six New Playes* of 1653, occurs this advertisement:

> These Books I have now in the Presse, ready to come forth.

130.   Six new Playes, viz.

The ⎰ BROTHERS.
⎱ SISTERS.
⎰ DOUBTFUL HEIR.
⎱ IMPOSTURE.
⎰ CARDINALL.
⎱ COURT SECRET.

By James Shirley, Gent. in 8°. Being all that ever the Author made for the Private house in Black-Fryers.

"Being *all* that ever the Author made for the Private house in Black-Fryers": if these indeed be "all," then must one of these six be the play licensed as *The Politique Father*—for that Shirley wrote *The Politique Father* for any but the King's men, is unlikely. By a process of elimination, we can account for every play in the list except the first: *The Court Secret* we know was never acted; *The Doubtful Heir* was licensed as *Rosania,* the name of its heroine; *The Sisters, The Imposture,* and *The Cardinal* were licensed under the names by which we know them. Only *The Brothers* remains to be accounted for among the published plays; only *The Politique Father* among the dramas licensed. If Moseley, publishing in Shirley's lifetime, told the truth—if these six plays be "all"—and if, as we have every reason to believe, *The Politique Father* was licensed for the King's men: then must *The Politique Father* be *The Brothers* of 1652.

For these five reasons, then—that *The Brothers* of 1652 was published as the first of six "new" plays; that it contains what appears to be an allusion to the Spanish plot of 1641; that it was acted by the King's men, for whom we have every reason to suppose that Shirley wrote only from 1640 to 1642; that it was dedicated to Thomas Stanley, Esq., who was but one year old in 1626, but who entered the university in 1639; and that Moseley's advertisement eliminates all possibilities save Fleay's conclusion—for these five reasons, I agree with Fleay that *The Brothers* of 1652 is to be identified not with *The Brothers* of 1626 but with *The Politique Father* of 1641.

Two of Fleay's propositions we have now considered: (1) that *The Politique Father* is not *The Politician;* and (2) that *The Brothers* of 1652 is not *The Brothers* of 1626 but is rather *The Politique Father*. Are these two propositions now established? As we review our discussion, we note that a majority of our strongest arguments in support of both propositions involve the premise that Shirley in no instance wrote for the King's men previous to his return from Ire-

[61]

land, and that he in no instance wrote for the Queen's men after his return. This premise we cannot positively affirm; for we no longer possess the office-book of the Master of the Revels; and an inference based solely upon the title-pages now extant establishes only a reasonable presumption. When, however, we combine the arguments that involve this premise, with arguments that are not thus brought in doubt, we have, I believe, sufficient ground for accepting Fleay's conclusions.[64b]

III

My acceptance, however, applies only to Fleay's first and second propositions. His third proposition—that the play licensed as *The Brothers* in 1626 is to be identified with the play which Bullen, in 1883, pub-

[64b] On December 10, 1914, while the second proof-sheets of this book were still in my possession, I had the pleasure of receiving from Dr. Robert Stanley Forsythe a copy of his able work *The Relations of Shirley's Plays to the Elizabethan Drama,* fresh from the press. Naturally, I read with much attention the section (pages 173–177) in which Dr. Forsythe endeavors to maintain the identity of *The Brothers* of 1626 with *The Brothers* of 1652, and the identity of *The Politique Father* with *The Politician.* Should he convince the world that I am wrong in accepting Fleay's conclusions, he will but strengthen the principal thesis of my study, that Shirley, beginning as a realist, ended his career as a romanticist; for Dr. Forsythe would transfer this comedy of manners, *The Brothers,* from Shirley's third period—a period of romantic plays—to his first period, a period of realism, to which, for the sake of my thesis, I gladly would assign it. Unfortunately for me, however, I find Dr. Forsythe's arguments, on the points on which we differ, unconvincing. I am letting my chapter stand, therefore, just as it was before I saw his book.

lished under the title *Dicke of Devonshire*[65]—impresses me as much less certain. The arguments which tend to associate *Dicke of Devonshire* with the year 1626, seem to me not so conclusive as Fleay assumes; and then, even if we grant that *Dicke of Devonshire* was composed in 1626, we still lack definite grounds for identifying it with Shirley's play *The Brothers*.

As to the date of *Dicke of Devonshire,* one point must instantly be granted: that the play was composed not earlier than July 18, 1626; for so much of the play as relates to Richard Pike, or Peeke, of Tavistock, is based upon a pamphlet entered on that day in the Stationers' Register:

A booke cal[le]d *Three to one being and* [sic] *English Spanish combatt Performed by a westerne man of Tavestocke in Deuon: with an English quarter staffe against Three Spanish Rapiers and Ponyards at Sherres* [i.e., Xeres] *in Spayne the 15 of Nouember 1625.*[66]

[65] Bullen, *A Collection of Old English Plays,* II, 1–99; from Eg. MS. 1994.

[66] *S. R.,* IV, 125. The title-page of the pamphlet, as reprinted in Arber's *English Garner,* I, 621–639, reads thus: *Three to One. Being an English-Spanish combat performed by a Western Gentleman of Tavistock in Devonshire, with an English quarterstaff, against three Spaniards* [at once] *with rapiers and poniards; at Sherries* [Xeres] *in Spain, the 15th day of November, 1625: in the presence of Dukes, Condes, Marquises, and other great Dons of Spain; being the Council of War. The author of this book, and the actor in this encounter; R*[ichard] *Peeke. Printed at London for I. T. and are to be sold at his shop.* [n.d.]

That the play was written not later than the close of 1626, is indicated—possibly—by a passage in the play itself. In a conversation concerning the Spanish Armada, in Act I, scene ii, the second merchant says to the first:

> . . . Stay; Eighty Eight,—
> Thirty eight yeares agoe; much about then
> Came I into the world.—Well, sir, this fleete?[67]

Thirty-eight years added to 1588 place this conversation definitely in the year 1626; and Shirley's *The Brothers* was licensed November 4, 1626. But does the passage prove that *Dicke of Devonshire* was composed in 1626? May it not rather prove that the dramatist, writing perhaps years later, thought of the events of his play as occurring in or about the year 1626? To this conclusion, some support is given by a passage in Act III, scene i. The hero, in his pamphlet, speaking of an attempt to ransom him, says only: "The town, thinking me to be a better prize than indeed I was, denied me, and would not part from me."[68] In the play, however, we find the following dialogue:

JEWELL: . . . Sure they hold him for some great noble purchace.

[67] *Dicke of Devonshire*, in Bullen's *Collection of Old English Plays*, II, 16.
[68] *Three to One*, in Arber's *English Garner*, I, 631.

SECRETARY: A Barronet at least, one of the lusty blood, Captaine.

CAPTAINE: Or perhaps, Mr. Secretary, some remarkable Commonwealths man, a pollitician in Government.[69]

Is this reference to "some remarkable Commonwealths man, a pollitician in Government" likely to occur so early as 1626?

But even if we grant that *Dicke of Devonshire* was composed in 1626, the year when *The Brothers* was licensed for presentation, this does not prove the two identical. If we knew that *Dicke of Devonshire* were Shirley's, then the coincidence of date would be significant. If we possessed the office-book of the Master of the Revels, and by it could account for every play of 1626 except *The Brothers,* then we might infer that *The Brothers* is *Dicke of Devonshire.* But no such process of elimination is possible. We do not know that Shirley wrote *Dicke of Devonshire.* We do not know that it may not have been licensed by another dramatist under some title now lost with the lost office-book. For that matter, we cannot be sure that it ever was either licensed or presented. We know only that it has survived as "Eg. MS. 1994."

Even, then, if we grant that *Dicke of Devonshire* was composed in 1626, we still need evidence to connect the play with Shirley's *The Brothers.* And on

[69] *Dicke of Devonshire,* in Bullen's *Collection,* II, 45.

this point, the evidence is not conclusive. The plot, indeed, fits well enough the title of *The Brothers;* for so much of the play as does not concern Richard Pike, deals with the relations of Manuel and Henrico, sons of Don Pedro Gusman. But to how many plots is such a title applicable! Again, as Fleay has pointed out, *Dicke of Devonshire* "is expressly called (near the end) 'the story of Two Brothers.' ":[70]

> Macada. Letters shall forthwith fly into Madrid
> To tell the King the storyes of Two Brothers,
> Worthy the Courtiers reading.[71]

But what does this prove? Even in a single year, how many dramas might offer such a phrase? With almost as much reason might we identify Shirley's lost play *Look to the Lady,* entered in the Stationers' Register, March 11, 1639/40,[72] with the play published as *The Politician;* for that very phrase, "Look to the Lady!" occurs in *The Politician,* Act V, scene ii.[73] Clearly, the mere presence of the words "the storyes of Two Brothers" in *Dicke of Devonshire,* is no proof of its identity with Shirley's *The Brothers* of 1626.

Again, how do those critics who suppose our dramatist a Roman Catholic, reconcile the anti-Romanist

[70] Fleay, *English Drama,* II, 236–237; cf. *Anglia,* VIII, 406.
[71] *Dicke of Devonshire,* v, i; in Bullen's *Collection,* II, 99.
[72] *S. R.,* IV, 475.
[73] *The Politician,* v, ii; *Works,* v, 172.

speeches in this play with the alleged religious sympathies of Shirley? Would so recent a convert to Catholicism permit his hero, even for dramatic effect, to scorn the sacrament of confession as does Dicke of Devonshire in Act IV, scene ii? [74] To allege that the episode occurs also in the pamphlet on which the play is based, is not a sufficient answer. [75]

As for the style of the play, I find in it little that resembles Shirley's. In so far as the play concerns Richard Pike, it follows so closely the substance of the pamphlet paragraph by paragraph, that the playwright's style is lost in that of the original. For the rest—the portions dealing with Manuel, Henrico, and Eleonora—much of it is in blank verse not unworthy of Shirley in his lesser works, yet in no wise marked by anything peculiar to our dramatist. The poetic atmosphere usually belonging to the romantic plays of Shirley, I do not find in *Dicke of Devonshire*.

In short, although we cannot, in this instance, prove beyond question that Fleay's hypothesis is wrong, we are quite as far from proving that his hypothesis is right. The argument based on the plot of *Dicke of Devonshire* and on the alleged allusion to the title in the license-list, is of little weight: "storyes

[74] In Bullen's *Collection*, II, 70–71.
[75] In Arber's *English Garner*, I, 632–633.

of Two Brothers" occur too often in this world to be distinctive. The anti-Romanist speeches in *Dicke of Devonshire* ill agree with Shirley's supposed conversion to Catholicism. The style of the play has not been unmistakably associated with the style of Shirley. And, finally, as to the date of the two plays, although *Dicke of Devonshire* cannot have been written earlier than the year of the licensing of *The Brothers,* not only could it have been written later, but the seeming allusion to the Commonwealth makes a later date more probable. For these four reasons, I must decline to receive *Dicke of Devonshire* into the Shirley canon, and must be content to assume that *The Brothers* of 1626 was never published. But that Fleay is right in assuming that *The Politique Father* of 1641 is to be identified not with *The Politician* but with *The Brothers* of 1652, I hold to be not only probable but well-nigh certain.

To sum up, then, our record of Shirley from 1625 to 1632, what have we determined? In the first place, we have recognized that the record of the christening of "Mathias, sonne of Mr. James Shurley, gentleman," at St. Giles, Cripplegate, February 26, 1624/5, must refer to the Mathias mentioned in the will of the dramatist as his "eldest son"; and upon this recognition we have based the inference that, on or before this date, James Shirley had probably taken up his residence in London. In the second place, we have noted the dates of the licensing of *Love Tricks with Complements* and *The Maid's Revenge;* of the probable presentation of *The Wedding;* and of the licensing of *The Brothers, The Witty Fair One, The Faithful Servant, The Traitor, The Duke, Love's Cruelty, The Changes, Hyde Park,* and *The Ball;* and we have noted the dates of the publication, or of the entry for publication, of *The Wedding, The Grateful Servant (The Faithful Servant), The School of Complement (Love Tricks),* and *Changes, or Love in a Maze.* And finally, we have shown—conclusively, I trust—that the play licensed as *The Brothers* in 1626 is to be identified neither with the play published under that title in 1652 nor with that published in 1883 as *Dicke of Devonshire.* Upon this chronology, we may safely, in Chapters VI to IX, base our inferences concerning the development of Shirley during his first dramatic period.

CHAPTER III

SHIRLEY'S SECOND DRAMATIC PERIOD

1632–1636

IN *The Arcadia* of Shirley, Act III, scene i,[1] Thumb, the miller, protesting against a rebel plot, declares:

We met together to drink in honour of the king's birthday, and though we have tickled the cannikins, let us be merry and wise, that's my opinion; no treason, the king is an honest gentleman, and so is the queen.[2]

A moment later, the discussion is interrupted by the arrival of the king himself. In the embarrassment that results, Thumb makes himself the spokesman:

King, by your leave,—Which is the king? my eyes twinkle—We have been playing the good fellows to celebrate your majestical birthday; will your grace see a song?[3]

[1] Not Act III, scene ii, as Fleay has it, in his *English Drama,* II, 239. His error is occasioned by the misprint in the running title in *Works,* VI, 205.

[2] *Works,* VI, 201–202.   [3] *Ibid.,* 205.

Now these two references to the king's birthday have no bearing whatever upon the action; nor is there in the play good reason why Thumb should doubt the identity of the king, for the king's retinue, at the moment, consists solely of his queen, his daughter, and a prince disguised as an amazon. Evidently, we must seek, for these passages, an external explanation; and this explanation is found in the theory advanced by Fleay, that Shirley's *Arcadia* was first presented at court on the birthday of King Charles. This would account for the references to "your majestical birthday"; it would account also for Thumb's uncertainty. Evidently he addressed his second speech not to King Basilius but to King Charles. And this theory that *The Arcadia* was a play written for the court, would account also for the fact that it appears never to have been licensed by Sir Henry Herbert. Since the hypothesis is Fleay's, I will quote his argument:

The Arcadia, a Pastoral, was acted by the Queen's servants at Drury Lane, but was evidently originally presented at Court on a King's Birthday, 19th Nov.; cf. iii. 2 [read: III, i], "to celebrate your majestical birthday." It was not in 1633, for then *The Young Admiral* was presented. It was before Nabbes' *Covent Garden,* 1632, for that contains an allusion to the actor who personated Mopsa. Heywood's *Love's Mistress,* the scene of which is also in Arcadia, which was the King's day play of 19th

Nov. 1634, is filled with allusions to it. The most likely
date is, therefore, 19th Nov. 1632. This play, being a
Court play, does not appear in Herbert's license-list. I
suspect it was written by "command." [4]

That Fleay's argument is not absolutely conclusive,
must be admitted; and yet, so far as I am aware, no
evidence has been found to cast doubt upon his rea-
soning. Tentatively, therefore, I set the date of *The
Arcadia* as November 19, 1632; and with this date,
I begin my account of Shirley's second dramatic
period.

The following year, 1633, saw the production of
three more of Shirley's plays: *The Bewties,* licensed
January 21, 1632/3, [5] and, a few months later, published as *The Bird in a Cage;* [6] *The Young Admiral,*
licensed July 3, 1633; [7] and *The Gamester,* licensed
November 11. [8] Besides these, there was *The Night*

[4] Fleay, *English Drama,* II, 239.

[5] Malone's *Shakspere,* 1821, III, 232, note. Gosse, in his introduction to the *Mermaid Shirley,* p. xx, gives the year as 1632, without
specifying that it is Old Style; and then, forgetful of that fact, he
places the play before *Hyde Park* and *The Ball,* both of which pre-
cede *The Bewties* by nearly a year.

[6] The identity of the play licensed as *The Bewties* and that published as *The Bird in a Cage,* we need not question. Their dates
agree; the original title fits the subject of the published play; and the
reason for the change of title is made evident by the ironical dedication to William Prynne, then in confinement. Cf. Fleay, *Anglia,* VIII,
407, and *English Drama,* II, 239–240.

[7] Malone's *Shakspere,* 1821, III, 232, note.

[8] *Ibid.*

Walker, "a play of Fletchers corrected by Sherley," licensed May 11, 1633.[9]

Concerning *The Young Admiral* and *The Gamester,* interesting entries appear in the office-book of the Master of the Revels. Under date of July 3, 1633, he writes:

The comedy called *The Yonge Admirall,* being free from oaths, prophaness, or obsceanes, hath given mee much delight and satisfaction in the readinge, and may serve for a patterne to other poetts, not only for the bettring of maners and language, but for the improvement of the quality, which hath received some brushings of late.

When Mr. Sherley hath read this approbation, I know it will encourage him to pursue this beneficial and cleanly way of poetry, and when other poetts heare and see his good success, I am confident they will imitate the original for their own credit, and make such copies in this harmless way, as shall speak them masters in their art, at the first sight, to all judicious spectators. It may be acted this 3 July, 1633.

I have entered this allowance, for direction to my suc-

[9] Malone's extracts from Herbert's office-book include two references to *The Night Walker,* in both of which the title is given in the plural:

(1) "'For a play of Fletchers corrected by Sherley, called *The Night Walkers,* the 11 May, 1633, £2. 0. 0. For the queen's players.'"

(2) "'*The Night-Walkers* was acted on thursday night the 30 Janu. 1633 [i.e., 1633/4] at Court, before the King and Queen. Likt as a merry play. Made by Fletcher.'"

Malone's *Shakspere,* 1821, III, 236, and note.

cessor, and for example to all poetts, that shall write after the date hereof.[10]

Four months later, he records:

On tusday the 19th of November, being the king's birth-day, *The Yong Admirall* was acted at St. James by the queen's players, and likt by the K. and Queen.[11]

And the following February, there appears this entry:

On thursday night the 6 of Febru. 1633 [i.e., 1633/4], *The Gamester* was acted at Court, made by Sherley, out of a plot of the king's, given him by mee; and well likte. The king sayd it was the best play he had seen for seven years.[12]

This royal opinion—though open to suspicion of partiality—appears to have been well founded; for Shirley's *The Gamester* and its successive revisions held the stage well into the nineteenth century.

Shirley's publications for the same year, 1633, were a second edition of *The Wedding;* a dramatic allegory entitled *A Contention for Honor and Riches,* entered in the Stationers' Register for W. Cooke the previous autumn, November 9, 1632;[13] *The Witty Fair One,* entered for the same publisher on January 15, 1632/3;[14] and *The Bird in a Cage,* also for W.

---

[10] Malone's *Shakspere,* 1821, III, 232–233. [11] *Ibid.,* 234. [12] *Ibid.,* 236. [13] *S. R.,* IV, 262. In the entry, the title reads: *A Dialogue of Riches and honor by J: S.* [14] *S. R.,* IV, 265.

Cooke, March 19, 1632/3.[15]   Of these four publications, the title-pages, transcribed from the copies belonging to the late Robert Hoe, Esq., read as follows:

The Wedding. As it vvas lately Acted by her Maiesties Seruants, at the Phenix in Drury-Lane. Written by Iames Shirley, Gent.   Horat.—Multaq, pars mei Vitabit Libitinam—London; Printed for Iohn Groue, and are to be sold at his Shop in Chancery-Lane, neere the Rowles, ouer against the Suppeny-Office. 1633.

A Contention for Honovr and Riches. By J. S.—ubi quid datur oti, illudo chartis—London, Printed by E. A. for William Cooke, and are to be sold at his shop neere Furnivals Inne gate in Holborne. 1633.

The Wittie Faire One. A Comedie. As it was presented at the Private House in Drvry Lane. By her Maiesties Servants. By Iames Shirley. . . . London Printed by B. A. and T. F. for Wil. Cooke, and are to be sold at his shop, neere Furnivals-Inne Gate, in Holborne. 1633.

The Bird in a Cage. A Comedie. As it hath beene Presented at the Phœnix in Drury-Lane. The Author Iames Shirley, Servant to Her Majesty. Iuven. Satyra. 7. Et Spes, & ratio Studiorum, in Cæsare tantum. London Printed by B. Alsop. and T. Fawcet. for William Cooke, and are to be sold at his Shop neere Furnivals-Inne Gate, in Holborne. 1633.

[15] *S. R.,* IV, 267. Fleay, in *Anglia,* VIII, 407, misprints this as March 10. In the entry in the Stationers' Register, the title reads, *The Bird in the Cage,* not *"a" Cage.*

The publication of *The Bird in a Cage* incidentally presented Shirley in the rôle of champion of the queen against the Puritan satirist William Prynne. In the year 1632, Henrietta Maria and her ladies had taken part, at court, in the presentation of Montague's pastoral drama, *The Shepherds' Paradise*.[16] Their participation may, or may not, have been the actual occasion of Prynne's obscene abuse of women players in his *Histriomastix*, published shortly afterward;[17] but the Court of the Star Chamber so interpreted his

[16] See Schelling, *Elizabethan Drama*, II, 173. Fleay once suggested (*Anglia*, VIII, 407) that the play in which the queen participated might have been Shirley's *Arcadia*.

[17] *Histrio-Mastix. The Players Scovrge, or, Actors Tragædie, . . . Wherein it is largely evidenced . . . That popular Stage-playes (the very Pompes of the Divell which we renounce in Baptisme, if we beleeve the Fathers) are sinfull, heathenish, lewde, ungodly Spectacles. . . . By William Prynne, an Vtter-Barrester of Lincolnes Inne. . . . London, . . . 1633.*

The passages concerning women actors occur on pp. 162, 214–215, 1000, 1002, 1003, and in the index entry under "W." Of these, the index entry shall be sufficient illustration:

"*Women-Actors*, notorious whores. p. 162, 214, 215, 1002, 1003. Unlawfull. *Ibid.* Hence Justinian. Autenticorum Collat. 5. Tit. 4. f. 46. enacted this Law: Scenicas non solum si fidejustores prestent, sed etiam si jus-jurandum dent quod observabunt & *impiam complebunt operationem*, & quod nunquam *ab impia illa & turpi operatione cessabunt*, possent sine periculo discedere. Et tale jus-jurandum à scenica præstitum, & fide jussoris datio non tenebit. And good reason: for S. *Paul* prohibits women to speake publikely in the Church. 1 Cor. 14. 34. 1 Tim. 2. 12. And dare then any Christian women be so more then whorishly impudent, as to act, to speake publikely on a Stage, (perchance in mans apparell, and cut haire, here proved sinfull and abominable) in the presence of sundry men and women? *Dii talem terris avertite pestem.* O let such presidents of impudency, of impiety be never heard of or suffred among Christians."

attack, and sentenced the unhappy reformer to lose his ears in the pillory, to pay a fine of five thousand pounds, and to be imprisoned for life.[18] How bitterly James Shirley, "Servant to her Majesty," resented the attacks of Prynne, appears in his address to Prynne, in the verses prefixed to Ford's *Love's Sacrifice*, 1633:

> Look here, thou, that hast malice to the stage
> And impudence enough for the whole age;
> Voluminously ignorant! be vext
> To read this tragedy, and thy own be next.[19]

Even more bitter, however, was Shirley's ironical dedication of *The Bird in a Cage*:

To Master William Prynne,
    Utter-Barrister of Lincoln's-Inn.

Sir:

The fame of your candour and innocent love to learning, especially to that musical part of humane knowledge, Poetry, and in particular to that which concerns the stage and scene, (yourself, as I hear, having lately written a Tragedy) doth justly challenge from me this Dedication. I had an early desire to congratulate your happy retirement; but no poem could tempt me with so fair a circumstance as this in the title, wherein I take some delight to think (not without imitation of yourself, who have ingeni-

[18] *Works*, II, 367, note.   [19] *Ibid.*, VI, 509.

ously fancied such elegant and apposite names for your own compositions as *Health's Sickness, The Unloveliness of Love-locks,* &c.) how aptly I may present you at this time, with the *Bird in a Cage,* a comedy, which wanteth, I must confess, much of that ornament, which the stage and action lent it, for it comprehending also another play or interlude, personated by ladies, I must refer to your imagination, the music, the songs, the dancing, and other varieties, which I know would have pleas'd you infinitely in the presentment. I was the rather inclined to make this oblation, that posterity might read you a patron to the muses, and one that durst in such a critical age, bind up the wounds which ignorance had printed upon wit and the professors: proceed (inimitable Mecenas) and having such convenient leisure, and an indefatigable Pegasus, I mean your prose (which scorneth the road of common sense, and despiseth any style in his way), travel still in the pursuit of new discoveries, which you may publish if you please, in your next book of Digressions. If you do not happen presently to convert the organs, you may in time confute the steeple, and bring every parish to one bell.

This is all I have to say at this time, and my own occasions not permitting my personal attendance, I have entreated a gentleman to deliver this testimony of my service; many faults have escaped the press, which your judgment will no sooner find, than your mercy correct, by which you shall teach others a charity to your own volumes, though they be all errata. If you continue where you are, you will every day enlarge your fame, and beside the engagement of other poets to celebrate your Roman constancy, in particular oblige the tongue and pen of your devout honourer,

JAMES SHIRLEY.[20]

Doubly appropriate, in view of this dedication, was the selection of Shirley to be the author of a masque in which the four Inns of Court should voice their abhorrence of the attitude of Prynne and their loyalty to the king and queen. This masque, which was presented at Whitehall on February 3, 1633/4, and again at Merchant Taylors' Hall on February 11, was a spectacle of the utmost magnificence. The participants, splendidly costumed, assembled at Ely and Hatton Houses, and proceeded in gorgeous procession, attended by torch-bearers and musicians, to the palace. Twice the chariots of the "Grand Masquers" and the attendant cavalcade passed under the window where stood the king and queen; then, dismounting, the participants entered the banqueting-house of Whitehall. There, with elaborate scenery and stage effects designed by "Inigo Jones Esquire, Surveyor of his Majesty's works,"[21] and to the accompaniment of music composed "by Mr. William Lawes and Mr. Simon Ives, whose art," says the modest dramatist, "gave an harmonious soul to the other-

[20] *Works*, II, 367–369.   [21] *Ibid.*, VI, 284.

wise languishing numbers,"[22] the gentlemen of the four Inns of Court presented James Shirley's masque *The Triumph of Peace*. It was an entertainment of dances, songs, and spectacle, set in dramatic dialogue and diversified with many an antimasque humorous or satiric; an entertainment, says the printed copy, "which was, for the variety of the shows and richness of the habits, the most magnificent that hath been brought to court in our time."[23] Of the expenses of this masque, Mr. Whitelocke, one of the committee in charge, has left the following record:

For the Musicke, which was particularly committed to my charge, I gave to Mr. Ives and to Mr. Lawes 100£ a piece, for their rewards; . . . and the whole charge of the Musicke came to about one thousand pounds. The clothes of the horsemen reckoned one with another at 100£ a suit, att the least, amounted to 10,000£. The charges of all the rest of the masque, which were borne by the societies, were accounted to be above twenty thousand pounds.[24]

What reward came to Shirley for his services, Whitelocke does not state.[25]

[22] *Works*, VI, 284.

[23] *Ibid.*, VI, 283–284.

[24] From a MS. by Whitelocke, quoted by Dyce in *Works*, I, xxviii, note.

[25] Concerning *The Triumph of Peace*, Malone (*Shakspere*, 1821, III, 236) gives the following extract from the office-book of the Master of the Revels:

Besides this masque, *The Triumph of Peace,* Shirley produced in the year 1634 two comedies: *The Example,* licensed June 24, and *The Opportunity,* licensed November 29.[26] In the same year, *The Traitor,* destined to be published in 1635, was entered in the Stationers' Register for W. Cooke, November 3.[27] *The Triumph of Peace,* entered for the same publisher on January 24, 1633/4, passed through three editions within the year.[28] The title-page of the copy in the Hoe Collection reads:

The Trivmph of Peace. A Masque, presented by the Foure Honourable Houses, or Innes of Court. Before the King and Queenes Majesties, in the Banquetting-house at White Hall, February the third, 1633. Invented and Written, By James Shirley, of Grayes Inne, Gent. Primum hunc Arethusa mihi—London, Printed by Iohn Norton, for William Cooke, and are to be sold at his Shop, neere Furnivals-Inne-gate, in Holborne. 1633.

The year 1635 adds four items to our chronology: the publication of *The Traitor,* which had been en-

"The Inns of court gentlemen presented their masque at court, before the kinge and queene, the 2 [*sic*] February, 1633 [i.e., 1633/4], and performed it very well. Their shew through the streets was glorious, and in the nature of a triumph.—Mr. Surveyor Jones invented and made the scene; Mr. Sherley the poett made the prose and verse."

[26] Malone's *Shakspere,* 1821, III, 232, note.

[27] *S. R.,* IV, 303.

[28] The entry, *S. R.,* IV, 287, reads: "The Maske of the four Inns of Court with the Sceane as it is to be presented before his Maiesty at Whitehall the third of ffebruary next."

tered in the Stationers' Register on the third of November previous; and the licensing of *The Coronation,* February 6, 1634/5;[29] of *Chabot, Admiral of France,* by Chapman and Shirley, April 29;[30] and of *The Lady of Pleasure,* October 15.[31]

For this edition of *The Traitor,* the title-page of the copy in the Hoe Collection reads:

The Traytor. A Tragedie, vvritten by Iames Shirley. Acted By her Majesties Servants. London: Printed for William Cooke, and are to be sold at his Shop at Furnivals Inne-gate in Holborne. 1635.

This was the last work of Shirley to be published before he went to Ireland.

Concerning the presentation of one of the plays licensed in this year, Collier quotes from the manuscript diary of Sir Humphrey Mildmay the following entry:

8 Dec. [1635.] Dined with Rob. Dowgell, and went to the *La. of Pleasure,* and saw that rare playe.[32]

Of the other plays licensed in 1635, both have suffered from disputed authorship. The earlier of these, *The Coronation,* was published, but five years after

[29] Malone's *Shakspere,* 1821, III, 232, note.
[30] *Ibid.*   [31] *Ibid.*
[32] Collier's *History of English Dramatic Poetry,* II, 70, note.

[82]

its presentation, as "Written by John Fletcher, Gent." [33] Shirley reclaimed it in his "Catalogue of the Authors Poems already printed" appended to *The Cardinal,* 1652. In this list, against the title of *The Coronation,* he prints the note:

> Falsely ascribed to *Jo. Fletcher.*[34]

The play was again printed as Fletcher's in the Beaumont and Fletcher folio of 1679; but in view of Shirley's explicit statement, and in view of the fact that Fletcher had been dead nearly ten years before the play was licensed, we need not hesitate to assign the play to Shirley.

Concerning *Chabot, Admiral of France,* the truth is not so evident. Malone's summary of Herbert's license-list gives no hint that the play is by any hand but Shirley's. In "A Catalogue of such things as hath beene Published by James Shirley Gent.," printed in *The Maides Revenge,* 1639,[35] and again in "A Catalogue of the Authors Poems already printed," appended to *The Cardinal,* 1652,[36] the titles *"Chabot Admirall of France"* and *"Philip Chabot Admirall of France"* appear without mention of a collaborator.

[33] From the title-page of the copy belonging to the late Robert Hoe, Esq.

[34] From the copy in the possession of the present writer.

[35] From the copy belonging to the late Robert Hoe, Esq.

[36] From the copy in the possession of the present writer.

On the other hand, although the Stationers' Register names only Shirley as the author,[37] the title-page of the first edition reads:

The Tragedie of Chabot Admirall of France: As it vvas presented by her Majesties Servants, at the private House in Drury Lane. Written by George Chapman, and James Shirly. London Printed by The [Tho.] Cotes, for Andrew Crooke and William Cooke. 1639.[38]

When, from this external evidence, we pass to the internal evidence of style, we find that those critics who are best qualified to judge, attribute the larger portion of the play to Chapman. Dyce, in his account prefixed to Shirley's *Works,* expresses the opinion that "nearly the whole of this tragedy is evidently from Chapman's pen"; [39] and in the note prefixed to the play, he adds: "Chapman seems to have written so large a portion of it, that I . . . thought it scarcely admissible in a collection of Shirley's works." [40] Fleay was of the opinion that "Chapman wrote I, II, and the prose speeches in III, 1, V, 2, of the Proctor and Advocate. . . . Shirley altered and rewrote the latter part, III, IV, V." [41] Swinburne held that "of

[37] *S. R.,* IV, 415.

[38] From the facsimile title-page in the edition by Lehman, *Publications of the University of Pennsylvania,* 1906.

[39] Dyce, in *Works,* I, xxxii.

[40] *Ibid.,* VI, 87.

[41] Fleay, *English Drama,* II, 241.

the authorship of Chabot there can be no question; the subject, the style, the manner, the metre, the characters, all are perfectly Chapman's." [42] Ward, in his *English Dramatic Literature,* remarked: "Most readers will be inclined to follow Dyce in concluding 'nearly the whole'—or at least the body—of it to be from Chapman's pen"; [43] and in his article on Shirley in the *Dictionary of National Biography,* Ward further said: "Although Shirley may have made some not immaterial additions to this fine tragedy, which Chapman may have left incomplete at his death in 1634, there can be little doubt but that in substance it is to be reckoned among Chapman's works, to some of the most characteristic of which it exhibits an undoubted affinity." [44] Lehman, in the introduction to his edition of *Chabot,* sums up his own impressions thus:

After a careful comparative study of Chapman's and Shirley's styles and methods, I have reached the conclusion that the play was originally written by Chapman and subsequently revised by Shirley. There is scarcely a page upon which the peculiarities of the former's style are not discernible. The principal of these peculiarities are: involved sentences, tortuous thought, and the tendency to

[42] Swinburne, *Essay on George Chapman's Poetical and Dramatic Works,* xxxii.
[43] Ward, *English Dramatic Literature,* II, 444.
[44] Ward, in *DNB.,* LII, 133.

[85]

philosophize. On the other hand, the evidence of revision is to be found in many places. The angular gram-
matical constructions are not so numerous as in other
plays of Chapman, the thought is somewhat clarified, and
there is greater degree of dramatic unity than is common
in Chapman's plays.[45]

Parrott, in his introduction to *Chabot*, in his edition of *The Plays and Poems of George Chapman*,
1910, agrees with Lehman that "the play was originally composed by Chapman and revised by Shirley."
Parrott believes that "this revision was very careful,
and amounted occasionally to the complete rewriting
of a scene"; and that, to state briefly his conclusions,
"three scenes of the eleven composing the play,
namely, I, i, II, iii, and V, ii, remain essentially as
Chapman wrote them; that II, i, and III, i, are practically new scenes by Shirley, displacing, in the first
case at least, older work by Chapman; and that all
the rest of the play presents a groundwork of Chapman, revised, cut down, and added to by Shirley."[45a]
And then, after a plausible hypothesis as to how the
revision of this play by Chapman fell to Shirley, Parrott adds:

Shirley would cut down the long epic speeches, cut out

[45] Lehman, *The Tragedy of Chabot*, introduction, p. 25.
[45a] Parrott, *The Plays and Poems of George Chapman. The
Tragedies*, p. 633.

as much as possible the sententious moralizing, fill in with lively dialogue, introduce, or at least strengthen, the figures of the Wife and the Queen to add a feminine interest to the play, and in general make it over for the stage of his day. And it is impossible to compare *Chabot* with such plays as *The Revenge of Bussy* or the Byron tragedies without feeling more and more strongly that this is exactly what happened. The amount of its difference from Chapman's earlier work is the measure of Shirley's revision. But the original design and the groundwork of the play as it now stands is Chapman's.[45b]

The most adequate and most recent discussion of this question, is that by Schipper, in his *James Shirley, Sein Leben und Seine Werke,* 1911. Of the authorship of *Chabot,* he says, in part:

That the play in its essence cannot come from Shirley, will be clear immediately to every attentive reader. Against Shirley's authorship speak not alone the peculiarities of style, e.g., the often long-spun periods, or the peculiarities of verse-construction, such as the repeated occurrence of rhymed verses, and, on the other hand, the long-extended use of prose, but also the content and the construction of the action. . . . The question how far Shirley may have collaborated in the play is difficult to answer.[46]

And then, after citing conflicting opinions as to the

[45b] *Ibid.*
[46] Schipper, pp. 180–181.

authorship of particular portions, Schipper continues:

One sees, therefore, how large a part the subjective feeling plays here, and how extremely uncertain are its tests of authorship. We must content ourselves, therefore, with the fact that, in some way, Shirley collaborated in this play, which, however, in respect to its substance and its style, bears essentially the characteristic marks of Chapman's authorship.[47]

Upon the details of this discussion, I shall here venture no opinion: like Schipper, I have too little confidence in subjective feeling as a test of authorship. That Shirley had some hand in this tragedy, external evidence appears to show; but that his share was considerable may yet be doubted. During the twelve months preceding the licensing of *Chabot,* April 29, 1635, Shirley had produced *The Example, The Opportunity,* and *The Coronation.* What time would remain to him for work upon *Chabot?* The history of France, moreover, was Chapman's favorite field;[48] and the play possesses at once an almost classical unity of structure and, in the opening act, an almost pre-Shaksperian crudity of exposition, that

---

[47] Schipper, p. 182.

[48] E.g., *Bussy D'Ambois,* 1607; *The Conspiracy and Tragedy of Charles, Duke of Byron,* 1608; and *The Revenge of Bussy D'Ambois,* 1613.

are both foreign to the work of Shirley. In view of
these considerations, therefore, and in view of the approximate unanimity of opinion among those critics
who have studied the style of Chapman and of Shirley, I feel justified in the position that, whatever the
precise contribution of Shirley to *The Tragedy of
Chabot,* its importance is not such as to warrant its
consideration in a study of Shirley's development as
a dramatist. From the critical portions of this monograph, I shall therefore omit all discussion of *Chabot.*

But one more play of Shirley's belongs to this his
second dramatic period: *The Duke's Mistress,* licensed January 18, 1635/6.[49] Five weeks later, according to Sir Henry Herbert, the play received the
honor of a presentation at court; for he entered in his
office-book:

> *The Dukes Mistres* played at St. James the 22 of Feb.
> 1635 [i.e., 1635/6]. Made by Sherley.[50]

This is the last reference to Shirley or his affairs
prior to his change of residence to Ireland. In May
of that year, the outbreak of the plague in London
occasioned the temporary closing of the theaters;[51]
and Shirley, to all appearances, shortly transferred
his activities to Dublin.

[49] Malone's *Shakspere,* 1821, III, 232, note.
[50] *Ibid.,* 238.　　　　　　　[51] *Ibid.,* 239.

What, then, are our conclusions concerning the chronology of Shirley's second dramatic period?

First, we have accepted Fleay's hypothesis that *The Arcadia*—of the licensing of which we have no record—was probably first acted on the king's birthday, November 19, 1639. Second, we have noted from the official records the dates of the licensing of *The Bewties, The Young Admiral, The Gamester;* the presentation of *The Triumph of Peace;* and the licensing of *The Example, The Opportunity, The Coronation, Chabot, The Lady of Pleasure,* and *The Duke's Mistress;* and we have noted the publication or the entry for publication of a second edition of *The Wedding,* and of *A Contention for Honor and Riches, The Witty Fair One, The Bird in a Cage (The Bewties), The Triumph of Peace,* and *The Traitor.* And, lastly, we have concluded that, although *The Coronation* is to be ascribed (despite its title-page) to Shirley, yet *Chabot Admiral of France* is probably in too large a part the work of Chapman to warrant its consideration in our study of Shirley's development as a dramatist. Upon these premises we shall base, in Chapters X to XIII inclusive, our conclusions concerning Shirley's growth from 1632 to 1636.

CHAPTER IV

SHIRLEY'S THIRD DRAMATIC PERIOD

1636–1642

ALTHOUGH Wood, in his *Athenæ Oxonienses,* makes no mention of Shirley's residence in Ireland, the fact that the dramatist spent about four years in Dublin is well established. That the date of his departure from England is 1636 —not 1637, as Dyce supposed—is generally accepted. Dyce based his argument on a letter from Octavius Gilchrist printed in Wilson's *History of Merchant Taylors' School,*[1] in which Gilchrist states that "in 1637 Shirley went to Ireland, under the patronage of George, Earl of Kildare."[2] As Dyce, however, immediately questions the authority of the second part of Gilchrist's statement, we may well inquire whether it were more accurate with respect to the date 1637. On the same page, moreover, on which Dyce quoted from this letter, he also quoted—and then failed to understand—two lines by Shirley himself in a pro-

[1] Part ii, p. 673.
[2] Dyce, in *Works,* I, xxxiv.

[91]

logue written for Middleton's *No Wit, no Help like
a Woman's* on the occasion of its Dublin presentation:

> I'll tell you what a poet says: *two year*
> *He has liv'd in Dublin.*[3]

As the Dublin presentation of this play occurred in
1638,[4] this passage can mean only that Shirley had
lived in Dublin since 1636.

The motive for Shirley's change of residence to
Dublin is probably to be found in the prevalence of
the plague in London in 1636, and in the closing of
the theaters that resulted. Of this, Sir Henry Herbert writes in his office-book:

> At the increase of the plague to 4 within the citty and
> 54 in all.—This day the 12 May, 1636, I received a war-
> rant from my lord Chamberlin for the suppressing of
> playes and shews, and at the same time delivered my sev-
> erall warrants to George Wilson for the four companys
> of players, to be served upon them.[5]

Nine months later, Herbert writes again:

> On thursday morning the 23 of February the bill of
> the plague made the number at forty foure, upon which

---

[3] *Works,* VI, 493.
[4] As shown by reference to the date in Act III, scene i, as revised
by Shirley.
[5] Malone's *Shakspere,* 1821, III, 239.

decrease the king gave the players their liberty, and they began the 24 February, 1636 [i.e., 1636/7].[6]

Presently, however, without date, he adds:

The plague encreasing, the players laye still untill the 2 of October, when they had leave to play.[7]

This prevalence of the plague in London and the consequent closing of the theaters from May 12, 1636, to October 2, 1637, may not be the true or the only reason why Shirley was desirous to leave the capital; but the explanation seems sufficiently probable to be made a matter of record.

In the Irish capital, John Ogilby, for whom Shirley was destined later to perform much miscellaneous work, had opened in 1635 a theater in Werburgh Street, the first in Dublin. For this theater, Shirley appears to have begun dramatic work, writing new plays and revising old. Among his poetical works, we find eight prologues written for plays presented before Dublin audiences: "A Prologue to Mr. Fletcher's play in Ireland"; "A Prologue to *The Alchemist,* acted there"; "A Prologue to *The Irish Gent.";* "A Prologue to a play there, called, *No Wit to a Woman's";* "A Prologue to another of Master Fletcher's plays there"; "A Prologue to a play there,

[6] Malone's *Shakspere,* 1821, III, 239. [7] *Ibid.*

[93]

called *The Toy"; "To another play there"*; and "To a play there, called *The General."* [8] Of Shirley's own plays written during his residence in Ireland, we shall speak in course.

Without further introduction to Shirley's third dramatic period, I shall now proceed to the details of the chronology. To this end, as in former chapters, I shall first record those facts which are well known or readily established, and shall then consider, one after another, the questions in dispute. For example, there is the possibility that the date on which Shirley's romantic comedy *The Royal Master* was presented before the Lord Deputy of Ireland, was not, as has been supposed, the evening of New Year's Day of 1637/8, but the evening of New Year's Day of 1636/7; and again it is by no means impossible that Shirley's alleged visit to England in 1637 is as unreal as his once-accepted resumption of residence in London in 1638. These matters, therefore, belong not to our immediate record of established fact, but rather to the later pages of this chapter, our discussion of possibilities.

Whatever be the date of the presentation of *The Royal Master,* and whatever be the truth as to Shirley's alleged visit to London, the year 1637 affords abundant certainties. *The Lady of Pleasure, Hyde*

[8] *Works,* VI, 490–496.

Park, and *The Young Admiral* were entered in the Stationers' Register for W. Cooke and A. Crooke on April 13, 1637, and were published in the same year.[9] Their title-pages read:

The Lady of Pleasvre. A Comedie, As it was Acted by her Majesties Servants, at the private House in Drury Lane. Written by James Shirly. London, Printed by Tho. Cotes, for Andrew Crooke, and William Cooke. 1637.[10]

Hide Parke a comedie, As it was presented by her Majesties Servants, at the private house in Drury Lane. Written by James Shirly. London, Printed by Tho. Cotes, for Andrew Crooke, and William Cooke. 1637.[11]

The Yovng Admirall. As it was presented By her Majesties Servants, at the private house in Drury Lane. Written by James Shirly. London, Printed by Tho. Cotes, for Andrew Crooke, and William Cooke. 1637.[12]

In the autumn of the same year, two more of Shirley's plays were entered in the Stationers' Register for the same publishers: *The Example,* entered October 18, 1637;[13] and *The Gamester,* entered November 15.[14] For these two plays, the title-pages read:

[9] *S. R.,* IV, 355.
[10] From the copy belonging to the late Robert Hoe, Esq.
[11] *Ibid.*
[12] From the copy belonging to the present writer.
[13] *S. R.,* IV, 369.
[14] *Ibid.,* 373. Not October 18, as stated by Fleay in *English Drama,* II, 233 (not *Anglia,* VIII, 408), and by Nissen.

The Example. As it vvas presented by her Majesties Servants At the private House in Drury-Lane. Written by Iames Shirly. London. Printed by Iohn Norton, for Andrew Crooke, and William Cooke. 1637.[15]

The Gamester. As it vvas presented by her Majesties Servants At the private House in Drury-Lane. Written By Iames Shirly. London. Printed by Iohn Norton, for Andrew Crooke, and William Cooke. 1637.[16]

In this same year, 1637, were issued new editions of *Love Tricks* and *The Grateful Servant.* Their title-pages read:

The Schoole of Complement. As it vvas acted by her Majesties Servants at the Private house in Drury Lane.— Hæc placuit semel. By I. S. London Printed by I. H. for Francis Constable, and are to be sold at his shop under Saint Martins Church neere Ludgate. 1637.[17]

The Gratefvll Servant. A Comedie. As it was lately presented with good applause in the private House in Drury-Lane. By her Majesties Servants. Written by James Shirley Gent.—Usque ego postera Crescam laude recens. London: Printed by I. Okes for William Leake, and are to be sold at his shop in Chancery-lane neere the Roules. 1637.[18]

[15] From the copy belonging to the late Robert Hoe, Esq.
[16] *Ibid.*
[17] *Ibid.*
[18] *Ibid.*

For the year 1638, the facts of record concern chiefly publication and entries for publication. On March 13, 1637/8, *The Royal Master* was entered in the Stationers' Register—not for W. Cooke and A. Crooke, as Fleay asserts,[19] nor for Andrew Cooke & Rich. Serger, as Nissen states,[20] but for Master Crooke, John Crooke, and Richard Searger.[21] From these discrepancies, one infers that Fleay and Nissen did not, on this point, consult the Stationers' Register itself, but were content to accept the statements of the title-pages—sources often at variance with one another and with the Register. For example, the copies of *The Royal Master* belonging to the late Robert Hoe, Esq., give two further statements as to the publishers—statements which agree neither with Fleay's version nor with Nissen's, nor with the Stationers' Register. One reads, "by Thomas Allot and Edmond Crooke"; the other, "by Iohn Crooke and Richard Serger." In full, these title-pages read as follows:

The Royall Master; As it was Acted in the new Theater in Dublin: and Before the Right Honorable the Lord Deputie of Ireland, in the Castle. Written by Iames Shirley.—Fas extera quærere regna. Printed by T.

---

[19] Fleay, in *Anglia,* VIII, 412, and *English Drama,* II, 233.
[20] Nissen, p. 21.
[21] *S. R.,* IV, 385.

Cotes, and are to be sold by Thomas Allot and Edmond Crooke, neere the Castle in Dublin. 1638.[22]

The Royall Master; As it was Acted in the new Theater in Dublin: and Before the Right Honorable the Lord Deputie of Ireland, in the Castle. Written by Iames Shirley—Fas extera quærere regna. London, Printed by T. Cotes, and are to be sold by Iohn Crooke, and Richard Serger, at the Grayhound in Pauls Church-yard. 1638.[23]

These two copies have the same sheets and, except for the imprint, the same title-pages. The first was intended for sale in Dublin, the latter for sale in London. Evidently, each bookseller was supplied with copies with a separate imprint, even though he was not one of those who joined to enter the book for publication.

On the same day, March 13, 1637/8, Shirley's *The Duke's Mistress* was entered in the Stationers' Register for W. Cooke and A. Crooke.[24] Nissen notes that, upon the title-page of the copy of this play in the Hamburg City Library, A. Crooke alone is given as publisher.[25] On the other hand, the Hoe copy bears the name of William Cooke:

[22] From the copy of the Irish issue of the first edition belonging to the late Robert Hoe, Esq.

[23] From the copy of the London issue of the first edition belonging to the late Robert Hoe, Esq.

[24] *S. R.,* IV, 385.   [25] Nissen, p. 21, note 2.

The Dvkes Mistris, As it vvas presented by her Majesties Servants, At the private House in Drury-Lane. Written by Iames Shirly. London, Printed by John Norton, for William Cooke, 1638.[26]

This is but another example of joint entry and separate imprint: its only moral is that knowledge of a title-page will not warrant an inference as to the entry in the Stationers' Register.

Six weeks later, on April 23, 1638, *The Royal Master* was licensed for London presentation.[27]   Fleay, in 1885, asserted that it was "licensed for the Queen's men at Salisbury Court."[28]   In 1891, he changed this to "at Salisbury Court, by the Queen's men, I suppose."[29]   As no extant record shows for what company the play was licensed, Fleay's last two words are wisely added; yet his supposition is probably correct: so far as we know, *The Doubtful Heir* and *The Imposture,* licensed in 1640, were the first plays that Shirley gave to the King's men; and if he had given *The Royal Master* to Beeston's Boys in Drury Lane, the play would certainly have been included in the list of Cockpit plays, August 10, 1639. The title-page of *The Royal Master* mentions, as we have noted, only its presentations "in the new Theater in Dublin:

---

[26] From the copy belonging to the late Robert Hoe, Esq.

[27] Malone's *Shakspere,* 1821, III, 232, note.

[28] Fleay, in *Anglia,* VIII, 408.

[29] Fleay, in *English Drama,* II, 242.

and Before the Right Honorable the Lord Deputie of Ireland, in the Castle."

In the autumn of the same year, 1638, were entered for W. Cooke and A. Crooke, *The Ball* and *Chabot, Admiral of France.* The date of entry is not, as Fleay asserts, December 24, 1638,[30] but October 24, 1638.[31] The actual printing of these plays is dated 1639. Both, according to their title-pages, were the joint work of Chapman and Shirley; but the Stationers' Register mentions Shirley only. *The Ball* we have reason to believe is chiefly Shirley's; *Chabot,* except for slight revision, Chapman's.[32]

In the year 1639, three more of Shirley's plays were printed: *The Ball* and *Chabot,* which had been entered in the Stationers' Register for W. Cooke and A. Crooke the previous October; and *The Maid's Revenge,* entered for W. Cooke alone, April 12, 1639.[33] The title-pages of these three plays read thus:

The Ball: a Comedy; As it vvas presented by her Majesties Servants, at the private House in Drury Lane. Written by George Chapman, and James Shirly. London, Printed by Tho. Cotes, for Andrew Crooke, and William Cooke. 1639.[34]

The Tragedie of Chabot Admirall of France: As it

[30] Fleay, in *Anglia*, VII, 408; but not in *English Drama*, II, 234.
[31] *S. R.*, IV, 415.   [32] Cf. pp. 83–89, *supra*.
[33] *S. R.*, IV, 437.
[34] From the copy in the British Museum.

vvas presented by her Majesties Servants, at the private House in Drury Lane. Written by George Chapman, and James Shirly. London, Printed by The Cotes, for Andrew Crooke, and William Cooke. 1639.[35]

The Maides Revenge. A Tragedy. As it hath beene Acted with good Applause at the private house in Drury Lane, by her Majesties Servants. Written by Iames Shirley Gent. London. Printed by T. C. for William Cooke, and are to be sold at his shop at Furnivalls Inne Gate in Holbourne. 1639.[36]

Less than two weeks later, on April 25, 1639, four more of Shirley's plays were entered in the Stationers' Register for W. Cooke and A. Crooke: *The Coronation, The Opportunity, Love's Cruelty,* and *The*

[35] From the facsimile title-page in the edition by Lehman, *Publications of the University of Pennsylvania,* 1906.

[36] From the copy belonging to the late Robert Hoe, Esq. Upon the verso of folio A2 of this copy of *The Maid's Revenge,* is printed:

"A Catalogue of such things as hath beene Published by James Shirley Gent.

"Traytor	Example
Witty Faire one	Dukes Mistresse
Bird in a Cage	Ball
Changes, or Love in a Maze	Chabot Admirall of France
Gratefull Servant	Royall Master
Wedding	Schoole of Complements
Hide Park	Contention for Honour and Riches
Young Admirall	Triumph of peace, a Masque
Lady of Pleasure	Maides Revenge"
Gamester	

This catalogue is an absolutely complete list of all the works of Shirley that are known to have been published down to and including the year 1639.

Night Walker.[37] The play last named is merely one of Fletcher's, revised by Shirley. None of these four plays was published until the following year. The same is true of the other plays of Shirley entered in the Stationers' Register in 1639: *The Humorous Courtier,* entered for W. Cooke alone on July 29;[38] and *The Arcadia,* entered for John Williams and Francis Egglesfeild, November 29.[39] On the latter date, Williams and Egglesfeild also entered *Love's Cruelty;* but to this, Cooke and Crooke had a prior claim.[40]

The Humorous Courtier, mentioned in the foregoing paragraph, had never been licensed under that title; but, as the plot turns on the question of who shall become the Duke of Mantua, and as the successful suitor proves to be the Duke of Parma in disguise, we are accustomed to assume that the play entered and printed as *The Humorous Courtier* is identical with the play licensed as *The Duke,* May 17, 1631.[41] I find no ground, however, for identify-

[37] *S. R.,* IV, 438. Nissen, p. 21, asserts that *Love's Cruelty* was published by A. Crooke alone. Perhaps he is quoting not the Stationers' Register but a title-page.

[38] *Ibid.,* 447. Fleay, in *Anglia,* VIII, 409, and in *English Drama,* II, 234, misprints July 29 as July 20.

[39] *Ibid.,* 465. Fleay, in *Anglia,* VIII, 412, twice misprints "Egglesfeild" as "Egglestone"; and Nissen, p. 21, spells it "Egglesseild."

[40] Cf. *S. R.,* IV, 438, with *S. R.,* IV, 465.

[41] Fleay, in *Anglia,* VIII, 406, and in *English Drama,* II, 237, misprints this date as May 7 for May 17. Cf. Malone's *Shakspere,* 1821, III, 232, note.

ing either *The Humorous Courtier* or *The Duke*
with the play entitled *The Conceited Duke,* mentioned in the list of "Cockpitt playes appropried,"
August 10, 1639.[42] Were *The Conceited Duke* the
play licensed as by Shirley, it would be likely to stand
with his fourteen other plays, which are grouped in
the middle of the list. Instead, it stands next to the
last, among plays of various authorship. Were *The
Conceited Duke* the play published as *The Humorous Courtier,* we should expect to find the disguised
Duke of Parma a man conspicuous for his conceits.
Instead, we find him the sanest of the suitors. For
these reasons, I account Fleay's identification of *The
Conceited Duke* with *The Duke* of Shirley far from
warranted; but I account his identification of *The
Duke* and *The Humorous Courtier* wholly probable.[43]

The only other fact of record for this year 1639, is
that on October 30, Shirley's play *The Gentleman
of Venice* was licensed for London presentation.[44]
When the play was printed, sixteen years later, it was
described on its title-page as "Presented at the Private
house in Salisbury Court by her Majesties Servants." [45] This is the only one of Shirley's plays of

[42] Malone's *Shakspere,* 1821, III, 159–160, note.

[43] Fleay, in *Anglia,* VIII, 406, and in *English Drama,* II, 237.

[44] Malone's *Shakspere,* 1821, III, 232, note.

[45] From the title-page of the copy belonging to the present writer.

which we know positively that it was presented at Salisbury Court: in the case of *The Politician,* we have the assertion of the title-page that it was there presented; but, as no record of the license is extant, we must admit the possibility that the title-page is incorrect: in the case of *The Royal Master,* we have a record of the license; but, as the play was printed before it was put upon the stage, we have no title-page to tell us at what theater it was presented. Probably, however, all three of these plays were presented by the Queen's men at Salisbury Court.

Early in the year 1640, there were entered upon the Stationers' Register the titles of two plays otherwise unknown: *"The Tragedy of Saint Albons,* by Master James Shirley,"entered for W. Cooke, February 14, 1639/40; [46] and *"Looke to the Ladie,* by James Shirley,"entered for Williams and Egglesfeild, March 11, 1639/40.[47] Why these plays were never published does not appear.

Some six weeks later, on April 28, 1640, two more plays, *St. Patrick for Ireland* and *The Constant Maid,* were entered in the Stationers' Register for R. Whitaker.[48] Neither of these had been licensed for

[46] *S. R.,* IV, 472.

[47] *Ibid.,* 475. Fleay, in *Anglia,* VIII, 409, misprints this date as March 10 for March 11; on page 412, moreover, he gives the publisher's name as "Egglestone."

[48] *Ibid.,* 482. Fleay, in *Anglia,* VIII, 412, misprints the date of *St. Patrick* as October 28 for April 28.

London presentation; they are supposed to have been written for the Dublin theater.

Of the plays that had been entered in the Stationers' Register in the previous year, *The Humorous Courtier, Love's Cruelty, The Arcadia, The Opportunity,* and *The Coronation* were all published in 1640. Possibly to this list we ought to add *The Maid's Revenge,* which bears upon its title-page the date 1639. As the year 1639 (Old Style) did not end until March 25, and as the play contains a dedication that may have been added by Shirley in the spring of 1639/40 rather than at the time when the play was entered in the Stationers' Register, April 12, 1639, it is possible that the date on the title-page really means 1639/40. The title-page of this play, *The Maid's Revenge,* we quoted with those of the publications of 1639.[49] The title-pages of the plays of 1640 are as follows:

The Hvmorovs Covrtier. A Comedy, As it hath been presented with good applause at the private house in Drury-Lane. Written by Iames Shirley Gent. London. Printed by T. C. for William Cooke, and are to be sold by James Becket, in the Inner Temple. 1640.[50]

Loves Crveltie. A Tragedy, As it was presented by her Majesties Servants, at the private House in Drury

---

[49] See p. 101, *supra.*
[50] From the copy belonging to the late Robert Hoe, Esq.

Lane. Written by James Shirley Gent. London, Printed by Tho. Cotes, for Andrew Crooke. 1640.[51]

A Pastorall called the Arcadia. Acted by her Majesties Servants at the Phœnix in Drury Lane. Written by Iames Shirly Gent. London, Printed by I. D. for Iohn Williams, and F. Eglesfeild and are to be sould at the signe of the Crane in Pauls Church-yard. 1640.[52]

The Opportvnitie a comedy, As it was presented by her Majesties Servants; at the private House in Drury Lane. Written by Iames Shirley. London. Printed by Thomas Cotes for Andrew Crooke, and Will. Cooke, and are to be sold at the Signe of the Greene Dragon in Pauls Church-yard. 1640.[53]

The Coronation a comedy. As it was presented by her Majesties Servants at the private House in Drury Lane. Written by John Fletcher. Gent. London, Printed by Tho. Cotes, for Andrew Crooke, and William Cooke. and are to be sold at the signe of the Greene Dragon, in Pauls Church-yard. 1640.[54]

Sometime in this same year 1640, were published also *St. Patrick for Ireland* and *The Constant Maid,* entered, as we have already noted, on April 28. Their title-pages are as follows:

[51] From the copy belonging to the late Robert Hoe, Esq.
[52] *Ibid.*
[53] From the copy belonging to the present writer—identical with that belonging to the late Robert Hoe, Esq.
[54] From the copy belonging to the late Robert Hoe, Esq.

St. Patrick for Ireland. The first Part. Written by James Shirley. London, Printed by J. Raworth, for R. Whitaker. 1640.[55]

The Constant Maid. A Comedy. Written by James Shirley. London, Printed by J. Raworth, for R. Whitaker, 1640.[56]

The two plays of Shirley that appear to have received London presentation in this year, are *The Doubtful Heir,* licensed June 1, 1640,[57] and *The Imposture,* licensed November 10.[58] Both of these, according to their title-pages of 1652, were acted at the private house in Black Friars, i.e., by the King's men. The significance of Shirley's change, at this time, from the Queen's men to the King's, I shall presently discuss.

Sometime in this year 1640, most probably in the spring, Shirley returned from Dublin and resumed his residence in London. As the precise date of his return is one of the debatable points in the Shirleian chronology, I reserve its detailed consideration for the latter portion of this chapter, and here proceed to record such matters as are certain.

For the year 1641, all that we know of Shirley concerns two plays then licensed for presentation: *The*

[55] From the copy belonging to the late Robert Hoe, Esq.
[56] *Ibid.*
[57] Malone's *Shakspere,* 1821, III, 232, note.
[58] *Ibid.*

Politique Father, May 26, 1641,[59] and *The Cardinal,* November 25.[60] The former was never published under that title; but, as we have shown in Chapter II, in our discussion of the identity of *The Brothers* of 1626, we have every reason to suppose that *The Politique Father* of 1641 has survived as the play mentioned as *The Brothers* in the Lord Chamberlain's list of August 7, 1641, and published under that name in 1652. That play, according to its title-page, was acted "at the private House in Black Fryers."[61] *The Cardinal,* according to its title-page of 1652, was also acted by his Majesty's Servants.[62] In the prologue, Shirley ventured the opinion that "this play might rival with his best";[63] and in the dedication, 1652, he declared it to be, in his conception, the best of his flock.[64] Certainly, it shares with *The Traitor* the honor of being his ablest production in romantic tragedy.

The year 1642, which ends Shirley's career as dramatist, was marked by but two plays: *The Sisters,* licensed April 26,[65] and *The Court Secret,* never licensed. The former, according to its title-page of

---

[59] Malone's *Shakspere,* 1821, III, 232, note.
[60] *Ibid.*
[61] From the copy belonging to the present writer.
[62] *Ibid.*
[63] *Works,* v, 275.
[64] *Ibid.,* 273.
[65] Malone's *Shakspere,* 1821, III, 232, note.

1652, was "acted at the private House in Black Fryers"; [66] the latter, according to its title-page of 1653, was "Never Acted, But prepared for the Scene at Black-Friers." [67] Thus concludes Shirley's third and last dramatic period.

From the certainties of Shirleian chronology for this third dramatic period, we pass now to questions in dispute. What was the date of the presentation of *The Royal Master* before the Lord Deputy in Dublin Castle? Did Shirley visit London in the spring of 1636/7? Did he visit London in the spring of 1638/9? At what time did Shirley resume his residence in London? What did Shirley mean by writing, in the dedication of *The Maid's Revenge,* "Some say I have lost my preferment"? And, finally, must we assume, with Fleay and Nissen, that the reason why Shirley, on his return, ceased writing for the Queen's men and began writing for the King's, was that the Queen's men, during his absence, had published his plays without his knowledge and consent? These several questions we shall in turn consider.

I

FIRST among these six problems, is the question: What was the date of the presentation of *The Royal*

[66] From the copy belonging to the present writer.
[67] *Ibid.*

Master before the Lord Deputy in Dublin Castle?
The evidence in the case consists of the entry in the
Stationers' Register, on March 13, 1637/8; the licensing of the play (for presentation) on April 23, 1638;
and the publication of the play sometime within the
year 1638 with a title-page, dedication, and epilogue,
all bearing upon the date of the Dublin presentation.
The title-page, as we have noted, asserts that the play
was "Acted in the new Theater in Dublin: and Before the Right Honorable the Lord Deputie of Ireland, in the Castle"; the epilogue is "as it was spoken
to the Lord Deputy on New-Year's-Day, at night, by
way of vote, congratulating the New Year";[68] and
the dedication, which was presented to George, Earl
of Kildare, reads as follows:

My Lord:

It was my happiness, being a stranger in this kingdom,
to kiss your lordship's hands, to which your nobleness, and
my own ambition encouraged me; nor was it without justice to your name, to tender the first fruits of my observance to your lordship, whom this island acknowledgeth
her first native ornament and top branch of honour. Be
pleased now, my most honourable lord, since my affairs in
England hasten my departure and prevent my personal
attendance, that something of me may be honoured to wait
upon you in my absence: this poem. 'Tis new, and never

[68] *Works,* IV, 187.

yet personated; but expected with the first, when the English stage shall be recovered from her long silence, and her now languishing scene changed into a welcome return of wits and men. And when, by the favour of the winds and sea, I salute my country again, I shall report a story of the Irish honour, and hold myself not meanly fortunate to have been written and received

The humblest of your lordship's servants,

JAMES SHIRLEY.[69]

This dedication, it will be noted, contributes four facts to our stock of information: (1) that *The Royal Master* was Shirley's first composition after coming under the patronage of the Earl of Kildare; (2) that, at the time when Shirley wrote this dedication, the play had not been acted—was "new, and never yet personated"; (3) that, at that time, Shirley was on the point of leaving Ireland—his affairs in England hastened his departure, and he hoped, by the favor of winds and sea, to salute his country again; and (4) that, when he penned the dedication, the English stage had not yet recovered from its long silence—i.e., that the date of writing was some time after May 12, 1636, the date when the theaters closed because of the plague, but prior to October 2, 1637, the date of the reopening. In view of these four facts, where shall we place the presentation of *The Royal*

---

[69] *Works,* IV, 103.

Master before the Lord Deputy? Shall it be on New Year's Day of 1636/7 or on New Year's Day of 1637/8?

From the evidence here cited, Fleay [70] and Nissen [71] have inferred that the presentation of *The Royal Master* "Before the Right Honorable the Lord Deputie" occurred on January 1, 1637/8. Nissen deems it probable, for example, that Shirley paid a visit to London in March or April, 1637, lured by some report of the reopening of the theaters on February 23; that he brought with him the manuscript of *The Royal Master* with the dedication already written; that he left it in England to be printed; that its publication was then deferred (as we know) until the spring of 1638; and that meanwhile, on January 1, 1637/8, the play was presented before the Lord Deputy at the Castle. [72]

This hypothesis is entirely plausible; yet it involves two assumptions that we may well avoid: the assumption, namely, that in the last few weeks before the play issued from the press in the spring of 1638, Shirley despatched from Dublin a copy of the New Year's epilogue and a new title-page mentioning the production of the play in Dublin; and the still greater

[70] Fleay, in *Anglia,* VIII, 408.
[71] Nissen, p. 18.
[72] *Ibid.,* pp. 18–19.

assumption that Shirley would give *The Royal Master* to a publisher before it had been staged.

Both of these difficulties we may avoid if we but place the New Year's presentation on January 1, 1636/7, instead of 1637/8; i.e., if we suppose that the presentation occurred not after Shirley's visit to London but before. Suppose that Shirley wrote his dedication, and sent it with the manuscript of his play to the Earl of Kildare sometime in December, 1636. He might then, with far more likelihood, call it the "first" fruits of his observance; yet he could still say that, since the previous May, the English stage had been languishing in "long" silence; that the play was never yet personated; and that his affairs in England hastened his departure. Suppose then that, either with or without the influence of Kildare, Shirley's play was presented before the Lord Deputy at the Castle, on January 1, 1636/7. For this presentation, Shirley would write the epilogue; and the play, with title-page, dedication, and epilogue complete, he could then take with him immediately to London. There the hope of the reopening of the theaters might well have detained him until after February 23; and in this time he could have arranged for the publication of the three plays that were entered in the Stationers' Register on April 13, 1637, to each of which, as we know, he prefixed a dedication. Then—possibly for the convenience of the London actors, possibly for the convenience of the publishers—the printing of *The Royal Master* waited until the spring of 1638. Such is our chronology if we assume that the presentation before Strafford was on January 1, 1636/7; a chronology more plausible than that made necessary by the date usually assumed. That Fleay and Nissen are wrong in assuming the year to be 1637/8, we cannot prove; but more in keeping with all the facts we know, is the earlier date, 1636/7.

II

FOR this year 1637, one further problem remains to be considered: Did Shirley visit London in that year? In our hypothetical chronologies for *The Royal Master,* we allowed for such a possibility in the spring of 1637; but whether Shirley made such a visit, we do not surely know. We know only that, when he wrote the dedication lately quoted, his affairs in England hastened his departure. Nissen offers in evidence the fact that, on April 13, 1637, three of Shirley's plays —*The Lady of Pleasure, Hyde Park,* and *The Young Admiral*—were entered in the Stationers' Register for W. Cooke and A. Crooke;[73] and the fact that each of these plays as published bears Shir-

[73] *S. R.,* IV, 355.

ley's dedication.[74]   Equally tenable, however, is
Fleay's hypothesis: that the presence of these dedications indicates not that Shirley was in London on
April 13, 1637, but rather that he had prepared for
the printer both his manuscripts and his dedication
before leaving for Ireland in 1636.[75] In none of these
dedications does Shirley refer to Ireland, or to his life
in Dublin.   That Shirley, late in 1636 or early in
1637, intended soon to visit England, his dedication
of *The Royal Master* shows; that he ultimately fulfilled his purpose, we cannot demonstrate.

III

THE third of our six problems concerning Shirley's
last dramatic period, is the question whether the poet
visited London in the spring of 1639.   If the fact that
the three plays entered in the Stationers' Register on
April 13, 1637, were prefaced with dedications,
means that Shirley was personally in London on that
date, then the fact that *The Maid's Revenge,* entered
on April 12, 1639, has likewise a dedication, means
that on that date Shirley was again in London.
Moreover, one might argue that the dedication itself
supports this supposition.   "It is," wrote Shirley, of

[74] Nissen, p. 18.
[75] Fleay, in *Anglia,* VIII, 408.

the play, "a Tragedy which received encouragement and grace on the English stage; and though it come late to the impression, it was the second birth in this kind, which I dedicated to the scene. . . . It is many years since I saw these papers, which make haste to kiss your hand." [76] This passage—especially the word "papers"—suggests the hypothesis that Shirley had discovered either among his own manuscripts or among those belonging to the Cockpit company, a copy of *The Maid's Revenge,* first played in 1625/6, and had caused it to be entered, April 12, 1639, for publication. All this, however, is but supposition: the passage quoted fits almost as well a second hypothesis presently to be offered; and as for the fact that the play has a dedication—that is no proof of the personal presence of the dramatist in London. In short, Shirley may have visited England in the spring of 1639; but the evidence available does not prove the visit.

The second hypothesis accounting for the presence of the dedication with *The Maid's Revenge,* is that it resulted not from a visit to London about April 12, 1639, but from Shirley's return in the spring of 1639/40. The date "1639" upon the title-page means —translated into New Style—that the play was published between March 25, 1639, and March 25, 1640.

[76] Dedication, in *Works,* I, 101.

The dedication, therefore, may have been supplied not just subsequent to the former date, but rather just prior to the latter. This second hypothesis we should keep in mind as we consider our fourth problem, the date of Shirley's resumption of residence in London.

IV

ON what date did Shirley end his Dublin residence? The date of his return to London appears to fall somewhere within the year 1640. Dyce, by carelessly assuming that the dedication to *The Royal Master* was penned, as it was printed, in 1638, and that Shirley's purposed "departure" from Ireland, mentioned in that dedication, was for permanent residence rather than for a business visit, gives the impression that Shirley's Dublin period terminated in 1638.[77] That this cannot be the case is evident, as Fleay has pointed out,[78] from the opening lines of the prologue to *The Imposture,* licensed November 10, 1640:

> He [the poet] knows not what to write; fears
>   what to say.
> He has been stranger long to the English scene.[79]

[77] Dyce, in *Works*, I, xxxiv–xxxv.
[78] Fleay, in *Anglia*, VIII, 409, and in *English Drama*, II, 246.
[79] *Works*, V, 181.

Shirley would not have written thus in 1640 if he had been resident in London since 1638. Moreover, in his dedication of *The Opportunity* (entered in the Stationers' Register April 25, 1639, but not published until 1640), Shirley thus addresses his traveling companion, Captain Richard Owen:

> This Poem, at my return with you from another kingdom (wherein I enjoyed, as your employments would permit, the happiness of your knowledge and conversation), emergent from the press, and prepared to seek entertainment abroad, I took boldness thus far to direct to your name and acceptance. . . .[80]

Since this play, which was "emergent from the press" on Shirley's return from Ireland, bears the date 1640, we must infer that Shirley returned either in 1640, or, at earliest, late in 1639 (Old Style), i.e., in February or March of 1639/40. The fact that *The Maid's Revenge,* which bears the date 1639, has, like *The Opportunity* of 1640, a dedication, may be best explained on the assumption that Shirley returned to London early in the spring of 1639/40. Such an assumption, moreover, harmonizes well with the fact that *The Doubtful Heir,* licensed as *Rosania* June 1, 1640, was presented not by her Majesty's Servants, but by the King's men at Black Friars: a change of such consequence as to indicate (it would seem) the

[80] *Works,* III, 369.

presence of the dramatist. The assumption harmonizes also with the supposition that Shirley's poem *To the E[arl] of S[trafford] upon his Recovery* [81] has reference to Strafford's illness of the spring of 1640.[82] Nissen argues that "from the circumstance that the plays *St. Patrick for Ireland* and *The Constant Maid,* entered in the Stationers' Register on the 28th of April, 1640, appeared without dedication, one may be inclined to draw the conclusion that he [Shirley] had not yet settled again in the capital of England." [83] But although the presence of a dedication in these plays might indicate that Shirley had some hand in their publication, the absence of a dedication does not indicate that they were published without his knowledge and consent—much less does it indicate that Shirley had not arrived in London. All the evidence seems to warrant the conclusion that Shirley arrived in London not later than the opening weeks of 1640, perhaps even before the twenty-fifth of March, the date when the year (Old Style) legally began.

V

OUR fifth problem for Shirley's third dramatic period is the significance of a passage in his dedication

[81] *Works*, VI, 428.
[82] Nissen, p. 20.
[83] *Ibid.*

to *The Maid's Revenge:* "I never affected the ways of flattery: some say I have lost my preferment by not practising that Court sin."[84] Dyce, by quoting this passage early in his *Account,*[85] leads the casual reader to suppose that Shirley's words refer to something in the first part of his career—as if they dated from the original presentation of *The Maid's Revenge,* licensed February 9, 1625/6, not from its publication in 1639 or 1639/40. Such, however, cannot be their application. They must refer rather to a loss of preferment subsequent, at earliest, to the years 1633 and 1634, when, as author of *The Young Admiral, The Gamester,* and *The Triumph of Peace,* Shirley certainly was high in favor. Shall we suppose that Shirley's removal to Ireland in 1636 and his continuance there even after the reopening of the London theaters in October, 1637, were due not alone to the ravages of the plague in London and to the opportunity offered by John Ogilby in Dublin, but also to loss of preferment at court? Had Shirley's satires upon fashionable society offended others than Sir Henry Herbert? Why should the sometime favorite of king and queen be drudging for Ogilby in Dublin?

In support of such a possibility, we may cite two bits of documentary evidence: Herbert's entry con-

[84] Dedication to *The Maid's Revenge,* in *Works,* I, 101.
[85] Dyce, in *Works,* I, viii–ix.

cerning *The Ball,* November 18, 1632; and Shirley's allusion to the same matter in *The Lady of Pleasure,* licensed October 15, 1635. The first of these (already quoted in our second chapter) is from the office-book of the Master of the Revels:

18 Nov. 1632. In the play of *The Ball,* written by Sherley, and acted by the Queens players, ther were divers personated so naturally, both of lords and others of the court, that I took it ill, and would have forbidden the play, but that Biston promiste many things which I found faulte withall should be left out, and that he would not suffer it to be done by the poett any more, who deserves to be punisht; and the first that offends in this kind, of poets or players, shall be sure of publique punishment.[86]

Three years later, with evident reference to *The Ball,* Shirley inserted in *The Lady of Pleasure* the following lines:

> Another game you have which consumes more
> Your fame than purse: your revels in the night,
> Your meetings call'd *The Ball,* to which repair,
> As to the court of pleasure, all your gallants
> And ladies, thither bound by a subpoena
> Of Venus, and small Cupid's high displeasure.
> 'Tis but the Family of Love translated
> Into more costly sin! There was a play on't;
> And, had the poet not been bribed to a modest

[86] Malone's *Shakspere,* 1821, III, 231–232.

Expression of your antic gambols in't,
Some darks had been discovered, and the deeds too.
In time he may repent, and make some blush
To see the second part danced on the stage.[87]

Thus runs the play licensed for presentation in the autumn of 1635. In the spring of 1636, Shirley took up his residence in Dublin. Have we, in these lines, an explanation of his departure, and of his words in 1639: "I never affected the ways of flattery: some say I have lost my preferment by not practising that Court sin"?

On the other hand, may we not rather assume that the loss or alleged loss of preferment—"some *say* I have lost my preferment"—has reference not to London but to Dublin? Had Shirley, for the moment, offended either Strafford or Kildare? Was Shirley returning to London because in Ireland he had lost his preferment? These questions I must be content to leave unanswered.

VI

OUR final problem for Shirley's third dramatic period is to discover why Shirley ceased to write for her Majesty's Servants, and prepared his last six plays

[87] *The Lady of Pleasure*, I, i; *Works*, IV, 9.

for the King's men. Concerning this matter, Fleay
wrote in 1885:

It appears that a dozen plays were printed during
Shirley's absence in Ireland undedicated by him and without his supervision. . . . Whether he was annoyed, as I
think, that the Queen's men should have made his writings public in this way or for some other reason, he wrote
no more for them; but joined the King's company.[88]

By 1891, Fleay's conjecture has become a certainty.
He writes:

The Queen's men in the plague trouble had evidently
been selling Shirley's plays without his knowledge or consent; and, worse still, they had sold *Love's Cruelty* twice
over, and *The Coronation* as a play of Fletcher's. . . .
No wonder that Shirley left writing for a company that
had treated his works in this way during his absence.[89]

And in 1901, Nissen states the assumption still more
positively:

Upon his arrival in London, our author was to make
the unpleasant discovery that during his absence no less
than twelve of his plays had been published by others.
The Queen's men had published not only the pieces played
in the Cockpit Theatre before his departure to Dublin,
not yet edited by him, but had also given to the press two

[88] Fleay, in *Anglia*, VIII, 409.
[89] Fleay, in *English Drama*, II, 243–244.

of those dramatic works sent back from Ireland, *St. Patrick for Ireland* and *The Constant Maid*—two dramas which evidently they had not acted at all. All these plays appeared, therefore, without dedications; and, since the author did not supervise the printing, the text in many of them is very inaccurate. . . . The Queen's men had not only sold the dramas of Shirley in their possession without his knowledge and approval—*Love's Cruelty* even twice; namely to the firm of W. Cooke and A. Crooke, as well as to Williams & Egglesfeild—they had, what is perhaps still worse, sold *The Coronation* as a work of Fletcher's and *Look to the Lady,* a piece which it is highly probable was not written by him, as his own. That our poet was indignant over such treatment, one can imagine. He broke off his relations with the players of the Queen. The last of the dramas composed and acted in Ireland, *Rosania,* which he brought with him to England in the year 1640, he offered to the King's Servants playing in the Black Friars and Globe Theatre. This company, whose playwright he became when Heywood ceased to write for the stage, brought out his later dramatic works.[90]

What is this argument of Fleay and Nissen? During Shirley's residence in Ireland, twelve of his plays (including *Chabot* and *The Night Walker* as by Shirley) were published in London without his dedication: therefore these plays were published without his knowledge or consent: therefore he had grounds for anger—anger against the Queen's players: for

[90] Nissen, pp. 20–21.

this reason he ceased writing for the Queen's players, and wrote thenceforth only for the players of the King.

Let us examine certain of the links in this long argument. We might, perhaps, inquire whether absence of dedication is adequate proof of absence of knowledge or consent to publication; but we will let that point pass. Let us grant that all twelve of these plays were put in print unknown to Shirley. Does it follow that he had grounds for anger? Was Shirley the man that had been wronged? In short, was the playwright the owner of the play for the purposes of publication?

One document that has survived to us from the year 1637, appears to uphold a different interpretation. In a long letter directed by the Lord Chamberlain, Philip, Earl of Pembroke and Montgomery, to the Master and Wardens of the Company of Printers and Stationers, dated June 10, 1637, the Lord Chamberlain distinctly states that the companies of players owned plays, "bought and provided at very dear and high rates"; that the printing of these plays without the authority of the players resulted not only in "much prejudice" to the actors, but in "much corruption" to the books, "to the injury and disgrace of the authors"; and that, since "some copies of plays belonging to the King and Queen's servants, the players, . . . having been lately stolen, or gotten from them by indirect means, are now attempted to be printed," the Lord Chamberlain commands that the Stationers see that no play be printed without the express permission of the company of players concerned.[91] In a similar letter, dated August 7, 1641, the Earl of Essex, successor to the Earl of Pembroke and Montgomery in the office of Lord Chamberlain, is equally specific.[91a] If the Lord Chamberlain's order be good law, then not Shirley but the company of actors would be the aggrieved party in case of the unauthorized publication of a play.

But let us waive this point also. Let us assume that Shirley was justly angry at the publication of his plays without his knowledge or consent. Against whom should he be angry? Against the Queen's players, say Fleay and Nissen.

The objection to this assumption is that the company of her Majesty's Servants who, during Shirley's residence in Ireland, presented certain of his plays at Salisbury Court, and whom he abandoned in favor of the King's men on his return from Dublin, is not the company of the same name that, before Shirley's

[91] This letter is printed, wholly or in part, in Chalmers's *Apology*, pp. 513–514, note *v;* Collier's *English Dramatic Poetry*, II, 83–84, note; and Malone's *Shakspere*, 1821, III, 160–161, note.

[91a] Reprinted by Chambers in *The Malone Society Collections, Parts IV & V*, pp. 364–369.

Dublin period, brought out his plays at the Private House in Drury Lane; and there is no evidence that the new company inherited any of Shirley's manuscripts from the original company.

Down to the year 1637, all of Shirley's plays with one exception[92] had been acted by the Queen's men under Christopher Beeston, acting in the Private House in Drury Lane, otherwise known as the "Phœnix" and the "Cockpit." When the plague of 1636–1637 occasioned the long closing of the theaters, Christopher and William Beeston organized a company of boys for acting plays at court.[93] It was with such a company, not with the adult "Queen's men," that the Beestons reopened the Cockpit on October 2, 1637. As a result, Turner, Perkins, Sumner, and Sherlock, of the old company, united with the best of the former Revels Company at Salisbury Court.[94] This new organization under Turner,[95] adopted the

[92] See the title-pages in the Bibliography. The exception is *Changes, or Love in a Maze*, acted "at the Private House in Salisbury Court, by the Company of His Majesties Revels."

[93] See Herbert's entries for February 7 and 14, 1636/7, in Malone's *Shakspere*, 1821, III, 239.

[94] See Herbert's entries of October 2, 1637, quoted by Malone, *Shakspere*, 1821, III, 240.

[95] Turner's managership is inferred from the following entry quoted in Chalmers's *Apology*, p. 511, note, from a manuscript book in the Lord Chamberlain's office:

"6th March 1639/40—A warrant for £80, unto Henry Turner &c. the Queen's players, for seven plays by them acted at court in 1638, & 1639; whereof £20 for one play at Richmond."

name of "her Majesty's Servants." They presented Shirley's *The Gentleman of Venice,* and, presumably, *The Royal Master* and *The Politician;* but they were not her Majesty's Servants of the Cockpit, the Phœnix, the Private House in Drury Lane. The old company had ceased to be.[96]

Nor can it be shown that the new company at Salisbury Court inherited, from its namesake of the Cockpit, any of the plays of Shirley. The number of plays by Shirley acted before he went to Dublin, is twenty-three. Of these, the Lord Chamberlain's list of August 10, 1639, names fifteen as the property of William Beeston as governor of the young company at the Cockpit.[97] Among these fifteen, stand five plays which Fleay and Nissen assert were sold to the publishers by the Queen's men! Are we to assume that the actors of Salisbury Court stole these five plays from the Cockpit children to sell to the stationers?

And what grounds has Nissen for the assumption that the Queen's men "had also given to the press two of those dramatic works sent back from Ireland, *St. Patrick for Ireland* and *The Constant Maid"?* How do we know that the Queen's men ever had these plays in their possession?

[96] On the history of the several companies mentioned, see especially, Murray, *English Dramatic Companies.*

[97] The MS. is quoted by Collier, *English Dramatic Poetry,* II, 92, note. Cf. Malone's *Shakspere,* 1821, III, 159–160, note.

And what of the plays that were acted, or presumably were acted, at Salisbury Court? Were they likewise published without Shirley's knowledge and consent? On the contrary, *The Royal Master, The Gentleman of Venice,* and *The Politician*—the only plays assignable on any ground to Salisbury Court—all were published with dedications signed by Shirley: two of them after a wait of over fifteen years.

In short, even if we assume that the twelve plays published without dedication during Shirley's absence, were published without his knowledge and consent—an assumption of the utmost liberality—and even if we assume further that, in such publication, Shirley was the man aggrieved—an assumption that appears contrary to the Lord Chamberlain's letter of June 10, 1637—we are yet unable to discover why Shirley's anger should be directed against the Queen's men of Salisbury Court; for, of the plays of Shirley known to have been in their possession, not one was published without Shirley's dedication, and of the twelve plays published without dedication, not one can be shown to have been in their possession. Under these circumstances, let us not accuse her Majesty's Servants of literary larceny.

But, one asks, if the Salisbury Court men had not made Shirley angry, presumably by disposing of his manuscripts, why then did he sever his connection with them and begin writing for the King's men at Black Friars?

The answer, it seems to me, is to be found in the changes which the old "Queen's men" had undergone in Shirley's absence. He returned from Ireland in the spring of 1640, to find that his old manager, Christopher Beeston of the Phœnix—the Cockpit—the Private House in Drury Lane—had transferred his attention to a company of boys, and, presently, had been superseded in the management of these young players by William Beeston, who, in turn, was about to be superseded, June 27, 1640, by William Davenant.[98] Shirley returned to find that the old "Queen's men" that he had known, had ceased to be; and that the name "her Majesty's Servants" was now borne by a new organization under Turner, an organization consisting of four of the old "Queen's men" joined with the best of the former Revels Company of Salisbury Court. This new company had presented, during Shirley's residence in Dublin, his *Gentleman of Venice,* and probably also *The Politician* and *The Royal Master;* but it could have had for Shirley no especial interest. These actors were not the Queen's men of the Cockpit in Drury Lane, the players under Beeston who had produced almost

[98] See the document quoted by Collier in *English Dramatic Poetry,* II, 101, note.

[130]

every play of Shirley from the day when the modest schoolmaster of St. Albans had "retired to the Metropolis, lived in Greys inn, and set up for a playmaker." They were merely a new company of actors under a new manager, who, during Shirley's absence in Ireland, had presented three plays that he had sent to them. Why should he continue to write for this new company? Why should he not seek a position with a better company? The King's men were well established at Black Friars and the Globe. With the death of Massinger,[99] they would welcome such a dramatist as Shirley. For this reason, I believe, and not from indignation that the Queen's men had published his plays without his knowledge and consent, Shirley in 1640 began writing for his Majesty's Servants at Black Friars.

What, then, are our conclusions concerning the chronology of Shirley's last dramatic period? In the first place, we have noted Shirley's removal to Dublin in the year 1636, the probable motive for his removal (the plague in London), and his establishment in Dublin as dramatist to John Ogilby's new theater in Werburgh Street. Secondly, we have verified from Malone's transcript of the office-book of Sir Henry Herbert, Master of the Revels, from the Stationers' Register, and from the title-pages of the published

[99] Died March, 1639/40.

plays, the available facts concerning the presentation of *The Royal Master, The Gentleman of Venice, The Politician, St. Patrick for Ireland, The Constant Maid, Rosania (The Doubtful Heir), The Imposture, The Politique Father (The Brothers of 1652), The Cardinal, The Sisters,* and *The Court Secret;* and concerning the publication of *The Lady of Pleasure, Hyde Park, The Young Admiral, The Example, The Gamester, The Royal Master, The Duke's Mistress, The Ball, Chabot, The Maid's Revenge, The Coronation, The Opportunity, Love's Cruelty, The Night Walker, The Humorous Courtier (The Duke), The Arcadia, St. Patrick for Ireland,* and *The Constant Maid.* And finally, with respect to questions in dispute, we have concluded: (1) that the date of the presentation of *The Royal Master* before the Lord Deputy in Dublin Castle, may have been the evening of January 1, 1636/7, rather than January 1, 1637/8, as has been usually assumed; (2) that Shirley's alleged visit to London in the spring of 1637 may have taken place but, on the basis of extant evidence, is incapable of proof; (3) that the same is true of Shirley's alleged visit in the spring of 1639; (4) that the date of Shirley's ultimate return to London is 1640, probably in the spring, and perhaps even before March 25, the date when the new year (Old Style) legally began; (5) that Shirley's references to his having lost his preferment must refer to a misfortune subsequent to 1633 and 1634, and may refer either to loss of preferment at court—possibly as a result of his personal satire in *The Ball* and in *The Lady of Pleasure*—in 1635, or to loss of preferment in Ireland in 1639, or to neither; and (6) that Shirley's reason for ceasing to write for the Queen's men on his return from Ireland, was probably not his indignation over the publication of certain plays, but merely the fact that the original company of her Majesty's Servants was no longer in existence, and that the King's men offered him a more promising position than could the new company of her Majesty's Servants at Salisbury Court. With these facts as a basis and a background, we shall endeavor in Chapters XIV to XVIII inclusive, to complete our study of Shirley's development as a dramatist.

I cannot better conclude my record of Shirley's third and last dramatic period, than by quoting the prologue of his last acted comedy, *The Sisters:*

Does this look like a Term? I cannot tell;
Our Poet thinks the whole Town is not well,
Has took some physic lately, and, for fear
Of catching cold, dares not salute this air.
But there's another reason. I hear say
London is gone to York; 'tis a great way.

[133]

Pox o' the proverb, and of him, say I,
That look'd o'er Lincoln! 'cause that was, must we
Be now translated north? I could rail, too,
On Gammar Shipton's ghost; but 'twill not do:
The town will still be flecking; and a play,
Though ne'er so new, will starve the second day.
Upon these very hard conditions,
Our Poet will not purchase many towns;
And if you leave us too, we cannot thrive:
I'll promise neither Play nor Poet live
Till ye come back. Think what you do. You see
What audiences we have, what company
To Shakspere comes, whose mirth did once beguile
Dull hours, and, buskin'd, made even sorrow smile.
So lovely were the wounds, that men would say
They could endure the bleeding a whole day.
He has but few friends lately: think of that!
He'll come no more; and others have his fate.
Fletcher, the Muses' darling, and choice love
Of Phœbus, the delight of every grove;
Upon whose head the laurel grew: whose wit
Was the time's wonder, and example yet:
'Tis within memory, trees did not throng,
As once the story said, to Orpheus' song.
Jonson, t'whose name wise art did bow, and wit
Is only justified by honouring it;
To hear whose touch, how would the learned quire
With silence stoop! and when he took his lyre,
Apollo dropp'd his lute, asham'd to see
A rival to the god of harmony:

You do forsake him too. We must deplore
This fate; for we do know it by our door.
How must this Author fear then, with his guilt
Of weakness, to thrive here, where late was spilt
The Muses' own blood; if, being but a few,
You not conspire, and meet more frequent too?
There are not now nine Muses, and you may
Be kind to ours. If not, he bad me say,
    Though while you careless kill the rest, and laugh,
    Yet he may live to write your epitaph.[100]

Thus runs the prologue of the last play of Shirley
acted before the Civil War: "London is gone to
York"; but the poet hopes that "yet he may live to
write your epitaph." Ten years later, in a dedication
addressed to William Earl of Strafford, son of the
greater Earl of Strafford—that unhappy minister of
an unhappy king—Shirley described the catastrophe
in four pregnant words: for Shirley, for Shirley's patron, and for that patron's patron, "the stage was
interdicted." [101]

[100] *Works,* v, 356–357.
[101] Dedication of *The Court Secret; Works,* v, 428.

CHAPTER V

SHIRLEY'S POST-DRAMATIC PERIOD

1642–1666

AFTER eighteen brilliant years as dramatist to court and public, Shirley, at the age of forty-six, entered upon the closing period of his career—a quarter century of anticlimax: cavalier, schoolmaster, literary drudge. For his life as soldier, our sole authority is Wood's *Athenæ Oxonienses*. This account may well be as inaccurate as it is inadequate; but it is all we have:

When the rebellion broke out, and he [was] thereupon forced to leave London, and so consequently his Wife and Children (who afterwards were put to their shifts), he was invited by his most noble Patron, William, Earl (afterwards Marquess and Duke) of Newcastle, to take his fortune with him in the wars, for that Count had engaged him so much by his generous liberality toward him, that he thought he could not do a worthier act than to serve him, and so consequently his Prince.[1]

[1] Wood, 1691–1692, II, 261; cf. 1817, III, 737.

This, I repeat, is all that we know of Shirley's soldiering; and even this may be as dubious as is the imaginative account in Shiels's *Cibber's Lives of the Poets* or Gosse's assertion that Shirley accompanied his lord to France.[2] Ward, to be sure, insists that "the lines *To Odelia*[3] certainly imply that Shirley took personal part in the 'war' in which Newcastle was concerned from November, 1642, till July, 1644, when (after Marston Moor) he quitted England."[4] And Nissen, who, as we have seen before, believes in a most literal interpretation of lyric poetry, declares that, from this poem *To Odelia,* we learn that Shirley tarried many months far from her in the North; and that he entreats her for speedy news, for " 'tis far, and many accidents do wait on war."[5] Perhaps—but are all the lyrics of the Cavaliers to be accounted autobiographic documents? If so, how did Shirley, in his *Poems* of 1646, venture to address by name so many mistresses? What did Odelia think? What said his good wife Frances? By all means, let us return to our Wood!

After the Kings cause declined, he [Shirley] retired obscurely to London, where among other of his noted friends, he found Tho. Stanley, Esq., who exhibited to

[2] Introduction to the *Mermaid Shirley,* xxvi.
[3] *Works,* VI, 408.
[4] Ward, in *DNB.,* LII, 128.
[5] Nissen, p. 22.

him for the present. Afterwards, following his old trade of teaching School, which was mostly in the White Fryers, he not only gained a comfortable subsistence (for the acting of plays was then silenced) but educated many ingenious youths, who afterwards proved most eminent in divers faculties.[6]

The substantial accuracy of these assertions, we need not question. Shirley's publications for the years 1646 and 1647 are such as would be appropriate to the pensioner of Thomas Stanley, Esq.; his publications from the year 1649 onward, include several that are appropriate to a schoolmaster; and in Shirley's will of July, 1666, which I shall quote later in this chapter, he describes himself as "of Whitefriars, London, gentleman."

Shirley's *Poems* of 1646 is a small octavo volume in three parts, paged as if each part were to be issued separately. The several title-pages read:

Poems &c. By James Shirley. Sine aliquâ dementiâ nullus Phœbus. London, Printed for Humphrey Moseley, and are to be sold at his shop at the signe of the Princes Armes in St. Pauls Church-yard. 1646.

Narcissus, or, The Self-Lover. By James Shirley. Hæc olim— London, Printed for Humphrey Moseley, and are to be sold at his shop at the signe of the Princes Armes in St. Pauls Church-yard. MDCXLVI.

[6] Wood, 1691–1692, II, 261; cf. 1817, III, 737–738.

Hæc summum vatem Shirleium pingit Imago,
Solem sic reddit debilis umbra suum:
At si nativâ fulgentem luce videbis,
Exhibet en propriâ picta Tabella manu.

W. Marshall sculpsit. 1646.

JAMES SHIRLEY

From the engraving by W. Marshall, 1646

The Trivmph of Beavtie. As it was personated by some young Gentlemen, for whom it was intended, at a private Recreation. By James Shirley. London, Printed for Humphrey Mosely, and are to be sold at his shop, at the Signe of the Princes Armes in St. Pauls Churchyard. MDCXLVI.[7]

Prefixed to the first of these divisions is a portrait of Shirley framed in a wreath of bay, supported by Tragedy and Comedy. Beneath it are engraved the lines:

Hæc summum vatem Shirleium pingit Imago;
  Solem sic reddit debilis umbra suum:
At si nativâ fulgentem luce videbis,
  Exhibet en propriâ picta Tabella manu.

The engraving is signed "W. Marshall sculpsit, 1646." Appended to this division of the volume is the following "Postscript to the Reader":

I had no intention upon the birth of these poems, to let them proceed to the public view, forbearing in my own modesty to interpose my fancies, when I see the world so plentifully furnished. But when I observed most of these copies corrupted in their transcripts, and the rest fleeting from me, which were by some indiscreet collector, not acquainted with distributive justice, mingled with other men's (some eminent) conceptions in

[7] From the copy belonging to the late Robert Hoe, Esq.

print, I thought myself concerned to use some vindication, and reduce them to my own, without any pride or design of deriving opinion from their worth, but to shew my charity, that other innocent men should not answer for my vanities.

If thou beest courteous, reader, there are some errors of the press scattered, which thy clemency will not lay to my charge; other things I remit to thy judgment: if thou beest modest, I repent not to have exposed them and myself to thy censure. J. S.[8]

The second portion of the volume—*Narcissus, or The Self-Lover*—is supposed to be identical with the poem that was entered in the Stationers' Register on January 4, 1617/18, under the title: *Ecc[h]o and Narcissus the 2 unfortunate lovers written by Jeames Sherley.*[9] Paged with *Narcissus* are "Prologues and Epilogues, written to several Plays presented in this Kingdom and elsewhere."

In 1647, the year following the publication of his *Poems*, we have a further glimpse of Shirley. This time the retired dramatist appears as dramatic critic —the author of an address "To the Reader" prefixed to the plays of Beaumont and Fletcher:

Comedies and Tragedies Written by Francis Beavmont And Iohn Fletcher Gentlemen. Never printed be-

[8] *Works*, VI, 461–462.
[9] *S. R.*, III, 286.

fore, And now published by the Authours Originall Copies. Si quid habent veri Vatum praesagia, vivam. London, Printed for Humphrey Robinson, at the three Pidgeons, and for Humphrey Moseley at the Princes Armes in St Pauls Church-yard. 1647.[11]

This was a volume of no small importance. For plays, a folio was still a rarity; and the number of commendatory verses goes to show that, as a literary undertaking, it was accounted notable. That the tone of Shirley's introduction should be cordial was inevitable; but that it was sincere as well we need not doubt: from Rare Ben Jonson, the "acknowledged master" of Shirley's early years, he had long since transferred his allegiance to these romantic dramatists "whom but to mention is to throw a cloud upon all former names and to benight posterity."[12]

And now, reader [says Shirley], in this tragical age, where the theatre has been so much out-acted, congratulate thy own happiness that, in this silence of the stage, thou hast liberty to read these inimitable plays, to dwell and converse in these immortal groves.[13]

Alas, that one who could write thus of his predecessors in romantic drama must next produce a *Via ad Latinam Linguam Complanata!*

[11] From the copy in the possession of Ernest Dressel North, Esq.
[12] *Ibid.*
[13] *Ibid.*

[141]

This text-book has a most marvelous frontispiece-title, engraved by T. Cross: Grammatica enthroned, and, below on either side, Etymologia and Syntaxis. The printed title reads:

Via ad Latinam Linguam Complanata. The Way made plain to the Latine Tongue. The Rules composed in English and Latine Verse: For the greater Delight and Benefit of Learners. By James Shirley. Avia Pieridum peragro loca. Lucret. London, Printed by R. W. for John Stephenson, at the signe of the Sun on Ludgate-Hill. 1649.[14]

Four years later, in 1653, Shirley again appears. In this year he published *Six New Playes,* a volume which included: *The Doubtful Heir,* licensed, as *Rosania,* June 1, 1640; *The Imposture,* licensed November 10, 1640; *The Brothers,* which we believe to be identical with *The Politique Father,* licensed May 26, 1641; *The Cardinal,* licensed November 25, 1641; *The Sisters,* licensed April 26, 1642; and *The Court Secret,* "never acted, but prepared for the scene at the Black-Friers," 1642. The title-page of this volume bears, as the date of publication, the year 1653. The title-pages of the individual plays, however, with the exception of *The Court Secret,* are dated not 1653 but 1652. They are as follows:

[14] From the copy belonging to the late Robert Hoe, Esq.

Six New Playes, Viz. The Brothers. Sisters. Doubtfull Heir. Imposture. Cardinall. Court Secret. The
Five first were acted at the Private House in Black Fryers
with great Applause. The last was never Acted. All
Written by James Shirley. Never printed before. London, Printed for Humphrey Robinson at the Three Pigeons, and Humphrey Moseley at the Prince's Armes in
St. Paul's Curch-yard. 1653.[15]

The Brothers, A Comedie, As It was Acted at the
private House in Black Fryers. Written By James Shirley. Never Printed before. London, Printed for Humphrey Robinson at the Three Pigeons, and Humphrey
Moseley at the Prince Armes in St. Paul's Church-yard.
1652.[16]

The Sisters, A Comedie, As It was acted at the private
House in Black Fryers, Written By James Shirley. Never
Printed before. London, Printed for Humphrey Robin-
son at the Three Pigeons, and Humphrey Moseley at the
Prince's Arms in St. Paul's Church-yard. 1652.[17]

The Doubtful Heir. A Tragi-comedie, As It was
Acted at the private House in Black Friers, Written By
James Shirley. Never Printed before. I ondon, Printed
for Humphrey Robinson at the three Pigeons, and Humphrey Moseley at the Prince's Arms in St. Paul's Church-
yard. 1652.[18]

[15] From the copy belonging to the present writer.
[16] *Ibid.*
[17] *Ibid.*
[18] *Ibid.*

The Impostvre A Tragi-Comedie, As It was Acted at the private House in Black Fryers. Written By James Shirley. Never Printed before. London, Printed for Humphrey Robinson at the Three Pigeons, and Humphrey Moseley at the Prince's Armes in St. Paul's Curch-yard. 1652.[19]

The Cardinal, A Tragedie, As It was acted at the private House in Black Fryers, Written By James Shirley. Not Printed before. London, Printed for Humphrey Robinson at the Three Pigeons, and Humphrey Moseley at the Prince's Arms in St. Paul's Church-yard. 1652.[20]

The Court Secret, A Tragi-comedy: Never Acted, But prepared for the Scene at Black-Friers. Written By James Shirley. Never printed before. London, Printed for Humphrey Robinson at the three Pigeons, and for Humphrey Moseley at the Prince's Armes in Saint Paul's Church-yard, 1653.[21]

Appended to *The Cardinal* in this volume of *Six New Playes,* is "A Catalogue of the Authors Poems Already Printed." It includes all of his published works up to that time except, strangely, *The Young Admiral* and *The Arcadia.* Also unmentioned are three of the *Six New Playes—The Doubtful Heir, The Cardinal,* and *The Court Secret;* two plays subsequently published—*The Politician,* and *The Gen-*

[19] From the copy belonging to the present writer.
[20] *Ibid.*
[21] *Ibid.*

tleman of Venice; and certain minor pieces.[22] A similar list of publications was appended, as the reader may recall, to *The Maid's Revenge,* 1639.

To this same year, 1653, belong also both the act-

[22] This list of publications appended to *The Cardinal* reads as follows:

"A CATALOGUE OF THE AUTHORS POEMS ALREADY PRINTED

Tragedies

The Traytour
Philip Chabot Admirall of France
Loves Cruelty
The Maids Revenge
Dukes Mistris
The Cardinal

Comedies and Tragi-comedies

The School of Complement
The Lady of Pleasure
Hide-parke
The Constant Maid
*The Coronation   * Falsely as-
The Changes, or Love in a Maze   cribed to
The Gratefull Servant   *Jo. Fletcher.*
The Patron of Ireland
The Humorous Court[ier]
The Wedding
The Ball, or French Dancing Master
The Gamester
The Example
The Bird in a cage
The Royall Master
The Opportunity
The Witty Fair one
The Imposture
The Brothers
The Sisters
A Masque of the four Honorable Innes of Court, presented before
    the King and Queens Majesty at Whitehall in the Banqueting house.
Poems."

[145]

ing and the publication of Shirley's *Cupid and Death*. Its title reads:

Cvpid and Death. A Masque. As it was Presented before his Excellencie, The Embassadour of Portugal, Upon the 26. of March, 1653. Written by J. S. London: Printed according to the Authors own Copy, by T. W. for J. Crook, & J. Baker, at the Sign of the Ship in St. Pauls Church-Yard, 1653.[23]

The last plays that Shirley printed appeared two years later, in 1655. These were *The Politician* and *The Gentleman of Venice,* both of which, according to their title-pages, had been presented at Salisbury Court by her Majesty's Servants. *The Gentleman of Venice,* as we noticed above, had been licensed for presentation on October 30, 1639. Later, according to Shirley's dedication, "it lost itself, till it was re-covered after much inquisition."[24] This passage means, I take it, that either because Shirley had ceased to write for the players of Salisbury Court, or because of the closing of the theaters, or perhaps merely because the Queen's men insisted upon their rights of ownership, Shirley was long unable to re-gain possession of the play. Such may have been the history also of *The Politician,* published, like *The*

[23] From the copy in the British Museum.
[24] *Works,* v, 3.

Gentleman of Venice, by Humphrey Moseley, in 1655, and, like that play, ascribed on its title-page to her Majesty's Servants of Salisbury Court. Of the licensing of *The Politician,* we have no record; but this may be the fault of Malone's transcript rather than the laxity of Manager Turner or of Sir Henry Herbert. The ill-advised attempt to identify this play with *The Politique Father,* I have sufficiently discussed in connection with *The Brothers* of 1626. In respect to its publication, it was, as Shirley prophesied in his dedication, "the last" of his plays "to salute the public view." [25] The title-pages of these two plays read thus:

The Gentleman of Venice A Tragi-Comedie Presented at the Private house in Salisbury Court by her Majesties Servants. Written by James Shirley. London, Printed for Humphrey Moseley and are to be sold at his Shop at the Princes Armes in St. Pauls Church-yard. 1655. [26]

The Polititian, A Tragedy, Presented at Salisbury Court By Her Majesties Servants; Written By James Shirley. London, Printed for Humphrey Moseley and are to be sold at his Shop at the Princes Armes in St. Pauls Church-yard. 1655. [27]

[25] *Works,* v, 91.
[26] From the copy belonging to the present writer.
[27] *Ibid.*

Shirley's second Latin text-book appeared in 1656, and was reissued under a new title in 1660. The two title-pages read:

The Rudiments of Grammar. The Rules Composed in English Verse, For The greater Benefit and delight of young Beginners. By James Shirley. Vtile dulci. London, Printed by J. Macock for R. Lownds, and are to be sold at his shop at the white Lyon in Paul's Church-Yard, 1656.[28]

Manductio: or, A leading of Children by the Hand Through the Principles of Grammar. The second Edition, Enlarged. By Ja: Shirley. Perveniri ad summum nisi ex principiis non potest. London, Printed for Richard Lowndes, at the White-Lion in S. Pauls Church-Yard. 1660.[29]

Of greater interest is the little volume of 1659 containing *Honoria and Mammon* and *The Contention of Ajax and Ulysses for the Armor of Achilles*. The title-pages of the volume and of the parts read thus:

Honoria and Mammon. Written by James Shirly Gent. Scene Metropolis, or New-Troy. Whereunto is added the Contention of Ajax and Ulisses, for the Armour of Achilles. As it was represented by young Gentlemen of quality at a private entertainment of some Per-

---

[28] From the copy in the British Museum.
[29] *Ibid.*

sons of Honour. London, Printed for John Crook, and are to be sold at his shop at the signe of the Ship in S. Pauls Church-yard, 1659.[30]

Honoria and Mammon. Written by James Shirley [Three lines in Latin.] London, Printed by T. W. for John Crook, at the sign of the ship in S. Pauls Church-yard. [n.d.][31]

The Contention of Ajax and Ulysses, for the Armor of Achilles. As It was nobly represented by young Gentlemen of quality, at a private Entertainment of some persons of Honour. Written By James Shirley. London, Printed for John Crook, at the sign of the ship in S. Pauls Church-yard. [n. d.][32]

The Contention of Ajax and Ulysses is especially to be remembered for containing that noble dirge that seems destined for all time to represent the work of Shirley in our anthologies: the poem beginning,

> The glories of our blood and state
> Are shadows, not substantial things.

Spoken as it is by Calchas to the six princes, Agamemnon, Diomedes, Menelaus, Thersander, Nestor, and Ulysses, as they bear the body of Ajax to the temple, the poem is especially affecting:

[30] From the copies belonging to the late Robert Hoe, Esq.
[31] *Ibid.*   [32] *Ibid.*

[149]

JAMES SHIRLEY, DRAMATIST

The glories of our blood and state
   Are shadows, not substantial things;
There is no armour against fate;
   Death lays his icy hand on kings:
      Scepter and crown
      Must tumble down,
And in the dust be equal made
With the poor crooked scythe and spade.

Some men with swords may reap the field
   And plant fresh laurels where they kill;
But their strong nerves at last must yield;
   They tame but one another still:
      Early or late
      They stoop to fate,
And must give up their murmuring breath,
When they, pale captives, creep to death.

The garlands wither on your brow.
   Then boast no more your mighty deeds;
Upon Death's purple altar now,
   See, where the victor-victim bleeds:
      Your heads must come
      To the cold tomb;
Only the actions of the just
Smell sweet, and blossom in their dust.

In the library of the late Robert Hoe, Esq., were three copies of this volume, in one of which occurred the rare engraving of Shirley dated 1658. It shows head and shoulders mounted upon a pedestal: dark

Iacobus Shirlæus:

G Phenik pinx: R. Gaywood fecit 1658

JAMES SHIRLEY

G. Phenik pinx: R. Gaywood fecit 1658

skull-cap, wavy black hair falling upon a soft white collar, round face, scant light mustache, conspicuous eyes. Clearly emblazoned in the upper left-hand corner, a shield displays the arms of the Warwick Shirleys, but differenced with a crescent: paly of six, presumably *or* and *azure,* a quarter ermine.[33] Beneath the bust appear the words: "Jacobus Shirlaeus: G. Phenik pinx: R. Gaywood fecit 1658."

The similarity of this engraving to the oil portrait of Shirley in the Bodleian, was noted by Dyce in 1833. This painting, which has been but inaccurately copied by Lupton in the engraving prefixed to the first volume of Shirley's *Dramatic Works,* shows Shirley seated in a massive chair, leaning slightly upon his right elbow with his right hand at his cheek. It shows the same black skull-cap, the same flowing hair—or wig—the same soft white collar, the same scant light mustache (not black, as Lupton makes it), and the same fine eyes, as in the Phenik-Gaywood portrait. Clearly the two pictures belong to the same period of Shirley's life, even if they be not more vitally related.[34]

[33] A student familiar only with the modern method of engraving arms, might read this shield "paly of six *azure* and *argent";* for the odd pales are shaded horizontally and the even pales are without line or dot. That such is the significance of the lines, however, is most unlikely. The modern method of indicating tinctures in black and white, was very new in England in 1658.

[34] Cf. Dyce's note in *Works,* I, lviii.

Shirley's few remaining publications may be chronicled in a paragraph. In 1657, the unsold sheets of *The Constant Maid* and *St. Patrick for Ireland,* of 1640, were reissued with new title-pages. In 1659, was reprinted Shirley's *Cupid and Death* of 1653. *The Wedding* and, according to Ward, *The Grateful Servant*[35] were reprinted in 1660; *The Night Walker,* in 1661. In the latter year, *The Constant Maid* appeared for a third time, but with the unexpected title-page:

Love will finde out the Way. An Excellent Comedy. By T. B. As it was Acted with great Applause, by Her Majesties Servants, at the Phœnix in Drury Lane. London: Printed by Ja: Cottrel, for Samuel Speed, at the Signe of the Printing-Press in St. Paul's Church-yard. 1661.[36]

The play appeared a fourth time in 1667, but under a combination title: *"The Constant Maid: or, Love will finde out the Way. . . . By J. S."*[37] Thus ends the list.

We have, however, from the pen of Wood, one further note upon the work of Shirley:

[35] Ward, in *DNB.,* LII, 130, gives this date, but with a question-mark, borrowed, perhaps, from the catalogue of the British Museum.

[36] From the title-page of the copy belonging to the late Robert Hoe, Esq.

[37] From the copy in the British Museum.

Our author Shirley did also much assist his generous Patrone William, Duke of Newcastle, in the composure of certain Plays which the Duke afterwards published; and was a Drudge for John Ogilby in his translation of Homers *Iliads* and *Odysses,* and some of Virgils works, into English verse, with the writing of annotations on them.[38]

Of the accuracy of these statements we have no proof; but we know that the year 1649—in which Ogilby published the first edition of his Virgil—was the year in which Ogilby contributed complimentary verses to Shirley's *Via ad Latinam Linguam Complanata.* We remember also the statement made by Wood that, in preparation for his translation of the *Iliad,* 1660, and of the *Odyssey,* 1665, Ogilby studied Greek under Shirley's usher, David Whitford. Concerning Shirley's relation to the plays of William, Duke of Newcastle, the only evidence is the presence of a catch, "Come, let us throw the dice,"[39] both in Shirley's *Poems,* 1646, and in Newcastle's comedy, *The Country Captain.*

In the years immediately following the Restoration, the work of Shirley was again upon the stage. As Wood expresses it,

After his Majesties return to his Kingdoms, several of

[38] Wood, 1691–1692, II, 262; cf. 1817, III, 739–740.
[39] *Works,* VI, 439.

his [Shirley's] plays which he before had made, were acted with good applause, but what office or employ he had confer'd upon him after all his sufferings, I cannot now justly tell.[40]

In both of these assertions, the modern biographer has only to concur with Wood. Of office or employment conferred on Shirley "after all his sufferings," we have no evidence. Possibly the aged dramatist was still, as in 1639, unable to affect "the ways of flattery."[41] Possibly, at the age of sixty-four, he was indifferent. We have, however, ample evidence of the revival of the plays of Shirley on the London stage. In a list of the plays presented by the Red Bull actors, 1660–1663, quoted by Malone,[42] appear *The Traitor* and *Love's Cruelty;* and in a list which, according to Malone, "appears to have been made by Sir Henry Herbert in order to enable him to ascertain the fees due to him, whenever he should establish his claims,"[43] we find: "1660. . . . Tuesday the 6 Nov. *The Traytor* . . . Thursday the 15 Nov. *Loves Cruelty* . . . Thursday the 22 Nov. *The Traytor* . . . Monday the 26 Nov. *The Opportunity.* . . . 1662. . . . May 17, *Love in a Maze.* . . . July 6.

[40] Wood, 1691–1692, II, 261; cf. 1817, III, 739.
[41] Dedication to *The Maid's Revenge; Works,* I, 101.
[42] Malone's *Shakspere,* 1821, III, 272–273.
[43] *Ibid.,* 273.

The Brothers. . . . July 23. *The Cardinall.*"[44]
Pepys, in his diary for October 10, 1661, records:

> Sir W. Pen, and my wife and I, to the Theatre, . . .
> where the King came to-day, and there was *The Traytor,*
> most admirably acted; and a most excellent play it is.

And again, October 2, 1662, he writes:

> At night, . . . hearing that there was a play at the
> Cockpit, (and my Lord Sandwich, who came to town last
> night, at it), I do go thither, and by very great fortune
> did follow four or five gentlemen who were carried to a
> little private door in the wall, and so crept through a
> narrow place, and come into one of the boxes next the
> King's, but so as I could not see the King or Queen, but
> many of the fine ladies, who yet are not really so hand-
> some generally as I used to take them to be, but that they
> are finely dressed. Here we saw *The Cardinall,* a trag-
> edy I had never seen before, nor is there any great matter
> in it. The company that came in with me into the box
> were all Frenchmen that could speak no English: but,
> Lord! what sport they made to ask a pretty lady that they
> got among them, that understood both French and Eng-
> lish, to make her tell them what the actors said.

These two plays, *The Traitor* and *The Cardinal,* together with *The Opportunity, The Example,* and

[44] Malone's *Shakspere,* 1821, III, 273–276.

Love in a Maze, are mentioned by John Downes, in his *Roscius Anglicanus,* as among the plays acted at the New Theater in Drury-Lane in 1663:

These being Old Plays [he writes], were Acted but now and then; yet, being well Perform'd, were very Satisfactory to the Town.[45]

The next mention of a play by Shirley occurs in Pepys's diary for August 18, 1664:

Dined alone at home, my wife going to-day to dine with Mrs. Pierce, and thence with her and Mrs. Clerke to see a new play, *The Court Secret.* . . . My wife says, the play she saw is the worst that ever she saw in her life.

In 1666, Downes thus resumes the record:

After this the Company [of Sir William Davenant, in Lincoln's Inn Fields] Reviv'd Three Comedies of Mr. Sherly's viz. *The Grateful Servant, The Witty Fair One, The School of Complements.* . . . These Plays being perfectly well Perform'd; especially Dulcino the Grateful Servant, being Acted by Mrs. Long; and the first time she appear'd in Man's Habit, prov'd as Beneficial to the Company, as several new Plays.[46]

Upon one of these plays, the comment of Pepys, August 5, 1667, is not quite so favorable:

[45] Downes, *Roscius Anglicanus,* 1708; reprint of 1886, p. 9.
[46] *Ibid.,* p. 27.

To the Duke of York's house, and there saw *Love's Trickes, or the School of Compliments;* a silly play, only Mis's [Davis's] dancing in a shepherd's clothes did please us mightily.

The lines just quoted have taken us a year beyond the death of Shirley; but I insert here two more passages from Pepys, the first from his diary for December 30, 1667, the second, an entry for July 11, 1668:

Thence with Sir Philip Carteret to the King's play house, there to see *Love's Cruelty,* an old play, but which I have not seen before; and in the first act Orange Moll came to me . . . to tell me that . . . I was desired to come home. So I went out presently, and by coach home, and . . . after a very little stay with my wife, I took coach again, and to the King's playhouse again, and come in the fourth act: and it proves to me a very silly play, and to everybody else, as far as I could judge.

To the King's playhouse, to see an old play of Shirly's, called *Hide Parke;* the first day acted; where horses are brought upon the stage: but it is but a very moderate play, only an excellent epilogue spoke by Beck Marshall.

The foregoing list of Shirleian revivals recorded by Pepys and by Downes, we may supplement from two title-pages of the year 1667: *The Constant Maid: or, Love will finde out the Way . . . As it is now Acted at the new Play-house called the Nursery, in Hatton-*

Garden . . . ; [47] and *Love Tricks, or, the School of
Complements; As it is now acted by his Royal Highnesse The Duke of York's Servants At the Theatre in
Little Lincolns-Inne Fields.* [48] Evidently Wood's
assertion that "several of Shirley's plays . . . were
acted with good applause," has some foundation.

Concerning the family of Shirley and his worldly
estate in his declining years, his will of July, 1666,
preserved at Somerset House, bears interesting witness. As this document has not heretofore appeared
in print, I quote it here entire. The blank spaces
were left unfilled in the original:

I, James Shirley of White Fryers, London, gentleman,
being of perfect mind and memory, Doe make and declare
this my last Will and Testament in the manner and forme
following.

First, I resigne my Soule into the hands of Almighty
God, my Creator, with full beliefe to have remission of all
my Sinnes by the Meritts, death, and Passion of my Re-
deemer Jesus Christ.

My body I remitt to the earth to be decently buried
according to the Discretion of my Executor hereafter
named.

As to the Disposition of my worldly estate, I give and
bequeath the same (my Debts, if any shall appeare, and
funerall Charges first defraid) as followeth:

---

[47] From the copy in the British Museum. See Bibliography.
[48] *Ibid.*

I give and bequeath to my eldest Son, Mathias Shirley, 200£ Sterl. to bee paid him within six moneths after my Decease. I likewise give him my Cornelian seald ring, my silver watch, and my best wearing clothes.

I give and bequeath to my son Christopher Shirley 100£ to be paid him likewise within 6 monthes after my decease.

I give and bequeath to my son James Shirley the some of 150£ Sterl. to bee paid him within 6 monthes as aforesaid.

I give and bequeath to my Daughter Mary, now wife of Standerdine Shirley, *als.* Sachell, the some of 200£ Sterl. to bee paid as aforesaid. I alsoe give her a Silver Tanckard marked.

I give unto Standerdine above named One gold ring with fine Turkey stones, and I doe release and forgive to him a Debt of Fifty pounds which I lent him upon his Bond dated [   ].

I give and bequeath to my Daughter Lawrinda, the Relict of Howard Fountaine, the some of Two Hundred pounds. Item. I give to her my little Diamond.

I give and bequeath to George Shirley, *als.* Sachell, son of the said Standerdine and Mary, the sume of Thirty pounds to bee paid as above said.

I give and Bequeath to my worthy friend Mr. John Warter of the Inner Temple, the sume of [   ].

I give to Mistris Warter, wife of the said Mr. John Warter, to buy her a Ring [   ].

I give to Mr. George Warter, sonne of the said Mr. John [   ] the sume of [   ].

I give to Mr. Vincent Cane, my loveing friend, the sūme of Twenty pounds to be Disposed by him according to a former agreement betwixt Us.

And I doe by this my will, give and bequeath unto my loveing wife, Frances Shirley, all the Remainder of my Estate, Specialtyes, plate, moneys, Jewells, Linnen, Woollen Bedding, brass, Pewter, or goods of any Kind whatsoever, my debts and Legacyes being first paid, in confidence that shee wilbe kind to my Children, and at her Death, if it shall please God that any of them Survive her, I doubt not but that shee will leave upon them some Testimony of her love for my sake.

And I doe hereby nominate, Constitute, and appoint my said loveing wife, Frances Shirley, Executrix of this my last Will and Testament.

In Witness whereof I have subscribed my name and affixed my Seale, the [   ] Day of July Anno Dm̄ 1666, And in the Eighteenth yeare of the Raigne of our Soveraigne Lord, King Charles the Second.

JAMES SHIRLEY.

Signed, Sealed, and published in the presence of [   ].[49]

The will of Shirley, July, 1666, brings us to the

---

[49] Prerogative Court of Canterbury [Somerset House], Mico, folio 170. The will bears the following endorsement:

"3 November 1666 commission issued to Mary Poulton, wife of Richard Poulton, daughter of the sister of Frances Sherley deceased, while she lived relict and executrix named in the will of the testator James Shirley, late of White Fryers, London, but deceased in the parish of St. Giles in the Fields, co. Middlesex, to administer the goods, etc., of the said James Shirley, the said Frances having died before taking upon her the execution of the above will."

record of his death in October of the same year; but before we make this final entry, it is fitting that we summarize our chapter on Shirley's Post-dramatic Period.

Although this chapter covers a period of twenty-four years, from 1642 to 1666, its content may be briefly stated. We have noted the probability that Shirley served with Newcastle in the Civil War, and that he was pensioner to Thomas Stanley, Esq., and literary collaborator with Newcastle and with Ogilby. We have noted that he was a successful schoolmaster in Whitefriars. We have chronicled the publication of his *Poems,* his *Via ad Latinam Linguam Complanata,* his *Six New Playes,* his *Cupid and Death, The Politician, The Gentleman of Venice,* and his *Honoria and Mammon* and *The Contention of Ajax and Ulysses.* We have noted and described the engraving of Shirley by W. Marshall, 1646; the oil portrait in the Bodleian; and the Phenik-Gaywood engraving, 1658. We have quoted from Herbert, from Pepys, and from Downes, the record of Shirleian revivals after 1660. Finally, from the records of the Prerogative Court of Canterbury, we have reproduced in full the will of Shirley, a document not previously in print.

In September, 1666, some two months after Shirley made his will, occurred the Great Fire of London.

Of the misfortunes that it brought upon Shirley and his wife Frances, Wood shall speak:

At length, after Mr. Shirley had lived to the age of 72 years at least [Wood should have written "seventy"] in various conditions, and had seen much of the world, he with his second Wife, Frances, were driven by the dismal conflagration that hapned in London an. 1666, from their habitation near to Fleetstreet, into the Parish of St. Giles in the Fields in Middlesex; where, being in a manner overcome with affrightments, disconsolations, and other miseries occasion'd by that fire and their losses, they both died within the compass of a natural day: whereupon their bodies were buried in one grave in the yard belonging to the said Church of S. Giles's on the 29 of Octob. in sixteen hundred sixty and six.[50]

In the register of burials of "St. Giles in ye Fields, 1638–68," occurs the following entry:

October 1666.
29 { Mr. James Sherley.
{ Mris. Frances Sherley his wife.

[50] Wood, 1691–1692, II, 262; cf. 1817, III, 740.

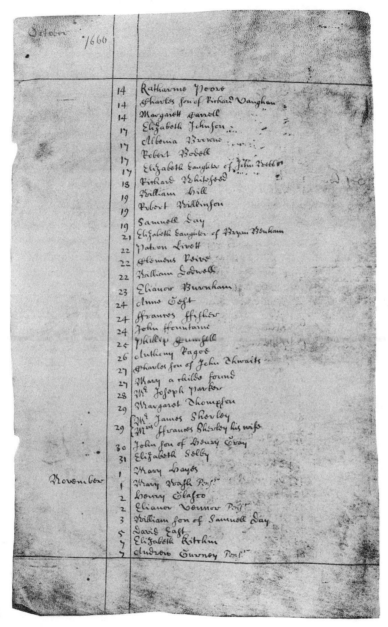

October	1666	
	14	Katharine Moore
	14	Charles son of Richard Vaughan
	14	Margarett Garroll
	17	Elizabeth Johnson
	17	Alberua Browne
	17	Robert Bodell
	17	Elizabeth daughter of John Wettor
	18	Richard Whitehead
	19	William Hill
	19	Robert Wilkinson
	19	Samuell Day
	21	Elizabeth daughter of Bryan Benham
	22	Nathan Livett
	22	Clemens Poive
	22	William Lodwell
	23	Elianor Burnham
	24	Anne Oost
	24	ffrances ffisher
	24	John ffountaine
	24	Phillipp Grimgell
	26	Anthony Pagot
	27	Charles son of John Thwaits
	27	Mary a chilld found
	28	Mr Joseph Parker
	29	Margaret Thompson
	29	Mr James Shorley
	29	Mris ffrances Shorley his wife
	30	John son of Henry Gray
	31	Elizabeth Selby
November	1	Mary Hayes
	1	Mary Wash Pest
	2	Henry Glasco
	2	Elianor Vernon Pest
	3	William son of Samuell Day
	5	David Eagt
	7	Elizabeth Kitchin
	7	Andrew Gurney Pest

RECORD OF THE BURIAL OF "MR. JAMES
SHERLEY" AND OF "MRIS. FRANCES
SHERLEY HIS WIFE"

From the Register of St. Giles in the Fields, October 29, 1666

PART II
THE PLAYS OF SHIRLEY

THE FIRST
DRAMATIC PERIOD

CHRONOLOGY OF PLAYS

FIRST DRAMATIC PERIOD

1625–1632

1624/5, February 10. *Love Tricks, with Comple-ments* licensed. Subsequently published as *The School of Complement.*

1625/6, February 9. *The Maid's Revenge* licensed.

1626, May 31. *The Wedding* (according to the hypothesis of Fleay) acted.

1626, November 4. *The Brothers* licensed. A lost work, to be identified neither with *The Brothers* of 1652 nor with *Dicke of Devonshire.*

1628, October 3. *The Witty Fair One* licensed.

1629, November 3. *The Faithful Servant* licensed. Subsequently published as *The Grateful Servant.*

1631, May 4. *The Traitor* licensed.

1631, May 17. *The Duke* licensed. Subsequently published as *The Humorous Courtier.*

1631, November 14. *Love's Cruelty* licensed.

1631/2, January 10. *The Changes* licensed. Subsequently published as *Changes, or Love in a Maze.*

1632, April 20. *Hyde Park* licensed.

1632, November 16. *The Ball* licensed.

CHAPTER VI

THE FIRST DRAMATIC PERIOD—BEGUN

FROM *LOVE TRICKS* TO *THE WEDDING*

FROM our examination of the life of Shirley, we pass now to a consideration of his dramatic works and of his development as a dramatist. Our endeavor, in the five chapters just concluded, has been to weigh anew the evidence concerning his career, and thereby to establish, with greater accuracy than has been hitherto attained, the chronology of Shirley's plays. This chronology being established, our endeavor now becomes twofold: first, to ascertain the character of his dramatic works, both individually and in their several kinds, realistic and romantic; and, second, to ascertain the direction of his growth from play to play, from period to period. With respect to their character, we shall find that Shirley was not without interest in the realistic comedy of manners and of humors; but that he gave himself even more earnestly to dramatic romance, to romantic comedy, and to romantic tragedy. With respect to the direction of his growth, we shall find

[167]

that Shirley, although originally a follower of the realistic school, gradually shifted to the writing of romantic plays: that the career of James Shirley, dramatist, is itself a drama, in which the contending forces are realism and romanticism, and in which romanticism is ultimately triumphant.

Of the realistic plays of Shirley, *Hyde Park, The Ball,* and *The Gamester* are typical examples. Their purpose was to satirize conditions and characters that actually existed, and, to this end, not only to depict with accuracy the manners and the men of court and town, but, on occasion, to magnify an actual characteristic into a humor. In their use of humors, in their realism, in their careful attention to technique, Shirley's comedies of manners show conspicuously the influence of the realistic comedy of his predecessors and contemporaries—the influence of such plays as *Every Man in His Humor* and *The Wild Goose Chase.* The Jonsonian influence Shirley himself cordially and reverently admitted when, in the dedication of *The Grateful Servant,* he made reference to "our acknowledged master, learned Jonson."

Of the romantic plays of Shirley, *The Traitor, The Young Admiral,* and *The Royal Master* are representative. Their purpose was to present, on the far coast of some Bohemia, intrigues of statecraft or of love; scene after scene of amazement or poetic charm.

Occasionally one of these romantic plays may introduce a character of humor, just as a realistic play may lay its scene in Mantua or Ferrara. But, despite such minor inconsistencies, the type is clear: a romantic type that reminds us now of the romantic comedy and the romantic tragedy of Shakspere, of a *Much Ado* or of a *Romeo and Juliet;* now of the dramatic romance of Fletcher and of Shakspere, of a *Philaster* or of a *Cymbeline.*

In Shirley's first dramatic period—from the licensing of his first play, *Love Tricks,* February 10, 1624/5, to the licensing of *The Ball,* November 16, 1632—realism is increasingly triumphant. Indeed, out of the eleven surviving plays that belong surely to this period,[1] only three *The Maid's Revenge, The Grateful Servant,* and *The Traitor*—are definitely romantic. *Love Tricks* is a mixture of romanticism and realism; and the remaining seven plays— *The Wedding, The Witty Fair One, The Humorous Courtier, Love's Cruelty, Changes, Hyde Park,* and *The Ball*—are definitely realistic. Five of these seven

[1] From this estimate, I omit the play licensed as *The Brothers,* November 4, 1626. For reasons stated in my second chapter, I am convinced that it is not the play published as *The Brothers* in 1652. That *The Brothers* of 1626 may be identical with *Dicke of Devonshire* is possible, but has not been proved. That the play is no longer extant is quite as probable. As for the play published as *The Brothers* in 1652, I shall consider it in this work as identical with the play licensed as *The Politique Father,* May 26, 1641.

realistic plays, moreover, fall in the last two years of the period, in swift succession.

Realism and romanticism, the two forces that in the drama of Shirley were to struggle for the mastery, make their appearance together in his first dramatic work. Of the three plays that form the subject of this chapter, *The Maid's Revenge* is a romantic tragedy; *The Wedding* is a realistic comedy of manners and of humors; and *Love Tricks, or The School of Complement,* which chronologically I should have mentioned first, is a glorious mixture of elements that range from the Fletcherian pastoral of the closing scenes to the Jonsonian humors of the compliment-school.

For a career in which so many elements were successfully to mingle, *Love Tricks, or The School of Complement,* licensed February 10, 1624/5, affords an introduction thoroughly appropriate. It well-nigh exemplifies, indeed, the type of play once mentioned by Polonius—the "tragical-comical-historical-pastoral." Like a modern musical comedy, the play consists of a multitude of episodes emotionally diverse and intellectually incoherent, strung on a thread that only by courtesy can be called a plot.

Such as it is, the story deals with the fortunes of two families. The first consists of an ancient gentleman named Cornelio, his son Antonio, and his daugh-

[170]

ter Selina. Formerly he had had another daughter, Felice; but she, forbidden to marry Gasparo, had abandoned both her father and her lover, and had utterly disappeared. The second family consists of an old merchant named Rufaldo and his daughter Hilaria. Rufaldo desires to marry Cornelio's daughter Selina; and he commands his own daughter, Hilaria, to give her love to Bubulcus, a wealthy country gull. She, however, prefers the suit of Cornelio's son Antonio.

Into this situation there comes, as a complicating force, the servant, Gorgon. By him inspired, old Rufaldo imagines he is young again, and in this belief, presses his love upon Selina. Refusing a more desirable suitor, Infortunio, she consents, without apparent motive, to the marriage. Her father, Cornelio, does not like the match; but, remembering the loss of Felice, he consents to let her have her will. On the wedding morn, however, Selina comes to her senses, disguises herself as a shepherd, and slips away. Her absence occasions alarm; but her brother, concluding that she has but played a joke upon them all, disguises himself in Selina's clothes and becomes Rufaldo's bride. This gives him access to his own love, Rufaldo's daughter. His first act, however, is to quarrel with Rufaldo and administer a beating.

At this point, the play becomes a pastoral. Selina,

disguised as a shepherd, has met a shepherdess who is really her lost sister, Felice. To them comes Selina's lover, Infortunio, distracted because he thinks her married to Rufaldo. Presently Gasparo arrives, recognizes his lost love Felice, and reveals himself. Selina takes the same occasion to reveal herself to Infortunio; but Gasparo, insisting that Selina is married to Rufaldo, declares her statement false. Realizing that her brother, Antonio, has assumed her part at home, Selina sends for him to join her in the forest. A general assembly of the characters, a mutual recognition scene, and the union of the three pairs of lovers, end the play.

Such is the plot—the very slender plot—of *Love Tricks,* Shirley's earliest play. The real interest, fortunately, consists in episodes that present the comic characters. There is Rufaldo's self-deception and its cure at the hands of his supposed bride Antonio. There is the boasting of Bubulcus, the country gull, and his fear when Antonio, taking him at his word, causes his arrest for murder. There is the "business" of Gorgon as a shepherdess and the betrayal of his would-be lovers. There is the masque in the pastoral scene, as a device effecting the final recognitions. And lastly, most notable of all, there is the scene in which Gasparo and Gorgon conduct the School of Complement. This is a satire upon the contemporary books of polite instruction. The master and his usher teach their pupils elaborate speeches for various occasions. Presently they require all their pupils to rehearse at once. At that moment enters Infortunio, temporarily insane, and assumes the pupils to be lost souls in hell. They, by Gasparo's direction, explain to him in turn why each was damned. Excellent in itself, this scene conspicuously exemplifies the weakness of the play: the fact, namely, that the best part of the play is utterly unrelated to the major plot.

Love Tricks, as every critic notes, is full of echoes. Gorgon is the typical witty servant of Latin comedy. Selina's disguise as a shepherd suggests Rosalind and many more. The Welshman, Jenkin, recalls Fluellen of *Henry V;* and the two scenes in which he carries on a lively conversation with an echo are of a piece with the echo scenes in *The Old Wives' Tale,*[2] in *Cynthia's Revels,*[3] and in *The Duchess of Malfi,*[4]— the classical joke of an answer that echoes the final syllables of the question. Finally, the quarrel between Bubulcus, Gorgon, and Jenkin, as to which shall speak the epilogue, recalls a similar quarrel in *Cynthia's Revels* as to which of three children shall be prologue; and the entire scene devoted to the School of Complement is in the style of Jonson.

[2] Peele, *The Old Wives' Tale,* line 372 et seq.
[3] Jonson, *Cynthia's Revels,* I, i.
[4] Webster, *The Duchess of Malfi,* v, iii.

To conclude: *Love Tricks* is a patchwork of romance, humors, manners, farce, pastoral, and masque. It may be, as Swinburne says, a "feebly preposterous and impotently imitative abortion, . . . the product of second-hand humor and second-rate sentiment"; [5] yet I cannot help believing that, perhaps for this very reason, it needs only appropriate music, costuming, and scenery, to make it an acceptable rival to the latest Broadway "show."

Very different from *Love Tricks,* both in subject and in unity of effect, is Shirley's "second birth," *The Maid's Revenge,* licensed February 9, 1625/6. Dyce has said of this, "Though *The Maid's Revenge* has some impressive scenes, it is perhaps the worst of Shirley's tragedies." [6] Taken literally, this criticism of Dyce is not untrue; yet it gives the casual reader an erroneous impression. Let us admit that this play is "the worst of Shirley's tragedies." Should we wish it otherwise? Would we not have our apprentice least successful in his first attempt? Let us grant that it is not so well written as *The Traitor* or *The Cardinal.* May it not be, none the less, a fairly good tragedy, especially for so young a dramatist?

The story deals with two noble families of Portu-

[5] A. C. Swinburne, "James Shirley," in *The Fortnightly Review,* XLVII (n.s.), 462–463.

[6] Dyce, in *Works,* I, xi.

gal: the one consisting of the old lord Gaspar de
Vilarezo, his two daughters, Catalina and Berinthia,
and his son Sebastiano; the other, of Antonio and his
sister, Castabella. Antonio loves Berinthia; but,
finding that her father insists that Berinthia shall
receive no suitors till her older sister is married, he
pretends to pay court to Catalina. The latter falls
in love with him, and then discovers his duplicity.
She locks up Berinthia, and arranges to have her carried off by Antonio's rival and then poisoned. Antonio, warned by his servant, arrives first upon the
scene and bears off Berinthia to his own castle, where
his sister Castabella receives her in all honor. Sebastiano, who is at once Berinthia's brother and Antonio's dearest friend, comes to demand satisfaction,
accepts their explanation, and remains to woo Antonio's sister, Castabella.

Catalina, however, insists upon revenge. At her
instigation, old Vilarezo orders Sebastiano, on pain
of a father's curse, to kill Antonio; and here we have
the tragic situation: two young men, close friends,
each about to marry the other's sister, compelled to
fight to the death over a matter in which they, personally, are in absolute accord. Despite the implor-
ing protests of Berinthia and Castabella, their brothers and lovers fight. Both seconds are slain, and
then Antonio.

The final act deals with Berinthia's revenge upon her brother and sister, whom she holds jointly responsible for the death of her lover. She poisons the latter, stabs the former, and then stabs herself. Meanwhile Castabella, sister of the dead Antonio, has come, disguised as a page, to offer her services to her mourning lover. Scarcely has she arrived ere Sebastiano falls by Berinthia's hand: Castabella is left with the aged Vilarezo to mourn the dead.

For the second production of a youthful schoolmaster, *The Maid's Revenge* is a successful melodrama. The plot is based upon a struggle genuinely tragic, and is presented without serious violations of unity. Even the comic scene at the apothecary's gives facts essential to the story and at the same time affords necessary relief. The serious characters, although not greatly conceived, are yet acceptably done; and the comic characters, such as the braggart suitor and the blunt soldier, are pleasing examples of types which Shirley especially enjoyed. The larger portion of the play, moreover, is expressed in smooth blank verse. Against the disparaging criticism of Dyce, already quoted, I am glad to set the words of Schelling: *"The Maid's Revenge* . . . is a tragedy of much promise, swift in action, capably plotted, and fluently and lucidly written."[7]

[7] Schelling, *Elizabethan Drama,* II, 322.

The Wedding, acted—if Fleay be right[8]—on May
31, 1626, is a comedy of London life and manners.
Unlike *Love Tricks, The Wedding* is no mere med-
ley but a well-constructed play. It is, moreover, a
play representative of Shirley's comedies of manners
at their best: a realistic picture not of the coarser
side of London life but of fashionable society; a picture, witty, "humorous," but not satiric; with a realism which, in the scenes of deepest feeling, the poet's
alchemy well-nigh transmutes into romanticism.

The major plot is characterized by strong scenes
and striking situations. As the hero, Beauford, is
on the point of marrying Gratiana, his cousin Marwood declares to him that he, Marwood, has sinfully
enjoyed the bride. In the duel resulting from this
accusation, Marwood falls, but with his dying breath
affirms the truth of his assertion. Beauford, returning to the house where all are waiting for the ceremony, takes Gratiana apart, repeats Marwood's accusation, and refuses to credit her denials. He then
withdraws to await his own arrest for the slaying of
Marwood. Gratiana, meanwhile, has found a champion in Captain Landby, nephew of Justice Landby,
a figure in the minor plot. Captain Landby conceals
Gratiana in his uncle's house, and then takes from her
to Beauford a letter stating that, by the time he re-

[8] Fleay, in *Anglia*, VIII, 405.

ceives it, she will be dead by drowning. The captain, however, is not her only supporter. Millicent, her page, claims to have knowledge bearing on the case, and advises that Gratiana examine Cardona, her waiting-woman. As a result, Millicent goes presently to Beauford's lodging, and places before him a great chest in which, says Millicent, is Marwood's body. As Marwood's relative, the page demands satisfaction for his death; but first he insists that Beauford listen to the evidence of Cardona, whom, to gain Gratiana, Marwood had corrupted. This evidence proves that Marwood enjoyed not Gratiana but Cardona's daughter Lucibel. Beauford, now conscious of his fatal error, opens the chest, finds within it not the dead Marwood but the living Gratiana, and then, just as all joy seems to have returned, is once more driven to despair: officers enter to arrest him for the murder of Marwood. Brought before Justice Landby, Beauford offers no defense. Gratiana pleads for him without avail. When all hope seems vanished, the justice asks the whereabouts of Marwood's body, and, at that, Marwood himself steps forward living. They then demand that he admit his error and Gratiana's innocence. When he refuses, they summon in Cardona. She, repeating her testimony, adds the circumstance that, since that night, her daughter Lucibel has not been seen. At that, Millicent the page steps forward and reveals himself as Lucibel disguised. Marwood—a libertine reformed—declares that he will begin his recompense by marrying Lucibel.

The subplot of *The Wedding* concerns the rivalry of three suitors for the hand of Jane, daughter of Justice Landby. Two of these suitors are characters of humor: Lodam, fat and ever eating; Rawbone, a usurer, thin as a result of his penurious abstinence. The third is Haver, a young gentleman of good birth and character but restricted means, who, disguised under the name of Jasper, has become servant to Rawbone that he may be employed as a messenger to Mistress Jane. In the minds of Jane and of her father, Haver is the favored suitor; but the justice, desiring to test his daughter, pretends to favor Rawbone. Haver, knowing both his rivals to be cowards, inspires Rawbone to challenge Lodam to a duel, promising to fight disguised in Rawbone's place. Lodam, knowing Rawbone to be as much of a coward as he is himself, makes great boasts, but yields at Haver's first attack. Captain Landby, who has watched the duel for his uncle, then brings all the participants before the justice. Before Rawbone can make Haver reëxchange clothes, Justice Landby commands Jane instantly to marry the supposed Rawbone. The protests of the real Rawbone are fruitless; and the lovers, never suspecting that Jane's father knows the identity of the victorious duelist, hasten to be married before he shall discover his mistake.

To the critic in pursuit of echoes, *The Wedding* has more than one Shaksperian detail. Just as Selina in *Love Tricks* suggested, in her shepherd weeds, the figure of Rosalind in *As You Like It,* so Millicent-Lucibel, the page, recalls Julia of *Two Gentlemen of Verona* and Viola of *Twelfth Night.* Yet she might with equal propriety recall Beaumont and Fletcher's Euphrasia-Bellario of *Philaster* or Shirley's own Castabella of *The Maid's Revenge.* But for chronology, Massinger's Maria-Ascanio of *The Bashful Lover* (licensed 1635) might have been added to the list. The complaints of Camelion, Rawbone's starving servant, suggest remotely the similar complaints of Launcelot Gobbo, famished in the house of Shylock. Beauford's accusation against his bride Gratiana and his subsequent belief that she is dead may be compared with Claudio's accusation in *Much Ado About Nothing* and Hero's period of concealment; but in Shirley's play, the bridegroom is less of a blackguard, and the *dénouement* a bit more plausible. Most nearly Shaksperian are the duel between Lodam and the supposed Rawbone, and the challenge that precedes it—both scenes strongly reminiscent of *Twelfth Night.* The real atmosphere of

the play, however, is not that of Shakspere but that
of Jonson or that of Fletcher—in his realistic work.
Most evident in the humors of Lodam and of Rawbone, this realistic atmosphere permeates the entire
play and is especially perceptible in the Landby
household: above all else, *The Wedding* is a comedy
of London life and manners.

Our outline of *The Wedding* has made evident, I
hope, the strength of the play with respect to dramatic struggle and surprise. In another respect,
however, it is less successful: although each of its
plots taken by itself is well constructed, the play as
a whole lacks unity in the highest sense. Between the
two plots there is no inevitable relation: Justice
Landby and his nephew are the only characters that
appear in both, and they are vital to neither. In
short, the play is merely salt and sugar in the same
receptacle; a physical mixture, not a chemical com-
pound; two plays, not one. This fault is frequent in
non-Shaksperian comedy; but we must remember its
existence when we read the otherwise acceptable criticism of Dyce: "This comedy is one of Shirley's most
perfect productions, equally admirable in its serious
and in its broadly humorous scenes; its plot is conducted with infinite art, and its characters are
strongly drawn and happily contrasted." [9]

[9] Dyce, in *Works,* I, xiii.

Slight as are the three plays considered in this chapter, they indicate something of the scope, if not of the strength, of Shirley's subsequent work. In the more serious portions of *The Wedding,* we note a faint influence of Shaksperian romantic comedy: an echo, perhaps, from *Much Ado.* In the masque and pastoral of *Love Tricks,* in the girl page of *The Wedding* and *The Maid's Revenge,* and in the love, the hate, the duel, the poisoning, the stabbing, and the suicide of the latter play, we note the influence of Fletcherian pastoral, and dramatic romance, and romantic tragedy. And, most conspicuous of all, in the witty servant and the country gull of *Love Tricks,* in the usurer of *The Wedding,* in the school of complement in the former play, and in the low-comedy scenes in the latter, we note the influence of Jonsonian, of Fletcherian—and possibly Middletonian—comedy of manners and of humors. Shirley, unquestionably, is a student of his predecessors. Unquestionably, also, he is as yet divided in his allegiance between realism and romanticism. How far he is to profit by his study, and with which school he is ultimately to cast his lot, shall be considered in the chapters following.

CHAPTER VII

THE FIRST DRAMATIC PERIOD—CONTINUED

THE WITTY FAIR ONE AND
THE GRATEFUL SERVANT

FROM February 10, 1624/5, to November 4, 1626, Shirley, as we have noted, had produced three tolerably successful plays— *Love Tricks, The Maid's Revenge,* and *The Wedding,*—together with a fourth play, *The Brothers* of 1626, the identity of which is now uncertain. Four plays, however, within so brief a time, meant hasty work. We are glad to note, therefore, that, in the years immediately following, our dramatist allowed himself to write more leisurely. In the four years and a half from November 4, 1626, to May 4, 1631, Shirley contented himself with the production of three plays: *The Witty Fair One, The Faithful Servant* (published as *The Grateful Servant*), and *The Traitor.* These three, unlike the plays before considered, show careful workmanship. Like them, however, they represent continued experiment in several types of drama: *The Witty Fair One* is a realistic comedy of manners and of humors; *The Grateful Servant* is romantic comedy with a realistic under-plot; and *The Traitor* is romantic tragedy. Of these three plays, *The Traitor,* because of its importance, I reserve for Chapter VIII; *The Witty Fair One* and *The Grateful Servant* are the subject of the present chapter.

The Witty Fair One, licensed October 3, 1628, is a comedy of London life and manners. Its major plot presents the stratagems of the rich and witty Violetta to avoid marriage with the rich and witless Sir Nicholas Treedle—her father's choice—and to bestow her hand upon her poor but adoring lover Aimwell. Against her purpose, the principal obstacle is the watchfulness of Brains, her father's servant. Through a friend, she sends to Aimwell an oral message which seems to say to him his love is hopeless. He, how-ever, finds in her purposed ambiguities a favorable interpretation, and succeeds in sending her a letter. Brains hears her read it, and presently detects her maid delivering to Aimwell a reply. That night, Brains steals from Violetta's chamber what he sup-poses to be Aimwell's letter. When Aimwell boasts to a friend his note from Violetta, he opens it to find that it is the note he sent to her, seemingly returned in scorn. He resolves to love no more. Brains, on the other hand, discovers that the letter he has stolen

is not Aimwell's note to Violetta but her intended
answer—the best evidence that Brains could wish.
He addresses it to her father, and sends it to him by
Sensible, Violetta's maid. Violetta, worried at the
loss of her letter—the note from Aimwell, as she
thinks,—offers to deliver the missive that the maid is
taking to her father, so that the maid may search for
the missing note. As a result, Violetta hands her father the note that she has written to Aimwell: an
acceptance of Aimwell's love and an exhortation to
prevent her marriage to Sir Nicholas. Her father
reads it, rages, discharges Sensible, summons Brains
to stand guard over Violetta, and orders that the marriage to Sir Nicholas take place next morning. Violetta, however, sends to Aimwell by Sensible a further message; and he prepares accordingly. She,
meanwhile, pretends to be reconciled to the marriage; obtains, through Sir Nicholas, permission to
go shopping—with Brains as escort; and stirs up the
vain tutor of the foolish knight to waylay Brains and
bear her off. When the tutor attacks, he receives a
beating from the efficient Brains; but during the
scuffle, Sensible, masked and dressed like her mistress, takes Violetta's place. Presently, accompanied
by officers, the tutor pursues Brains, causes his arrest,
and—as he thinks—valiantly bears off his lady-love.
He, however, is waylaid in turn by Sir Nicholas and

his servants; and the knight, likewise supposing that Sensible is Violetta, carries her off to the parson who shall "divide" them into man and wife. Violetta, meanwhile, has been duly married to the waiting Aimwell. Such is the major plot; and of it, well may Schelling say: "Seldom in the old drama has the principle of climax and surprise been so cleverly employed." [1]

I wonder, however, whether Schelling has assumed correctly that Violetta is "the witty fair one." Shirley's own auditors, it seems to me, would have applied that title rather to Penelope, Violetta's cousin. This ingenious maiden, who makes the minor plot revolve about her, is in love with Fowler, a well-born libertine. She realizes fully that Fowler—like many another hero of the comedy of manners—intends only to betray her; but she resolves to outwit him, and to lead him to the altar. His pretext—that of Volpone in his pursuit of Celia, Corvino's wife[2]—she seemingly accepts. She consents to a meeting in her chamber, admits him, puts him to shame; and then pretends that he is dying in her presence. Her friends assist her in the jest. Fowler hears that he is dead; that his funeral is about to be solemnized. He attends it, hears his evil life discussed, and for a time

[1] Schelling, *Elizabethan Drama*, II, 289.
[2] Jonson, *Volpone*, II, iii; III, vi.

he imagines that he is really dead. He reads the elegies and epitaphs prepared for his solace by the witty fair one. Among them are the touching lines:

> How he died, some do suppose;
> How he lived, the parish knows.
> Whether he's gone to Heaven or hell,
> Ask me not; I cannot tell.[3]

Presently he addresses Penelope, and she answers him. He asks her whether she is talking to a dead man. She answers, Yes, to a man dead to all noble thoughts and—until his reformation—dead to her. As she is about to vow utter renunciation of him, he interrupts her with a promise to reform his life and an offer of honorable marriage. Her father approves the match, and she accepts. If such an elaborate pleasantry be wit, Penelope is the witty fair one.

The plot-structure of this play is excellent; and yet, with all its excellences, two faults appear. The first—a fault appearing in many comedies of the day —is the same as that which we noted in *The Wedding:* major and minor plots exist each for itself. As Sir Nicholas would put it, they have been *divided* into man and wife. Between the action centering about Fowler and Penelope and that centering about Brains, Aimwell, and Violetta, there is no necessary

[3] *The Witty Fair One,* v, iii; *Works,* I, 357.

connection. The second fault is that, in order to preserve suspense, Shirley violates all reasonable chronology. In Act III, scene iii, he makes Aimwell open
for the first time a letter that was handed him at the
end of Act II. Yet, as appears from Brains's all-night
watch in Violetta's chamber (III, i), and from Sir
Nicholas's morning greeting to his tutor (III, ii), a
whole night has passed between the time of Aimwell's
receipt of the letter and his opening it. Shall we
believe that a letter from Violetta meant no more to
Aimwell? If it were so, it was a grievous fault. If
not, what think you of the dramatist?

In Shirley's characters we find less to censure.
Most interesting among them all, are the witless Sir
Nicholas and the omniscient Brains. The former
first appears under the ministrations of his tutor. As
for the divisions of the continent into peninsula, isth-
mus, and promontory, he remembers some such
things, but has forgotten them. As for his globe, he
will have it stand in his hall, for his tenants to wonder
at, instead of the Book of Martyrs. As for studying
England, he is resolved to be ignorant of his own
country; say no more on it.[4] After this we are prepared to accept Aimwell's "character" of the knight:
". . . His inward senses are sound, for none comes

[4] *The Witty Fair One*, II, i; *Works*, I, 293–294.

from him; he speaks words, but no matter. . . ."[5]
From such a character flow errors innumerable. He
begins by saluting not his betrothed but her cousin:

> SIR NICHOLAS [*to Penelope*]. Lady, and mistress of
> my heart, which hath long melted for you,—
>   RICHLEY. This is my daughter.
>   SIR NICHOLAS. Then it melted for you, lady.[6]

His tutor has supplied him with verses for his lady-
love; but Sir Nicholas presently admits they are not
his, and offers in comparison some absurd lines that
he has made himself:

> Her foot is feat with diamond toes,
> But she with legs of ruby goes.
>
> .   .   .   .
>
> Her head is opal, neck of sapphire,
> Breast carbuncles, shine like a fire;
> And, the naked truth to tell ye,
> The very mother of pearl her belly.
> How can she choose but hear my groans,
> That is composed of precious stones?[7]

After much display of wit and valor, which makes
one think that perhaps Sir Nicholas is himself the
witty fair one, he ends, as we have noted, by marrying

[5] *The Witty Fair One*, II, ii; *Works*, I, 306.
[6] *Ibid.*, p. 307.
[7] *Ibid.*, III, ii; *Works*, I, 312–313.

Violetta's maid—poor thing!—and, fearing to be jeered for his mistake, he maintains that he has not been cheated and that Sensible shall be his own lady-bird; for "a lady is a lady, a bargain is a bargain, and a knight is no gentleman." [8]

As for Brains the watch-dog, Brains the omniscient, Brains the argus-eyed, I cannot better express his character and, at the same time, his humor and its cure, than by quoting one of his later speeches:

It was my boast that I was never cozened in my life. Have I betrayed so many plots, discovered letters, deciphered characters, stript knavery to the skin, and laid open the very soul of conspiracy, deserved for my cunning to be called Brains both town and country over, and now to forfeit them, to see them drenched in a muddy stratagem, cheated by a woman, and a pedantical lousy word-monger! It is abominable; patience, I abhor thee. I desire him that bids me go hang myself, which is the way to Surgeon's Hall? I will beg to have my skull cut. I have a suspicion my brains are filched, and my head has been late stuffed with woodcocks' feathers.[9]

Such is *The Witty Fair One*. Like *The Wedding* —even more than *The Wedding*—it is a comedy of London life and manners: a play in the style of Jonson, with Jonson's careful structure, Jonson's truth

[8] *The Witty Fair One*, v, iii; *Works*, I, 361.
[9] *Ibid.*, p. 359.

to life, Jonson's comic characters of humor; yes, and the repulsive intrigue of Jonson's *Volpone*. From a dramatic point of view, the play is excellent. Morally, however, the underplot is a body of material that not all the wit of Penelope can fumigate, and that could be expurgated only by annihilation. That the editor of the *Mermaid Shirley* should include *The Witty Fair One* among his five "Best Plays," is a matter for regret. With all the wealth of Shirley's romantic plays from which to choose, why should Gosse select but comedies of manners—and of manners so abhorrent?

Unlike *The Witty Fair One, The Grateful Servant,* licensed as *The Faithful Servant* November 3, 1629, is in its main plot a pure romantic comedy, comparable in subject-matter and in poetic charm with the story of Shakspere's Viola. In its underplot, however, it is a realistic picture of a cynical libertine and of his reformation by means of an elaborate jest —a picture in which the repulsiveness of the theme is all but forgotten amid the grimness of the humor.

The Duke of Savoy, indignant that Milan has denied him the once-promised hand of Princess Leonora, announces that he will woo to be his wife a beautiful gentlewoman of Savoy, Cleona. At the duke's capital have just arrived Foscari, a nobleman formerly betrothed to this Cleona but by her believed

[191]

to have died in foreign travel, and Dulcino, a beautiful youth whom Foscari has rescued from a band of outlaws and who, in gratitude, has become Foscari's page. Foscari, ignorant of the duke's addresses, sends Dulcino to Cleona to announce his own arrival. At Cleona's, Dulcino meets the duke; and the latter is so strongly reminded of his lost Leonora that, for the moment, he breaks off his wooing. Cleona, although flattered by the duke's addresses, is true to Foscari and is rejoiced to find him living. Foscari, however, in exaggerated devotion, resolves to show his love to her by withdrawing his claim in favor of the duke. To this end, he arranges himself to enter a Benedictine monastery, informs the astonished duke of his resolution and its motive, and orders Dulcino to tell Cleona that the news that Foscari was alive is false— a tale intended only to gain her momentary favor— and that Dulcino now reveals the deception lest it prevent her marriage to the duke. This message Dulcino presently delivers, and then, urged by Foscari, consents to become with him a Benedictine, and fearfully awaits the arrival of the holy father who is to arrange for their admission. The holy father proves to be Valentio, with whom Dulcino had been traveling when the outlaws set upon them; and he immediately greets Dulcino as "dear Leonora." When the duke, Cleona, and all the lords and ladies of the court, have assembled by invitation of the abbot to witness the admission of Foscari and Dulcino to the Benedictine order, Father Valentio reveals the identity of the latter to the duke:

Leonora, daughter to the late Gonzaga, Duke of Milan, fearing she should be compell'd to marry her uncle, in the habit of a page and the conduct of Father Valentio, came to Savoy to try the love and honour of his excellence, who once solicited by his ambassador—[10]

The joyous duke reveals the whole situation to Cleona; and the play ends with the union of the disguised princess to the duke and of Cleona to Foscari.

Side by side with this romantic plot is set the realistic picture of the duke's brother, Lodwick the libertine, his depravity and its reformation. At the opening of the play we find him refusing to accompany the duke a-wooing, because his wronged wife Astella is living with Cleona; and presently we find him commanding his follower Piero to commit adultery with his wife so that he may have adequate grounds for a divorce. His former guardian, the aged lord Grimundo, undertakes his reformation. Grimundo, after fruitless exhortation, pretends that he has all this time but played the hypocrite, and offers to take the libertine to a mistress more glorious than any he has

[10] *The Grateful Servant*, v, ii; *Works*, II, 90.

yet enjoyed. In fulfilment, Grimundo brings him to a wondrous garden. A masque of nymphs and satyrs welcomes them. Strange music sounds. The lady of the garden fascinates him with her beauty. But Lodwick is conscious rather of the uncanny horror of the place and of its mistress: she hints at strange powers, promises him unlimited dominion, and finally admits she is a devil. Shuddering, he begs permission to depart. He hurries home, only to find that Piero is with Astella. Piero insists that he has fulfilled his master's orders, and looks for his reward. Lodwick responds by an attempt to slay him. This brings Piero to the truth: Astella's virtue has resisted all entreaty. Taking his wife, Lodwick hastens to the duke his brother. They arrive close upon the discovery that the Benedictine candidates are Foscari and the princess. Before the abbot, duke, and court, Lodwick declares that he "new marries" Astella, and demands justice against Lord Grimundo. At that instant, to his horror, there enters the lady of the garden, the she-devil. Lodwick redoubles his vows of reformation. The she-devil throws back her veil and reveals herself as Grimundo's wife Belinda.

In both its minor and its major plot, this play is capitally conceived and executed. That the two plots have no inevitable relation, we may admit; but the skill with which they have been interwoven is likewise evident. In neither plot is there a moment's dullness. This interest results in part from the clever and effective dialogue; but it results even more from the striking nature of the situations. Scene after scene, the interest never wanes. The opening tilt between Lodwick and the duke, Grimundo's warning to Foscari, Cleona's welcome to Dulcino's message, the courtship of the duke and his departure, Foscari's resolution, Dulcino's second message and Cleona's grief, Grimundo's manœuvers against the libertine, Lodwick's instigation of Piero, Foscari's visit to the duke, his avowal of his renunciation, and the duke's acceptance of the sacrifice, Father Valentio's recognition of the princess, Lodwick's adventures with the supposed succuba, Piero's attempted adultery with Astella and his subsequent meeting with her husband, and, finally, the grand assembly at the abbey with its threefold revelation—each scene holds reader or auditor intent, a dramaturgic triumph.

In characterization, as in scene-conception, *The Grateful Servant* marks a forward step in Shirley's dramaturgy. In *The Witty Fair One*, Shirley was content to prepare for the entrance of Sir Nicholas by means of a lengthy "character" in the mouth of Aimwell. In *The Grateful Servant*, he relies rather upon innumerable minor touches—the chance remarks and action of all the persons of the play and especially of the one to be described. He makes his readers or auditors suppose that they are becoming acquainted with the people of the play precisely as they would become acquainted with people in real life. He even goes so far as to make Soranzo remark, when Lodwick has scarcely spoken once, "Still the same wild prince. There needs no character where he is, to express him."[11] Of the as yet unmentioned persons in this play, Jacomo is the one most entertaining. He is Cleona's steward, foolish and ambitious. He argues: "If his grace come hither a suitor to my lady, as we have some cause to suspect, and after marry her, I may be a great man, and ride upon a reverend mule by patent. There is no end of my preferment. . . . Methinks I talk like a peremptory statesman already; I shall quickly learn to forget myself when I am great in office; I will oppress the subject, flatter the prince, take bribes on both sides, do right to neither, serve heaven so far as my profit will give me leave, and tremble only at the summons of a parliament."[12] So he domineers over the household, and over Foscari's messenger, the princess; smiles or frowns according to the direction of the wind of favor; puts himself in the way to meet the duke, and so has an opportunity to show his

[11] *The Grateful Servant,* I, i; *Works,* II, 8.
[12] *Ibid.,* II, i; *Works,* II, 24–25.

statesmanship: "With your gracious pardon, if I were worthy to be one of your counsellors—" "What then?" "I would advise you, as others do, to take your own course. Your grace knows best what is to be done." [13]

If we compare *The Witty Fair One* and *The Grateful Servant* with the three plays previously discussed, we feel that Shirley is growing in his stage-craft and in his grasp of human life. In respect to unity of plot, he shows, to be sure, no consistency of standard: even after his tolerable attainment in *The Maid's Revenge,* he is content in general to follow the more loosely constructed models of his day. In respect, however, to effectiveness of scene, and in respect to comic characterization, Shirley is already achieving considerable success. Brains and Sir Nicholas in *The Witty Fair One,* and Jacomo, the Malvolio of *The Grateful Servant,* are memorable, if not wholly original, creations. Each play contains much that is repulsive; but, besides this, each contains much genuine and wholesome fun; and *The Grateful Servant,* in its romantic parts, manifests a delicacy of sentiment that we shall learn later to recognize as typical of Shirley.

[13] *The Grateful Servant,* III, ii; *Works,* II, 50.

CHAPTER VIII

THE FIRST DRAMATIC PERIOD—CONTINUED

THE TRAITOR

UNLIKE its two immediate predecessors, *The Witty Fair One* and *The Grateful Servant,* Shirley's *The Traitor,* licensed May 4, 1631, is a romantic tragedy.

In the interrelating of the several actions and in the high effectiveness of individual scenes, this play is conspicuously well constructed. Its central figure is Lorenzo—known to history as Lorenzino de' Medici —kinsman and favorite of Alexander, Duke of Florence. Lorenzo desires to become duke; and, to this end, besides creating a faction in the city, he begins two intrigues. One is to weaken his chief rival, Cosmo, by preventing his marriage to the wealthy Oriana; the other is to destroy the duke by involving him in deadly feud with a fiery noble named Sciarrha.

Up to the middle of the play, Lorenzo's fortunes rise triumphantly. He vindicates himself from a charge of conspiracy against the duke. He incites the duke to select as the object of his lust the beautiful sister of Sciarrha, Amidea. He informs Sciarrha of the duke's resolve and of the duke's command that Sciarrha be his pander, and plots with Sciarrha for vengeance on the duke. When Sciarrha tells his sister that he must kill the duke, she begs him rather to admit their sovereign to her chamber and leave the rest to her. Sciarrha consents, but hides behind the hangings. When the duke, deaf to her entreaties, attempts to force her to his will, Amidea draws a poniard, wounds her own arm, and declares that she will slay herself rather than be ravished. The duke interposes, turns penitent, and begs forgiveness. With that, Sciarrha comes forth, confesses his plot to slay the duke, and, to convince him, hides him behind the arras that he may overhear a conference with Lorenzo. The latter, however, is suspicious. When Sciarrha says that he has killed the duke, Lorenzo feigns utter ignorance and detestation of the deed, and starts to give the alarm. Sciarrha draws his sword upon Lorenzo; but the duke breaks forth and interposes, declares that they have misunderstood each other, and commands that they be friends. Thus is the first attempt of Lorenzo overthrown; but as yet he is himself secure.

Meanwhile, however, Lorenzo's second intrigue has made successful progress. Cosmo, on a pretense of friendship to Pisano, but chiefly influenced by his terror of Lorenzo, has yielded Oriana to Pisano; and Pisano, without the knowledge of Sciarrha, has broken his own engagement with Amidea, and has gained the consent of Oriana's mother to his new betrothal. When Sciarrha seeks vengeance on Lorenzo, the latter first places Sciarrha at the mercy of his swordsmen, then frees him with well-feigned generosity, and finally convinces him that the reformation of the duke should make them both again his loyal subjects. Then it is that Lorenzo (and Shirley), with consummate skill, brings his second intrigue to bear upon his first. He permits Sciarrha to discover Pisano's breach of faith to Amidea, stirs him to vengeance on Pisano, persuades the duke that he shall yet enjoy Amidea, follows Sciarrha as the latter stabs Pisano on his marriage morn, arrests him, promises a pardon on condition that he yield Amidea to the duke, threatens that, unless he yield, his sister shall be ravished, gains his pretended consent, and so leaves him maddening for a second murder. Lorenzo, seemingly, may yet be duke.

Sciarrha tells Amidea that he must yield her to the duke or slay her. To save her brother from the latter crime, she pretends that she will suffer the duke to have his will. Sciarrha stabs her. Dying, she explains that she did but *seem* consenting, to gain time; and to her younger brother she declares—like Desde-

mona—that her injury is self-inflicted. Intending
vengeance on the duke, Sciarrha causes her body to
be placed upon a bed in the room where the duke
expects to meet her. The duke enters, is left alone,
approaches, kisses the corpse, discovers she is dead.
As he cries out, Lorenzo and a confederate enter. "My
Amidea's dead!" exclaims the duke. "I prithee kill
me!" They both attack him. As he falls, Sciarrha
enters. Lorenzo tries to place on him the crime.
They fight. Sciarrha kills Lorenzo—and then dies.

Even so brief a summary as this, makes evident the
skill of our dramatist in plot-construction. As to the
interweaving of actions, *The Traitor,* in a modest
way, suggests even that masterpiece, *Othello.* It
needs but this comparison, however, to show the real
point of difference between the greater and the lesser
dramatist. The struggle in *Othello* is not primarily
that between Iago and the Moor, but rather that between Othello's jealousy and his love; and this struggle, the struggle that makes the play a tragedy, is
not external but internal. This concentration of the
contending forces within a single soul is what differ-
entiates the plot-structure of the psychological tragedy of Shakspere and of Webster from that of the
romantic tragedies of minor Elizabethans. Of this
internal struggle, *The Traitor* offers nothing; nothing of conflicting motives. The contest is merely be-

tween Lorenzo on the one hand and Sciarrha, the duke, and Amidea on the other; and in this contest, each unwaveringly performs his part and takes the consequences: neither Sciarrha, nor Lorenzo, nor Amidea, nor the pliant duke, hesitates or regrets. For each, the struggle is external, not within. This qualification we must keep in mind when we speak of *The Traitor* as a great tragedy. As to plot-structure, Shirley's conception has been greatly executed; but his conception itself is not the greatest. Only with the admission that it presents a struggle external, not internal, may the plot of *The Traitor* be accounted "great."

What is true of the plot, is true also of the characters: what Shirley attempts is not the highest; yet his achievement is such as to win even Swinburne's approbation. Lorenzo, Sciarrha, Amidea, each is a notable creation. Even the weakling duke is worth our study.

In Lorenzo, who plays the title rôle, Shirley has created a notable villain: resourceful, daring, plausible of tongue. Of his intrigue and its ambitious motives, Shirley gives us excellent exposition even in the dozen lines of conversation between Lorenzo and Petruchio in the opening scene. Of his resourcefulness and plausibility, Shirley presents a most brilliant example in the second scene: the scene in which Lorenzo, suddenly accused of treason, overwhelms his accusers by successive instances of his loyalty, and victoriously leads away his dupe to a night of dissipation. In the second act, Shirley again makes Lorenzo's skill of tongue victorious: having aroused Sciarrha's rage by telling him of the duke's lust for Amidea, Lorenzo aggravates it by telling Sciarrha that the duke wills that he, the brother, be pander; turns it to treason by admitting his own disloyal plots; and fires it to action by recalling to Sciarrha's mind the threatened rape of Amidea. Nor do Lorenzo's intuition and readiness desert him when, after the duke and Amidea and Sciarrha have made their peace (Act III, scene iii), Sciarrha endeavors to trap Lorenzo into a confession. But perhaps Shirley's characterization of Lorenzo shows to best advantage in the opening of Act IV, in which, after the soliloquy admitting the failure of his plots, Lorenzo seizes upon the visit of Sciarrha to persuade him that he, like Sciarrha, has become loyal at the duke's conversion; causes Sciarrha to discover Pisano's disloyalty to Amidea; and then, having revived the lustful desires of the duke, uses Sciarrha's purposed assassination of Pisano as a means for bringing Sciarrha, Amidea, and the duke once more within his power. The extent of this power, however, he at length miscalculates: and in this miscalculation, Shirley makes

occasion for Lorenzo's fall. When Lorenzo arrests
Sciarrha for the assassination of Pisano, and suggests
that Sciarrha purchase his pardon with his sister's
shame, Lorenzo fails to see that he is rousing vengeance not against the duke only, but against himself.
When Lorenzo stabs the duke's picture that he may
school himself to stab the duke, he presents not only
a bit of effective melodrama, but also conspicuous
evidence of his growing weakness. This weakness he
again presents when, in the assassination of the duke,
he stabs his victim not once but many times. Shirley
in this has prepared us well for the catastrophe: the
inability of the traitor longer to deceive Sciarrha or
even to penetrate Sciarrha's purpose, and his inability
to defend himself against Sciarrha's sword.

In Sciarrha, Shirley has created another powerful
figure: direct, fiery, easily deceived, yet ultimately
capable of matching himself in subtlety even against
the intrigues of Lorenzo. His fundamental characteristic, Shirley emphasizes in his first mention of
Sciarrha:

> Prepare Sciarrha, but be very wise
> In the discovery; *he is all touchwood*.[1]

We are not surprised, therefore, when, at the opening
of the second act, Shirley presents Sciarrha in the

[1] *The Traitor*, I, ii; *Works*, II, 110.

midst of his outburst to Lorenzo. To the suggestion
of Lorenzo, Sciarrha reacts so rapidly that he imagines each thought to be his own. The dishonor of
Amidea, the dishonor to himself, Lorenzo's alleged
enthusiasm for a commonwealth—all these motives
sweep Sciarrha forward to his resolution to assassinate the duke. He tells the duke's commands to
Amidea; he tests her constancy and that of Florio;
he rejoices in their virtue; and he vows that "the Tar-
quin shall be entertain'd." [2] Yet he consents to
Amidea's attempt to win the young monarch to a
nobler life, and, convinced of her success, defers his
purpose. His directness and credulity, manifested in
his inability to trick Lorenzo into a confession, become still more evident when, upon his visit of defiance to Lorenzo, he puts himself at the mercy of
Lorenzo's swordsmen and—more dangerous—of Lorenzo's words. He believes that Lorenzo has been
won to loyalty and virtue; and he never for a moment
suspects Lorenzo's purpose in permitting him to
learn, as if by accident, of Pisano's desertion of
Amidea and purposed marriage to Oriana. But with
his assassination of Pisano, Sciarrha begins to see the
light. He becomes convinced of Lorenzo's treachery; he realizes at last that Amidea has no hope but
death. He resolves to trick Lorenzo and the duke:

[2] *The Traitor*, II, i; *Works*, II, 120.

to send them not Amidea but Amidea's body; to seize that moment when his sister shall be nearest heaven, and by slaying her to save her honor. When, to save her brother from such guilt as this, Amidea pretends that she will pay Lorenzo's price, Sciarrha strikes. Too late they learn each other's motives:

> Again, again forgive me, Amidea,
> And pray for me. Live but a little longer,
> To hear me speak. My passion hath betray'd
> Thee to this wound, for which I know not whether
> I should rejoice or weep, since thou art virtuous.
> The duke, whose soul is black again, expects thee
> To be his whore.—Good Death, be not so hasty.—
> The agent for his lust, Lorenzo, has
> My oath to send thee to his bed: for otherwise,
> In my denial, hell and they decree,
> When I am dead, to ravish thee—mark that,
> To ravish thee!—and I confess, in tears
> As full of sorrow as thy soul of innocence,
> In my religious care to have thee spotless,
> I did resolve, when I had found thee ripe
> And nearest heaven, with all thy best desires,
> To send thee to thy peace. Thy feign'd consent
> Hath brought thy happiness more early to thee,
> And saved some guilt. Forgive me altogether.[3]

Victorious in this, Sciarrha pursues his plan to lure the duke to Amidea's chamber. Lorenzo anticipates

[3] *The Traitor,* v, i; *Works,* II, 176.

Sciarrha in the slaying of the duke, but fails to deceive Sciarrha as to his ultimate intent. Sciarrha slays Lorenzo, and so dies the victor.

In Shirley's Lorenzo, we have seen a powerful character becoming ever weaker through the unnerving effect of his own villainy; in Shirley's Sciarrha, a character equally powerful attaining ever greater self-control and insight through suffering and struggle. No such development appears in Shirley's duke. He does not grow, either for good or ill; he merely vacillates. He believes Lorenzo's loyalty; he doubts it; he believes again. He desires Amidea; he turns virtuous; he desires again. He is unnerved by Amidea's dagger; unnerved by the mob; unnerved by Amidea's death; and he dies under the hands of his "best and dearest friend" Lorenzo, with penance on his lips. In short, Shirley's Duke Alexander is a figure of consistent vacillation and weakness.

In contrast with this vacillation and weakness in the duke, Shirley presents us, in Amidea, with a picture of consistent strength. That Amidea grows, we cannot say; all that she is at her death is present, potentially, in her first appearance. Yet this very consistency—especially in contrast with the development of Sciarrha and the disintegration of Lorenzo—is not without its charm. Her silent horror when Sciarrha first tells her of the duke's desires; her resolution to die rather than to yield her honor; her self-control when Pisano, without warning, cancels their betrothal; and her determination that Sciarrha shall not know of this dishonor: all manifest the nobility of her character. That this nobility is more than a passive capacity for suffering, appears in Act III, scene iii, in her control over Sciarrha and the duke. That her nobility is not without the softer virtue of forgiveness appears in her words to Pisano and Oriana upon their wedding morn:

AMIDEA.   Not for my sake, but for your own, go back,
Or take some other way; this leads to death.
My brother—
    PISANO.   What of him?
    AMI.   Transported with
The fury of revenge for my dishonour,
As he conceives, for 'tis against my will,
Hath vow'd to kill you in your nuptial glory.
Alas! I fear his haste. Now, good my lord,
Have mercy on yourself. I do not beg
Your pity upon me: I know too well
You cannot love me now; nor would I rob
This virgin of your faith, since you have pleas'd
To throw me from your love. I do not ask
One smile, nor one poor kiss; enrich this maid,
Created for those blessings; but again
I would beseech you, cherish your own life,
Though I be lost for ever.

ALONZO.   It is worth
Your care, my lord, if there be any danger.

   PIS.   Alas! her grief hath made her wild, poor lady.
I should not love Oriana to go back.
Set forward.—Amidea, you may live
To be a happier bride. Sciarrha is not
So irreligious to profane these rites.

   AMI.   Will you not then believe me?—Pray persuade
         him;
You are his friends.—Lady, it will concern
You most of all, indeed; I fear you'll weep
To see him dead, as well as I.

   PIS.   No more;
Go forward.

   AMI.   I have done; pray be not angry
That still I wish you well; may heaven divert
All harms that threaten you; full blessings crown
Your marriage! I hope there is no sin in this;
Indeed I cannot choose but pray for you.
This might have been my wedding-day—

   ORI.   Good heaven,
I would it were! My heart can tell, I take
No joy in being his bride, none in your prayers.
You shall have my consent to have him still;
I will resign my place, and wait on you,
If you will marry him.

   AMI.   Pray do not mock me;
But if you do, I can forgive you too.

   ORI.   Dear Amidea, do not think I mock
Your sorrow. By these tears, that are not worn

By every virgin on her wedding-day,
I am compelled to give away myself:
Your hearts were promised, but he ne'er had mine.
Am I not wretched too?
    AMI.   Alas, poor maid!
We two keep sorrow alive then, but I prithee,
When thou art married, love him, prithee love him,
For he esteems thee well; and once a day
Give him a kiss for me; but do not tell him
'Twas my desire; perhaps 'twill fetch a sigh
From him, and I had rather break my heart.[4]

The nobility of character here evident in Amidea's forgiveness and resignation, appears again in her meeting with her brother after he has slain Pisano. Weeping both for the dead and for the living, she begs that her own death may purchase pardon for Sciarrha. When he says that he must slay her to preserve her, she tries to save him from the deed by pretending that she will yield her honor to the duke; when he stabs her, she forgives him; and to their brother Florio declares that she herself "drew the weapon" to her heart.

Such, then, are the leading characters in Shirley's *Traitor:* Lorenzo, Sciarrha, the duke, and Amidea. In Amidea, Shirley has created a character beautiful for its consistent virtue and its pathos; in the duke, a

[4] *The Traitor,* IV, ii; *Works,* II, 163–165.

[210]

character contemptible for its weakness and its vacillation; in Sciarrha, a character primarily emotional that grows in wisdom; in Lorenzo, a character primarily intellectual that disintegrates from its own villainy. That none of these characters is built on an internal struggle, we must admit. And this externality of struggle makes Shirley's characterization, like Shirley's plot-structure, less notable than that of Shakspere. This granted, however, Shirley's characterization in *The Traitor* deserves our highest praise. Each of the major figures is living and distinct, clearly contrasted with his fellows. With each re-reading of the play, we follow them with stronger interest.

Before we leave *The Traitor,* two topics remain to be considered: the comic relief, and the verse. The comic element centers about the figure of Depazzi, a *parvenu* ennobled by Lorenzo's favor. In his case, perhaps, we should modify our judgment that the play shows no instance of internal struggle. In him, his loyalty to Lorenzo's interest struggles most comically with his fears. When Lorenzo is accused of treason, Depazzi's frightened "asides" admitting all the charges, make spicy comment on his lord's denial. When his patron's plots have involved him more deeply still in treason, he causes his page to arraign him before an imaginary court; and when the page, rising to the occasion, charges him with a series of wholly imaginary crimes, Depazzi is so thoroughly alarmed that he forgets himself, begins a real confession, beats the page, and finally dismisses him with gold. When Lorenzo's first attempt against the duke has failed, Depazzi brings him fifteen hundred crowns for permission to resign his post and flee the city. Not only is all this comic matter admirable fooling in itself, but it is far more closely joined to the major plot than is usual outside of Shakspere.

With regard to the verse, let us first examine a typical passage from the opening act—the scene in which Lorenzo defends himself against the charge of treason. The passage following will serve our purpose:

> LORENZO.   . . . Ask this good counsellor, or these
> gentlemen,
> Whose faiths are tried, whose cares are always waking
> About your person, how have I appeared
> To them, that thus I should be rendered hateful
> To you and my good country? They are virtuous,
> And dare not blemish a white faith, accuse
> My sound heart of dishonour. Sir, you must
> Pardon my bold defence; my virtue bleeds
> By your much easiness, and I am compelled
> To break all modest limits, and to waken
> Your memory (if it be not too late

To say you have one) with the story of
My fair deservings. Who, sir, overthrew
With his designs, your late ambitious brother,
Hippolito, who, like a meteor, threatened
A black and fatal omen?

    DUKE.   'Twas Lorenzo.

    LOR.   Be yet as just, and say whose art directed
A countermine to check the pregnant hopes
Of Salviati, who, for his cardinal's cap,
In Rome was potent, and here popular?

    DUKE.   None but Lorenzo.

    DEPAZZI.   Admirable traitor! [*Aside.*]

    LOR.   Whose service was commended when the exiles,
One of whose tribe accuseth me, had raised
Commotions in our Florence? When the hinge
Of state did faint under the burthen, and
The people sweat with their own fears, to think
The soldier should inhabit their calm dwellings,
Who then rose up your safety, and crushed all
Their plots to air?

    DUKE.   Our cousin, dear Lorenzo.

    LOR.   When he that should reward, forgets the men
That purchased his security, 'tis virtue
To boast a merit. With my services
I have not starved your treasury; the grand
Captain Gonzales accounted to King Ferdinand
Three hundred thousands crowns for spies; what bills
Have I brought in for such intelligence?

    DEP.   I do grow hearty.   [*Aside.*]

    DUKE.   All thy actions

[213]

Stand fresh before us, and confirm thou art
Our best and dearest friend; thus we assure
Our confidence; they love us not that feed
One jealous thought of our dear coz, Lorenzo.[5]

Now this is not a "purple passage" but a group of lines that, in most respects, is thoroughly representative of the play throughout. It is not great poetry; yet, if read aloud, it will be found metrical, melodious, and, above all, dramatically effective. As to the meter, it is varied but not irregular. The position of the pause changes pleasantly from line to line. Inversions, substitutions, and elisions occur, but not too often. In this particular passage, the percentage of run-on lines chances to be high. Had we examined a longer passage, however, we should have found that Shirley's use of run-on lines in *The Traitor* closely corresponds to that of Shakspere in his later plays. As to his meter, therefore, Shirley is here no anarchist. As for melody, the passage quoted is not conspicuous; yet surely it is pleasing to the ear, as in the lines:

A countermine to check the pregnant hopes
Of Salviati, who, for his cardinal's cap,
In Rome was potent, and here popular.

[5] *The Traitor,* I, ii; *Works,* II, 108–110.

[214]

And finally, as for dramatic effectiveness, read the lines aloud and note how well they are adapted to delivery. Observe especially how frequently the final word of an unstopped line is one that logically deserves distinction. *Gentlemen, waking, appeared, hateful, virtuous, accuse, must, bleeds, compelled, waken, too late, overthrew, brother, threatened, Lorenzo:* in sixteen consecutive lines, but one concludes with an unemphatic ending. When the logical stress comes thus upon the final word, we need no longer pause to keep the verse-form perfect.

In respect to mastery of verse, however, Shirley in *The Traitor* does something more than maintain this passing standard of acceptability. When occasion serves, as in the sad farewell of Amidea, his muse is genuinely poetic:

Your fathers knew him well: one who will never
Give cause I should suspect him to forsake me;
A constant lover; one whose lips, though cold,
Distil chaste kisses. Though our bridal bed
Be not adorned with roses, 'twill be green;
We shall have virgin laurel, cypress, yew,
To make us garlands; though no pine do burn,
Our nuptial shall have torches; and our chamber
Shall be cut out of marble, where we'll sleep,
Free from all care for ever. Death, my lord,

I hope, shall be my husband. Now, farewell.
Although no kiss, accept my parting tear,
And give me leave to wear my willow here.[6]

Swinburne, who held that "as a rule" Shirley's
plays are "wearisome and conventional, anæmic and
invertebrate,"[7] accounted *The Traitor* "the one play
which gives its author a place among the tragic poets
of Shakespeare's age and country."[8] In view of this
all but entire disapproval of the plays of Shirley—a
disapproval due, as we shall find, too often to his
ignorance of the plays discussed—Swinburne's cordial interest in and favorable opinion of the plot, the
characterization, and the verse of Shirley's *Traitor,*
holds a significance that warrants some quotation:

"The gravest error or defect of Shirley's work as
a dramatist," writes Swinburne, "is usually perceptible in the management of his underplots; his hand
was neither strong enough to weld nor skilful enough
to weave them into unity or harmony with the main
action; and the concurrent or alternate interests,
through lack of coherence and fusion, become a
source of mere worry and weariness to the distracted
attention and the jaded memory. But the main plot
of *The Traitor,* founded on the assassination or im-

[6] *The Traitor,* IV, ii; *Works,* II, 165.
[7] In *The Fortnightly Review,* LIII (n.s., XLVII), 462.
[8] *Ibid.,* 467.

molation of Alessandro de' Medici by his kinsman Lorenzino, . . . is very neatly and happily interwoven with a story which at first sight recalls that of the fatal marriage and breach of promise through which the name of Buondelmonti had attained a significance so tragical for Florence three hundred and twenty-two years earlier. . . . This . . . is skilfully and delicately adapted to bring into fuller relief the most beautiful figure on all the overcrowded stage of Shirley's invention. His place among our poets would be very much higher than it is if he could have left us but one or two others as thoroughly realized and as attractively presented as the noble and pathetic conception of Amidea. There is something in the part which reminds us of Beaumont's Aspatia; but even though the forsaken heroine of the elder poet has yet more exquisite poetry to utter than any that Shirley could produce, her character is less noble and attractive, the manner of her death is less natural and far less touching. The lover in either case is equally contemptible; but the heroic part of Sciarrha is as superior in truthfulness as it was inferior in popularity to the famous but histrionic part of the boastful martialist Melantius. The king in *The Maid's Tragedy* is certainly not better drawn than his equally licentious but less tyrannous counterpart in *The Traitor;* and the very effective scene in which

Calianax denounces Melantius to the king, only to be stormed down and put to silence by the denial of his accomplice and the laughing incredulity of the victim, is surpassed by the admirable device in which the chief conspirator's superb and subtle audacity of resource confounds the loyalty of Sciarrha and confirms the confidence of Alessandro. A more ingenious, natural, and striking situation—admirable in itself, and more admirable in its introduction and its assistance to the progress of evolution of the plot—it would be difficult to find in any play. The swiftness and sharpness of suspicious intuition, the promptitude and impudence of intelligent hypocrisy, which distinguish the conduct of Shirley's ideal conspirator, are far above the level of his usual studies or sketches of the same or a similar kind. Nor is there, if I mistake not, so much of really beautiful writing, of pure and vigorous style, of powerful and pathetic simplicity, in any earlier or later work of its author. Of Shakespeare or of Marlowe or of Webster we can hardly hope to be reminded while reading Shirley; but we are reminded of Fletcher at his best by the cry of sympathy with which Amidea receives the assurance that the rival who has unwittingly and reluctantly supplanted her is also the victim of her lover's infidelity and ingratitude:

"Alas, poor maid!
We two keep sorrow alive then.

This indeed, if I may venture to say so, seems to me a touch not unworthy of Webster himself—the nearest of all our poets to Shakespeare in command of spontaneous and concentrated expression for tragic and pathetic emotion." [9]

Whether or not we accept this enthusiastic opinion of Swinburne in its entirety, our estimate of *The Traitor* may well be highly favorable. Its verse is acceptable and, at times, genuinely poetic; its comic relief is entertaining, original, and skilfully correlated with the serious plot; its characters, although embodying no internal struggle, are nobly conceived and clearly delineated; its tragic plot, although based upon external struggle, is conspicuously well constructed; its individual scenes are notably effective. In the lustful tyrant, in the depraved villain, in the brother as pander, and in the use of the corpse, the play presents the familiar material of Webster-Tourneurian tragedy of lust and horror; but does so without repulsiveness. In the emphasis upon love, in the contrast of the idyllic-sentimental with the tragic-horrible, in the clever use of surprise, and in the Amintor-Aspatia personages, it presents, but with far

[9] A. C. Swinburne, "James Shirley," in *The Fortnightly Review,* LIII (n.s., XLVII), 467–468.

more probability, the material of Beaumont and Fletcher in romantic tragedy. The elements indeed are old; but the effect is new. For a major dramatist at the height of his career, *The Traitor* would have been a creditable production; for a minor dramatist scarce out of his apprenticeship, *The Traitor* is a memorable achievement.

CHAPTER IX

THE FIRST DRAMATIC PERIOD—CONCLUDED

FROM *THE HUMOROUS COURTIER* TO *THE BALL*

OF the six plays thus far considered, three— *The Maid's Revenge, The Grateful Servant* and *The Traitor*—belong to the romantic school of Shakspere and of Fletcher; one, *Love Tricks,* is a mixture of realism and romanticism; and the remaining two, *The Wedding* and *The Witty Fair One,* belong primarily to the realistic school of Jonson. Of the five plays that we must now consider, the five plays following *The Traitor* in 1631 and 1632, all, for one reason or another, must be classed as further essays in the realistic style. *The Humorous Courtier,* licensed as *The Duke,* May 17, 1631, has been called by Schelling[1] a romantic comedy. To most readers, however, notwithstanding its Italian setting, the play will seem primarily a comedy of humors. *Love's Cruelty,* licensed November 14, 1631, has likewise an Italian scene; but, in subject and in atmosphere, this tragedy is to be classed with the realistic plays of London life and manners.

[1] Schelling, *Elizabethan Drama,* II, 313–314.

Changes, or Love in a Maze, licensed January 10, 1631/2; *Hyde Park,* licensed April 20, 1632; and *The Ball,* licensed November 16, 1632, are all indisputably comedies of manners. That Shirley, after producing so excellent a romantic tragedy as *The Traitor,* should devote himself to the writing of realistic plays, is indicative of the popularity of this type of drama. Realism in comedy—derived from that of Fletcher and of Jonson—was leading onward toward the realism of the Restoration. In this movement, Shirley had his part: in the five successive plays with which we are now to conclude our account of Shirley's first dramatic period, his dominant characteristic is realism and not romanticism.

In *The Humorous Courtier,* licensed as *The Duke,* May 17, 1631, Shirley produced a new and more poetic version of Jonson's *Every Man out of his Humour:* a version in which a duchess of Mantua plays the physician to her entire court. "They are mad humours," she says, "and I must physic them."[2] The theme is productive of a well-knit plot. Foscari, Duke of Parma, who has been wooing the Duchess of Mantua, suddenly disappears from her court; and the duchess announces her intent to choose a husband from among her lords. Encouraged by her new favorite, Giotto, each courtier believes himself the

---

[2] *The Humorous Courtier,* v, iii; *Works,* IV, 600.

chosen man, and displays in his wooing his characteristic weakness. Volterre, like Lodam in *The Wedding,* but with a better right, boasts of his fluency in
foreign tongues; Depazzi practises set speeches, such
as Shirley had ridiculed in *The School of Complement,* six years before; Contarini, who has the misfortune to be married, endeavors—happily without
success—to bribe Giotto to commit adultery with
his wife so that he may divorce her—a device previously used by Shirley in *The Grateful Servant;*
and Orseolo, the humorous courtier *par excellence,*
whose humor it has been to pretend abhorrence of all
women, confesses now the utmost licentiousness in the
expectation that this will make him a suitor more
acceptable. In the final scene, the duchess makes
sport of each in turn, and then announces that her
servant, Giotto, who has been assisting in the jest, is
really the missing Duke of Parma in disguise and her
accepted husband. To the modern reader, this play
is far from pleasing: its mirth is flat; its episodes are
repulsive. To an audience, however, that was fond
of humors and that found nothing offensive in immorality, *The Humorous Courtier* may well have been
diverting. The main conception certainly is clever.
The old title-page—a witness, however, not above
suspicion—asserts that the play had been "presented
with good applause."

The other play belonging to this year is *Love's Cruelty,* a tragedy licensed November 14, 1631. Schelling refers to its "romantic Italian atmosphere"; [3] yet its scene might well have been contemporary London, and its tone differs but little from that of the more serious and poetic of Shirley's comedies of manners. Indeed, as we shall note presently in connection with *The Example,* realism and romance in Shirley are ofttimes closely blended. Typical of this blending is the passage in which Shirley pays tribute to "the soul of the immortal English Jonson." [4]

The scene of *Love's Cruelty* is Ferrara. Clariana, betrothed to Bellamente, is curious to meet his much-praised friend Hippolito. Concealing her identity, she visits him. He, called away by a summons from the duke, locks her in his room; then, finding himself delayed, sends Bellamente to release her. Although astonished to find his betrothed in such a situation, Bellamente accepts her explanation, and marries her. Clariana, however, leads on Hippolito to commit adultery. Bellamente takes them in the act, and, after a sensational scene, dismisses them unpunished. Meanwhile, the Duke of Ferrara has been endeavoring to seduce Eubella, a charming little country girl,

[3] Schelling, *Elizabethan Drama,* II, 324.
[4] *Love's Cruelty,* II, ii; *Works,* II, 213.

daughter of Sebastiano; and to effect his ends, the duke has employed Hippolito as his spokesman. Hippolito, however, overcome with shame for his crime against Bellamente and won by the virtue of Eubella, ceases to plead the duke's lust, and for himself makes an offer of honorable marriage to Eubella. The duke discovers the treachery of his ambassador, and, himself ashamed, confirms their purposed marriage. To prevent this marriage, Clariana, pretending that she is to reveal a plot by Bellamente against Hippolito, summons him to her chamber on his wedding morn. She finds him, however, true to Eubella and indignant at the deception. At that moment, they are found by Bellamente. Clariana stabs Hippolito, and he wounds her with his sword. She lives only long enough to beg forgiveness of her husband; Hippolito, only until the arrival of Eubella. Bellamente dies from the shock of the discovery. The duke resolves to console Eubella by marrying her himself.

As compared with *The Traitor,* this tragedy is a backward step: the theme has less of tragic grandeur; the verse is less notable; the comic relief is savorless; and the scene in which the lustful monarch renounces his pursuit of the maiden and confirms her betrothal to her lover, seems, when compared with Shirley's later handling of the situation in *The Royal Master,* poor indeed. Nevertheless, *Love's Cruelty* is not

[225]

mediocre. The two plots are skilfully combined; the main action affords occasion for several truly effective scenes; and the psychology of the Clariana-Hippolito intrigue is far from conventional. Moreover, the use of realism in tragedy, although not unprecedented, is sufficiently unusual to invite remark, both for its unflinching truth and for its severe morality. Although I cannot rate this play as highly as have some,[5] I account it a most interesting experiment in realistic tragedy.

To the next year, 1632, belong four plays: *Changes, or Love in a Maze, Hyde Park,* and *The Ball,* all comedies of London life and manners, and a light romantic play, *The Arcadia.* The last of these, I reserve for the opening chapter on Shirley's Second Dramatic Period; the others shall be considered here.

Changes, or Love in a Maze, was licensed January 10, 1631/2. Its plot amply justifies its title. Gerard, a young gentleman of fashion, finds himself in love with two sisters, Chrysolina and Aurelia; and, although both return his affection, he is unable to make choice between the two. He begs his friend Thornay to love either of the sisters so that he himself may choose the other. The two friends, however, soon have a disagreement; and the sisters dismiss them

---

[5] Compare, however, Swinburne, "James Shirley," in *The Fortnightly Review,* LIII (n.s., XLVII), 468–469.

both. Now Thornay, as we learn, was previously betrothed to a third maiden, Eugenia. His rival, Yongrave, in that exaggerated devotion which Shirley has already depicted in Foscari of *The Grateful Servant* and, less sincerely, in Cosmo of *The Traitor,* recalls Thornay to Eugenia, and brings about their marriage. Then, finding that his self-sacrifice has inspired a love for him in Chrysolina, Yongrave rises to the occasion and marries her. This marriage relieves Gerard of the necessity of making choice between the sisters; and he contentedly marries Aurelia, the one remaining.

As a supplement to this somewhat complicated plot, we have a group of characters of humor: Caperwit, a poetaster; Caperwit's page disguised as Lady Bird; and Sir Gervase Simple, a newly knighted country gull—all of whom are intended to provide diversion of the Jonsonian variety. There is also, in the final scene, a masque. The play is clean enough, but slight in value.

Of a much more notable quality is *Hyde Park,* licensed April 20, 1632. Its plot is loosely knit; but its characters and setting constitute a marvelously realistic picture of the fashionable life of Shirley's day. The structure of the play involves three stories which fail to unite but which sometimes intersect. The first is merely the return of a seven-years-lost husband, Bonavent, to find his wife about to marry Lacy, and the steps by which he recovers Mistress Bonavent—to her entire satisfaction. The second story deals with a Mistress Carol, whose avowed humor it is to jeer her suitors and put them all to scorn:

> I will not have my tongue tied up, when I've
> A mind to jeer my suitors. . . .
> For I must have my humour; I'm sick else.[6]

Finally one of her lovers, Fairfield, desires a boon: that Mistress Carol, after setting aside anything that she would not willingly grant, will permit him anything else that he may ask. She agrees; makes all the exceptions she can think of—to love him, to marry him, and so forth; and then finds that his request is this: that she shall never desire his company. She soon finds, of course, that she cannot do without him; and her efforts to call him back without appearing so to do, form one of the most amusing elements in the play. The third story is another of the familiar themes of Shirley: the reformation of a libertine. Frank Trier, to test the virtue of Julietta, his betrothed, introduces her to Lord Bonvile with the implication that she is a lady of pleasure. She, however, arouses his lordship's better self, rewards her lover's want of faith by annulling their betrothal, and ends

[6] *Hyde Park*, II, iv; *Works*, II, 490.

by receiving the young lord's offer of honorable marriage.

These plots, as I have said, are without logical connection: even *Love in a Maze* has more of unity. In other respects, however, *Hyde Park* marks an advance in Shirley's workmanship. The characters in this play are more distinct than those of earlier plays; and they are more like real people. Unlike the characters in *The Witty Fair One,* they inspire in us at least a beginning of human sympathy; we rejoice with them in their good fortune. Additional interest arises from the fact that the third and fourth acts are laid in Hyde Park on a racing day. Here the betting and the races—foot and horse—form a lively setting for the action. Pepys records, in 1668, two years after Shirley's death, that in this scene horses were brought upon the stage—"the earliest record," thinks Dyce, "of horses being introduced."[7] We may note also that these Hyde Park scenes vaguely suggest the *Bartholomew Fair* of Jonson, and that the women have something in common with Fletcher's witty heroines; but we must not press this similarity too far.

Dyce calls *Hyde Park* a "very lively and elegant comedy";[8] but Ward is more exact in saying that

[7] Dyce, in *Works,* I, xvii–xviii.
[8] *Ibid.,* xviii.

"only in so far as it is descriptive of . . . the realities of contemporary life and manners,"[9] is the play of special interest. Its importance for us is as a forward step in the career of Shirley as a dramatist: a greater mastery in character-drawing and in the depiction of a realistic setting.

Hyde Park, as we have noted, is a realistic sketch of the fashionable citizen society of London; *The Ball,* licensed November 16, 1632, is an equally realistic picture of the life and manners of the nobility. In *Hyde Park,* the women are addressed as "Mistress," and are immensely flattered by the presence of even one real lord; in *The Ball,* the women are addressed as "Lady," and the least among their suitors claims to be cousin to an earl. This difference gives to the latter play a certain elegance of tone that is lacking in the former: an elegance—according to the standards of the day. In the seventeenth century, it must be remembered, the manners of even the most polite society still possessed a coarseness that is to-day well-nigh inconceivable. The wit of Lady Lucina in *The Ball* is as remote from modern gentlehood as is the wit of Mistress Carol in *Hyde Park.*

That Shirley's unflattering pictures in *The Ball* gave offense to at least one follower of the court, appears from the official entry, previously quoted,

[9] Ward, *English Dramatic Literature,* III, 106.

from the office-book of Sir Henry Herbert, Master
of the Revels:

18 Nov. 1632. In the play of *The Ball,* written by
Sherley, and acted by the Queens players, ther were
divers personated so naturally, both of lords and others
of the court, that I took it ill, and would have forbidden
the play, but that Biston promiste many things which I
found faulte withall should be left out, and that he would
not suffer it to be done by the poett any more, who deserves to be punisht; and the first that offends in this kind,
of poets or players, shall be sure of publique punishment.[10]

If, then, the printed version of *The Ball* is but a di-
luted version, what was the original? Even in the
revised form, society makes a sorry showing. If, in
the original, "ther were divers personated so naturally, both of lords and others of the court," need we
wonder that some should take offense at Shirley's
realism?

Shirley's own opinion on this question, as expressed in *The Lady of Pleasure,* licensed three years
later, and the possible bearing of these satires upon
Shirley's departure for Dublin shortly after, we have
considered in Chapter IV, above. Our immediate
interest in these comments by Herbert and by Shirley

[10] Malone's *Shakspere,* 1821, III, 231–232.

is rather in relation to certain criticisms which Swinburne has seen fit to pass upon Shirley's character-drawing in *The Ball*. Herbert, we have seen, complained that divers lords and others of the court were personated too "naturally," and commanded that these natural touches be "left out." Shirley testifies that

> . . . had the poet not been bribed to a modest
> Expression of your antic gambols in't,
> Some darks had been discover'd, and the deeds too.[11]

This passage from *The Lady of Pleasure*, Swinburne knew; but its real meaning, as indicated by the passage in the office-book of Sir Henry Herbert, he most unfortunately perverts:

> The ladies and their lovers [says this critic], are so lamentably shadowy and shapeless that a modern reader has no difficulty in understanding the curious admission of the poet in a later and better and less reticent play that he had been "bribed to a modest admission [12] of their antic gambols." Had he rejected the bribe, supposing it to have ever been offered, a less decorous and a less vacuous comedy might have been better worth our reading: but possibly, if not probably, the assertion or imputation

---

[11] *The Lady of Pleasure,* I, i; *Works,* IV, 9.

[12] Swinburne, be it noted, is inaccurate even in his quotation: Shirley wrote "expression," not "admission."

may be merely the part of the character to whom it is assigned.[13]

That the lines quoted by Swinburne are to be interpreted rather as Shirley's protest against the censorship of Herbert, must be evident to any careful student. Had Swinburne been more familiar with his subject, and especially with the office-book of the Master of the Revels, a less clever and less superficial criticism might have been better worth our quoting.[14]

"The main purpose of this comedy," says Ward, "seems to have been to give the lie to the scandalous reports which had arisen in connection with the first attempts at establishing Subscription Balls."[15] Whether the aim of the dramatist were so kindly, we have reason to doubt; but he certainly took advantage of popular interest in these gatherings. For his enveloping action Shirley chose the preparations for the ball, including frequent dancing-lessons conducted by Monsieur Le Frisk; and, for the scene of his closing act, the ball itself. His plots, such as they are, Shirley built up around Lady Lucina, a rich young

[13] A. C. Swinburne, "James Shirley," in *The Fortnightly Review,* LIII (n.s., XLVII), 470–471.

[14] The general subject of the value of Swinburne's critical essay upon Shirley—his frequent superficiality of acquaintance with the plays discussed, his tendency to substitute adjectives for specific facts, and his seeming indifference to accuracy in matters of exact scholarship—I must reserve for a note in the Bibliography.

[15] Ward, *English Dramatic Literature,* III, 107.

widow, and her many suitors, and around the rivalry of Lady Rosamond and Lady Honoria for the attentions of Lord Rainbow. Lady Lucina gives audience in turn to each of her suitors, Sir Ambrose Lamont, Sir Marmaduke Travers, Bostock, cousin to Lord Rainbow, and Colonel Winfield. Of each of the first three she makes a fool, and then sends him to procure a marriage license; the fourth she jeers directly. He, however, by the connivance of her maid, has overheard her conference with the others. He tells them how they are deceived, and agrees with them on vengeance. When they return to her, however, Bostock, their spokesman, is so discourteous to Lucina that Winfield interferes and overwhelms him in her presence. Winfield remains with Lucina, and renews his suit. She offers to marry him on one simple condition: that he will make oath to her that he has been "honest," i.e., that he has lived a moral life. He refuses. She says that his refusal to perjure himself for a fortune proves his honesty in another sense, and she will marry him. First, however, she must introduce him to her six children, to whom the bulk of her estate belongs. Surprised but unshaken, Winfield bids her bring the children in. She confesses that she was but testing his devotion; and declares that nothing now remains but to prove to him that the ball, which he had thought of questionable morality, is really innocent. Together, in the final act, they view the ball; and Winfield is convinced.

The second action, the rivalry of Rosamond and Honoria for the attentions of Lord Rainbow, opens with a quarrel between the ladies. He overhears them, vows that he loves both equally, and leaves it for them to decide whose servant he shall be. In his absence, they are visited by Sir Ambrose and Sir Marmaduke. Smarting under their repulse by Lady Lucina, Sir Marmaduke offers his love to Lady Rosamond; Sir Ambrose, his to Honoria. Each replies by telling her suitor that the other is desperately in love with him. The suitors then offer themselves to their supposed admirers, only to be told that they have been deceived; that the statement was but a test of their devotion. The arrival of Monsieur Le Frisk for the inevitable dancing-lesson saves the situation. The ladies then turn their attention to Lord Rainbow. At the ball, they tell him that, unable to agree as to which most deserves his love, they have decided to ask him to draw lots. He declares that he will draw both lots. He does so, and finds each a blank. Outwitted, he gracefully admits defeat; and begs of each lady the acceptance of a jewel.

As these outlines indicate, the effectiveness of this comedy consists neither in the strength of the characters nor in the structure of the plot, but rather in the amusing situations and in the opportunities for lively repartee. All these Shirley handles well; and to them, he adds a further element, a group of comic characters of humor. Monsieur Le Frisk, the French dancing-master; Barker, who rails at all the world; Bostock, who boasts of noble blood, but who, under the great-est provocation, is too cowardly to draw his sword; and Jack Freshwater, the pretended traveler, who lends his money on condition that he receive five for one at his return, and whose astonishing ignorance proves that he has never quitted England: all these add a pleasant seasoning to the salad. Were Barker taster to his Majesty, he perhaps would say that many of the ingredients of the salad were a trifle stale; that the mistress who makes a sport of all her lovers had done duty in *Hyde Park* the previous April; that the two ladies loving the same man had appeared in *Changes, or Love in a Maze* but the January before; and that Jack Freshwater, who did most politicly disburse his sums, to have five for one at his return from Venice,[16] is in this but an echo of Jonson's Pun-tarvolo, who put forth some five thousand pound, to be paid him five for one upon the return of himself and his dog and his cat from the Turk's court in Con-stantinople.[17] And Barker might add, if he were but

---

[16] *The Ball*, II, i; *Works*, III, 21.
[17] Jonson: *Every Man out of his Humour*, II, i; IV, iv.

a prophet, that the scene of the lovers who attempt to revile their mistress and are put to shame by another, is but a preliminary sketch for a scene in Shirley's *The Lady of Pleasure,* 1635. If his Majesty were wise, however, he would reply to Barker that, in this comedy, Shirley has at least served up several tolerably entertaining humors, a goodly number of amusing episodes, plenty of sprightly conversation, several dances, and a masque. His Majesty might add that, for the audience of November, 1632, Shirley's local and personal allusions were vastly entertaining.

SUMMARY

BEFORE we proceed to our study of Shirley's second period, let us glance back for a moment over the eleven plays extant from the less than eight years between February 10, 1624/5, and November 16, 1632. *Love Tricks, or the School of Complement, The Maid's Revenge, The Wedding, The Witty Fair One, The Grateful Servant, The Traitor, The Humorous Courtier, Love's Cruelty, Changes, or Love in a Maze, Hyde Park, The Ball:* these eleven plays afford as much variety as do those of either of Shirley's later periods, and, occasionally, as high effectiveness. For plot-construction, we find grounds for commendation in *The Witty Fair One,* in *The Grateful Servant,* in *Love's Cruelty,* and in *Hyde Park;*

for character-delineation, in Sir Nicholas and Brains, in Foscari, Cleona, Leonora, and Jacomo, in Bella-mente, Clariana, Hippolito, and Eubella, in Fair-field and his Mistress Carol. Above all, both for character and for plot, we find artistic satisfaction in *The Traitor* and in its Lorenzo, Sciarrha, and Amidea.

But during these eight years, in what fields has Shirley done his work? Of the five plays that we have just recalled, two are romantic, three are realistic; but of the eleven plays surviving from Shirley's first dramatic period, only three are primarily romantic. One, the earliest, is a mingling of the types; and the remaining seven are plays of London life and manners. In short, although Shirley's ablest drama of the period—*The Traitor*—is a romantic tragedy, the larger number of his plays are realistic studies in the style of Jonson and of Fletcher.

THE SECOND
DRAMATIC PERIOD

CHRONOLOGY OF PLAYS

SECOND DRAMATIC PERIOD

1632–1636

1632, November 19. *The Arcadia* probably acted.

1632/3, January 21. *The Bewties* licensed. Subsequently published as *The Bird in a Cage*.

1633, July 3. *The Young Admiral* licensed.

1633, November 11. *The Gamester* licensed.

1634, June 24. *The Example* licensed.

1634, November 29. *The Opportunity* licensed.

1634/5, February 6. *The Coronation* licensed.

1635, October 15. *The Lady of Pleasure* licensed.

1635/6, January 18. *The Duke's Mistress* licensed.

CHAPTER X

THE SECOND DRAMATIC PERIOD—BEGUN

FROM *THE ARCADIA* TO *THE YOUNG ADMIRAL*

FROM *Love Tricks, or The School of Complement,* licensed February 10, 1624/5, to *The Ball,* licensed November 16, 1632, the plays of Shirley had been dominated by the style of "our acknowledged master, learned Jonson." Indeed, of the eleven extant plays belonging to this his first dramatic period, only three—*The Maid's Revenge, The Grateful Servant,* and *The Traitor*—are romantic. The other eight, with the exception of that hermaphrodite, *Love Tricks,* are realistic. Beginning, however, with *The Arcadia,* Shirley entered upon a period in which, without wholly abandoning the realistic style, he devoted himself primarily to romantic plays. Of the nine original plays,[1] belonging to this his second dramatic period, only three—*The Gamester, The Example,* and *The Lady of Pleasure* —are comedies of London life and manners; the

---

[1] I am ignoring, in this estimate, *The Night Walker* ("a play of Fletcher's corrected by Shirley"), *The Triumph of Peace* (a masque), and *Chabot, Admiral of France* (by Chapman and Shirley).

other six—*The Arcadia, The Bird in a Cage, The Young Admiral, The Opportunity, The Coronation,* and *The Duke's Mistress*—are romantic. From a period in which only one third of his work was romantic, Shirley passed to a period in which only one third was not romantic. This comparison between his first and second periods becomes doubly significant when we observe that, out of a total of eleven extant dramas belonging to his third and last dramatic period, Shirley produced but two non-romantic plays.[2]

From *The Ball,* licensed on the sixteenth of November, 1632, to *The Arcadia,* acted on the nineteenth of the same month, the change is almost startling. Not only had *Changes, or Love in a Maze, Hyde Park,* and *The Ball* been comedies of manners; but to their realism they had added, in each instance, a group of Jonsonian characters of humor. *The Arcadia,* on the other hand, is Fletcherian romance in treatment and in material; not romantic comedy, but dramatic romance of the type of *Philaster* and of *Cymbeline.* Nothing could be farther from the Jonsonian comedy of humors. In short, we may take *The Arcadia* as a turning-point in the career of Shirley.

[2] *The Politique Father,* i.e., *The Brothers* of 1652, and *The Constant Maid.*

The Arcadia of Shirley is a dramatic version of *The Arcadia* of Sidney. To avoid fulfilment of an oracle, Basilius, King of Arcadia, Gynecia, his queen, and his daughters, Pamela and Philoclea, withdraw to a lodge in the forest. Hither follow them two princely suitors: Pyrocles, son of the King of Macedon, in love with Philoclea, disguised as an amazon, Zelmane; and his cousin, Musidorus, Prince of Thessaly, in love with Pamela, disguised as a shepherd, Dorus. King Basilius falls in love with the supposed amazon Zelmane; his queen, penetrating the disguise, becomes infatuated with the Prince of Macedon. To escape from the importunities of their lust, the prince appoints with the king and with the queen a meeting at a cave; and while they seek him there, he renews his vows to their daughter Philoclea. His cousin Musidorus, meanwhile, is endeavoring to elope with their other daughter, Pamela. When the king and queen, having met each other at the cave, have made their peace, the king drinks a wine that the queen, in the belief that it would insure permanence in love, had brought for Pyrocles. He finds it to be poison, and falls dead. As guilty of his death, the officers of state arrest the queen, Prince Pyrocles, Philoclea, and the eloping Musidorus and Pamela. Euarchus, King of Macedon, sits as judge, and sentences to various deaths the queen and princes. Too late he discovers the latter to be his son and nephew: the decree must stand. As they are passing to their execution, the murdered Basilius stirs upon his bier and comes to life. The oracle has been fulfilled.

When Williams and Egglesfeild published *The Arcadia* in 1640, they called it "a pastorall." Whether Shirley himself called it a pastoral, we do not know; but the modern student of the drama must call it not primarily a pastoral but a typical "romance." The story of an oracle and its fulfilment; a prince disguised as an amazon; another as a shepherd; the pure love of the princes for the princesses; the lustful love of the king for the supposed amazon, and of the queen for the disguised prince; the masque of the shepherds; the comic business of Dametas, Miso, Mopsa; the elopement of a prince and princess; the rebellion; the love-potion that appears a poison; the seeming death of the king; the tragic fate that threatens all the leading characters; the discovery that the judge has sentenced his own son and nephew; his unexpected confirmation of the sentence; the amazing recovery of the king thought dead; and his recognition of the fulfilment of the oracle: all these varied and surprising incidents are the typical material of a Fletcherian "romance," and as such they are presented. When Schelling says that *The Arcadia* is conspicuous among Shirley's dramas only "for its close following of his chosen material," [3] and that "it is memorable for no other reason," [3] he is considering the play as an isolated phenomenon, not as a step in Shirley's development as a dramatist. For Shirley, *The Arcadia* marks his complete acceptance of romanticism.

The second in this group of three romantic plays is *The Bird in a Cage,* licensed as *The Bewties* January 21, 1632/3. To previous critics this play has seemed of interest chiefly for its political allusions and especially for its satirical attack on William Prynne, then in confinement. To us, the play is more of interest as gay romanticism run mad: another contribution to the school of Fletcher. The Duke of Mantua, wishing to marry his daughter Eugenia to the heir of Florence, banishes her noble lover Philenzo and shuts up Eugenia in a closely guarded tower. The lover, returning in disguise, boasts in the duke's court that, if he be granted money enough, he can accomplish any task assigned him. As a jest, and to test the fidelity of his guards, the duke grants him unlimited treasure for a month, commands him to gain access to the princess, and decrees death as the penalty for his failure. Bribes prove of no avail; and the lover, despairing, resolves to immortalize himself by releasing all poor debtors from the prison. One of these, in gratitude, invents a device to help the

[3] Schelling, *Elizabethan Drama,* II, 315.

lover. He presents to the duke a cage full of rare birds; and the duke, as he anticipated, sends it to his daughter. When she opens the cage, her lover steps from its central pillar. Next day the lover, still disguised, reports to the duke that he has performed the task assigned him; that he has gained access to the princess. Summoned as a witness, the princess confirms his assertion, and begs, moreover, that she may have him as her husband. The duke is furious that she should love a stranger, a man of no birth. When the lover, however, reveals himself as the banished Philenzo, the duke, fearing that Florence will break off the marriage treaty, orders him to instant execution. As he is led out, there comes a letter from the Duke of Florence. Florence has heard of the love of the princess for Philenzo; he has no further interest in the alliance; he recommends that Mantua marry the princess to Philenzo. The Duke of Mantua resolves to act on the advice: Eugenia may have her chosen lover. His leniency, however, comes too late: Philenzo has taken poison on the way to execution; he is brought in—dead. When the dead Philenzo, however, hears that he should have had the princess as his bride, he comes to life, and they live happily ever after. In short, *The Bird in a Cage* is Fletcherian dramatic romance turned into extravaganza.

Except to indicate Shirley's change of interest

from realistic to romantic drama, *The Arcadia* and *The Bird in a Cage* are of but secondary importance. Even in the romantic field, Shirley had done better work before, in *The Grateful Servant* of 1629 and in *The Traitor* of 1631. In *The Young Admiral,* however, licensed July 3, 1633, Shirley once more produced a play of primary importance, a tragicomedy that ranks among the most successful of his romantic dramas.

The Young Admiral, as has been shown by Stiefel, [4] borrows the complication and climax of its major plot from that of Lope de Vega's *Don Lope de Cardona.* The resolution of this plot, however, with the minor actions and the general treatment of the material, is Shirley's own. Vittori, admiral of the fleet of Naples, on returning from victory against the fleet of Sicily, finds that the son of the King of Naples, Prince Cesario—whose misbehavior while a suitor at the court of Sicily has brought on the war—has taken advantage of Vittori's absence to attempt the honor of his wife Cassandra, has imprisoned his father on a false charge of treason, and has shut the gates of Naples against his returning army. The young admiral, appealing to the aged king, secures the release of his father, Alphonso, upon condition

[4] Stiefel in *Archiv für das Studium der neueren Sprachen und Literaturen,* CXIX, 309–350.

that Vittori, Alphonso, and Cassandra go into banishment. Before they can escape, Alphonso is again imprisoned by the prince; and Vittori and Cassandra, driven back by storm upon the coast of Naples, are made captive by the King of Sicily, who has just arrived before Naples with a second fleet. To Vittori, Sicily gives the choice of commanding the army against his native city or of suffering the death of his Cassandra. Love and loyalty struggle for mastery; but rather than let Cassandra die, Vittori resolves to sacrifice his honor. When the Prince of Naples hears of this, however, he warns Vittori that Vittori's first attack upon the city shall be the signal for Alphonso's execution. While the young admiral is facing this awful alternative—the death of wife or father—he enters the tent of Rosinda, the Sicilian princess, and there discovers his wife Cassandra with the Prince of Naples. The prince, made prisoner, tauntingly shows Vittori the letter of Cassandra that had lured him thither. Vittori is convinced. Heart-broken, he begs the king that he fulfil his threat to decapitate Cassandra; then, seeking the princess, Vittori begs that she secure from her father an order for his own execution. Rosinda, however, solicits his service in a dangerous enterprise. Consenting, he, at her request, escorts the princess from the camp of Sicily to the palace of the King of Naples. There she avows her

identity, declares her love for the captured prince
Cesario, and offers herself as hostage for his safety.
Vittori now realizes that Cassandra's letter was but
an artifice to lure Cesario to the princess. Joyously
he throws off his disguise, and seeks and obtains the
pardon of the King of Naples. In the Sicilian camp,
meanwhile, the king discovers the disappearance of
his daughter. Wild with alarm, he commands the
beheading of Cassandra and the prince, but is
checked with a warning that Naples holds the princess as a hostage. A conference between the kings
results in a renewal of the treaty for the marriage of
the prince and princess. Vittori, meanwhile, loses
no time in reclaiming his beloved Cassandra.

As the foregoing summary makes evident, the plot
of *The Young Admiral* consists not of a struggle between contending passions within the hero's mind,
but merely of a struggle between the hero and various
external forces. Such is Shirley's management, however, that, scene by scene, this mere external struggle
finds expression in a struggle that is internal: the
struggle between love of wife and love of country;
the struggle between love of wife and love of father;
and, in the mind of the father, the struggle between
love of king and love of son. These several internal
conflicts, as a comparison will show, are original with
Shirley, not borrowed from his Spanish source, *Don*

Lope de Cardona. They are, moreover, additions of great value. Shirley, like his predecessors in dramatic romance, sought, above all else, for the emotional effectiveness of individual scenes. For such effectiveness, nothing could contribute more than this element of internal struggle.

In his characterization, also, Shirley has done well. He has made Cesario a princely and efficient villain, whom we admire even in his villainy; he has made Rosinda every inch a princess; Cassandra, a devoted wife and loyal friend; Vittori, a much tried and tolerably heroic hero. To realize fully the success of Shirley's characterization, we have only to compare these four well-rounded figures with the wooden puppets that play the corresponding parts in *Don Lope de Cardona.*

As for the minor actions, neither Shirley's comic characters nor his comic scenes lack originality and effectiveness. Didimo, the mischievous page; Pazzorello, the foolish steward who desires to be made, by witchcraft, bullet-proof; and Fabio, the courtier who speaks much but never to the point, and whose unfortunate bargain with Captain Mauritio lends savor to the final scene: all these are matter foreign to Shirley's Spanish source, and matter genuinely delightful.

In versification, also, Shirley's *The Young Ad-*

miral is not without success. In the lesser plays of
Shirley, the verse is often commonplace; but in his
major plays, especially in passages of deep feeling,
it is not unworthy. Such a passage is the latter part of
Act III, scene i, of *The Young Admiral,* from which
I venture to quote a single speech:

VITTORI [*to Cassandra*].   Do not say so!
Princes will court thee then, and at thy feet
Humble their crowns, and purchase smiles with provinces.
When I am dead, the world shall doat on thee,
And pay thy beauty tribute. I am thy
Affliction; and when thou art discharg'd
From loving me, thy eyes shall be at peace.
A sun more glorious shall draw up thy tears,
Which, gracing heaven in some new form, shall make
The constellations blush, and envy 'em.
Or, if thy love
Of me be so great that, when I am sacrificed,
Thou wilt think of me, let this comfort thee:
I die my country's martyr, and ascend
Rich in my scarlet robe of blood; my name
Shall stain no chronicle, and my tomb be blest
With such a garland time shall never wither;
Thou, with a troop of wives as chaste as thee,
Shalt visit my cold sepulchre, and glory
To say, This doth enclose Vittori's dust
That died true to his honour and his country.
Methinks I am taking of my leave already,

[251]

And, kissing the wet sorrows from thy cheek,
Bid thee rejoice Vittori is a conqueror,
And death his way to triumph.[5]

   The high seriousness and poetic beauty of these
lines suggest more adequately than could any criticism the character of this tragicomedy, *The Young
Admiral,* and, with some qualification, the character
of all the romantic plays of Shirley: a wistful con-
sciousness of the pathos and, at times, of the tragedy
of life; a yearning for conditions more happy and
more noble than the world he knew.   In the extravaganza *The Bird in a Cage,* in the Fletcherian romance *The Arcadia,* and in the tragicomedy *The
Young Admiral,* Shirley presents various species of
this romantic genus: species that range in tone almost from tragedy to farce.   Yet in each, whether
seemingly frivolous or serious, he gives us something
more than the cynical satire of his comedies of London life and manners: he gives us, in the place of wit,
a heart.

   [5] *The Young Admiral,* III, i; *Works,* III, 134–135.

CHAPTER XI

THE SECOND DRAMATIC PERIOD—CONTINUED

THE GAMESTER AND *THE EXAMPLE*

NOT without occasional "backsliding" did Shirley abandon the realistic school. In the very year of the licensing of *The Young Admiral,* and again in the following spring, Shirley was guilty of a fall from grace. In the first of these instances, however, his tempter was no less a person than the king.

In two respects, moreover, these comedies of manners—*The Gamester* and *The Example*—differ from Shirley's previous work in the realistic school. In the first place, the incidents, although not always more decent, are at least more moral. In the Penelope-Fowler scenes of *The Witty Fair One,* Shirley had used repulsive situations merely for comic effect; in *The Gamester,* and even more emphatically in *The Example,* he places the emphasis not on the evil but on the reformation. Shirley has evidently come to feel the tragic side of the immorality he pictures, and no longer accounts it a subject for heartless jesting or for indifference. In the second place, both in *The Gamester* and in *The Example,* amid the realism and amid the characters of humor, Shirley has introduced an element of romance. In *The Gamester,* the Beaumont-Delamore action is romantic comedy—well-nigh romantic tragedy—though the scene be London; in *The Example,* the extravagant "honor" of Sir Walter Peregrine and of Lord Fitz-avarice in the major plot gives a romantic tone to the entire play, and makes it—if such a thing be possible —a romantic comedy of manners.

The earlier of these two comedies, *The Gamester,* was licensed November 11, 1633. From a dramatic —as distinct from an ethical—point of view, its plot is well worthy of its royal source. Wilding, neglectful of his loving wife, makes dishonorable suit to Penelope, her ward, and even commands his wife to solicit Penelope in his behalf. The wife, for purposes of her own, prevails on Penelope to promise him a meeting. When, however, the appointed hour arrives, Wilding, unwilling to leave the gaming-table, sends his friend Hazard to keep the appointment with Penelope. In the morning, smarting from his loss at cards, Wilding hears from Hazard a glowing account of his meeting with the ward. Doubly smarting, Wilding presently discovers from his virtuous wife that it was she and not Penelope that kept the assignation. Wilding's first impulse is to keep both his wife and his friend Hazard in ignorance of the truth. To this end, he offers to double Penelope's dowry if Hazard will marry her. As the two are in love already, they hasten to the priest. Then, at the last, the repentant Wilding finds that his fears are groundless: that Hazard had found both women waiting to shame the erring husband, and that with them Hazard had arranged the plot that brought Wilding to his senses. If the reader can adopt the Gallic attitude which makes adultery a fit subject for a jest and accounts a wronged husband the height of the ridiculous, then this main plot of *The Gamester* is a capital theme capitally presented. As Schelling says: "The popularity of *The Gamester* . . . is based not solely on its appeal to the pruriency of its auditors, but likewise on the admirable knitting of its plot and the success with which the dramatic suspense is sustained to the very end." [1]

The two other actions in the play, however, are probably more acceptable to the Anglo-Saxon mind.

[1] Schelling, *Elizabethan Drama*, II, 293. I am glad, however, that Professor Schelling adds: "To pick and choose this play as typical of the comedy of its age, and of Shirley in particular, is almost as unfair as it would be to select the discourse of Mistress Overdone and her tapster Pompey as characteristic of Shakespeare's dialogue at large, or hold up the device by which Helena wins her husband, Bertram—a device, by the way, not altogether dissimilar to that employed by Mistress Wilding under similar conditions—as typical of the master dramatist's prevalent ethics of conduct."—*Ibid.*, 293–294.

The first of these, allied to the main plot both by the presence of Wilding and by the active participation of Hazard, is especially interesting for its realistic pictures of gaming-houses, gamblers, and men about town. Old Barnacle, a wealthy citizen, desires his heir and nephew to gain a reputation among the gallants. To this end, he bribes Hazard, a known man of valor, to allow Young Barnacle to strike him in a gambling-house. So successful is the plot that Young Barnacle gains a mighty reputation as a bully, and believes himself as valiant as he seems. As a result, he quarrels upon all occasions, until Old Barnacle, fearful lest his hopeful nephew be killed, offers to Hazard another hundred pounds to humble the young gallant. Hazard willingly administers the required thrashing, and then reveals the jest.

The connection between this second plot and that first given seems closer in the play than in this abstract; but the connection between these and the third plot is slight even in the play. This third plot deals with the romantic loves of Beaumont and Violante, Delamore and Leonora. On the charge of slaying Delamore in a duel, Beaumont is imprisoned under sentence of death. Sir Richard Hurry, father of Leonora, commands her to marry Beaumont, though the latter has slain her betrothed and is himself betrothed to her dearest friend. When Sir Richard

promises to obtain Beaumont's pardon on condition
that he marry Leonora, Beaumont refuses to abandon
Violante. Urged by Violante to accept Sir Richard's
offer and so save his life, Beaumont declares himself
doubly obliged to be true to Violante. At a final
hearing, Sir Richard again offers Leonora and her
wealth to Beaumont. He refuses. Sir Richard thereupon sentences Beaumont—to marry Violante. Delamore, he assures them, is alive and out of danger,
and has his consent to marry Leonora. This story,
beginning with a supposedly fatal duel and ending
happily in a court of justice, is somewhat suggestive
of the Beauford-Marwood action in *The Wedding*.
Its effect, however, depends less on startling situations and more on romantic emotionality.

Although the three plots are not vitally related, each
by itself is so carefully constructed that, in surprise
and in suspense, it is genuinely effective. Of the characterization less is to be said; yet it is tolerably successful. Hazard and Wilding make a well-con-
trasted pair: the latter unable to resist the temptation
of the moment, whether for gaming or for women;
the former sane and self-controlled even in his vices,
able to dissuade his companions from committing
assault upon the officers, able to leave the gaming-
table while yet a winner, able to discern virtue in
womanhood and to respect it. Young Barnacle, too,

makes a distinct and interesting figure, not only in his swaggering but also in his humor of speech—so exquisitely caricatured by Wilding's page. The women of the play are, to the modern reader, less attractive. True to the manners of their time, they lack the modern sense of the indelicate: they have a looseness of phrase, and an undue tolerance for the viciousness of their acquaintances. In themselves, however, they seem not immoral; and Shirley's increased ability to characterize has made them real enough somewhat to enlist our sympathy. In short, although *The Gamester* is by no means great, its popularity is not ill deserved. In view of Herbert's record that the play was "made by Sherley out of a plot of the king's," we need not wonder at the further note: "The king sayd it was the best play he had seen for seven years."[2]

The Example, licensed June 24, 1634, is to modern taste the most acceptable of Shirley's comedies of London life and manners. Its two minor actions are conspicuously in the style of Jonson. The first of these concerns the humors of Vainman and Pumice-stone, suitors to Jacinta, who requires the former never to speak while in her presence, the latter always to perform the opposite of what she bids.[3] The second concerns the humors of Sir Solitary Plot, a char-

[2] Malone's *Shakspere,* 1821, III, 236.
[3] *The Example,* IV, ii; *Works,* III, 337–339.

acter compounded of Jonson's Morose in *Epicœne,*
and Jonson's Sir Politic Would-be in *Volpone.* Like
the latter,[4] he suspects a plot in every circumstance;
like the former, he shuts himself up in his rooms, and
is cured of his humor only by a practical joke. His
servants, Oldrat and Dormant, add their humors to
his own; and when Oldrat, playing constable, attempts to "reprehend" the traitors, he becomes a very
Dogberry.[5]

The real interest, however, centers in the action
involving Sir Walter Peregrine, Lady Peregrine,
and Lord Fitzavarice. Sir Walter, because of heavy
debts, especially to Lord Fitzavarice, has taken service in the wars. In his absence, Lord Fitzavarice
endeavors to corrupt Lady Peregrine, and offers even
to cancel all her husband's debts as a reward for her
infidelity. Finally, in admiration of her constancy,
he presents her with the mortgage and with "a
wealthy carkanet." At that moment, Sir Walter, ven-
turing arrest, comes home, hears from his wife from
whom the mortgage and the jewels come, and will
listen to no explanation. Passionate in his imagined
wrong, he sends a challenge to Fitzavarice. The
latter asks his follower, Confident Rapture, to be his
second. The follower, to avoid fighting, instigates

---

[4] *Volpone,* II, i.
[5] *The Example,* v, i; *Works,* III, 354.

Fitzavarice's scrivener to arrest Peregrine for debt. Naturally, Sir Walter believes that the arrest was at the suit of Lord Fitzavarice. His lordship, however, is indignant at the trick. He pays Sir Walter's debts, secures his freedom, and goes in person to see him at the prison. Overwhelmed by this generosity, Sir Walter both withdraws his suspicions that Fitzavarice occasioned the arrest and accepts his assurance of his noble purposes toward Lady Peregrine. Lord Fitzavarice, however, lest it be said that he has bought Sir Walter's consent to Lady Peregrine's dishonor, or even his consent to drop the duel, insists that they fight. For form's sake, then, they fight the duel. Both draw blood. The second intervenes. And the play ends—in the betrothal of Lord Fitzavarice to a sister of Lady Peregrine, Jacinta.

Extravagant as all this sounds in abstract, it makes a thoroughly effective play, full of strong scenes and appealing characters. Indeed, *The Example* has won the approbation of even Swinburne, who not only singles it out as "the best of Shirley's comedies," but adds: "To have written such a tragedy as *The Traitor,* such a comedy as *The Example,* should be sufficient to secure for their author a doubly distinguished place among the poets of his country." [6] "A

[6] A. C. Swinburne, "James Shirley," in *The Fortnightly Review,* LIII (n.s., XLVII), 472.

judgment unblinded by perversity, prepossession, or malevolence," continues Swinburne, "must allow that the noble tone of this poem is at least as typical of its author's tone of mind as the baser tone of a preceding play. . . . The noble, high-spirited, simple-hearted, and single-minded heroine would suffice to sweeten and redeem an otherwise condemnable or questionable piece of work; her husband is a figure not unworthy to be set beside her; and the passionate young tempter, whose chivalrous nature is so gracefully displayed in the headstrong, punctilious, perverse, and generous course of conduct which follows on the fact of his conversion, would be as thoroughly successful and complete a study as either, if it were not for the luckless touch of incongruous melodrama which throws the lady of his love into a swoon at the sight of his preposterous poniard and the sound of his theatrical threats. But all that can be done to redeem this conventional and sensational error is admirably well done in the sequel of this noble and high-toned play: a model of simple construction and harmonious evolution, in which the broad comedy of the underplot is rather a relief than an encumbrance to the progress of the more serious action."

Whether one agree with Swinburne's opinion in its entirety, and especially with his assertion that *The Example* is "the best of Shirley's comedies," will be in part a matter of personal taste. Others would prefer, perhaps, to select for that honor one of the romantic comedies. It is significant, however, that much of the excellence of this realistic comedy results from qualities that are found more frequently in romantic drama. Indeed, although the scene of this play is laid in London, and although its minor actions concern Jonsonian characters of humor, its major plot is marked by such high seriousness and its major persons are dominated by such lofty motives that one is tempted to classify *The Example* not as comedy of manners but as romantic comedy.

Even in comedy of manners, Shirley here shows the influence of the romantic drama.

CHAPTER XII

THE SECOND DRAMATIC PERIOD—CONTINUED

THE OPPORTUNITY AND *THE CORONATION*

IN the two winters remaining before Shirley went to Dublin, he produced four new plays: *The Opportunity* and *The Coronation* in the season of 1634–5; and *The Lady of Pleasure* and *The Duke's Mistress* in the season of 1635–6.[1] The first two constitute the subject of the present chapter; the second two, of that which follows. Of these four plays, one, *The Lady of Pleasure,* is a comedy of manners; but the others are contributions to the romantic school: a romantic comedy, a dramatic romance, and a romantic tragicomedy respectively.

The Opportunity, licensed November 29, 1634, is a capital little comedy, fairly bubbling over with clever situations and charming character. Like its source—*El Castigo del Penséque* by Tirso de Molina[2]—Shirley's play presents the maddening per-

[1] I omit from this critical discussion *Chabot, Admiral of France,* licensed April 29, 1635, because of the doubt whether Shirley was more than its reviser. See Chapter III, above.

[2] See A. L. Stiefel, "Die Nachahmung spanischer Komödien in England unter den ersten Stuarts," in *Romanische Forschungen,* v, 193–220.

plexities of a young adventurer torn between his love for a beauteous gentlewoman who believes herself his sister, and his coincident opportunity to win the hand of an equally beautiful and equally infatuated duchess. Unlike its Spanish original, however, Shirley's play does not end in the marriage of the hero to the maiden who had imagined herself to be his sister, but, with greater poetic justice, in his loss of both the duchess and her gentlewoman.

In Shirley's version, Aurelio Andreozzi, a young gentleman of Milan, comes with his friend Pisauro to Urbino. Here he discovers that he is mistaken for one Borgia: that he is the supposed son of an aged nobleman, Mercutio; the supposed brother of the charming Cornelia; and the supposed murderer of a brother of Ursini, favorite of the duchess. In short, he finds himself received as one who rashly has returned from banishment, and who is liable to pay, as the price of his temerity, his head.

From this danger he is freed by the intercession of Ursini. Ursini loves Cornelia; and therefore, to establish himself in the good graces of Cornelia and her family, he forgives, as the mischance of a duel, the killing of his brother, and from the duchess secures the hero's pardon. This pardon, however, throws Aurelio-Borgia into further difficulties. He is urged to consent to Ursini's marriage with

Cornelia. As Borgia, he cannot well refuse; as Aurelio, he is himself in love with fair Cornelia. Cornelia, he discovers, is as madly infatuated with him; yet she is horrified, he sees, at a passion which she deems unnatural. The duchess, moreover, begins to shower him with favor. Her infatuation for the supposed Borgia becomes the scandal of the court. He sees before him the possibility of a ducal coronet; nor is he indifferent to the duchess's personal charms. He finds that his standing with the duchess has aroused the sexual jealousy of Cornelia and the political jealousy of Ursini. To cap the climax, the ambassador of the Duke of Ferrara—really no other than the duke himself disguised—breaks off his negotiations for a marriage between duke and duchess, and prepares to leave the court.

That night, divided between his growing affection for Cornelia and his desire to take advantage of the favor of the duchess, Aurelio-Borgia stands beneath the palace window. Unknown to him, behind him stands the duke. From the window, Cornelia, pretending to be the duchess, warns him not to presume upon her favor, for she plans to marry with Ferrara. The duke, overhearing, joyfully departs. At this moment the duchess takes Cornelia's place. Surmising what has passed, she pretends to be Cornelia, and begs him to consent to her marriage with Ursini.

Desperate lest he lose both the duchess and Cornelia, Aurelio declares that he is not her brother Borgia, and in his own person avows for her his love. The duchess, fearing now lest he leave the country in despair, gives him some slight encouragement, and leaves him still wondering whether, after all, he would rather marry Cornelia or the duchess.

Next morning the duchess renders Aurelio more perplexed than ever. She does her best to lead him to avow his love, and promises to see him married to any mistress whom he may desire, "be she the proudest, greatest in our duchy, without all limitations." As Aurelio is on the point of taking the duchess at her word, Cornelia enters to announce the Duke of Ferrara. She attempts to court Aurelio, but the jealous duchess summons her away. Aurelio glories; the duchess loves him; Cornelia loves him—but he must give her no encouragement; her Grace is much the better woman! Then, within a moment, all his hopes are dashed. The duchess reënters with the duke and train; and Ursini tells Aurelio that Ferrara has claimed the duchess by a promise made "last night," and that it is the duchess's pleasure that the marriage of Ursini to Cornelia wait on hers.

Not yet, however, is the story done. The duchess denies all knowledge of the "promise." Cornelia confesses the impersonation. The duke withdraws, indignant. Again the duchess stirs Aurelio to renew his suit. He sees the opportunity, but hesitates. At length he asks her—*if she loves him!* She lectures him gloriously, and then—pardons him! And then she has him write for her a letter—a letter to an unnamed suitor—a letter avowing her love and promising a midnight meeting in her garden and their marriage in the morning! This she signs, and commands Aurelio to deliver it "to him that loves her best." This letter the faint-hearted Aurelio delivers—to the duke!

The duke declares this joy beyond his hope. Aurelio, discovering his error, tries to gain access to the duchess's garden. He arrives too late: the duke is in possession. He then resolves to win Cornelia. She listens to him, and, in his presence, accepts Ursini's suit. The duke and duchess publish their betrothal. Aurelio leaves Urbino.

Whether as intrigue or romance, *The Opportunity* is a delightful comedy. Without an instant's dullness, the action rushes on. It has a zest, a joyous freshness that gives life even to time-worn situations —yes, even to mistaken identity! And the characters —the infatuated duchess, the charming Cornelia, the testy Mercutio, the bewildered Aurelio—they, too, are a joy. Even Shirley's rascally servant and mischievous page in the underplot (of which I have said nothing) contribute to the general delectability. Concerning the content of *The Opportunity,* we have but one regret: that Shirley failed to copy from the Spanish the scene in which Aurelio is permitted to help the duchess don her glove.[3]

As to the relation of the play of Shirley to its source, I cannot do better than to quote from the concluding paragraphs of the article by Stiefel:[4]

"As we review the whole, we find that Shirley has made abundant use of his model. To it he is indebted not only for the idea of the play, but also for the principal points of his plot, the arrangement of the materials, the best and most effective scenes. But the imitation is not slavish. Not many literally translated passages are found. Even where he has faithfully copied a scene, he has preserved his own individuality in the expression as far as possible. . . . The scenes invented by Shirley are numerous; and, although they are inferior in humorous effect to those of the original, nevertheless they are still strong enough for the part. At the head we place the Pimponio scenes (the comic underplot), which sometimes develop an excellent humor. But Shirley does not really attain to the geniality of the Spaniard.

[3] The availability of *The Opportunity* for modern presentation is suggested by its revival, some eight years ago, at the University of Illinois. See *The Nation,* June 14, 1906.

[4] Stiefel, *Romanische Forschungen,* v, 218–219.

This is best indicated when one compares the imitated scenes with the original. How clumsy everything there appears beside the spirited, charming Spaniard!

"In respect to character, Shirley goes his own way; and herein he surely surpasses his original. The men especially receive a pronounced individuality. Masterly is the character of Mercutio, which is the poet's own creation. 'The waspish vanity and perverse exultation of the old man,' according to Dyce's opinion (III, 411, note), 'are, in truth, very skilfully and humorously portrayed.' The jealous Ursini, the cynical Pisauro, the imperious duke, the clown Pimponio, are figures that stand forth more sharply than any in *Castigo*. In a more remarkable manner, the leading characters, especially the women, lose under Shirley's hands. There is wanting in the latter, that grace and roguishness, that intense personal charm which make us, in Tirso, indulgent toward their weakness and folly. Don Rodrigo, also, has suffered in his English costume. In Tirso he appears as a noble, knightly figure. It is not his exterior alone that prepossesses the countess in his favor. Brave in battle, he has defended her against the hostile attack of Casimiro. The love of the condesa is also an overflow of her gratitude and, at the same time, founded upon the inner worth of the tested man. On the other hand, what does Aurelio do in Shirley to deserve the passion of the duchess? Nothing; absolutely nothing. She sees him, and is in love with him; she sees him, and wishes to possess him.

"The English play, through the greater variety of characters, through the introduction of subordinate characters, and through the underplot, is richer and more exciting in treatment than is the Spanish; but, in exchange for this, the chief action—the relation between princess and adventurer—has lost as well in breadth as in depth. The idea of the piece remains the same. Both poets represent in a delightful manner how close-lying happiness is forfeited by too timorous reflection; both learn 'occasio ægre offertur, facile amittitur.' . . . Taking everything together, we must estimate Shirley's comedy as an excellent imitation enriched with many original features. Still we believe that, in the whole work, it has not equalled, much less, then, surpassed its model."

Slighter than *The Opportunity,* yet, in its own way, charming, is *The Coronation,* a Fletcherian dramatic romance, licensed February 6, 1634/5. The story of the play is a blending of two actions: first, the attempt of Cassander, the Lord Protector of Epire, to control the crown; second, the love-affair of Arcadius and Polidora. The interest comes from the complications that result from a succession of revelations concerning the purpose of the young queen, Sophia, and the identity of her rivals for the throne.

Cassander, the Lord Protector, plans to marry his son, Lisimachus, to the youthful queen. To this, Sophia seemingly consents; but asks that, as a preliminary to the marriage, she be fully invested with her royal power. Cassander, confident that she loves his son, agrees to the coronation. But no sooner is she in control than she avows her purpose to wed not Lisimachus but a young noble of the court, Arcadius. This avowal confounds not only the purposes of Cassander but also the intentions of Arcadius; for the latter has accounted himself deeply in love with Polidora, with whom he has exchanged vows within the hour. Arcadius, however, is too weak to resist the temptation offered by the queen; forgetful of Polidora, he consents without a protest. Even her letter disturbs him but a moment. When, however, he is about to be married to Sophia, Macarius, his supposed uncle,[5] intervenes. Arcadius, he says, is Prince Demetrius, Sophia's younger brother, supposed dead, whom the late king had intrusted in infancy to Macarius, lest Cassander, the lord protector, cut him off. To the truth of this, the late king's signature and the evidence of the bishop both bear witness. Sophia

[5] Arcadius-Demetrius is not, as Dyce says in the *Dramatis Personæ*, III, 460, the "supposed son" of Macarius, but rather the supposed nephew. Cf. pp. 464, 465, 476, 478, 500, 501, etc.

has lost both her expected husband and her crown; Arcadius-Demetrius is the rightful king. With that, the new king remembers his first love, Polidora, and goes in state to lead her to his throne. She will have none of him—as king. Sophia, likewise, recalls her former love, Lisimachus. He has found, he says, a new mistress. Sophia's suspicions turn to Polidora. Meanwhile, Cassander, the baffled lord protector, seeks for an engine against Demetrius. He finds it in the imprisoned Seleucus, long Demetrius's rival. He declares that Seleucus is Prince Leonatus, an elder brother of Sophia and of the new-crowned king, hidden, like the latter, while a babe. Seleucus believes the tale a lie, but resolves to profit by it. By an energetic coup, he gains the crown—and dismisses his instigator. When Cassander in revenge declares him an impostor, Eubulus, the supposed father of Seleucus, reveals that he is indeed Leonatus and the rightful king: Cassander's fabrication was unconscious truth. So the play ends: Arcadius-Demetrius, repentant and no longer king, regains his Polidora; Princess Sophia discovers that the "new mistress" of Lisimachus is—herself; Seleucus-Leonatus reigns.

As compared with other work of Shirley, the characterization in this play is second-rate: no character is especially appealing; no character is especially well drawn. The individuals are, indeed, clearly differentiated; but the characterization is sketchy. Cassander, throughout, is merely the ambitious, unscrupulous would-be king-maker; Lisimachus is merely his modest son, "too good to be the son of such a father";[6] Seleucus-Leonatus, the elder prince, is ever proud and violent and scornful; Arcadius-Demetrius, his younger brother, is no coward, indeed, but is fickle of love and weak of will; Polidora is loving, but sentimentally romantic; Princess Sophia is "wise above her years,"[7] but, to the reader, unattractive. In not one of these characters—not even in Arcadius when Sophia tempts him from his former love[8]—is there a hint of internal struggle. No one of the characters is developed sufficiently to grip our interest. In short, Shirley's character-drawing in *The Coronation* is the typical characterization of Fletcherian dramatic romance—sufficient only for the moment, effective solely for the scene in which it falls.

Like other Fletcherian romance, however, *The Coronation* does not lack effective situations. The scene in which Sophia grants Seleucus the privilege of combat with Arcadius;[9] that in which Arcadius

[6] *The Coronation*, I, i; *Works*, III, 462.

[7] *Ibid.*, II, ii; *Works*, III, 482.

[8] *Ibid.*, II, iii; *Works*, III, 488–489; and *Ibid.*, III, ii; *Works*, III, 495–501.

[9] *The Coronation*, I, i.

and Polidora exchange their vows;[10] that in which the combat is interrupted, and the queen chooses as husband not Lisimachus but Arcadius;[11] that in which Seleucus scoffs at Arcadius's praises of the queen, and Arcadius is revealed as Prince Demetrius;[12] the scene in which Polidora, with her masque of Fortune, Love, and Honor, rejects the wooing of the king;[13] and, finally, that scene which proves Seleucus-Leonatus to be the rightful heir:[14] each of these scenes is, for the moment, strikingly effective. Considered as a whole, however, *The Coronation* is memorable only as being one further play by Shirley in the style of Fletcher.[15]

Whether or not we count the romantic tragedy *Chabot, Admiral of France,* among the plays of Shirley, we see that, thus far, the dramas of this his second period are overwhelmingly romantic. *The Arcadia* we found to be a dramatic romance of the type of *Philaster* and of *Cymbeline; The Bird in a Cage,* a dramatic romance turned into an extravaganza. *The*

---

[10] *The Coronation*, II, i.   [12] *Ibid.*, III, ii.   [14] *Ibid.*, v, iii.
[11] *Ibid.*, II, iii.   [13] *Ibid.*, IV, iii.

[15] Not only in the original quarto, but also in the folio of Beaumont and Fletcher, 1679, and in subsequent editions of their works, this play, *The Coronation,* is ascribed, as the reader will recall, to John Fletcher. The title-page of the quarto (I quote from the copy in the Hoe Collection) reads: *The Coronation, a comedy. . . . Written by John Fletcher, Gent. London, . . . 1640.* In view of its superficial resemblance to the work of Fletcher, this attribution of the play is not surprising. The proof that the play is Shirley's, I have presented in a former chapter (see pp. 82–83).

Young Admiral we found to be a romantic tragicomedy, effective in plot, effective in internal struggle scene by scene, effective in its characterization of Cesario, Rosinda, Cassandra, and Vittori, effective in its departures from its Spanish source. *The Coronation* we found to be a Fletcherian dramatic romance, sketchy in its characterization—as Fletcherian dramatic romance ought to be—but striking in situation and surprising in the successive revelations of its plot. *The Opportunity* we found to be a sparkling romantic comedy, delightful both for its situations and for its characters. Against these five romantic plays—at least two of which are among the most satisfying of the plays of Shirley—we have found in this period but two that are comedies of manners; and these two—*The Gamester* and *The Example*—are, with one exception, the last important contributions of Shirley to the realistic school. In the chapter that follows, we shall consider in detail two plays, one a romantic tragicomedy, the other a satiric comedy of manners. Each, in its own way, typifies a large body of the work of Shirley. Of the two, perhaps the comedy of manners is the greater. But whichever of these plays we may prefer, we must remember that the period which they conclude was, for Shirley, a period of conversion to the romantic school.

[275]

CHAPTER XIII

THE SECOND DRAMATIC PERIOD—CONCLUDED

THE LADY OF PLEASURE AND *THE DUKE'S MISTRESS*

FOR the winter of 1635–36, the last winter before Shirley went to Dublin, the plays of our dramatist were two in number: *The Lady of Pleasure,* licensed October 15, 1635; and *The Duke's Mistress,* licensed January 18, 1635/6. These plays, as typical of Shirley's work at the close of his second dramatic period, we shall consider somewhat at length.

The Lady of Pleasure, the last, with but two exceptions,[1] of Shirley's comedies of manners, is a bitter but clever satire upon the wilder lords and ladies of the court; their extravagance, their gaming, their drunkenness, and their licentiousness. Brilliant as

---

[1] These two comedies of manners are *The Brothers* of 1652 and *The Constant Maid* of 1640. The former is believed, by many critics, to be identical with the play of the same name licensed in 1626; the latter, although usually assigned to the Dublin period, gives internal evidence of being among the earliest of Shirley's plays. I shall discuss them both as productions of Shirley's third dramatic period; for the evidence for placing them earlier appears to me inadequate. Nevertheless, for a study of Shirley's comedy of manners at its best, we must turn rather to *The Example* and *The Lady of Pleasure,* in his second period.

Restoration comedy, it is equally unreadable; and yet, although it is among the most offensive of the plays of Shirley, it is, at the same time, among the most severely moral.

The plot of *The Lady of Pleasure* centers about a young woman of fashion, Aretina, wife of Sir Thomas Bornwell. Him she has persuaded to sell their country estates and to move to town; and there she wastes her husband's substance in fast society. A direct ancestress of Lady Teazle,[2] Aretina quarrels with her husband for opposing her extravagance; scorns the well-meant warning of a kinsman against the wiles of a procuress; recalls her nephew from the university to train him in fashionable dissipation; and herself takes the initiative in a particularly unworthy intrigue. Her husband, in an effort to bring her to her senses, endeavors to frighten her by his own prodigality and to arouse her jealousy by dancing attendance upon Celestina, a merry widow of sixteen. These excesses, however, Aretina welcomes as warrant for her own misdoings. Nor does she stop short of actual adultery. When, however, her husband, returning from the gaming-table, announces gaily that their fortune will last them but a month, his levity arouses her attention. And when her worth-

[2] Compare *The Lady of Pleasure,* I, i, with *The School for Scandal,* II, i.

less gallant, Master Kickshaw, who knows not the identity of the lady of the darkened chamber, boasts to Aretina of the gold his mistress gave him and confesses that he believes his mistress a she-devil,[3] then at last she realizes the horror of her situation and prays her husband for forgiveness.

The other figures in the play contribute variously to the sorry picture. Celestina, the widow of sweet sixteen, is not, indeed, immoral; yet in wit and word she is unbridled beyond the possibilities of expurgation. Lord A, the nameless libertine mourning his dead mistress, descends from his noble pedestal to attempt the honor of Celestina. Madam Decoy, the procuress, plies her trade. Master Frederick, the somber university student, plays the drunkard with repulsive variations. Sir William Scentlove, Master Kickshaw, and Master Littleworth, like the "worm" of Cleopatra, do their kind. In fact, the only character that emerges from the play with honor is Haircut, the barber. He, at least, receives our hearty sympathy when, in revenge for a trick that Scentlove plays on him, he forces Sir William to remove his periwig and stand bare for half an hour:

> Or this, or fight with me.
> It shall be no exception that I wait
> Upon my lord. I am a gentleman;

[3] Cf. *The Grateful Servant*, IV, v; *Works*, II, 76 et seq.

You may be less, and be a knight. The office
I do my lord is honest, sir. How many
Such you have been guilty of, heaven knows.[4]

And yet, despite repulsive subject-matter, we cannot but admit that, as a play, *The Lady of Pleasure*
is excellently done. The several threads of the story
are closely interwoven; the scenes are lively and
amusing; the moral teaching is unmistakable. The
language, too, is varied and appropriate. Celestina's
stinging characterization of Kickshaw and Littleworth, her parody of Lord A's poetic flights, and her
eloquent defense of womanly honor in repulsing his
solicitations: all, in their several ways, are notable.
Especially conspicuous in contrast with the method
in *Chabot,* is the skilful manner in which, in *The
Lady of Pleasure,* Shirley presents his character-de-
scriptions. He does not, indeed, confine himself to
the modern method of incidental presentation. He
uses passage after passage of direct characterization.
But in *The Lady of Pleasure,* these descriptions arise
as if of necessity from the circumstances. Aretina
quarrels with her husband, and he draws her picture.
Celestina, administering a tongue-lashing to the impertinent gallants, tells them what they are. The
steward, forgetful of a caller's name, describes him

[4] *The Lady of Pleasure,* v, i; *Works,* IV, 97.

to identify him to his mistress. As a result, the play is conspicuous for satiric characterization.

In short, as Neilson has remarked, *The Lady of Pleasure* is "a good example of Shirley's comedy of manners"; and since, as he continues, "this type of Shirley's comedies is important in measuring the approach made toward the Restoration comedy before the Puritan Revolution,"[5] we, as students of Shirley, should be grateful to Neilson for including *The Lady of Pleasure* in his recent collection, *The Chief Elizabethan Dramatists*.

The Duke's Mistress, licensed January 18, 1635/6, is Shirley's last play before he went to Ireland—his last play among those belonging to his Second Dramatic Period. It is not, as Dyce declared, a tragedy,[6] but a tragicomedy in which the underplot of Horatio and Fiametta is humor run mad, and the serious portion a somber romantic tale of court intrigue ending in no deaths save those of the major and the minor villain. Because the play stands thus at the end of Shirley's second period; because it is a romantic tragicomedy; because in this period, and even more in the period to follow, romantic plays were Shirley's favorite form; and because this particular play is, to an unusual degree, typical of Shirley's matter and

---

[5] Neilson, *The Chief Elizabethan Dramatists,* p. 860.
[6] *Works,* I, xxxv; and IV, 190.

manner in this particular field; for all these reasons, *The Duke's Mistress* especially merits our attention.

The action of the play may be resolved into three elements: (1) the attempt of Dionisio Farnese, Duke of Parma, to cast off his loyal wife, Euphemia, and to obtain as his mistress Ardelia, the betrothed of Bentivolio; (2) the attempt of the duke's kinsman and heir, Leontio,[7] to obtain the love of the duchess and to supplant the duke; and (3) as comic underplot, the wooing of Fiametta by Horatio, whose humor it is to value a mistress in proportion to her exceeding ugliness.

The material is typical of Shirley's romantic tragicomedies. The play opens with revels in honor of Ardelia, "the duke's mistress." As these are at their height, the duchess enters, and begs the duke, since she has lost his love, to sentence her to death. Ardelia, who has not heard the plea, innocently begs that it be granted: "Do not, sir, deny your duchess her desires, so just and reasonable!" Euphemia, horrified, vows to be revenged on duke and mistress. In reply, the duke commands the close confinement of the duchess; and, that he may have grounds for further action, he appoints as jailer his kinsman and next heir, Leontio, whose passion for the duchess he suspects.

[7] Also spelled "Leonato"; see Gifford's note in *Works,* IV, 271.

To this distracted court has returned Bentivolio, formerly the betrothed lover of Ardelia. As he is reproaching her for her faithlessness, the duke appears. Ardelia hides her lover, and then, from the duke, forces a confession (which neither Bentivolio nor the court would have believed from any other), that, notwithstanding all the duke's solicitations, Ardelia has not yielded him her honor. Convinced of her innocence, Bentivolio studies to protect her. He has need; for already he has revealed his secret to Valerio. The latter, having first betrayed Bentivolio and Ardelia to the duke, demands that Ardelia buy his silence with her shame. Fearful lest her refusal cost Bentivolio's life, Ardelia, to gain time, promises Valerio a meeting.

Meanwhile, Leontio, kinsman of the duke, has solicited without success the virtuous duchess. Realizing that he can achieve nothing while her husband lives, but that, were he duke, he might accomplish all, Leontio bribes Pallante, a disaffected captain, to assassinate Farnese. Valerio overhears his secret, convinces Leontio of his loyalty, and, for Leontio, prevails upon Bentivolio, also, to slay the duke. Leontio, as heir, will pardon him.

That night Fiametta, Ardelia's ugly waiting-woman, insists that Ardelia give the duke's lust immediate satisfaction. While she is protesting,

Valerio arrives to claim her. He gets rid of Fiametta by means of a pretended summons from Horatio, and, finding Ardelia obdurate, attempts to force her. With that, she covers him with a pistol. Some one knocks. Supposing it the duke, Valerio hides behind the hangings. Bentivolio enters. Believing that the rat in the arras is the duke, he runs Valerio through; and then, still ignorant of the truth, attempts, with Ardelia, to leave the palace.

Leontio, kinsman of Farnese, meanwhile waits for the explanation of the shouts of "Treason!" Pallante comes, and reports that he has slain the duke. In the midst of his account—which lays strange stress upon the duke's repentance—officers enter with Bentivolio and Ardelia prisoners. Bentivolio, like Pallante, asserts that he has slain the duke. Leontio, though puzzled at the second confession, sees in it an opportunity to shift the blame from his retainer, and forthwith orders Bentivolio and Ardelia both to prison. Believing that the duke is dead, Leontio hastens to force the duchess to his will. Entering her room, he finds with her the duke—spared by Pallante—repentant and reconciled. For the moment, however, Leontio does not recognize Farnese, but mistakes the duke for one of his own servants. He tells Euphemia that the duke's death leaves her free to love him. The duchess will have none of him, and cries out "Treason!" The disguised duke, being unarmed, repeats the cry. Leontio threatens to kill him, but is convinced that the second cry was but an echo. That he may force the duchess, Leontio hands the duke his sword to keep the door. The duke reveals himself, and attacks Leontio. The latter uses the duchess's body as a shield; but the duke's shouts bring Pallante and the guard. Leontio falls wounded; admits his treasons; dies. Word comes that Valerio has been found slain in Ardelia's chamber. All is explained; and the duke and duchess, reunited, joyfully sanction the marriage of Bentivolio to the duke's innocent mistress, fair Ardelia.

That *The Duke's Mistress* is, in its subject-matter, typical of the tragicomedies of Shirley, must be evident from the foregoing summary: it is a tale of lust and intrigue at an Italian court, a tale in which innocence is ultimately triumphant and in which villainy suffers death or reformation. In the management of this material, likewise, *The Duke's Mistress* is representative of Shirley's tragicomedies. In the first place, the exposition is typical. The play opens with a single rapid scene that—interesting in itself—gives us an instant grasp of the situation. Valerio jests about the duke's desertion of the duchess and passion for Ardelia, and twits Leontio about his despondency and the duke's suspicions; Leontio addresses the neg-

lected duchess, is overheard by Strozzi, retains Pallante, and pays his respects to the now doubly suspicious duke; Ardelia enters and is welcomed by the
duke: all this in a single scene, and the play is on.

Besides being typical for its skilful exposition, *The
Duke's Mistress* is typical for its well-knit plot. The
comic subplot, to be sure, is united to the serious action only by the fact that its *dramatis personæ* play
also minor positions in the major plot: its Faust,
Horatio, is the comrade of Bentivolio; its Margaret,
Fiametta, is the companion of Ardelia; its Mephis-
topheles, Valerio, is the sub-villain of the major plot.
The two plots, however, that compose the major
action—that of the duke against Ardelia and that of
Leontio against the duke—these are inseparably
interwoven. The figure of Valerio, moreover, is
omnipresent, an aid to unity; for in all three actions
he plays a vital part. He it is that introduces Horatio to his first mistress, the ugly Fiametta, and that
then, as further complication, brings in her rival, the
uglier Scolopendra. He it is that discovers Leontio's
purpose to supplant the duke, pretends to join him,
and prevails on Bentivolio to be their agent in the
assassination of Farnese. He it is that betrays Bentivolio and Ardelia to the duke, that attempts himself
to force Ardelia's honor, and that, at last, mistaken
for the duke, falls by the avenging hand of Benti-

volio. Thus, by his mischievous participation in each action, Valerio links the three plots into one.

In choice of scenes, likewise, as in exposition and in unity of plot, *The Duke's Mistress* is typical of Shirley's tragicomedy. Both in the scenes that it includes and in the scenes that it omits, the play is typical. The effective scenes, the scenes essential to the plot, are present: the clash between the duke's mistress and the duchess in the presence of Bentivolio, Leontio, and the duke; the meeting of Ardelia and Bentivolio, followed by the confession of the duke in Bentivolio's hearing; the meeting between Leontio and the duchess; the two meetings between Valerio and Ardelia, and the slaying of Valerio by Bentivolio; and the final scene between Leontio, the duchess, and the duke. Yes, the *scènes à faire* are present —with one typical exception: where is the scene in which Pallante achieves the reformation of the duke? To secure a surprise—the duke's unexpected escape and reformation—Shirley has sacrificed an unusual opportunity for a scene of character-development.

In choice of subject-matter, in skill of exposition, in effectiveness of scenes, *The Duke's Mistress* is both typical and successful; but the result is only the romantic tragicomedy of Shirley, not the psychological tragedy of Shakspere.

SUMMARY

THE two plays considered in this chapter—*The Lady of Pleasure* and *The Duke's Mistress,* typical respectively of the realistic and the romantic plays of Shirley—summarize concretely the work of our dramatist from the autumn of 1632 to the spring of 1636. Of the nine extant plays, other than *Chabot,*[8] belonging to this period, three we have found to be comedies of London life and manners. Of these three plays, *The Gamester* is to be remembered for its highly complicated and effective plot and for its realistic pictures of London gaming-houses; *The Example,* for its striking scenes and its appealing characters; and *The Lady of Pleasure,* for its brilliant pictures of viciousness and extravagance in high life and for its skilful plotting and character-delineation. Each of these plays contains Jonsonian "characters of humor"— Oldrat, Dormant, Young Barnacle, the minor figures of *The Lady of Pleasure,* and, best of all, Sir Solitary Plot; each play is likewise Jonsonian both in its firm organization and in its unsparing and at times repulsive realism. Together, however, these three comedies of London life and manners rise above the earlier work of Shirley in the realistic school, both in their serious attitude toward life and in their severe morality. Each play offers, either in its major or in

---

[8] *Chabot,* which I ignore in this summary because of the probability that it is not wholly Shirley's, is romantic tragedy.

its minor plot, some person or some group of persons striving for more wholesome things; and in *The Example,* this striving produces characters genuinely noble.

The six remaining plays of Shirley's second period are, as we have noted, essays in the romantic style, plays that belong primarily to the school of Shakspere and of Fletcher. *The Bird in a Cage* is mere romantic nonsense flavored with satire upon contemporary politics; *The Arcadia* and *The Coronation* are typical Fletcherian dramatic romance, slight of characterization, improbable of plot, but full of unexpected turns, and pretty sentiment, and poetic charm; *The Opportunity,* a better play than either, gives sufficient attention to character to be accounted a romantic comedy rather than a Fletcherian dramatic romance; *The Young Admiral* and *The Duke's Mistress* are romantic tragicomedies. Each of these six, according to its kind, displays an excellent command of plot. The romantic comedy and the two romantic tragicomedies display, in addition, excellent character-delineation.

Although the best of these romantic plays—*The Young Admiral* and *The Opportunity*—are perhaps not greater than the best of the realistic plays—*The Example* and *The Lady of Pleasure*—we cannot help feeling that Shirley's interest and Shirley's ultimate success lie not in realism but in romanticism.

THE THIRD
DRAMATIC PERIOD

CHRONOLOGY OF PLAYS

THIRD DRAMATIC PERIOD

1636–1642

1638, April 23. *The Royal Master* licensed.

1639, October 30. *The Gentleman of Venice* licensed.

1639 (?). *The Politician* probably acted.

1640, April 28. *St. Patrick for Ireland* entered in the Stationers' Register.

1640, April 28. *The Constant Maid* entered in the Stationers' Register.

1640, June 1. *Rosania* licensed. Subsequently published as *The Doubtful Heir*.

1640, November 10. *The Imposture* licensed.

1641, May 26. *The Politique Father* licensed. Subsequently published as *The Brothers*.

1641, November 25. *The Cardinal* licensed.

1642, April 26. *The Sisters* licensed.

1642. *The Court Secret*. "Never acted, but prepared for the scene at Black-Friers."

CHAPTER XIV

THE THIRD DRAMATIC PERIOD—BEGUN

THE ROYAL MASTER

SHIRLEY'S third (and last) dramatic period extends from his departure for Ireland in 1636 to his return to London sometime in the spring or summer of 1640, and thence to the closing of the theaters in 1642. For much of this period, the precise chronology of Shirley's plays is far from certain: many of the plays were first produced in Dublin; and of the date of these presentations we have no record. My discussion, therefore, must follow the order in which the plays were licensed for presentation in London, or, when this record is wanting, the order in which the plays were entered in the Stationers' Register for publication. To this arrangement, however, I shall make one exception. *The Politician*, never licensed, was not published until 1655; yet, since it was "Presented at Salisbury Court By Her Majesties Servants,"[1] it must antedate Shirley's return from Dublin in 1640, the time when Shirley

---

[1] From the title-page of a copy of the 1655 edition, in the possession of the present writer.

[291]

severed his connection with the Queen's men. Since *The Gentleman of Venice* was, like *The Politician,* "Presented at the Private house in Salisbury Court by her Majesties Servants,"[2] and was likewise published in 1655, I shall assume, for purposes of arrangement, that the two plays belong to approximately the same time. *The Gentleman of Venice* was licensed for London presentation October 30, 1639. I shall place *The Politician* immediately after it. All other plays of the period I shall consider in the order of the earliest known date concerning them.

Taken as a whole, this third dramatic period is notable in two respects. In the first place, Shirley's work in the realistic style of Jonson and of Fletcher has all but given way to work in the romantic style of Fletcher and of Shakspere. Two plays, *The Constant Maid* and *The Politique Father* (i.e., *The Brothers* of 1652), are comedies of manners. The other nine of the eleven plays extant are all romantic. In the second place, the plays of this final period include several of the best of Shirley's works. *The Royal Master* and *The Cardinal* are ranked by many critics as Shirley's ablest work in romantic comedy and romantic tragedy respectively; and *The Doubtful Heir, The Imposture, The Court Secret,* and even

---

[2] From the title-page of a copy of the 1655 edition in the possession of the present writer.

that gay little farce *The Sisters,* are all deserving of cordial commendation. In short, the plays of Shirley's closing period confirm his mastery of romantic drama.

Earliest and most delightful of these eleven plays is *The Royal Master:* "Acted in the new Theatre in Dublin: and Before the Right Honorable the Lord Deputie of Ireland, in the Castle,"[3] "on New-yeares day at night,"[4] entered in the Stationers' Register, March 13, 1637/8; licensed April 23, 1638; and published the same year. It is a play notable for well-knit plot, effective scenes, pleasing characterization, clever dialogue, and poetic atmosphere.

The principal actions in the plot are two: first, the attempt of the king's favorite, Montalto, to strengthen his ascendancy by thwarting the purposed marriage of the king's sister to the Duke of Florence; and, second, Domitilla's misplaced infatuation for the king, and her recovery. To make his influence in the state secure, Montalto has desired for himself the hand of Theodosia, sister to the King of Naples. He finds, however, that the king intends the princess for the Duke of Florence, the brother of his deceased queen. To thwart this treaty, Montalto contrives a hunting-party that shall bring the king and duke to

[3] Title-page, 1638. From the copy belonging to the late Robert Hoe, Esq.
[4] Epilogue, in *Works,* IV, 187, and note.

[293]

dine at the country house of Simphorosa, a noble widow, in whose charming daughter, Domitilla, the favorite hopes to interest the duke. At the same time, he covertly informs the duke that Princess Theodosia is secretly contracted to another lover, even himself, and therefore must not wed the duke. Fascinated with Domitilla, the duke is not sorry for an excuse to cast off Theodosia; but yet he hesitates. At this, Montalto hints to the duke's secretary, Riviero, that the princess has already yielded him her honor. At the same time, Montalto reveals to Theodosia the interest of the duke in Simphorosa's daughter. All the contending forces thus aroused, Shirley, in the fourth act, brings together: the king reproaches the duke for his desertion; the duke brings his counter-charge against the princess; the king and princess clash; and then, as innocent little Domitilla falls in the way of the princess, she, for the moment, pays dearly for her imagined rivalry. Then Montalto, discovering that his charge against the princess is about to react upon himself, endeavors to keep all from access to the king until he can remove the only witness to his charge, Riviero. Through Montalto's sentries, Riviero, and then the duke himself, try without avail to gain conference with the king. Young Octavio, however, they allow to pass; for Montalto's creatures know him only as the favorite's favorite.

Then the king calls Montalto into counsel; he fears
that the duke's charge against the princess's chastity
is true; and he desires to find some nobleman who
will marry the princess to conceal her guilt. Montalto offers himself as sacrifice. The king embraces
him, and seeks to find for him some great reward.
He finds it: he will teach Montalto to distinguish
friends from foes; he will pretend to frown upon
Montalto; will order his confinement; he will encourage all who will to proffer charges; will note
who plead Montalto's cause; then he will summon
Montalto back to honor, and Montalto's enemies
shall stand revealed. Instantly, despite Montalto's
protest, the king begins to put his plan into execution: he orders Montalto and Montalto's faction into
confinement; he receives the accusations of Montalto's enemies. Among these accusations, Montalto's
plot against the duke, and his slandering of the princess, are now supplemented by proof, in Montalto's
own handwriting, that he was responsible for the
poisoning of Octavio's father several years before.
And yet, despite all this evidence, Octavio and the
duke's secretary Riviero, who are directing the attack, find to their amazement that the king supports
Montalto. They see Montalto welcomed back in
honor, and furnished with a list of all his enemies.
Then, in an instant, all is changed: the king over-

whelms Montalto with the charges and the evidence against him; the duke and the princess, who have made their peace, enter to add their adverse influence; the king orders Montalto to his doom.

This plot dealing with the intrigues of Montalto and their reaction upon their author, Shirley manages with great skill. The exposition and motivation; the climax, with its clash of duke and king, king and princess, princess and Domitilla; the suspense in the king's antechamber as man after man endeavors to achieve admission; the excitement of the falling action; the final suspense as the king heaps new honors on Montalto; the catastrophe, sudden and overwhelming: all these are capitally conceived. And then, after a scene devoted to the happy resolution of the Domitilla-action, Shirley returns for a moment to Montalto; reveals the fact that Montalto did not cause the poisoning of Octavio's father after all, that Montalto's letter had been intercepted, and that his intended victim lived among them in disguise—Riviero, the duke's secretary. And thus Shirley concludes the story of Montalto by commuting his sentence from death to banishment.

The second story—how Domitilla loved the king —equals the Montalto-action for dramaturgic skill, and excels it in poetic charm. At the opening we find Domitilla, a joyous unspoiled maiden of fifteen, living in the shelter of her mother's country house. The hunting dinner makes her known to all the court; and especially she attracts the notice of the king, the duke, and young Octavio. The king resolves to bestow her hand and fortune upon his favorite, Montalto. To this end, he finds opportunity to ask the maiden whether she will accept a husband of his choosing. She misunderstands him, thinks he means *himself,* and promises. The king, unconscious of the mischief wrought, summons Domitilla and her mother to his court, and directs Simphorosa to prepare her daughter for Montalto. Domitilla, meanwhile, in her own imagination begins to play the queen: when her mother attempts to mention Lord Montalto, she will not hear of him; when Octavio offers her his heart, she can think of him only as a subject; when the Duke of Florence presents a carcanet of diamonds, she fails to thank him and flies abruptly off to meet the king. Then follows the discovery of her mistake. The king does not love her; yet she can only love the king. The duke offers his love, and she rejects it. With her rejection, however, she couples something more: the reconcilement of the duke and princess. Her mother reveals the situation to the king, and begs his aid to break the infatuation. Having made certain that Domitilla is virtuous beyond temptation, he undertakes her cure. He

asks the little maid to be his *mistress*. The shock of
the proposal cures her love. She resists the king.
Octavio dares to intervene, her champion.

KING. How's this?
OCTAVIO. Sir, in a noble cause; if you to whom
In the first place truth flies, as to an altar,
Wave her religious defence, I dare die for her.
KING. You! so brave? to prison with him!—
We will correct your sauciness.
OCT.   You will grace
My first act, sir, and get me fame, by suffering
For so much sweetness.
DOMITILLA.   Let not your displeasure,
Great sir, fall upon him; revenge what you
Call disobedience, here.
KING.   You owe much to
His confidence; nor is there any punishment
Beyond your love and liking of his boldness;
You two should make a marriage with your follies.
OCT. Let Domitilla make Octavio
So blest.
DOM. My lord, you now deserve I should
Be yours, whom, with the hazard of the king's
Anger and your own life, you have defended.
There is a spring of honour here; and to it
In the presence of the king, his court, and heaven,
I dare now give my heart; nor is't without
My duty to a promise.

Oct.   Now you make
Octavio happy.
    King.   'Tis to my desires;
And I dare wish you joys. Forgive this practice;
—Nay, pretty Domitilla, I did this
But to divert more happily thy thoughts
Of me, who have not yet paid the full tribute
To my Cesaria's dust. Again let me
Congratulate thy choice in young Octavio,
Whose birth and forward virtue will deserve thee.[5]

In that part of the action that relates to Domitilla, Shirley enters upon a field that, as we have noticed, he too rarely touches—the field of character-development. Usually, as in most dramatic romances of the Fletcherian school, the characters in Shirley's plays are static: whatever be their nature in the opening act, that nature they retain without spiritual growth to the end of the play; or else, if change there be, it comes abruptly and without adequate preparation—a revolution, not an evolution. In *The Royal Master,* however, Shirley has given us in Domitilla a delightful picture of character-development. Through all the psychologic steps we follow her: from the happy but self-centered innocence of girlhood, through awakened love and sorrow, to an unselfish dedication to king, to princess, and to noble lover. We delight

[5] *The Royal Master,* v, i; *Works,* iv, 185–186.

in her not only for her strength or sweetness at any given moment but also for the growth she makes throughout the play.

Utterly different from the character of Domitilla, yet almost equally delightful in its way, is the character of her "secretary," as she calls him, Bombo. Unable either to read or write, he pores upon books he cannot understand—like many another chaplain, he declares. He has a pretty wit; but fears that his renown may spread abroad. When the king and his hunting-party stop to dine, he is sure that their visit was to search him out. The summons of the king confirms his fears. In attendance upon Domitilla at the court, he hides from all; and when Montalto falls, Bombo, to escape succession to the favorite's place, steals away home. In his humor thus to fly all worldly honors, Bombo makes an excellent foil for his ambitious little mistress, Domitilla.

Besides displaying Shirley's management of plot and character to best advantage, *The Royal Master* affords an excellent example of Shirley's sprightly dialogue. In illustration, I shall quote one passage —none the less willingly because it has been previously commended by Gifford.[6] It is from the first

---

[6] "It is impossible not to notice the feeling, gay good humour, and poetic excellence of this little dialogue."—Gifford, in *Works,* IV, 119, note.

meeting of Domitilla and Octavio, at the moment
before the arrival of the hunting-party at her
mother's country house:

Enter OCTAVIO.

OCT.   I kiss your fair hand, madam Domitilla.
The king and duke and all the jolly hunters,
With appetites as fierce as their own hounds,
Will be here presently.

DOM.   I hope they will not
Devour us, my good lord.

OCT.   But I would sit and feast, and feed mine eyes
With Domitilla's beauty.

DOM.   So, my lord!
Here was a gentleman—you could not choose
But meet him—spake your dialect.   I have
Forgot his name, but he was some great lord.

OCT.   Great lord! Fie! What an ignorance you live in.
Not to be perfect in a great lord's name!
There are few ladies live with us but know
The very pages.   Leave this darkness, madam,
And shine in your own sphere, where every star
Hath his due adoration.

DOM.   Where?
OCT.   The court.
Confine such beauty to a country-house!
Live among hinds, and thick-skinn'd fellows, that
Make faces, and will hop a furlong back
To find the t'other leg they threw away,
To shew their reverence! with things that squat,

[301]

When they should make a curtesy! To court, madam,
And live not thus, for shame! the second part
Of a fond anchorite. We can distinguish
Of beauty there, and wonder without spectacles;
Write volumes of your praise, and tell the world
How envious diamonds, 'cause they could not
Reach to the lustre of your eyes, dissolv'd
To angry tears! the roses droop, and gathering
Their leaves together, seem to chide their blushes,
That they must yield your cheek the victory!
The lilies, when they are censur'd for comparing
With your more clear and native purity,
Want white to do their penance in!—

    Dom.   So, so!
Have you done now, my young poetic lord?

    Oct.   There will be no end, madam, of your praises.

    Dom.   And to no end you have spent all this breath.
Allow all this were wit, that some did think us
The creatures they commend, (and those whom love
Hath curs'd into idolatry and verse,
May perhaps do so,) we do know ourselves
That we are no such things.

    Oct.   Is't possible?

    Dom.   And laugh at your chimeras.

    Oct.   You are the wiser.

    Dom.   If this be your court practice, let me dwell
With truth and plain simplicity.[7]

For such sprightly dialogue as this, for firm plot-
structure and effective scenes, for excellent character-

   [7] *The Royal Master*, I, ii; *Works*, IV, 118–119.

delineation and for the delineation of characters that grow, and finally, for poetic atmosphere and romantic charm, *The Royal Master* is not only one of the best of Shirley's plays but also one of the most attractive romantic comedies of the Elizabethan drama. We need not wonder that, out of all the plays of Shirley, Schipper has selected for translation into German *The Royal Master*.[8]

[8] *James Shirley, sein Leben und seine Werke, nebst einer Übersetzung seines Dramas "The Royal Master" von J. Schipper . . . Wien und Leipzig . . . 1911.* Schipper summarizes his impressions of *The Royal Master* as follows:

"Wie schon diese Analyse erkennen lässt, sind die beiden Handlungen des Dramas in vortrefflicher Weise aufgebaut und miteinander verknüpft worden. Auch die Characteristik der Personen desselben verdient alles Lob. Der edelmütige König und der schurkische Montalto, die leidenschaftliche Theodosia und die sanfte Domitilla sind in der glücklichsten Weise kontrastiert. Dies unschuldsvolle junge Mädchen erscheint in ihrer schwärmerischen Neigung für den edlen König, sodann in ihrer bitteren Enttäuschung über ihren Irrtum und schliesslich wieder in dem schönen Aufschwung womit sie dem für ihre scheinbar bedrohte Ehre mannhaft eintretenden Octavio sich zuwendet, als eine der anziehendsten Frauengestalten, die Shirley geschaffen hat.

"Der wackere Jüngling der sie gewinnt, ist ihrer würdig und sticht in seiner Ergebenheit und Treue vorteilhaft von dem wankelmütigen Herzog ab.

"Auch die komische Person des Stückes, der alte Bombo, ist eine anziehende Figur und, wenn man auch gelegentlich Züge teils von Shakespeares Falstaff, teils von dessen Malvolio an ihm entdeckt, dennoch eine originelle Persönlichkeit." (Page 199.)

CHAPTER XV

THE THIRD DRAMATIC PERIOD—CONTINUED

FROM *THE GENTLEMAN OF VENICE* TO *THE CONSTANT MAID*

THORNDIKE, in his suggestive work on English tragedy, remarks that, "in Shirley, as in Massinger, the most representative plays, and certainly those most satisfactory to our taste, are the tragicomedies. Bloodshed and horror and grossness of language and situation may all be absent, and the story of love and intrigue, even if it does not exalt the mind or purify the passions, may be altogether delightful. In *The Royal Master,* one of the best, the rôle of the lustful monarch is assumed for a single scene, only to cure a really charming heroine of her infatuation for royalty; and the intriguing favorite is foiled, the banished noble vindicated, and two love matches completed with gracefulness of language and dexterity of plot. Unfortunately Shirley's land of romance is rarely so wholesome as here, or the inhabitants so agreeable."[1]

[1] Ashley H. Thorndike, *Tragedy*, pp. 231–232.

Thorndike's concluding sentence is especially applicable to the two romances that we must next discuss: *The Gentleman of Venice* and *The Politician*. The former, licensed October 30, 1639, is another instance of what we have noted in *The Grateful Servant* and in other plays: an instance, namely, of the combination of a romantic action genuinely attractive with another action, romantic or realistic, conspicuously repulsive. The first of these two plots centers about Giovanni, the supposed son of the duke's gardener Roberto. Despite his lowly environment, Giovanni perfects himself in noble thought and deed, and attracts the attention of the duke's niece, Bellaura. When he resolves to take service in the wars, she provides him with armor and with a letter to her kinsman the commander. In an assault that follows, Giovanni so highly distinguishes himself that the duke urges him to name his own reward. With some hesitation, he asks the hand of Bellaura. Her pride forbids. Giovanni returns to his gardening. Meanwhile, however, Thomazo, the supposed son of the duke, has been convicted of high treason. To save Thomazo, his sometime nurse Ursula (the supposed mother of Giovanni) begs of the duke a pardon for *her* son. Then she reveals that *her* son is the worthless Thomazo, changed in infancy, and that Giovanni is the rightful heir. So the duke's true son is married to Bellaura.

The other principal action of this play centers about Cornari, his wife Claudiana, and an English gentleman, Florelli. Cornari—of great wealth but childless—is determined that his rascally nephew Malipiero shall not be his heir. To prevent this, he kidnaps Florelli and confines him in his palace, to the end that the foreigner shall get his wife with child. When Cornari, believing that he has forced his wife and his prisoner to do his will, is about to slay the latter, the confession of Florelli to the supposed priest (Cornari in disguise) proves to Cornari the virtue of them both, and shames him into the abandoning of his design. For this change of purpose, chance brings him his reward: the rascal nephew Malipiero is caught with Thomazo in attempted treason; and the outcome is his genuine reform.

The repulsiveness of this second action in *The Gentleman of Venice* warrants, perhaps, the silence with which Schelling treats the entire play.[2] And yet, if one can ignore the subject-matter and consider only the technique of the play, one can understand why, in the reign of Charles I, it did not lack "the best hands to applaud it in the theatre."[3] Although

[2] Although he discusses every other play of Shirley, Schelling names *The Gentleman of Venice* only in his "List of Plays" (*Elizabethan Drama*, II, 568) and in a foot-note reference to Fleay (*Ibid.*, II, 286, note).

[3] Dedication to *The Gentleman of Venice,* in *Works,* v, 3.

the two plots are not logically related, they are skilfully interwoven. Malipiero, especially, constitutes a lively connecting link between the two actions: he is the occasion of the Cornari-plot; and his escapade with the duke's supposed son, Thomazo, brings about the revelation that solves the Giovanni-plot. The play is more notable, however, for the effectiveness of individual scenes. Conspicuous among these, at least for realism, are Malipiero's quarrel with his uncle[4] and the night of riot at the courtezan's.[5] These scenes, indeed, are worthy of Restoration comedy at its best. And even better is the characterization. All the leading characters—Cornari, Claudiana, Florelli, Giovanni, Bellaura, Thomazo, Malipiero—are clearly drawn, but the duke's gardener, Roberto, and his froward wife, Ursula, are really notable creations. That such scenes and characters appear in the same play with the Cornari-story is most unfortunate.

The Politician, which, in the lack of definite information, we have ventured to place in the year 1639, is a somber and, at times, repulsive tragedy, in which political ambition is the motive, lust and assassination are the accepted means, and the miscarriage of the villain's plans is the cause of downfall. Gotharus, "the

---

[4] *The Gentleman of Venice,* I, i; *Works,* V, 5–10.
[5] *Ibid.,* III, iv; *Works,* V, 47–54.

politician," designing to control the throne of Norway, first despatches Turgesius, the prince royal, and Duke Olaus, the prince's granduncle, on a far campaign, with the purpose that the prince shall lose his life; then marries the lustful king to Marpisa, widow of Count Altomarus and long Gotharus's mistress; and plans that he will advance Marpisa's son, Haraldus—of whom Gotharus believes himself the father —as successor to the crown. Finding that Haraldus is too innocent to be his efficient tool and hearing that Prince Turgesius is marching home victorious, Gotharus resolves to debauch the character of the former and to cause the asassination of the latter. In this twofold attempt, however, Gotharus begins his downfall. Haraldus, made drunk by the politician's creatures and overwhelmed with the discovery of his mother's relations with Gotharus, dies of a fever and a broken heart. The supposed assassination of Prince Turgesius stirs the populace to riotous rebellion. The army clamors at the gates. Marpisa turns against Gotharus. To escape the rabble, he slays one of his confederates, and, after long and hopeless flight, takes refuge in a coffin prepared for Prince Turgesius. The rabble, finding the coffin, march forth to bury it with honors. They meet the army headed by Duke Olaus and the living Turgesius; and, opening the coffin, they find, within, the politician—dead.

Then comes Marpisa; boasts that she has poisoned Gotharus for the death of Haraldus, her son; and, from the same poison, dies before them all. Turgesius, who has escaped death through the loyalty of the supposed assassin, restores his penitent father to the throne, and announces his purpose to wed Albina, the wronged and virtuous widow of the politician.

Of the power of this play, from scene to scene, the following passage from the final act is a concrete illustration:

An Apartment in the Palace. Enter KING *and* MARPISA.

KING.   Oh, I am lost! and, my soul bleeds to think,
By my own dotage upon thee.

MARPISA.   I was curs'd
When I first saw thee, poor, wind-shaken king!
I have lost my son.

KING.   Thy honour, impious woman,
Of more price than a son, or thy own life.
I had a son too, whom my rashness sent
To another world, my poor Turgesius.
What sorcery of thy tongue and eyes betray'd me?

MARP.   I would I had been a basilisk, to have shot
A death to thy dissembling heart, when I
Gave myself up thy queen! I was secure,
Till thou, with the temptation of greatness,
And flattery, didst poison my sweet peace;
And shall thy base fears leave me now a prey
To rebels?

KING.   I had been happy to have left

Thee sooner. But begone! get to some wilderness
Peopled with serpents, and engender with
Some dragon like thyself.

MARP.   Ha! ha!

KING.   Dost laugh, thou prodigy, thou shame of
                woman!

MARP.   Yes, and despise thee, dotard. Vex till thy
                soul

Break from thy rotten flesh; I will be merry
At thy last groan.

KING.   O, my poor boy! my son!
His wound is printed here.—That false Gotharus,
Your wanton goat, I fear, practis'd with thee
His death.

MARP.   'Twas thy own act and timorous heart, in
                hope

To be secure. I glory in the mention,
Thou murderer of thy son!

Enter HORMENUS.

HOR.   Oh, sir, if ever, stand upon your guard!
The army, which you thought scattered and broke,
Is grown into a great and threat'ning body,
Led by the duke Olaus, your lov'd uncle;
Is marching hither; all your subjects fly to him.   [*Exit.*]

MARP.   Ha! ha!

KING.   Curse on thy spleen! Is this a time for
                laughter,

When horror should afflict thy guilty soul?
Hence, mischief!

MARP.   Not to obey thee, shadow of a king,

[310]

Am I content to leave thee; and, but I would not
Prevent thy greater sorrow and vexation,
Now I would kill thee, coward.

    KING.   Treason! treason!

    MARP.   Ay, ay; who comes to your rescue?

    KING.   Are all fled?

    MARP.   Slaves do it naturally.

    KING.   Canst thou hope to 'scape?

    MARP.   I am mistress of my fate; and do not fear
Their inundation, their army coming.
It does prepare my triumph. They shall give
Me liberty, and punish thee to live.

    KING.   Undone, forsaken, miserable king!

                          [Exeunt severally.][6]

No single scene, however, can give an adequate
conception of the cumulative effect of the entire play.
In theme and tone, *The Politician* is vaguely reminiscent both of *Hamlet* and of *Macbeth:* like the latter, it has for its protagonists an ambitious man and
woman who stop at nothing to attain their ends; like
the former, it deals with the corrupt conditions of a
northern court and with a series of attempts against
the rightful heir. In Marpisa and in Gotharus, we
note something of character-development from scene
to scene. Particularly in the closing act—in the scene
just quoted and in that which follows—the ferocity
of the erstwhile timorous Marpisa approaches to

    [6] *The Politician,* v, i; *Works,* v, 162–164.

magnificence.[7] But the play has nothing of the profound psychology of a Shaksperian masterpiece. It impresses one rather for its swift, tense scenes, its gloom, its horror. Nor does the survival of king and prince and duke and injured wife render *The Politician* less a tragedy. Shirley has not made these characters so interesting as to violate the unity of effect. Not these but the tragic figures are the protagonists. Gotharus and Marpisa aspire, suffer, die. Haraldus dies; and, ere he dies, he suffers. And permeating all is the atmosphere of social rottenness: the king's lust for Marpisa and for the chaste Albina; the double adultery of Gotharus and Marpisa; the piteous life and death of young Haraldus—the lawful issue of Marpisa and Count Altomarus, yet believed by Gotharus, by the court, and, for a tragic hour, by himself, to be the unlawful issue of Marpisa and Gotharus. Such is Shirley's *The Politician:* terrible, despite the survival of many innocent; effective, notwithstanding clap-trap and the absence of profound psychology; a romantic tragedy that is almost notable.

Whether the repulsive element that we have just

[7] Of the latter scene (*The Politician,* v, ii; *Works,* v, 164–176) Schelling writes: "Strained to the verge of improbability though much of it is, there is a holding power in the last scene of this tragedy, into which is crowded the unexpected discovery of the dead traitor, the pitiable lamentations of his miserable wife, the splendid Marpisa at bay, and the reconciliation of the prince and his father."—Schelling, *Elizabethan Drama,* II, 320.

noted in *The Gentleman of Venice* and in *The Politician,* was characteristic also of the two lost plays, *The Tragedy of St. Albans* and *Look to the Lady,* entered in the Stationers' Register on February 14 and March 11, respectively, in the year 1639/40, is a subject only for conjecture. We find, however, something of this same repulsiveness in that strange play *St. Patrick for Ireland,* entered in the Stationers' Register on April 28, 1640. Of this play, according to Schipper, the *dramatis personæ* may be classified as "christliche Priester und heidnische Barden und Magier; Engel, Geister und auch Schlangen."[8] Nominally a drama centering about the struggle between paganism and Christianity in Ireland, the play becomes, in fact, a jumble of lofty religious fervor, blood-and-thunder magic, miracles, licentiousness, and horse-play. On the one hand, two youths disguise themselves as statues in the temple, and thus gain opportunity to meet the king's daughters, their willing mistresses; another maiden is violated by a prince masquerading as a god; and a magic bracelet that renders the wearer invisible, enables a servant to play all sorts of pranks. On the other hand, the play presents a not unworthy picture of St. Patrick, includes the conversion of the royal family, and culminates gloriously in the expulsion of the snakes

[8] Schipper, *James Shirley, sein Leben und seine Werke,* p. 205.

from Ireland. Further description or discussion of the play would be superfluous. No wonder that *St. Patrick* was never licensed for the London stage, and that the promised "second part" [9] is non-extant!

From the tainted atmosphere of *The Gentleman of Venice, The Politician,* and *St. Patrick for Ireland,* it is refreshing to pass even to the triviality of *The Constant Maid.* As the licensing of this play is not recorded, and as the entry in the Stationers' Register was upon the same day as that of *St. Patrick for Ireland*—namely, on April 28, 1640—*The Constant Maid* has been usually assigned to the years of Shirley's residence in Dublin. Were we, however, to judge of the date of its composition by the emphasis upon complication and episode, by the absence of individual characterization—unless the conventional usurer and country gull be accounted individual— by the reversion in subject to London life and manners, and by the slightness of the play in all respects, we should be likely, on the strength of this internal evidence, to assign the play rather to the period of *Love Tricks* and other early imitative work.

Such as it is, the main action of *The Constant Maid*

[9] See the last line of the prologue, in *Works,* IV, 365, and the epilogue, *Works,* IV, 443. Krapp, in his monograph *The Legend of Saint Patrick's Purgatory, Its Later Literary History,* p. vi, note 2, is "inclined to think" that, "though there is no direct mention of the Purgatory, . . . it was to have been the subject of the second part" of Shirley's play.

is at least a clever series of variations upon the ancient proverb that the course of true love never did run smooth. Hartwell, a young gentleman of good birth and character but limited means, is the accepted lover of Frances, daughter of the wealthy widow Bellamy. The mother, however, abruptly withdraws her approval of the match, and commands Frances to accept instead the suit of Master Startup, a rich countryman who is half a fool. Then the widow offers herself and her fortune to her daughter's lover, Hartwell. He, by the advice of his friend Playfair (the hero of the second action), resolves to pretend to accept the widow's offer, in order that he may continue his attendance upon Frances. Frances's nurse, however, overhears this plot, and determines, in the interest of the countryman, to thwart it. Before Hartwell can explain the stratagem to his lady-love, the nurse sets on the foolish Master Startup to tell Frances that Hartwell woos her mother. By chance, Hartwell at that very moment avows to the widow his acceptance of her hand; and the daughter overhears them. To follow up this advantage, the nurse connives with Startup to admit him that night to Frances's chamber. Unwisely, however, the nurse reveals her purposes to Hartwell's servant; and he, in turn, reveals the plot to Master Hartwell. Hartwell, that he may test the true feeling of Mistress Frances, arranges to appear in Startup's stead. Startup, to avoid suspicion, has retired early; Hartwell's servant tells him that Hartwell is seeking him to slay him; and this so frightens Startup that he flees to the fields dressed only in his shirt. By this device, Hartwell obtains possession of his rival's clothes and opportunity. The nurse, meanwhile, to prove to Frances the worthlessness of Hartwell, tells her that her mother did but pretend an offer of love to test him, and that he instantly accepted. Frances, however, believing that Hartwell likewise counterfeited, remains constant. Then the nurse reënters, leading Hartwell disguised as Startup. This disguise Frances penetrates; but Hartwell, not comprehending this, believes that her vows of love for him are meant for Startup. Before she can explain, they are interrupted by an alarm: Hartwell, despairing, leaves the house; and Frances is left mourning. Startup, meanwhile, convoyed by Hartwell's servant, flies through the cold and terror of the fields, narrowly escapes a meeting with the raging Hartwell, and at last is arrested by the constable and watch. In the midst of the excitement occasioned by the disappearance of the rivals, a countryman arrives at Mistress Bellamy's. Startup, he declares, has trifled with his daughter, and must make amends by marriage. Frances rejoices at the prospect of being rid of Startup; but her mother quickly turns her joy to grief. At first, declares the mother, she did but pretend a love for Hartwell; but when he offered a return of her affection, her love became real: she, Bellamy, must marry Hartwell regardless of her daughter. As soon, however, as the mother has sufficiently tested Frances's love for Hartwell, she admits that she again has but pretended: she has now tested both, and the marriage of Hartwell and Frances soon shall be. This happy prospect, however, is shattered presently by awful news. The countryman and the watch, in search of Startup, have discovered Hartwell dressed in Startup's clothes, and have accused him of the death of Startup; and Hartwell has confessed the murder. In the court-room, in hearing of Frances and her mother, he again admits his guilt, and adds that the scorn of Frances was the cause. Then he discovers his mistake; he learns that Frances has been, throughout, the Constant Maid. He retracts his plea of guilty; and, at that moment, the watch bring Startup, living, into court.[10] Hartwell and Frances are at last united.

My relation of this the first action of *The Constant Maid* has resulted in a lengthy narrative; but by no other method could I show concretely the real nature of the play. Aside from the figure of the fool-

[10] Cf. the resolution in *The Wedding*, v, ii; *Works*, I, 445.

ish Startup, the interest results solely from the rapid and unexpected twists and turns of fortune. The setting and characters are those of the comedy of London life and manners; but the use of surprise upon surprise is almost the method of Fletcherian romance.

The second action, fortunately, may be more briefly told: a new and more realistic version of the elopement of Shakspere's Jessica and Lorenzo. As Hornet, the usurer, is about to poison a niece, his ward, that he may take her fortune, her lover, Playfair, learns of his intent. To cover her flight, Playfair arranges with a group of friends and servants to impersonate the king and a group of lords, to summon Hornet to their banquet, to knight him, and to entertain him with a masque. In the midst of this, Hornet discovers his eloping niece dancing with Playfair— only to be persuaded that she is not his niece but the daughter of his host, Sir Clement. Next morning, Hornet discovers his mistake, and surrenders to his niece her fortune lest his plot to poison her be charged against him.

Between these two actions of the play, the connection is but accidental. Playfair, the hero of the second action, is a friend of Hartwell, the hero of the first; Hornet, the usurer, appears in the opening scenes as a suitor to Widow Bellamy; and both actions end in the court of Justice Clement: these—these only —are the connecting links. Superficial in structure, the play shows equal haste in characterization: only in the stock characters of Startup and Hornet are the persons individual. These two figures, together with the succession of surprises in the Hartwell-Frances action, are what "make" the play. It is chiefly note-worthy as a reversion from the romantic plays of Shirley's final period to the realistic plays of Shirley's youth.

To synthesize our impressions of the four plays considered in this chapter, is not easy. They have too few points in common. *The Constant Maid* is clean, clever, but trivial and amateurish; to be remembered only as one more essay in the comedy of manners. *St. Patrick for Ireland* is beneath remark. *The Gentle-man of Venice,* in so far as it tells the story of Gio-vanni and his foster-parents, is delightful comedy; but in so far as it deals with the endeavors of Cornari, it has a repulsiveness that neither the dramaturgic skill of Shirley nor the virtue of Cornari's wife can soften. *The Politician,* on the other hand, notwith-standing its offensive theme, possesses a tragic power of plot, of situation, and of character, that places it among the abler plays of Shirley. Little in common, then, have these four plays; but three of them are repulsive in material, and yet they are not realistic but romantic.

CHAPTER XVI

THE THIRD DRAMATIC PERIOD—CONTINUED

FROM *THE DOUBTFUL HEIR* TO
THE BROTHERS OF 1652

THE plays considered in the two chapters just preceding vary materially in their artistic effectiveness and in their ethical acceptability. On the one hand, *The Royal Master* is a play both ably written and delightful. On the other hand, *The Gentleman of Venice* and, to an even greater extent, *The Politician* combine with excellence of treatment an extreme repulsiveness of subject-matter; *St. Patrick for Ireland,* except for the poetic beauty of an occasional passage, is pleasing neither artistically nor ethically; and *The Constant Maid,* although morally inoffensive, is dramaturgically a return to the amateurish efforts of our poet's youth. Now, however, in the three chapters that are to complete our discussion of Shirley's last dramatic period, we come to six successive plays—*The Doubtful Heir, The Imposture, The Politique Father* (i.e., *The Brothers* of 1652), *The Cardinal, The Sisters,*

[320]

and *The Court Secret*—all of which are both pleasingly and ably written, and one of which—*The Cardinal*—is a great tragedy not only in comparison with the other plays of Shirley but in comparison with the plays of any of the later Elizabethan dramatists. And of these six plays, all but one—*The Politique Father*—belong not to the realistic but to the romantic school.

The first of these, *The Doubtful Heir,* which was licensed June 1, 1640, is a capital bit of Fletcherian romance, swift of action, exciting of episode, fertile of surprise, and genuinely poetic. Just as Olivia, the Queen of Murcia, is about to be married to Leonario, the Prince of Arragon, their preparations are interrupted by the invasion of one Ferdinand who claims to be the rightful heir to the throne, a cousin of the queen, believed to have died in childhood. Against this pretender, the bridegroom leads the army, and returns victorious, bringing the claimant prisoner. With the pretender comes a gentle page, Tiberio; and this page a pretty love-scene in the prison reveals to the audience as Ferdinand's betrothed, Rosania. Summoned to stand trial for high treason, Ferdinand boldly avows himself the rightful king, and declares that one is present who could, if he would, attest his royal birth. When, however, the aged chancellor reproaches Ferdinand for endangering the lives of others, Ferdinand says no more. The queen, much moved by Ferdinand's noble bearing and by his words of parting to his page, commands the intermission of the trial during her absence from the room. The nobles, however, with the concurrence of the Prince of Arragon, are about to pass sentence on the pretender, when the queen, warned by the chancellor, returns. Highly indignant, the queen reproves her betrothed, the Prince of Arragon; pardons the pretender; declares that they may yet find Ferdinand's title to the kingdom clear, and commands him to escort her from the court!

As might have been expected in a Fletcherian romance, this seeming resolution is but the beginning of a further complication. Married to the pretender, the queen becomes wild at his neglect. She questions the page as to whether Ferdinand has not a mistress; and, seeing Ferdinand approach, she tries to arouse his jealousy by caressing this supposed Tiberio, and then leaves the two together. Then follows a sorrowful meeting between Ferdinand and his disguised Rosania. He explains that he consented to the marriage ceremony only to make possible his escape with her; and that with the queen his marriage never has been consummated. Ultimately, after Ferdinand has overruled Rosania's purpose to leave him to the queen, he prevails upon her to obey the queen's summons to her chamber and to leave to him the solution of the meeting. When the queen, smarting at Ferdinand's continued neglect and now assured that he has a mistress in the court, is endeavoring to woo his page (Rosania-Tiberio) to sinful love, Ferdinand brings the nobles to the royal chamber to take them in the fact. To his surprise, the queen receives his charges with composure; and, while her maid, in an inner room, is disguising the page in woman's garb, her Majesty reads the court a pretty lecture. And then, just as Ferdinand, breaking through the queen's pretense, is about to seize upon the "boy," a spy employed by the Prince of Arragon reveals the plot: the page in woman's dress is indeed a woman and—is Ferdinand's mistress!

Again imprisoned, and condemned to death, Ferdinand awaits his execution. Instead, he finds himself hailed by the chancellor and a throng of nobles as the rightful king. The chancellor it was that rescued him from death in childhood and arranged for his escape across the border; the chancellor, repenting his long silence, now testifies to Ferdinand's identity. Enthroned, King Ferdinand summons his sometime page, Rosania, to become his queen, and declares that it is now no blemish to Olivia still to be a virgin. Olivia, he announces, shall now be married to the Prince of Arragon. Suddenly, however, their joy is interrupted; the Prince of Arragon with an unexpected host has scaled the walls! King Ferdinand and his court are instant prisoners. With a command that Ferdinand be put to death, the victor sweeps Olivia to the chapel to be made his bride. For a last time Ferdinand and Rosania say farewell. The bearded general of the Prince of Arragon bears down upon them, tears off his false beard, and reveals —Rosania's father, kinsman of the chancellor, the guardian of the infant Ferdinand! The army that Arragon supposed to be his own is Valentia's army sent to the aid of Ferdinand upon his first repulse. It has intercepted Arragon's messengers, and has tricked him with its feigned support. And so, attended by a loyal and victorious host, King Ferdinand resumes his reign, and is married to his boyhood sweetheart, fair Rosania.

Such is the romantic story of *The Doubtful Heir:* swift, exciting, unexpected, with a final suspense that keeps one almost breathless. That it is a reworking of old material, we grant: the royal bridegroom leading to victory the army of the queen may have been (I do not say was) suggested by the unused portion of *El Castigo del Penséque*—the play from which Shirley drew much of his material for *The Opportunity;* the situation of a queen forcing her hand upon a prince previously contracted and ultimately true to

his first love, is but a better version of the Sophia-
Arcadius-Polidora action in *The Coronation;* the
scene in which the chancellor hails as king the imprisoned Ferdinand, is an echo of that in which the
lord protector in *The Coronation* hails the imprisoned Seleucus-Leonatus; the relation of the tricky
captain to the gullible citizens in the subplot (which
I have not attempted to describe) recalls the relation
of Captain Mauritio to the foolish Fabio in *The
Young Admiral;* the scene in which the queen, to woo
Tiberio (the disguised Rosania), assumes the part
of the man and requires Tiberio to play the maid,
might be accounted a new version of the scene in *As
You Like It,* in which Rosalind, disguised as a man,
requires Orlando to address her as a woman.[1]   Indeed, the entire foundation of *The Doubtful Heir*—
a prince concealed in infancy and a maiden playing
she-page to her lover—is almost as old as is romance
itself: all this we grant.   But above this seeming lack
of inventiveness stand out two facts: In the first place,
Shirley, like Shakspere, was shrewd enough, on finding an effective situation, to repeat it and to improve
upon it: as Shakspere, having attempted to portray
an inconstant lover in his Proteus of *Two Gentlemen
of Verona,* repeated the figure in his Lysander of *A
Midsummer Night's Dream* and bettered it by mak-

[1] Shakspere, *As You Like It,* IV, i.

ing it more reasonable—if fairy intervention can be accepted as a reason—so Shirley, having made the lover of Polidora marry Sophia in *The Coronation* of 1635, makes the lover of Rosania marry Olivia in *The Doubtful Heir* of 1640, and, in repeating the figure, betters it by supplying better motivation. In the second place, Shirley in his management of plot has learned to obtain a maximum of effect with a minimum of effort: to concentrate more complications upon fewer *dramatis personæ*. The story for which, in *The Coronation,* he used six major figures, he retold five years later in *The Doubtful Heir* with four. He condensed the lord protector and his son into the single figure of the Prince of Arragon; he condensed Seleucus-Leonatus and Arcadius-Demetrius into the single figure of King Ferdinand; he retained Sophia in Olivia, Polidora in Rosania; and to the latter he added the part of the faithful maiden playing page to a seemingly unfaithful lover. Such is the dramatic economy of Shirley: another excellent illustration of his mastery of technique.

As *The Doubtful Heir* is typical Fletcherian romance in its reliance upon unexpected situations and upon skilful management of plot, so is it typical in the limitation and nature of its characterization. The character-drawing in this play is not psychologically profound; it makes slight attempt to portray character-development; it realizes the several *dramatis personæ* only so far as they are essential to the story or to the scene of the moment; it accounts itself merely a means, not an end in itself. Rosania and Ferdinand and the Prince of Arragon, from prologue to epilogue, remain the same; they suffer, but they learn little from their sufferings; they are no older for their sad experience. As for the queen, with her startling change of passion from the prince to the pretender, from the pretender to the pretender's page, she is at least consistent in her inconsistency; but her first change is frankly without sufficient motive, and her return to her first love is the result of his victory, not of her volition. In all four major figures, the characterization is adequate and pleasing, but it is nothing more. To make it more would be to remove the play from the company of Fletcherian romance to—or at least *toward*—the society of Shaksperian tragicomedy; to shift the interest from episode to character.

And finally in language, as in character and plot, Shirley in *The Doubtful Heir* follows in the footsteps of his master Fletcher. Not strength but sweetness—of thought and of expression—is the characteristic quality of the more poetic passages in Shirley. In illustration, I quote some portions of the prison-scene in which Ferdinand is first hailed as king. My omissions are chiefly passages of explanation, not vital to my present purpose:

FERDINAND.   I have no heart to think of anything
But my Rosania; all devotion,
When I remember her, flies off, and leaves
My soul no contemplation but her safety.
They were too cruel to divide us.   Night
Itself looks now more black by this dim taper.
Rosania's eyes would brighten all; but they,
Weigh'd down with sleep and sorrow, are perhaps
At rest: a thousand angels watch about them!
And let some one whose office is to wait
On harmless love, present me to her dreams.
Oh let her hear me often call upon her,
As I am led to death! and when the stroke
Divides me from myself and from the world,
My heart shall pay her tribute, and my blood
Do miracles, when every crimson drop
My body bleeds shall not in vain be wept,
But fall into some letter of her name,
To keep alive our story.—What lights are these?
This place sure is not wont to be thus visited.
They are spirits.   Ha! yet if I have memory,
Those faces were but late familiar to me.
What mockery is this?   If you be substances
Of things I know, go tell the tyrant queen
She might allow me death without this scorn,
This jeering anti-masque.
   OMNES.   Long live the king!
   FERD.   What king?

OMNES.   Long live Ferdinand, king of
                    Murcia!

FERD.   A dream, a golden dream! What fancies wait
Upon our sleep! and yet I wake; they are
Apparitions; I'll shut my eyes, and lose them.
They will not vanish. Leandro, Rodriguez, Ernesto?

   OMNES.   All your subjects.

   LEANDRO.   Collect your scatter'd thoughts, my lord,
                    and be
Assured, we now pay real duties to you;
You are our king, and must be. . . .

   FERD.   I may command you then. Fetch me Rosania;
I'll be no king without her. Do not stay
To hear how much I love her 'bove the crown,
And all the glories wait upon it: she
That was my page, my fellow prisoner,
Rosania!
'Tis that name, next to heaven, I bow to.
Good my lord, follow him; and if she be
Awake, oh drop it gently by degrees
(The joy is mighty, she a sad weak virgin)
That I shall live to make her queen. . . .
She comes, she comes! . . .
See how the day that made
Haste to salute Rosania, and to wait
Upon thy triumph, blushes like a maid
When she is told she is in love! the stars
Are gone to tell the other world thy beauty,
Till now eclips'd with sorrow, hath thrown off

The imprisoning veil, and shines above their
   brightness. . . .
Come, my Rosania, time hath turn'd again
Our glass, and his keen scythe this comfort brings:
It cuts no sceptres down, but to make kings.[2]

This poetic element which we have just noted in
The Doubtful Heir appears again in *The Imposture,*
licensed five months later, November 10, 1640. In
The Imposture, we observe as well the emphasis
upon plot and situation rather than upon character.
The Imposture, however, differs from *The Doubtful
Heir* in that the action springs from the deliberate
initiative of the *dramatis personæ* rather than from
chance, and that the interest, scene by scene, results
not so much from surprise as from the struggle between contending characters. In short, *The Doubtful Heir* is merely a romance; *The Imposture* is a
comedy of romantic intrigue.

The plot of *The Imposture* centers about a struggle
between Flaviano, favorite of the Duke of Mantua,
on the one hand, and the duke's son and daughter on
the other, concerning the proposed marriage of the
latter to Prince Leonato of Ferrara. Lured by a
promise of Fioretta's hand, the Prince of Ferrara
has brought his army to the aid of Mantua. Flaviano, however, himself aspires to the hand of Fioretta;

  [2] *The Doubtful Heir,* v, ii; *Works,* IV, 342–346.

and therefore, taking advantage of the fact that her brother, Honorio, lies wounded, he persuades the duke that the Prince of Ferrara is a wild young man, morally unfit to marry Fioretta; removes Fioretta to a convent, and thence, secretly, to his mother's country house; and finally brings word to the expectant prince that Fioretta has vowed to remain in the convent for a year—to the postponement of the wedding. Prince Leonato, indignant at what he believes to be the perfidy of the duke, demands a personal interview with Fioretta. This interview they do not dare deny; but Flaviano, with the duke's consent, plots to provide a substitute for Fioretta. In the convent is a novice, Juliana, Flaviano's cast-off mistress; and her he persuades to play Fioretta's part. He instructs her even to wed Prince Leonato; but the duke, unwilling to abuse Ferrara thus, secretly commands Juliana to insist on the year's postponement of the marriage as before proposed. When the Prince of Ferrara comes to her at the convent, she pretends obedience to the duke's command. The prince, however, finds in her reply a hint that she is not unwilling to be carried off by force. With a picked company, therefore, he breaks into the convent, and bears off Juliana—the counterfeit Fioretta—as his bride-to-be.

The scene now changes to Ferrara, whither, suspicious of Flaviano's treatment, the real Fioretta has come under an assumed name, to become, as it happens, the guest of Prince Leonato's sister, Donabella. Hither also has come Honorio, to avenge what he supposes to have been the rape of his sister Fioretta. As he and Prince Leonato are about to fight, Juliana and the princess Donabella rush between their swords. Confronted by Honorio, Juliana so amazes him that she gains his temporary silence and so saves the situation. Left alone, Honorio is presently found and welcomed by his sister Fioretta. Juliana, meanwhile, resolves on self-destruction. She tells the prince that she is not Fioretta, but a noble virgin compelled by the Duke of Mantua to personate his daughter. That she is the cast-off mistress of Flaviano, she neglects to state; she stresses rather the fact that it was against her will that the prince bore her from the convent. At this moment, Honorio— whom Flaviano has followed from Mantua that he may slay him—breaks in upon the prince and Juliana with Flaviano prisoner. Honorio starts to tell Prince Leonato all of Flaviano's treachery. The prince, believing that Juliana's tale is all, cuts Honorio short; tells him that he will hear nothing from him; and declares his purpose to wed the noble virgin (Juliana) and to make war on Mantua for the duke's deceit:

LEONATO. . . . I know all the business,
And am resolved in my revenge.—Juliana,

Sweet suffering maid, dry thy fair eyes; 'tis I
Must make thee satisfaction. I thus,
By thy own name, receive thee to my bosom.—
But you, that practis'd cunning, shall, ere time
Contract the age of one pale moon, behold
The country I preserv'd, a heap of ruins. . . .

    HONORIO. Do you know
Whom you embrace? Flaviano has confess'd
Himself the traitor, and the black contriver
Of all this mischief. Leonato, hear me,
Or by thy father, newly fall'n to ashes,
I shall repent I had an honourable
Thought of thee. —Flaviano!—Madam witchcraft!
My rage will strangle my discourse; my soul
Is leaping forth to be reveng'd upon
That devil.—Prince, keep off; his very breath
Will stifle thee, and damn thy honour to
All ages. Fioretta's now in court.

    FLAV. Ha! in the court?
    LEO.   This is some new device.
    HON. I charge thee, by thy blood, throw off these
            harpies,
And do my sister justice, whom their treason
Hath made a scorn. That minute she usurps
Her name of bride, I shall forget the altar
And turn myself the priest, with all your blood
To make a purging sacrifice.

    LEO.   If, when we
Receive our rites, thou dost but frown, or whisper
To interrupt our ceremony, I

Will make thee hold the tapers, while the priest
Performs the holy office. Tell thy sister
Here I bestow what you have made me forfeit.
Present her to the nunnery, and counsel
Thy ignoble father, when I next see Mantua,
To be asleep in's coffin, and his vault
Deep, and thick ribb'd with marble: my noise else
Will shake his dust. Thy youth finds mercy yet;
Take the next whirlwind, and remove— Our guard!—
Petronio, we confine him to your house. . . . [*Exeunt.*][3]

For the moment, the intrigues of Flaviano seem
to triumph, but only for the moment. Flaviano's confederate, Claudio, betrays him to the prince. The
prince accuses Juliana; she begs for mercy; and he
casts her off. The Duke of Mantua arrives to save
his son. At the same moment enter Fioretta, Juliana,
and the princess Donabella. The old duke recognizes
his daughter. The princess—who, in her love for
Honorio, has mistaken his sister Fioretta for her rival
—runs joyously to find him. The prince, likewise
discovering the identity of Mantua's daughter, instantly resolves to have her for his bride. To Honorio he gives his sister Donabella. To a nunnery he
dismisses Juliana; to exile, the intriguing Flaviano.

This extended outline and the quoted scene have
given, I trust, an adequate idea of *The Imposture:* a

[3] *The Imposture,* IV, v; *Works,* V, 244–245.

romantic play characterized, both scene by scene and as a whole, by struggle and intrigue and poetic passion. The subplot, which presents a coward son, a masking mother, and a drinking-bout, need not detain us. But we must not dismiss the play without quoting the eight-line epilogue spoken by Juliana —an epilogue which, in its contrast between the real character of the actor and the part he plays, possesses a humor not unlike that of the more famous epilogue which Dryden wrote for that "little harmless devil," Nell Gwyn.[4] Fully to appreciate the fun, we must recall, first, that *The Imposture* was acted by the King's men at the private house *in Black Fryers,* and, second, that the part of Juliana—as of the other women in the cast—was played by *a man.*

Epilogue, spoken by JULIANA.

Now the play's done, I will confess to you,
And will not doubt but you'll absolve me too;
There is a mystery; let it not go far,
For this confession is auricular:
I am sent among the nuns, to fast and pray,
And suffer piteous penance; ha, ha, ha!
They could no better way please my desires:
I am no nun—but one of the *Black Friars*.[5]

[4] Dryden, Epilogue to *Tyrannic Love.*
[5] Epilogue to *The Imposture,* in *Works,* v, 269.

Six months after the licensing of *The Imposture,* appeared *The Politique Father,* licensed May 26, 1641. The grounds for identifying this with the play published as *The Brothers* in 1652, I have presented in an earlier chapter. If the latter be indeed *The Politique Father,* and not the play licensed as *The Brothers* in 1626, then we must account it not one of the earliest but the very last of Shirley's comedies of manners. Its scene and characters are nominally Spanish; but it affords no further grounds for not accounting it a comedy of London life.

If this play published as *The Brothers* in 1652 be, as we have concluded, *The Politique Father* of 1641, then the character from whom it first was named is Don Ramyres, the father of Fernando and Francisco.[6] This politic father desires to marry his eldest son and heir, Fernando, to Jacinto, daughter of the rich Don Carlos. To this plan, Ramyres gains the seeming acquiescence of Don Carlos; but when he brings Fernando for the wooing, the ungrateful heir takes the opportunity to woo Jacinta's penniless cousin Felisarda, while the younger brother pursues a long-standing love-affair with rich Jacinta. When Fernando, however, on being cross-questioned by Ramyres, admits his love for Felisarda and his bro-

---

[6] That Francisco, in the opening scene (*Works,* I, 195), speaks of *Don Carlos* as "a provident father," has been cited in support of a different interpretation. Fleay, *English Drama,* II, 246.

ther's standing with the heiress, the politic father, in a seeming rage, applauds the thriftiness of his younger son and heaps disinheritance and a father's curse upon the elder. To Francisco he immediately bequeaths his wealth to assure acceptability with Jacinta's father; and forthwith Ramyres politicly dies that the inheritance may take effect. The elder son hears that his father has been privately entombed within a convent, but that before his death he so far relented as to send his blessing to his sometime heir.

Meanwhile, Don Carlos, the father of Jacinta, has cast out Felisarda from his household, and has arranged to marry Jacinta to a wealthy and high-born libertine, Don Pedro. As Felisarda is returning to her father's house, she is waylaid by Don Pedro, and from him is rescued only by the timely appearance of Fernando. Despite Fernando's penniless condition, Felisarda would gladly marry him; but he is unwilling to accept such a sacrifice—to betray her to greater poverty. As for Jacinta, the heiress, who is being forced into marriage with Don Pedro, she elopes with Francisco on her wedding morn; and, when her father learns of the true character of Don Pedro and of the inheritance of Francisco, he is easily reconciled to the elopement. Then, from the concealment in the convent, appears the politic father, Don Ramyres. By his pretended death, he has se-

cured the marriage of Francisco to the heiress, and
has tested "Fernando's piety and his mistress' virtue."
He restores his elder son to fortune, and marries him
to Felisarda.

Around this major plot are grouped several interesting lesser characters and actions. There is the
grasping Carlos, father of Jacinta, who forbids the
attendance of the younger brother for his lack of fortune, but who welcomes successively the suit of
Alberto, of Fernando, and of Don Pedro, each
wealthier than his predecessor. There is the engag-
ing and irrepressible young scapegrace, Luys, Jacinta's brother, who, in return for commending them
to his sister, borrows money from her suitors, and
who finally secures uncounted money from his father
on pretext that he has slain Alberto and must flee the
country. There is the device by which Jacinta, with
the connivance of the noble widow Estefania, escapes
from Don Pedro on her wedding morn—a device not
unlike that by which Violetta in *The Witty Fair
One,* with the connivance of her maid, escapes from
marriage with Sir Nicholas. And, finally, there is
the high-born libertine Don Pedro, who makes love,
more or less honorable, to Jacinta, to Felisarda, and
to Estefania, only to find at the last that Jacinta is
married to Francisco, that Felisarda is safely affi-

anced to Fernando, and that Estefania is wedded to Alberto.

Although *The Politique Father* (*The Brothers* of 1652) is primarily a comedy of London life and manners, thinly disguised with Spanish names and setting, yet it differs materially from the well-nigh Middletonian realism of Shirley's other late realistic comedy, *The Constant Maid*. This difference results largely from the almost romantic treatment of the fortunes of the lovers in the major plot, and from the poetic quality of many passages in its more important scenes. Of this romantic treatment and poetic quality, the following extracts from the conclusion of Act IV, scene v, shall be example. It is the parting of Fernando and Felisarda:

FEL.   Shall I want fortitude to bid him welcome?—
Sir, If you think there is a heart alive
That can be grateful, and with humble thought
And prayers reward your piety, despise not
The offer of it here. You have not cast
Your bounty on a rock, while the seeds thrive
Where you did place your charity. My joy
May seem ill dress'd to come like sorrow thus;
But you may see through every tear, and find
My eyes meant innocence and your hearty welcome.
FER.   Who did prepare thee, Felisarda, thus
To entertain me weeping? Sure our souls
Meet and converse, and we not know't. There is

[339]

Such beauty in that watery circle, I
Am fearful to come near, and breathe a kiss
Upon thy cheek, lest I pollute that crystal.
And yet I must salute thee; and I dare,
With one warm sigh, meet and dry up this sorrow . . .
But first, I have a story to deliver,
A tale will make thee sad, but I must tell it:
There is one dead that loved thee not, . . . my
    father, . . .
Alas! I am no more Fernando; there
Is nothing but the empty name of him
That did betray thee. Place a guard about
Thy heart betime; I am not worth this sweetness.
    FEL.   Did not Fernando speak all this? alas,
He knew that I was poor before, and needed not
Despise me now for that.
    FER.   Desert me, goodness,
When I upbraid thy wants. 'Tis I am poor;
For I have not a stock in all the world
Of so much dust as would contrive one narrow
Cabin to shroud a worm. My dying father
Hath given away my birthright to Francisco;
I'm disinherited, thrown out of all,
But the small earth I borrow thus to walk on;
And, having nothing left, I come to kiss thee,
And take my everlasting leave of thee. . . .
    FEL.   'Tis . . . wealth first taught us art to
               surfeit by:
Nature is wise, not costly, and will spread

A table for us in the wilderness;
And the kind earth keep us alive and healthful,
With what our bosom doth invite us to.
The brooks, not there suspected, as the wine
That sometime princes quaff, are all transparent,
And with their pretty murmurs call to taste them.
In every tree a chorister to sing
Health to our loves; our lives shall there be free
As the first knowledge was from sin, and all
Our dreams as innocent.

    FER.   Oh, Felisarda!
If thou didst own less virtue I might prove
Unkind, and marry thee; but being so rich
In goodness, it becomes me not to bring
One that is poor in every worth, to waste
So excellent a dower. Be free, and meet
One that hath wealth to cherish it; I shall
Undo thee quite. But pray for me, as I,
That thou mayst change for a more happy bridegroom.
I dare as soon be guilty of my death
As make thee miserable by expecting me.
Farewell! and do not wrong my soul, to think
That any storm could separate us two,
But that I have no fortune now to serve thee.

    FEL.   This will be no exception, sir, I hope.
When we are both dead, yet our bodies may
Be cold, and strangers in the winding sheet,
We shall be married when our spirits meet.   [*Exeunt.*][7]

---

[7] *The Brothers*, IV, v; *Works*, I, 248–252.

Of this poetic element in *The Brothers* of 1652, another familiar example is the passage quoted by Farmer in his *Essay on the Learning of Shakespeare, 1766*, the description of the maid at prayers.[8]

Of the three plays considered in this chapter, two —*The Doubtful Heir* and *The Imposture*—are to be ranked among Shirley's most successful contributions to the romantic school. In neither is the characterization notable—nor is this to be expected in plays following so closely in the romantic, as distinguished from the realistic, style of Fletcher. But *The Imposture* is delightful for skilful intrigue and romantic atmosphere; and *The Doubtful Heir,* passionate, swift, astounding in surprise upon surprise, is a Fletcherian dramatic romance of highest quality. *The Brothers* of 1652, which we have identified with the play licensed as *The Politique Father,* 1641, is a comedy of manners of but minor interest—whether we compare it with the romantic plays which are its

[8] "Her eye did seem to labour with a tear
Which suddenly took birth, but, overweigh'd
With its own swelling, dropp'd upon her bosom,
Which, by reflection of her light, appear'd
As nature meant her sorrow for an ornament.
After, her looks grew cheerful; and I saw
A smile shoot graceful upward from her eyes,
As if they had gain'd a victory o'er grief;
And with it many beams twisted themselves,
Upon whose golden threads the angels walk
To and again from heaven."
                    The Brothers, I, i; *Works,* I, 202.

nearest neighbors, or with the realistic plays of Shirley's first and second periods. Even *The Brothers,* however, contains much pleasing verse. It is the poetical element that links this play not only with *The Doubtful Heir* and *The Imposture,* but also with the three plays still to be discussed.

CHAPTER XVII

THE THIRD DRAMATIC PERIOD—CONTINUED

THE CARDINAL

FOREMOST among the later plays of Shirley, and among the greatest that Shirley ever wrote, is *The Cardinal,* licensed November 25, 1641. In plot, this romantic tragedy is a struggle between the duchess Rosaura on the one hand and the cardinal on the other: the duchess being supported by a colonel named Hernando, and the cardinal being in alliance with his nephew Don Columbo. Opening in a struggle concerning the marriage of the duchess, the play concludes as a struggle for revenge.

The cardinal, for the strengthening of his own power, has persuaded the king to bestow the hand of the duchess upon Don Columbo. While Columbo is absent defending the kingdom against Arragon, the duchess writes him, demanding her release. Columbo, supposing it but a hint to hasten home, gives her her freedom. The duchess shows his letter to the king; and, on the strength of it, she secures the king's assent to her marriage with her long-time lover, Count d'Alvarez. Columbo returns upon their wedding night, stabs with his own hand Count d'Alvarez, and stays to justify his crime. His victory over Arragon pleads in his behalf; and this, by the cardinal's influence, wipes out all memory of the assassination. Columbo forces himself upon the duchess, and vows that, should she ever think to wed again, he will slay the next bridegroom as he has the last.

With this, the duchess accepts as her champion one Hernando, a colonel who has also personal grounds for hating both Columbo and the cardinal. In the duel that follows, Hernando slays Columbo. The duchess, meanwhile, seemingly insane, is made the cardinal's ward. He resolves to take revenge upon her by violating and then poisoning her. When, however, he attempts assault upon her, Hernando, concealed behind the arras, rushes to her rescue, stabs the cardinal, and then stabs himself and dies. To the king and court, the wounded cardinal confesses his treachery; and, in token of his penitence, he begs the duchess to accept an antidote for a poison which, he alleges, he administered to her at supper. In token of his good faith, he takes a portion of the antidote before her. She drinks, and finds it poison. He rejoices in the success of his deceit—and then learns that his own wound was not mortal. The cardinal and the duchess die together. Both have their revenge.

Upon and around this central story, Shirley has grouped a succession of strong and brilliant scenes. The departure of Columbo and the immediate meeting of d'Alvarez and the duchess;[1] the council of war, with Columbo's quarrel with Hernando, his receipt of the duchess's letter, and his answer;[2] her successful appeal to the king and resulting quarrel with the cardinal;[3] the celebration of the duchess's wedding to d'Alvarez, the "revels" by the unknown maskers, their murder of d'Alvarez, the unmasking of Columbo, his bold confession and defiance, and the duchess's cry for justice;[4] her subsequent meetings with Columbo, with Hernando, and with the cardinal;[5] the duel between Hernando and Columbo with their respective seconds, from which Hernando is the sole survivor;[6] the visit of Hernando and of the cardinal to the supposedly insane duchess, and the resulting deaths of all three:[7] all these scenes tell swiftly and vividly the story from which the remaining scenes—such as the comic episode of the servants dressing for the play, and the hinted amours of Columbo and Celinda—are but slight digressions. As a combination of emotional unity in each individual scene with intellectual unity in the play taken as a

[1] *The Cardinal*, I, ii.
[2] *Ibid.*, II, i.
[3] *Ibid.*, II, iii.
[4] *Ibid.*, III, ii.
[5] *Ibid.*, IV, ii.
[6] *Ibid.*, IV, iii.
[7] *Ibid.*, V, iii.

whole, *The Cardinal* stands first among Shirley's tragedies.

The Cardinal is notable, however, not solely for management of plot and for the high effectiveness of particular scenes; it is notable also for the interest of its characters. The duchess, Columbo, Hernando, and the cardinal: each is a powerful personality, powerfully conceived; each different from the others, and each finely delineated.

Most difficult of delineation was the character of the duchess Rosaura. Her, Shirley must present as guilty of the initial overt act that divorced her from her affianced lover, married her to that lover's rival, and led on to the assassination of d'Alvarez, the death of Columbo and two others in the resulting duel, the suicide of Hernando, and the death by poison of the cardinal and herself; and yet Shirley must so present the duchess that, from first to last, our sympathy shall be with her—the all but helpless soul struggling for life amid the cardinal's toils. This sympathy, Shirley skilfully builds up from scene to scene: he shows us how the anger of the lords runs high against the cardinal; how the love of the duchess for d'Alvarez antedated her forced alliance with the cardinal's nephew, Don Columbo; how, against the united power of the mighty general, the mightier cardinal, and the pliant king, naught could avail the duchess but a woman's stratagem; how, widowed on her wedding night, she cried in vain for justice against the murderer of her lord; how Columbo, more firm than ever in the king's support, drove her, by his threats, to desperation, and forced upon her, not for revenge or justice only, but even for self-preservation, her alliance with Hernando for the death of Columbo and the cardinal. Perhaps the finest touch—coming as it does between the death of Columbo in the duel and that of the cardinal by his own poison—is the scene in which the duchess, seemingly insane, receives her champion, Hernando:

> HERNANDO. Dear madam, do not weep.
> DUCHESS.   You're very welcome.
> I have done. I will not shed a tear more
> Till I meet Alvarez; then I'll weep for joy.
> He was a fine young gentleman, and sung sweetly.
> An you had heard him but the night before
> We were married, you would have sworn he had been
> A swan, and sung his own sad epitaph.
> But we'll talk of the Cardinal.
> HER.   Would his death
> Might ransom your fair sense! he should not live
> To triumph in the loss. Beshrew my manhood,
> But I begin to melt.
> DUCH.   I pray, sir, tell me,
> For I can understand, although they say
> I have lost my wits; but they are safe enough,

And I shall have them when the Cardinal dies;
Who had a letter from his nephew, too,
Since he was slain.

    HER.   From whence?

    DUCH.   I do not know where he is. But in some
             bower
Within a garden he is making chaplets.
And means to send me one. But I 'll not take it.
I have flowers enough, I thank him, while I live.

    HER.   But do you love your governor?

    DUCH.   Yes, but I'll never marry him; I am promis'd
Already.

    HER.   To whom, madam?

    DUCH.   Do not you
Blush when you ask me that? Must not you be
My husband? I know why, but that's a secret.
Indeed, if you believe me, I do love
No man alive so well as you. The Cardinal
Shall never know't; he'll kill us both; and yet
He says he loves me dearly, and has promis'd
To make me well again; but I'm afraid,
One time or other, he will give me poison.

    HER.   Prevent him, madam, and take nothing from
             him.

    DUCH.   Why, do you think 'twill hurt me?

    HER.   It will kill you.

    DUCH.   I shall but die, and meet my dear-loved lord,
Whom, when I have kiss'd, I'll come again and work
A bracelet of my hair for you to carry him,
When you are going to heaven. The poesy shall

Be my own name, in little tears that I
Will weep next winter, which, congeal'd i' the frost,
Will show like seed-pearl.   You'll deliver it?
I know he'll love and wear it for my sake.
 HER. She is quite lost.
 DUCH.   Pray give me, sir, your pardon;
I know I talk not wisely; but if you had
The burthen of my sorrow, you would miss
Sometimes your better reason.   Now I'm well.
What will you do when the Cardinal comes?
He must not see you for the world.
 HER.   He shall not;
I'll take my leave before he comes.
 DUCH.   Nay, stay;
I shall have no friend left me when you go.
He will but sup; he shall not stay to lie with me;
I have the picture of my lord abed;
Three are too much this weather.

Enter PLACENTIA.

 PLA.   Madam, the Cardinal.
 HER. He shall sup with the devil.
 DUCH.   I dare not stay;
The red cock will be angry.   I'll come again.[8]

By such devices as this does Shirley maintain our
sympathy for the duchess Rosaura; but, besides pic-
turing a character that holds our sympathy, he has
here—contrary to his custom—pictured a character
that grows.   From a timorous maiden, hiding her

---

[8] *The Cardinal*, v, iii; *Works*, v, 341–343.

heart from Columbo and the world, she becomes first the woman that dares demand her freedom, appeal to the king, and hurl defiance at the cardinal, and then, widowed of d'Alvarez and crushed beneath the threefold power, the woman that dares to draw Hernando to her aid against Columbo and, by feigned insanity, so to entrap the cardinal that she may "be Alvarez' justicer."

Strongly contrasted with the intriguing duchess on the one hand and with the intriguing cardinal on the other are the two bold, outspoken soldiers, Hernando and Columbo—the former calmly, the latter passionately brave. In Columbo, Shirley has depicted a commander that makes his very impetuosity a means to victory, and that thinks to take a wife as he would take a town—by storm. That the vanquished have rights, he cannot comprehend; nor can he comprehend the fine nobility of Count d'Alvarez. Against a valiant swordsman, he scorns a base advantage; yet he is on the point of resenting the message of the duchess by slaying the duchess's messenger, and he vents his rage upon the duchess with the same brutality as his revenge upon d'Alvarez. He is perhaps most nearly magnificent in the scene of the assassination at the wedding, when he stays to justify his deed; yet more characteristic is his subsequent visit to the duchess:

PLACENTIA. Madam, here's Don Columbo says he
must

Speak with your grace.

DUCHESS. But he must not, I charge you.
None else wait? Is this well done,
To triumph in his tyranny? . . .

ANTONIO. Sir, you must not see her.

COLUMBO. Not see her? Were she cabled up above
The search of bullet or of fire, were she
Within her grave, and that the toughest mine
That ever nature teem'd and groan'd withal,
I would force some way to see her.—Do not fear
I come to court your madam; you are not worth
The humblest of my kinder thoughts. I come
To show the man you have provok'd, and lost,
And tell you what remains of my revenge.
Live, but never presume again to marry.
I'll kill the next at the altar, and quench all
The smiling tapers with his blood. If after,
You dare provoke the priest and heaven so much,
To take another, in thy bed I'll cut him from
Thy warm embrace, and throw his heart to ravens.

CELINDA. This will appear an unexampled cruelty.

COLUMBO. Your pardon, madam; rage and my
revenge

Not perfect took away my eyes. You are
A noble lady; this not worth your eye-beam,
One of so slight a making and so thin
An autumn leaf is of too great a value
To play which shall be soonest lost i' the air.

[352]

Be pleased to own me by some name, in your
Assurance; I despise to be receiv'd
There. Let her witness that I call you mistress;
Honour me to make these pearls your carkanet.[9]

Against this valiant brutality of Columbo, Shirley
paints the valiant nobility of Hernando. He pictures Hernando's wisdom at the council-board, his
self-control in the face of Columbo's accusation, his
brave devotion to the dead d'Alvarez and to the living duchess, his victory in the duel, his rescue of the
duchess from the cardinal, and his self-inflicted
death. Any of these scenes would be worth quoting;
but, for the sake of illustrating at once the directness
of Hernando and the indirection—or, perhaps, the
crescent bravery of the duchess, I select his meeting
with her after d'Alvarez' death:

HERNANDO.   I know not how your grace will
                        censure so
Much boldness, when you know the affairs I come for.
    DUCHESS.   My servant has prepar'd me to receive it,
If it concern my dead lord.
    HER.   Can you name
So much of your Alvarez in a breath,
Without one word of your revenge? O, madam,
I come to chide you, and repent my great
Opinion of your virtue, that can walk,

---

[9] *The Cardinal,* IV, ii; *Works,* V, 320-321.

And spend so many hours in naked solitude;
As if you thought that no arrears were due
To his death, when you had paid his funeral charges,
Made your eyes red, and wet a handkerchief.
I come to tell you that I saw him bleed;
I, that can challenge nothing in his name
And honour, saw his murder'd body warm,
And panting with the labour of his spirits,
Till my amazed soul shrunk and hid itself:
While barbarous Columbo grinning stood,
And mock'd the weeping wounds. It is too much
That you should keep your heart alive so long
After this spectacle, and not revenge it.

    DUCH.   You do not know the business of my heart,
That censure me so rashly; yet I thank you:
And, if you be Alvarez' friend, dare tell
Your confidence, that I despise my life,
But know not how to use it in a service,
To speak me his revenger. This will need
No other proof than that to you, who may
Be sent with cunning to betray me, I
Have made this bold confession. I so much
Desire to sacrifice to that hovering ghost
Colombo's life, that I am not ambitious
To keep my own two minutes after it.

    HER.   If you will call me coward, which is equal
To think I am a traitor, I forgive it,
For this brave resolution, which time
And all the destinies must aid. I beg
That I may kiss your hand for this; and may
The soul of angry honour guide it—

DUCH.   Whither?

HER.   To Don Columbo's heart.

DUCH.   It is too weak, I fear, alone.

HER.   Alone? Are you in earnest? Why, will it not
Be a dishonour to your justice, madam,
Another arm should interpose? But that
It were a saucy act to mingle with you,
I durst, nay, I am bound in the revenge
Of him that's dead, (since the whole world has interest
In every good man's loss,) to offer it:
Dare you command me, madam?

DUCH.   Not command;
But I should more than honour such a truth
In man, that durst, against so mighty odds,
Appear Alvarez' friend and mine. The Cardinal—

HER.   Is for the second course; Columbo must
Be first cut up; his ghost must lead the dance:
Let him die first.

DUCH.   But how?

HER.   How! with a sword; and, if I undertake it,
I will not lose so much of my own honour,
To kill him basely.

DUCH.   How shall I reward
This infinite service? 'Tis not modesty,
While now my husband groans beneath his tomb,
And calls me to his marble bed, to promise
What this great act might well deserve, myself,
If you survive the victor. But if thus
Alvarez' ashes be appeas'd, it must
Deserve an honourable memory;
And though Columbo (as he had all power,

And grasp'd the fates) has vowed to kill the man
That shall succeed Alvarez—
    HER.   Tyranny!
    DUCH.   Yet, if ever
I entertain a thought of love hereafter,
Hernando from the world shall challenge it;
Till when, my prayers and fortune shall wait on you.
    HER.   This is too mighty recompense.
    DUCH.   'Tis all just.
    HER.   If I outlive Columbo, I must not
Expect security at home.
    DUCH.   Thou canst
Not fly where all my fortunes and my love
Shall not attend to guard thee.
    HER.   If I die—
    DUCH.   Thy memory
Shall have a shrine, the next within my heart
To my Alvarez.
    HER.   Once again your hand.
Your cause is so religious you need not
Strengthen it with your prayers; trust it to me.
    PLACENTIA.   Madam, the Cardinal.
    DUCH.   Will you appear?
    HER.   An he had all the horror of the devil
In's face, I would not baulk him.[10]

Last comes the cardinal; a subtle statesman subtly
drawn. Shirley shows us but little of his doings: his
means we know not; but we feel his might. How the

[10] *The Cardinal.* IV, ii; *Works,* V, 322–325.

cardinal forced the betrothal of the duchess to his nephew, and how, after the bold assassination, he secured that nephew's pardon—or, better still, release without a pardon—we are not told; we know only that the thing is done; we marvel and we fear. And just as Shirley makes us feel the cardinal's power without letting us behold its operation, so Shirley makes us feel the cardinal's wickedness almost without specific crime. With the exception of that portion of the final scene in which the cardinal endeavors to betray the duchess, he is ever the reverend churchman, full of regret at the evil he beholds. His hypocritical remorse before his death is typical of his life; his needless self-destruction, a dramatic master-stroke of irony:

CARDINAL.   I have deserv'd you should turn from me,
                    sir:
My life hath been prodigiously wicked;
My blood is now the kingdom's balm. Oh, sir,
I have abus'd your ear, your trust, your people,
And my own sacred office; my conscience
Feels now the sting. Oh, shew your charity
And with your pardon, like a cool soft gale,
Fan my poor sweating soul, that wanders through
Unhabitable climes and parched deserts.—
But I am lost, if the great world forgive me,
Unless I find your mercy for a crime
You know not, madam, yet, against your life,

I must confess, more than my black intents
Upon your honour; you're already poisoned.

 KING. By whom?

 CAR.   By me,
In the revenge I ow'd Columbo's loss;
With your last meat was mix'd a poison, that
By subtle and by sure degrees must let
In death.

 KING. Look to the duchess, our physicians!

 CAR.   Stay.
I will deserve her mercy, though I cannot
Call back the deed. In proof of my repentance,
If the last breath of a now dying man
May gain your charity and belief, receive
This ivory box; in it an antidote
'Bove that they boast the great magistral medicine:
That powder, mix'd with wine, by a most rare
And quick access to the heart, will fortify it
Against the rage of the most nimble poison.
I am not worthy to present her with it.
Oh, take it, and preserve her innocent life.

 1 LORD. Strange, he should have a good thing in such
      readiness.

 CAR. 'Tis that which in my jealousy and state,
Trusting to false predictions of my birth,
That I should die by poison, I preserv'd
For my own safety. Wonder not, I made
That my companion was to be my refuge.

    Enter SERVANT, *with a bowl of wine.*

 1 LORD. Here is some touch of grace.

CAR.   In greater proof of my pure thoughts, I take
This first, and with my dying breath confirm
My penitence; it may benefit her life,
But not my wounds.   Oh, hasten to preserve her;
And though I merit not her pardon, let not
Her fair soul be divorced.

The DUCHESS *takes the bowl and drinks.*

KING.   This is some charity; may it prosper, madam!
VALERIA.   How does your grace?
DUCH.   And I must owe my life to him whose death
Was my ambition?   Take this free acknowledgment;
I had intent, this night, with my own hand
To be Alvarez' justicer.
KING.   You were mad,
And thought past apprehension of revenge.
DUCH.   That shape I did usurp, great sir, to give
My art more freedom and defence; but when
Hernando came to visit me, I thought
I might defer my execution;
Which his own rage supplied without my guilt,
And, when his lust grew high, met with his blood.
1 LORD.   The Cardinal smiles.
CAR.   Now my revenge has met
With you, my nimble duchess!   I have took
A shape to give my act more freedom too,
And now I am sure she's poison'd with that dose
I gave her last.
KING.   Thou'rt not so horrid!
DUCH.   Ha! some cordial.
CAR.   Alas, no preservative

[359]

Hath wings to overtake it. Were her heart
Lock'd in a quarry, it would search, and kill
Before the aids can reach it. I am sure
You shall not now laugh at me.

   KING. How came you by that poison?

   CAR.   I prepar'd it,
Resolving, when I had enjoy'd her, which
The colonel prevented, by some art
To make her take it, and by death conclude
My last revenge. You have the fatal story.

   KING. This is so great a wickedness, it will
Exceed belief.

   CAR.   I knew I could not live.

   SURG. Your wounds, sir, were not desperate.

   CAR. Not mortal? Ha! Were they not mortal?

   SURG. If I have skill in surgery.

   CAR. Then I have caught myself in my own engine.

   2 LORD. It was your fate, you said, to die by poison.

   CAR. That was my own prediction, to abuse
Your faith; no human art can now resist it;
I feel it knocking at the seat of life;
It must come in; I have wreck'd all my own,
To try your charities: now it would be rare, —
If you but waft me with a little prayer;
My wings that flag may catch the wind; but 'tis
In vain; the mist is risen, and there's none
To steer my wand'ring bark.[11]

   In the creation and delineation of character, as in
the mastery of plot and scene, we have found reason

[11] *The Cardinal,* v, iii; *Works,* v, 348–351.

highly to commend the work of Shirley in *The Cardinal*. Were we likewise to discuss its language—its poetic form—we might add a commendation more; indeed, the frequent beauty of its verse must be already evident from incidental illustration. To say all this of a play that attempted, in the year 1641, to present once more the Websterian round of revenge, depravity, and rape, is no small praise. Shirley was correct in his opinion that this play might "rival with his best." [12] Save for his own modesty, he might have added that, even when measured with the best work of his contemporaries, Shirley's *The Cardinal* must be accounted a notable romantic tragedy.

[12] Prologue to *The Cardinal; Works*, v, 275.

CHAPTER XVIII

THE THIRD DRAMATIC PERIOD—CONCLUDED

THE SISTERS AND *THE COURT SECRET*

IN our series of eleven plays surviving from Shirley's third, and final, period, we come now to the last two of his productions: *The Sisters* and *The Court Secret*. These two plays—like his other dramas of this period, with the exception of *The Politique Father* and *The Constant Maid*—belong not to the realistic but to the romantic school. Neither play is a notable achievement; but each is thoroughly entertaining, and both are representative of the style of play that Shirley himself seems most to have enjoyed.

Last of the plays of Shirley to be acted on the stage, *The Sisters,* licensed April 26, 1642, is a gay mixture of romantic comedy and farce. Three stories mingle in its plot: the fortunes of a proud sister and a humble sister, of whom each comes to her reward; the amusing rogueries of a bandit chief, trapped at last in his own net; and the familiar but pretty romance of the maiden-page, who, sent a-wooing by the man she loves, becomes the object of his mistress's passion.

Rarely in the minor Elizabethan drama are three actions more effectively combined: each part seems absolutely essential to the others. No criticism apparently could be less apt than that of Ward, that *The Sisters* seems "rather hastily put together";[1] or than the similar remark of Dibdin that the play "is not well hung together."[2] Slight in substance, *The Sisters* is excellent in matters of technique, and especially in this matter of structural unity.

In the dominions of Farnese, Prince of Parma, dwell two noble sisters, Paulina and Angellina. The former, extravagant and insolently proud, drives to despair Antonio, their uncle. The latter, modest, gentle, and destined for a nunnery, he finds as difficult to convert to worldliness as her sister to true gentlehood. Paulina is resolved to wed no less a husband than the Prince of Parma; and in this ambition she is confirmed by the prophecy of a band of wandering astrologers. These astrologers, who in reality are Frapolo and his banditti in disguise, return presently to Paulina's castle, impersonating now the Prince of Parma and his train. Paulina, completely deceived, accepts Frapolo as her husband, and prepares to depart with him to court, with all her plate and jewels.

Meanwhile, however, the true Prince of Parma

[1] Ward, *English Dramatic Literature*, III, 118.
[2] Dibdin, *A Complete History of the Stage*, IV, 44.

has arrived, brought partly by a desire to behold Paulina in her pride, partly to win Angellina for his follower, Lord Contarini. At sight of Angellina, the prince falls in love with her himself, and, forgetful of his follower, becomes her suitor. She answers that she has already bestowed her heart upon Lord Contarini's page, Vergerio. Her avowal and the resulting discomfiture of prince and lord bring forth a revelation: Vergerio the page is Pulcheria, daughter of the Viceroy of Sicily and Lord Contarini's former mistress, whom he believed to be dead. Lord Contarini turns promptly to his regained Pulcheria; and as Pulcheria, unlike Shakspere's Viola, can supply no brother Sebastian in her stead, the loving Angellina makes shift to accept the hand and scepter of the Prince of Parma.

It remains, however, to unmask the bandit chieftain Frapolo at Paulina's castle; and so Farnese confronts his counterfeit. At first, Frapolo boldly plays the prince; but finding himself detected and escape cut off, he confesses the deception. The pride of Paulina takes a mighty tumble; but the worst—or best—is yet to come: her nurse—supposing that Paulina is about to be married to the *real* Farnese—reveals the fact that Paulina is but a supposititious child, own daughter to the nurse. The blunt old uncle voices the sentiments of all: "Why, there's a

baggage and a thief well met then!"[3]   The haughty
sister is married to the bandit chief; the gentle sister
to the Prince of Parma.

As compared with his mastery of plot, Shirley's
mastery of characterization in *The Sisters* is less conspicuous: as so often happens in these romantic plays,
the character-drawing is adequate rather than remarkable.   And yet, even in this character-drawing,
the work of Shirley in *The Sisters* is far from commonplace.   Antonio, the "old, blunt, brave" uncle of
the pair; the two sisters, admirably contrasted; Frapolo, the magnetic and audacious bandit; and, most
entertaining of all, the credulous, cowardly, unfilial
Piperollo: all these are not only clearly delineated
but capitally conceived.   Of Shirley's power both of
conception and delineation of character, the opening
scene, in which Frapolo rallies his frightened followers, is an excellent example; but an even better example is the scene in which Frapolo, at the very end,
attempts for a moment to outface the true Prince of
Parma and his following:

FRAPOLO.   Can you stand
The dazzling sun so long, and be not struck
Blind for this bold affront?   What wildness brought you,
In multitudes, to fright my happy peace,
And this good lady's, my most virtuous consort?

[3] *The Sisters,* v, ii; *Works,* v, 422.

LONGINO.   He bears up still!   [*Aside.*]

FRAP.   Have all my cares and watchings to preserve
Your lives and dearest liberties deserv'd
This strange return, and at a time when most
Your happiness is concern'd? since, by our marriage
With this sweet lady, full of grace and beauty,
You may expect an heir to bless your country.

CONTARINI.   Will you suffer him?

FRAP.   'Tis time your prince were dead; and when
                I am
Companion to my father's dust, these tumults,
Fomented by seditious men, that are
Weary of plenty and delights of peace,
Shall not approach to interrupt the calm
Good princes after death enjoy.   Go home,
I pray; depart: I rather will submit
To be depos'd, than wear a power or title
That shall not all be dedicate to serve you.
My life is but the gift of Heaven, to waste it
For your dear sakes.   My people are my children,
Whom I am bound in nature and religion
To cherish and protect.   Perhaps you have
Some grievance to present.   You shall have justice
Against the proudest here: I look not on
Nobility of birth, office, or fortunes;
The poorest subject has a native charter,
And a birthright to the laws and commonwealth,
Which, with an equal and impartial stream,
Shall flow to every bosom.

STROZZO.   Pious Prince!

FARNESE. I am at a loss to hear him. Sure I am
Farnese, if I be not lost by the way.

PIPEROLLO. Stand off, gentlemen,—let me see—
which? Hum! this?—no; th'other? Hum! send for a
lion, and turn him loose; he will not hurt the true prince.

FARN. Do not you know me, sir?

FRAP. Yes, I know you too well; but it stands not
with my honour. What composition?

FARN. Who am I?—Gentlemen, how dare you suffer
This thing to talk, if I be your Farnese?

FRAP. I say I am the prince.

FARN. Prince of what?

FRAP. Of rogues, an please your excellence.[4]

This passage shows something of Shirley's power
both for the conception and for the delineation of
comic character; yet even more delicious for character and for action are the two scenes in which Frapolo and his banditti as astrologers prophesy that
Lucio and Piperollo shall be robbed, and then, in
their own persons, carry out the prophecy. In the
first of these scenes, two of the banditti have prophesied that the steward, Lucio, shall be made a lord,
and that Piperollo his servant shall become a knight.
At that moment, Frapolo enters; and to him the steward and the knave appeal for a verification of their
respective fortunes:

[4] *The Sisters*, v, ii; *Works*, v, 420–421.

LUCIO.   Sir, if you please, till my lady return, to satisfy her steward and oblige him by your art—one of your under mathematics has given me a comfortable destiny.

FRAPOLO.   Your hand.   Where were you born?

LUC.   I know not, sir.

RANCONE.   A lord—   [RAN. *whispers* FRAP.]

FRAP.   No matter; Venus, in the ascendant with Sol, being lady of your seventh—hum! hum! with Jupiter, designs you to be a lord.

LUC.   They all agree; the miracle of learning!—One question more, I beseech you, sir.   I am to ride with my man to receive my lady's rent to-morrow, through the forest.

FRAP.   Go to!

LUC.   Now, I desire to know whether we shall be robb'd in our return, or no?

FRAP.   What time do you think precisely to come back, sir? for we should know the very minute.

LUC.   The money is ready, sir, and we do purpose— in your ear—

FRAP.   Yes, you shall be robb'd; there's nothing in nature to prevent it.

PIPEROLLO.   Will they kill us, an please you?

FRAP.   No, they shall not kill you; they shall only take your money, and break your pate; that will be all.

PIPEROLLO.   Why, let them rob us, sir; the loss of our money will be an evidence of our preferment, and you may have more assurance to be a lord, and I of my knighthood.[5]

[5] *The Sisters,* III, i; *Works,* v, 385–386.

Accordingly, on the morning following, Lucio and Piperollo, with their thousand pistoles of rent, pass through the forest; and Piperollo, fearful lest they escape the attention of the outlaws, sets up such a whooping that Frapolo and his men imagine, for the moment, that some stratagem is to be played upon them: then they grasp the situation—and the victims:

STROZZO. The gentleman is very merry. They that mean well, and have their wits about them, do not use to call upon our tribe. This is a plot, a very plot: and yet the coast is clear. . . . 'Tis my proud madam's steward and our quondam fellow thief; they were told their fortunes to be robb'd. Here had been a purchase lost, if I had not lain perdu.—You shall be dispatch'd presently, never fear it. [*He whistles.*]

LUC. What's that? I do not like that tune.

PIP. Hum! I am not in love with that quail-pipe. I could dwindle, but that I have a strong faith in the mathematics. Thieves, an't be thy will!

LUC. If they should cut our throats now—this is your folly. Would I were off!

PIP. Would I were a knight in an embroidered dishclout! Have a good heart, sir; there's no more to be said in't; let the stars take their course; 'tis my lady's money; and if we be robb'd, we are so much the nearer to preferment.

Re-enter FRAPOLO *and the rest, masked and disguised.*

LUC. Ah, sweet gentlemen, take but the money—

PIP. 'Tis ready told; nay, nay, we are friends. Give

us but a note under your hands for my lady's satisfaction, that you have received it, gentlemen.

LUC. You need not trouble yourselves to tell it, gentlemen; it is all right.

LONGINO. So, so! we'll take your words.

PIP. I should know that vizard; the garments that you wear too I have seen.—Old acquaintance!

FRAP. Does he know you? Cut his throat.

PIP. No, sir, I do not know him, nor any man, nor myself; I was not once robbed before, neither did I help any man to rob my own father and mother! I knew no cedar chest, I; I disclaim it; nor was any man that I knew left bound for the money. You are all honest gentlemen, and I congratulate our good fortune that you came so luckily in the very nick; we had carried home the money else in good sadness.—Sir, we are made for ever.—Rare mathematicians!

FRAP. What's that you talk, sirrah, of mathematicians?

PIP. It pleased some of the learned tribe to visit my lady not long since; but they are well, I hope; they told us we should be robb'd and 'tis done; blessed Chaldean!

FRAP. What became of them?

PIP. They 'scaped a scouring; for my lady's cynical uncle, in mere malice to learning, rais'd the clowns upon them, persuading the Hobbinols they came to rob the house; but honoured be the stars! they brought them off at the back gate.

FRAP. They seem honest fellows; let them live, and pass.

Luc. We humbly thank you, gentlemen.—Come, Piperollo.

Pip. And yet, now I remember, there wants a circumstance. My pate is not broke yet; there was a clause. The Chaldean was a little out.

Frap. I had forgot. [*Aside.*]—Will you be prating, sirrah? [*He breaks his head.*]

Pip. Now 'tis done; I thank you, dear gentlemen, I thank you; *go forth, and be a knight!* Mathematician, I adore thee. It bleeds. Where are you, sir? all is complete, and my head is broke, according to prophecy. Oh, admirable Chaldean![6]

These extracts, introduced to show Shirley's mastery of characterization in the persons of Frapolo and Piperollo, illustrate even more his mastery of wholesome comedy. From the farce of the supposed astrologers picking pockets while they decipher palms, to the pure character-comedy of Piperollo, complaining because his head has not been broken, Shirley, in these and other scenes, justifies amply the remark of Swinburne that *The Sisters* is a "very spirited and amusing comedy."[7] Professor Schelling, as if in echo of Dibdin and of Ward, speaks of the play as "hasty and unworthy."[8] That *The Sisters* is

[6] *The Sisters,* IV, i; *Works,* V, 394–396.

[7] A. C. Swinburne, "James Shirley," in *The Fortnightly Review,* LIII (n.s. XLVII), 476.

[8] Schelling, *Elizabethan Drama,* II, 322.

not Shirley's greatest comedy, we may readily concede; but, this granted, I for one am still of the opinion that, both for its fun and for its romance, *The Sisters* is at once well done and genuinely delightful.

Last of all the plays of Shirley is *The Court Secret,* a dramatic romance, or, as the title-page calls it, "A Tragi-Comedy: Never Acted, But prepared for the Scene at Black-Friers."[9] For romantic subject and for effectiveness of plot, this play is at once an appropriate and a worthy conclusion to the long list of Shirley's dramas.

Piracquo, a nobleman of Spain, has been forced in youth to play the pirate; but, having thus amassed great wealth and having long resided in high favor at the court of Portugal, he has been brought back from banishment by the Spanish prince Don Carlo, heir to the throne. With him has come Piracquo's son, Don Manuel, Prince Carlo's friend. The fortunes of this Don Manuel form the subject of the play.

On his arrival at the court of Spain, Don Manuel falls in love with Clara, daughter of Duke Mendoza. Clara returns his love, but various forces (as is necessary in dramatic romance) proceed to intervene. At the very outset, Maria the infanta falls in love with

[9] From the title-page of the copy of the 1653 edition in the possession of the present writer.

Manuel—despite the fact that a marriage is pending between Maria and Antonio, the Prince of Portugal. In the second place, Maria's royal brother Carlo—although all but betrothed to the Portuguese princess Isabella, sister of Antonio—is madly in love with Mendoza's daughter Clara. Thus the love of Manuel and Clara is from both sides royally assailed; Manuel must be rival to his patron, Prince Carlo; Clara to her bosom friend, Maria the infanta; and meanwhile, both Carlo and Maria are slighting the Portuguese alliance and the wishes of the king, their father.

This complicated situation, Shirley indicates rapidly and admirably in the opening scene; and even there he adds two further complications. The first of these is the interference of Roderigo, the king's brother: he reveals to the Prince of Portugal, Antonio, the fact that Prince Carlo courts Clara instead of Isabella; he makes Antonio suspicious of the relations of Maria and Manuel; he arouses Carlo's anger at Manuel's alleged presumption in thus courting Carlo's sister; and he attempts to blackmail Manuel's father, Piracquo, by threatening to prevent the sealing of his pardon. The second outside complication, barely hinted in the opening scene but destined to prove of great importance, is the fact that one Pedro, who is at once a kinsman of Piracquo and a servant to

[373]

Duke Mendoza, has possession of a certain secret. This secret appears to involve Mendoza in some long-hidden treason, and to concern the identity of Prince Carlo and our hero, Don Manuel.

As a result of his ill-founded jealousy of Manuel, Prince Antonio provokes him to a combat, and thus unintentionally occasions the imprisonment of Manuel. This imprisonment, in turn, brings about two meetings: one between Clara and Maria, the other between Manuel and Prince Carlo. The first reveals to Clara and the princess that they are rivals for the love of Manuel; and the second similarly reveals to Manuel and Prince Carlo that they are rivals for the love of Clara. Prince Carlo secures Don Manuel's release from prison and his reconciliation with Prince Antonio. Manuel in turn, moved by Carlo's generosity, promises Carlo to set Clara free and leave her to choose between him and the prince. She accepts her liberty—and forthwith renews her pledge to Manuel. Prince Carlo, vowing vengeance, secretly appoints a meeting with Don Manuel. Clara suspects; but Manuel assures her that the prince would never wound him basely and that nothing shall tempt him to lift sword against the prince. Repairing to the place appointed, Manuel hears loud cries for help: Prince Carlo's page runs toward him, declaring that a Moor has slain his master and that the Moor pursues. Manuel, hastening to Carlo's rescue, meets the Moor; they fight; the Moor falls—and proves to be Prince Carlo in disguise.

Meanwhile, the princess Isabella has arrived unheralded from Portugal—and Prince Carlo is nowhere to be found. The court is distracted at his untimely absence. His fate is announced in person by Don Manuel, himself the murderer! Duke Mendoza —even beyond Carlo's royal father—is clamorous for vengeance. Prince Antonio and Piracquo intervene: the former presents the testimony of the dying Carlo that Manuel fought believing himself the avenger of Carlo on the Moor; the latter declares that the man guilty of "the prince's loss" is not Don Manuel but Duke Mendoza! And thereupon, Mendoza, with Pedro as a witness, confesses what he knows of the court secret: the murdered prince is not the real Prince Carlo, but is Julio, Mendoza's son, substituted in infancy when the royal child was stolen from his nurse, Mendoza's wife.

Subsequently, from the imprisoned duke Mendoza, his daughter Clara hears in full the story: Prince Carlo, who has courted her, is in fact her brother; and the murderer of this brother is her lover, Manuel! And yet, she cannot curse him. She goes to Manuel's cell, and finds Maria there. He, ignorant of the identity of the slain prince Carlo, is using the murder as a means to cure the princess of her love for him. Maria declares that she can forgive him even the death of Carlo. Then Manuel, to bring the princess to her reason, asks Clara to play Maria's part; to answer as the princess how she can love the man that slew the prince her brother. And Clara, who knows that the slain man is not Maria's brother but her own, declares that she can still forgive and love the slayer. Manuel, fearful lest Clara's words encourage the princess, declares emphatically that their love can never meet; and Clara, forgetful that she but plays the princess, swoons at the words. The princess and Manuel soon revive her; and the princess, touched by the love of Manuel and Clara, resigns her rivalry for Manuel's love, and reveals the identity of the murdered Carlo. Maria's decision ultimately involves her acceptance of Prince Antonio.

But Julio, the pseudo-Carlo, is not dead. Despite the wounds inflicted by Don Manuel, he soon recovers; and Isabella, Princess of Portugal, to whom while lying wounded he has sent messages praying her forgiveness, decides that she loves the man and not the title: that Julio, son of Duke Mendoza, shall receive her hand. Since Julio-Carlo lives, Don Manuel is freed from prison to be joined by Clara. Only the king mourns: he has lost an heir, and he vows that Duke Mendoza, responsible for the infant Carlo's loss, shall pay the penalty. Again Piracquo intervenes and, with Pedro as a witness, reveals the second part of the court secret: the pirate that stole young Carlo was—Piracquo! the true prince Carlo lives; Piracquo's "son," Don Manuel, is this royal heir!

Such is *The Court Secret:* a dramatic romance turning upon a double imposture. Rarely among the complicated plots of Shirley is the complication at once more elaborate and more firmly knit. The mutual love of Manuel and Clara is assailed on the one hand by the love of the infanta Maria for Don Manuel—her brother, though she knows it not—and on the other hand by the love of the supposed prince Carlo for Clara—his sister, as he later finds. These two complicating passions are complicated in their turn by the pending alliance of Maria with Antonio, Prince of Portugal, and by that of the supposed Carlo with Antonio's sister Isabella. And all through the play, Piracquo, protector of the hero, and Roderigo, his arch-enemy, struggle for the mastery, and give visual embodiment to the contending fates; while Duke Mendoza, timorous of conscience, and his servant Pedro, mocking at his fears, keep ever before us the unknown but inevitable solution—the impending revelation of the fatal secret.

Perhaps it is in this very combination of suspense and of surprise as methods of holding the interest to the end, that Shirley, in *The Court Secret,* shows his greatest mastery. Coleridge, in listing the characteristics that, in his opinion, distinguish Shakspere from all other dramatic poets, places first Shakspere's use of "expectation in preference to surprise." [10] Surprise, on the other hand, seems the method most frequently employed in the dramatic romances of Fletcher. That Shirley, in *The Court Secret,* succeeds in combining these seemingly opposed devices into one: that he gains the interest of suspense by making us expect at any moment the revelation of the all-controlling secret, and yet at the same time gains the interest of surprise by keeping us utterly in the dark as to what this secret is: that Shirley succeeds in doing this, is, I feel, no small achievement. From the method of Shakspere and from the method of Fletcher, Shirley has seized the distinguishing essentials, has reconciled their seeming conflict, and has utilized them both in the plot-structure of this his final play.

Of the characterization of *The Court Secret,* little need be said. Except in the Mendoza-Pedro scenes, it is the characterization of Fletcherian romance, not

[10] Coleridge, *Complete Works* (edited by Shedd, New York, 1884), IV, 61.

the characterization of Shaksperian comedy: it exists
to tell the story, not to make it. The brave and generous princes, the devoted ladies, the stanch Piracquo,
the impotent king, the intriguing Roderigo: all are
pleasing embodiments of the familiar types. Even
the frightened duke Mendoza and his bold confederate Pedro—who at times lift the play into the realm
of comedy of character—are but an amusing reversal
of the audacious Lorenzo of *The Traitor* and his timorous Depazzi. Not in his characters but in his plot
lay Shirley's interest.

Thus, with a typical romance, we conclude our register of Shirley's plays. Allied in subject-matter, in
tone, and in method to *The Imposture* and to *The
Doubtful Heir, The Court Secret* represents far better than *The Sisters* or *The Cardinal* or *The Politique Father* the type of drama that Shirley most frequently produced: a type that presents not farce or
humors or manners on the one hand, or psychological
or even romantic tragedy on the other; but rather a
type of drama that leads hero and heroine into romantic complications seemingly inextricable, only to
end by lifting them out of prison or slaughter to a
throne; in short, the type of drama that springs from
Fletcherian romance, and that needs only a more
strenuous and blatant hero to be accepted as an ances-
tor of the "heroic" drama of the Restoration. For

the last play in a period dominated by romantic drama, for the last play in a career presenting, as we have seen, a struggle between realism and romanticism, and ending in the victory of the latter, no drama could be more appropriate than *The Court Secret*.

SUMMARY

FROM a consideration of Shirley's final play as typical of his interests and his art, I pass now to a reconsideration of his final period. Out of the eleven extant plays belonging to the years 1636–1642, only two —*The Constant Maid* and *The Brothers*—belong to the school in which Shirley began his work, the realistic school of Jonson and of Fletcher. Neither of these, moreover, is particularly effective work. *The Constant Maid,* although purporting to give a picture of London life and manners, is interesting only for the rather conventional usurer and country gull, and for the succession of surprises that constitute the plot. Were this frankly a romantic play, we might enjoy these perversities of fortune; but in a realistic setting, they are too improbable to be entertaining. *The Brothers,* although better than *The Constant Maid,* in that it has a fairly clever plot and a few tolerably amusing characters, is saved, after all, only by an infusion of romantic atmosphere and pleasing verse—an infusion which, in view of the nature of its subject, weakens rather than strengthens its artistic unity. Whatever merit belongs to the plays of Shirley's closing period, is not to be found in these two comedies of manners.

When, however, from these two comedies of the realistic school, we turn to the nine romantic plays belonging to this period, we find, beside the nonsense of *St. Patrick for Ireland* and the repulsiveness of *The Gentleman of Venice,* a list of plays distinctly worth our reading. The gay farce of *The Sisters;* the involved plots and surprising resolutions of the three Fletcherian dramatic romances, *The Doubtful Heir, The Imposture,* and *The Court Secret;* the exquisite romantic comedy of *The Royal Master;* the somber grandeur of *The Politician;* and, most notable of all, the tragic struggle and well-drawn protagonists of *The Traitor:* all these not only mark Shirley as a master playwright, but prove, beyond a doubt, our thesis that Shirley's strength and Shirley's interest lie ultimately not in the realistic but in the romantic school. He began his career as a follower of Jonson and of Fletcher in realism; he concluded it as a follower of Shakspere and of Fletcher in romance.

CHAPTER XIX

CONCLUSION

THE endeavor of the foregoing chapters has been threefold: first, to examine the little that we know of Shirley's life, to determine, fact by fact, the value of the evidence, and, on a basis of this critical examination, to construct a chronology more accurate than has been hitherto available; second, on a basis of this revised chronology, to restudy the dramatic works of Shirley in order to determine, if possible, the course of his development as a dramatist; and, third, from this same examination of the plays, to determine the distinctive characteristics of his dramatic works.

Extensive as is the field attempted, it covers, after all, but a small portion of the subject-matter suggested by the title "James Shirley, Dramatist." One would gladly consider, for example, not merely (as we have done) the *schools* to which Shirley's several plays belong, but also (as we have done but rarely) specific instances of his indebtedness to specific plays of his predecessors and contemporaries.[1] Particularly

[1] Since I wrote these lines, this topic has been ably treated in Forsythe, *The Relations of Shirley's Plays to the Elizabethan Drama*, 1914.

interesting, for instance, would be an examination of the probable influence of Webster upon Shirley's tragedies. Again, one would gladly dwell upon the topic announced, a dozen years ago, by Nissen:[2] the relation of Shirley to his sources. Especially would one dwell upon his use of material from the Spanish, a field opened by Stiefel in his comparison of *The Opportunity* with *El Castigo del Penséque* of Tirso de Molina, and continued in his comparison of *The Young Admiral* with Lope de Vega's *Don Lope de Cardona*.[3] Still more interesting and, I believe, less understood, is the relation of Shirley to his successors: the position of his comedies of London life and manners as a link between Elizabethan and Restoration comedy; and of his dramatic romances as a link between Fletcherian romance and the "heroic" plays of Dryden and of Otway. Adequately, however, to consider any one of these three topics, would demand a separate volume. The present monograph must be content to cover the field originally proposed: the chronology, the course of development, and the distinctive characteristics of the dramatic work of Shirley.

[2] Nissen, p. 26, note.
[3] A. L. Stiefel, "Die Nachahmung spanischer Komödien in England unter den ersten Stuarts," in *Romanische Forschungen,* v, 1890; and in *Archiv für das Studium der neueren Sprachen und Literaturen,* CXIX, 1907.

JAMES SHIRLEY, DRAMATIST

I

IN the chronological portion of our study, our endeavor has been not so much to gather new material
as to verify the data and weigh anew the inferences of
previous biographers. Important has it been to verify
even their citations from Herbert's license-list, from
the Stationers' Register, and from the title-pages of
the first editions of the works of Shirley; for, as we
have had occasion frequently to note, errors, typographical and otherwise, have crept in and have been
handed on: Fleay, in *Anglia,* has made at least seven
errors of mere date, and Ward, in the *Dictionary of
National Biography,* has made as many more.[4] Important also has it been to eliminate the imaginative touches that have appeared even in articles purporting to be contributions to exact scholarship—the
conjectures of one biographer that, in the work of his
successor, have strangely been transformed to certainties—and to distinguish, in the account of Wood
and other secondary sources, between the certain, the
probable, and the merely possible. Especially important has it been to analyze the logic of the arguments by which the Shirleian annalists have sought
to establish facts for which direct evidence is lacking:
to show wherein they have established their hypothe-

[4] Cf. the list of misprints under "Fleay" and "Ward" in the Bibliography.

[384]

ses, and to point out wherein their inferences are as yet unwarranted. By this twofold process of verification and logical analysis, we have built up a Shirleian chronology—differing not greatly from that heretofore accepted; not final, let us hope, for many interesting problems remain yet for solution; but, at least, typographically more accurate and logically more circumspect than any chronology of Shirley previously proposed.

Concerning the private life of Shirley, our conclusions have been very largely negative. We have seen that the old-time hypotheses concerning the parentage of Shirley are without foundation; that his life, from leaving Merchant Taylors' School in 1612 to the beginning of his dramatic career in 1625, is a subject of which we know with certainty almost nothing—unless we accept as certain the unsupported statements of Anthony à Wood, a generation subsequent to Shirley's death; that, in view of the distinction between Beeston's "Queen's men" of Drury Lane and Turner's "Queen's men" of Salisbury Court of later date, Shirley's alleged quarrel with the latter, upon his return from Ireland in 1640, is wholly mythical; that concerning his service under Newcastle, we have no reliable details: in short, that our certain knowledge of the private life of Shirley is limited, except for an occasional allusion in his dedications, to the contents of five documents: the record of the christening of "James the sonne of James Sharlie" and other entries referring to their family, in the register of St. Mary Woolchurch; the probation register of Merchant Taylors' School; the record of the christening of "Mathias, sonne of Mr. James Shurley, gentleman" at St. Giles without Cripplegate; Shirley's will —a document significant not only for the extensive bequests which it records but also for its specific mention of Mathias as Shirley's eldest son; and, finally, the passage in the burial register of St. Giles in the Fields for October 29, 1666.

With regard, however, to Shirley's life as dramatist, we have abundant data. Malone, in his extracts from the office-book of Sir Henry Herbert, Master of the Revels, has preserved an almost complete list of the dates when Shirley's plays were licensed for presentation. The dates on which his plays and other works were entered for publication are accessible in Arber's excellent transcript of the Stationers' Register. The dates of actual publication, the names of the companies by whom the dramas were presented, and many other facts of consequence, are preserved to us on the title-pages of the works themselves; and the lists of published works appended to *The Maid's Revenge,* 1639, and to *The Cardinal,* 1652, warrant the belief that all the works actually published, except the first edition of *Echo and Narcissus,* have survived. The most important of the questions in dispute—the truth of Fleay's hypothesis that *The Brothers* of 1652 is identical not with *The Brothers* of 1626 but with *The Politique Father* of 1641, has been determined, conclusively I trust, by Nissen's argument from the dedication to Thomas Stanley, Esq., and by the extract (first published in the present monograph) from Moseley's catalogue in the Hoe copy of the *Six New Playes.* In short, for our purposed study of Shirley's development as a dramatist, our chronology of his works is practically complete.

II

HAVING thus determined, so far as available evidence permits, the chronology of Shirley's life and works, we endeavored, secondly, to ascertain the course of Shirley's development as a dramatist. In the plays of Shirley, we distinguished two broad types: first, that in which Shirley's work is to be classed with the realistic plays of Fletcher and of Jonson; and, second, that in which it is to be classed with the romantic plays of Fletcher and of Shakspere. The emphasis given by some editors and critics to *The Witty Fair One, Hyde Park, The Gamester,* and *The Lady of Pleasure* has at times given the impression that Shir-

ley was chiefly a writer of comedy of manners—and
of manners most repulsive. How far from accurate
is this impression will appear from a recapitulation
of our critical survey.

In what we have called his first dramatic period—
from 1625 to 1632—the work of Shirley was, indeed,
chiefly realistic. Three and a half plays of this period may be counted on the romantic side: *The
Maid's Revenge* and *The Traitor* are romantic tragedies; *The Grateful Servant* is romantic comedy; and
Love Tricks, or The School of Complement is in part
romantic, especially in the pastoral scenes. But
against these must be reckoned seven and a half plays
belonging to the realistic school. At least half of
Love Tricks, and practically all of *The Wedding,
The Witty Fair One, The Humorous Courtier,
Love's Cruelty, Changes, or Love in a Maze, Hyde
Park,* and *The Ball,* are realistic. Moreover, were
we to accept the old assumption (which I trust we
have refuted) that the play published as *The Brothers* in 1652 is identical with the play licensed under
that title in 1626, we should but strengthen our gen-
eralization that Shirley began his career as a follower of the realistic school of Jonson and of
Fletcher.

In Shirley's second dramatic period, however, this
proportion of three and a half romantic plays to seven

and a half realistic plays is practically reversed. In this period from 1632 to 1636, only three plays—*The Gamester, The Example,* and *The Lady of Pleasure* —can be counted as realistic; the other six—*The Arcadia, The Bird in a Cage, The Young Admiral, The Opportunity, The Coronation,* and *The Duke's Mistress*—are romantic. Were we to include in our estimate, *Chabot, Admiral of France,* which we have concluded to be primarily by Chapman, we should have, for this second period, a total of seven romantic plays against but three that are realistic.

Shirley's growing interest in the romantic field, made evident by our summary thus far, is confirmed by our examination of his remaining work—his plays from his departure for Ireland in 1636 to the closing of the theaters in 1642. Of the eleven extant plays that we have assigned to this his final period, only two—*The Constant Maid* and *The Brothers*—are realistic; and, strangely enough, were we seeking only to demonstrate our thesis, we could find some ground for assigning these two plays not to the final but to the earliest period. *The Constant Maid* was entered in the Stationers' Register on April 28, 1640; but the date of its composition is unknown, and internal evidence would place it in Shirley's period of apprenticeship. *The Brothers* of 1652, which we have identified with *The Politique Father* of 1641, most critics

have been content to identify with *The Brothers* of
1626. However this may be, the other plays that we
have assigned to Shirley's final period are all roman-
tic--*The Royal Master, The Gentleman of Venice,
The Politician, St. Patrick for Ireland, The Doubtful Heir, The Imposture, The Cardinal, The Sisters,*
and *The Court Secret*—nine plays against a probable
two.

To take too literally and too absolutely the figures
in the preceding paragraphs, would be unfortunate.
The exact division between realism and romanticism
is difficult to make; and some critics, as we have
noted, divide the plays a little differently. With this
qualification, however, it is useful to express in definite figures our impressions of the course of Shirley's
development as a dramatist. Stated in tabular form,
they are as follows:

PERIOD		PLAYS PRIMARILY ROMANTIC	PLAYS PRIMARILY REALISTIC
First:	1625–1632	3½	7½
Second:	1632–1636	6	3
Third:	1636–1642	9	2
	Totals	18½	12½

For the popular impression that Shirley is primarily
a realistic dramatist, these totals, regardless of chronology, should have been sufficient refutation; but
when we see from our classification by periods, that

at least sixty per cent. of Shirley's realistic work falls in the first seven years of his career, the refutation becomes overwhelming. Shirley began his work as playwright as a realist; but the direction of his development was toward the romantic school: from Jonsonian and Fletcherian comedy of manners and of humors, he passed to Fletcherian and Shaksperean romantic comedy, dramatic romance, and romantic tragedy.

III

BESIDES reconstructing the chronology of Shirley's life and work, and tracing the course of his development as a dramatist, we have endeavored in our study to give some impressions of the characteristics of his drama. These characteristics we can best review by regrouping his plays under the two heads already indicated.

As a follower of the realistic school of Jonson and of Fletcher, Shirley's material is twofold: true but satiric pictures of the life of court and town; and the exaggerated sketches that we know technically as "characters of humor." Citizen life appears most fully in *The Constant Maid,* in *Hyde Park,* and in *The Gamester,* and life in somewhat higher circles in *The Witty Fair One, The Wedding, The Ball,*

Changes, or Love in a Maze, The Lady of Pleasure,
and *The Example.* To the same group, despite their
nominally Portuguese and Italian settings, belong
The Brothers of 1652, which we have identified with
The Politique Father, and *Love's Cruelty,* a tragedy
of adultery, which, notwithstanding the presence of
a duke of Ferrara and his court, is at most no more
romantic than *The Example.* Socially, these plays
present at times the commonness of Middleton, at
times the gentlehood of Fletcher. Morally they vary
from the repulsiveness of Jonson at his worst to the
wholesomeness of Shakspere at his best. Often offensive to our modern taste, they are not always immoral
in their influence: *The Lady of Pleasure* is a stinging
satire against extravagance, gaming, drunkenness,
and licentiousness; *Love's Cruelty* and *The Example*
preach even more eloquently of chastity and true
nobility.

Yet not alone as true pictures of the life of the
court and town do these plays attest the influence of
Jonson and his fellow realists: in these comedies of
manners—and in many a romantic play as well—
Shirley has inserted "characters of humor." Jacomo
of *The Grateful Servant,* Bombo of *The Royal
Master,* Piperollo of *The Sisters,* Young Barnacle
of *The Gamester,* Hornet and Startup of *The Constant Maid,* Rawbone and Lodam of *The Wedding,*

Depazzi of *The Traitor*, Bubulcus of *Love Tricks*,
Sir Gervase Simple and Caperwit of *Changes, or
Love in a Maze*, Sir Nicholas Treedle and the
omniscient Brains of *The Witty Fair One*, Orseolo
and others of *The Humorous Courtier*, Jack Freshwater, Bostock, Barker, and Monsieur Le Frisk
of *The Ball*, Vainman, Pumicestone, Oldrat, Dormant, of *The Example*, and, best of all, in the same
play, Sir Solitary Plot: each, to use the definition of
Dryden, is the embodiment of "some extravagant
habit, passion, or affection . . . by the oddness of
which he is immediately distinguished from the rest
of men";[5] each illustrates the wealth of adapta-
tion and creation of Shirley's "characters of humor."

Yet not in realism—whether "humorous" or satiric
—but in romance, did Shirley do his most distinctive
work: in dramatic romance, in romantic comedy, and
in romantic tragedy.

Dramatic romance—distinguished from romantic
comedy chiefly by stress upon surprising revelations
of the plot rather than upon the depiction or development of character—is Shirley's most frequent, though
not most fruitful field. It is, moreover, the type in
which Shirley's work most closely approximates the
work of Fletcher. Slightly suggested in the masque

[5] *Of Dramatick Poesie, an Essay. By John Dryden, Esq.* . . .
1668, in Ker, *Essays of John Dryden*, I, 85.

[393]

and pastoral element of *Love Tricks,* in the maiden-page of *The Wedding,* and in the miracles of *St. Patrick for Ireland,* this Fletcherian type is thoroughly exemplified in the oracle, the disguises, and the surprising dénouement of *The Arcadia;* in the incognito, the extravagance, and the startling resolution of *The Bird in a Cage;* in the concealed identity and kaleidoscopic changes of *The Coronation;* in the exchanged positions of Giovanni and Thomazo in *The Gentleman of Venice;* in the shifting love, the maiden-page, and the successive revolutions of *The Doubtful Heir;* and, finally, in the blending of surprise and of suspense in the double imposture of *The Court Secret.* Slight as several of these romances are, they are lacking neither in interest nor in poetic charm. At their best, they have a tensity of climax and an unexpectedness of outcome that hold one breathless. Whatever their weaknesses, they demonstrate at least Shirley's mastery of romantic plot.

Differing from the dramatic romances by virtue of attention rather to character than to plot, the seven romantic comedies of Shirley may be further divided into three groups. *The Sisters* and *The Opportunity* are fun run mad; *The Duke's Mistress,* on the other hand, and, to a less degree, *The Imposture* and *The Young Admiral,* are highly serious and almost tragic; and between these two extremes is a third group, characterized neither by laughter nor by death, but rather by exquisite delicacy of sentiment and of poetic charm: *The Grateful Servant* and *The Royal Master*. And what a delightful gallery of character these seven comedies present! The bold bandit Frapolo masquerading as Farnese, Prince of Parma; his haughty bride, Paulina, brought low by the revelation of her birth; Aurelio Andreozzi of Milan mistaken in Urbino for the banished Borgia, loving and beloved by both Cornelia and the duchess, yet unable to seize his "opportunity" in either suit; Ardelia of *The Duke's Mistress;* Juliana of *The Imposture;* Vittori of *The Young Admiral,* and, with him, Cassandra, Cesario, and Rosinda; Princess Leonora of *The Grateful Servant,* with Foscari and Cleona; and, best of all, the king, Montalto, Octavio, and little Domitilla of *The Royal Master:* these are characters worthy of our acquaintance—and remembrance. In these romantic comedies, Shirley produces something different from—and better than—his Fletcherian romances.

Least numerous, least representative of the work of Shirley, least adequate—if tried by the standard of the best that the English drama has produced—and yet, in themselves, notable contributions to that drama, are his romantic tragedies. Of these, *The Maid's Revenge* is admittedly least worthy; yet, with its struggle between love and filial duty, its wholesale slaughter, and its pathetic maiden-page, this play, the second that Shirley dedicated to the stage, is no mean production for the youthful dramatist. *Chabot,* with its fine unity and its sympathetic characterization, we must not claim for Shirley, for we know not how far he collaborated with Chapman in the drama. *The Politician,* however, somber in subject, powerful in scene, mighty in its protagonist, Marpisa, is a tragedy worthy of any but the greatest dramatist. Finally, most powerful if not most pleasing of all the plays of Shirley, stand his two tragedies, *The Traitor* and *The Cardinal:* the former masterly in plot and more than masterly in characterization; the latter masterly in character-delineation, but especially notable for management of plot. For, as the contest between the duchess and the cardinal, with its climax of madness, of poison, and of slaughter, is a struggle almost Websterian in its piteous horror, so, in *The Traitor,* the villainy of Lorenzo, the virtuous suffering of Amidea, and the noble vengeance of Sciarrha, make these characters a permanent contribution to our English tragedy.

Such was James Shirley, in life, in development, and in achievement: in life, a man of whose personal career we can establish little, but of whose literary chronology we have recorded much; in development, a convert from realism to romanticism; in achievement, a dramatist who, inheriting the best that his predecessors—Jonson, Fletcher, Shakspere—had to offer, combined their methods and their materials into a body of plays well worth our study. Let us dismiss him, therefore, as we introduced him, neither with the sometimes excessive commendation nor with the frequently ill-founded disparagement of Swinburne, but with the modest praise of Milton's nephew, Phillips: "James Shirley, a just pretender to more than the meanest place among the English poets, but most especially for Dramatic Poesy, in which he hath written both very much, and for the most part with that felicity that by some he is accounted little inferior to Fletcher himself." [6]

[6] Phillips, *Theatrum Poetarum,* 1675, pp. 80–81.

ANNOTATED BIBLIOGRAPHY

PART I

THE PUBLISHED WORKS OF JAMES SHIRLEY, CHRONOLOGICALLY ARRANGED

SHIRLEY, JAMES.   1618.

Eccho, or the Infortunate Lovers, a poem, by James Sherley, Cant. in Art. Bacc. Lond. 1618. 8vo.

Primum hunc Arethusa, mihi concede laborem.

Thus, in *Censura Literaria,* II, 382, Samuel Egerton Brydges quotes the title-page of Shirley's earliest work, "from a Ms. note to Astle's copy of Wood's *Athenæ.*" As no copy of this edition of *Eccho* has survived, we cannot judge of the accuracy of the transcript. In the Stationers' Register, the entry is as follows: "4 Januarij 1617 [i.e., 1617/18]. *Ecc[h]o and Narcissus the 2 Vnfortunate Louers* written by Jeames Sherley." See *S. R.,* III, 286.

SHIRLEY, JAMES.   1629.

The Wedding. As it was lately Acted by her Maiesties Seruants, at the Phœnix in Drury Lane. Written By Iames Shirley, Gent. Horat.—Multaq; pars mei Vitabit Libitinam—London. Printed for Iohn Groue, and are to be sold at his shop at Furniualls Inne Gate in Holborne. 1629.

From the copy belonging to the late Robert Hoe, Esq.

SHIRLEY, JAMES.   1630.

The Gratefvll Servant. A Comedie. As it was lately presented with good applause at the priuate House in Drury-Lane, By her Majesties Servants. Written by Iames Shirley Gent.—Vsque ego postera Crescam laude recens. London. Printed by B. A. and T. F. for John Groue, and are to be sold at his shop at Furnivals-Inne gate, 1630.

From the copy belonging to the late Robert Hoe, Esq.

[401]

SHIRLEY, JAMES. 1631.

The Schoole of Complement. As it vvas acted by her Maiesties Seruants at the Priuate house in Drury Lane.—Hæc placuit semel. —By J. S. London, Printed by E. A. for Francis Constable, and are to be sold at his shop in Pauls Church-yard, at the signe of the Crane. 1631.

From the copy belonging to the late Robert Hoe, Esq.

SHIRLEY, JAMES. 1632.

Changes: or, Love in a Maze. A Comedie, As it was presented at the Private House in Salisbury Court, by the Company of His Majesties Revels. Written by Iames Shirley, Gent. — — Deserta per avia dulcis Raptat Amor. London: Printed by G. P. for William Cooke, and are to be sold at his shop neere Furnivals Inne gate in Holborne, 1632.

From the copy belonging to the late Robert Hoe, Esq.

SHIRLEY, JAMES. 1633.

The Wedding. As it vvas lately Acted by her Maiesties Ser-uants, at the Phenix in Drury-Lane. Written by Iames Shirley, Gent. Horat.—Multaq, pars mei Vitabit Libitinam— London; Printed for Iohn Groue, and are to be sold at his Shop in Chan-cery-Lane, neere the Rowles, ouer against the Suppeny-Office. 1633.

Second edition. From the copy belonging to the late Robert Hoe, Esq.

SHIRLEY, JAMES. 1633.

A Contention for Honovr and Riches. By J. S.—ubi quid datur oti, illudo chartis— London, Printed by E. A. for William Cooke, and are to be sold at his shop neere Furnivals Inne gate in Holborne. 1633.

From the copy belonging to the late Robert Hoe, Esq.

SHIRLEY, JAMES. 1633.

The Wittie Faire One. A Comedie. As it was presented at

the Private House in Drvry Lane. By her Maiesties Servants. By Iames Shirley. . . . London Printed by B. A. and T. F. for Wil. Cooke, and are to be sold at his shop, neere Furnivals-Inne Gate, in Holborne. 1633.

From the copy belonging to the late Robert Hoe, Esq.

SHIRLEY, JAMES.   1633.

The Bird in a Cage. A Comedie. As it hath beene Presented at the Phœnix in Drury-Lane. The Author Iames Shirley, Servant to Her Majesty. Iuven. Satyra. 7. Et Spes, & ratio Studiorum, in Cæsare tantum. London Printed by B. Alsop. and T. Fawcet. for William Cooke, and are to be sold at his Shop neere Furnivals-Inne Gate, in Holborne. 1633.

From the copy belonging to the late Robert Hoe, Esq.

SHIRLEY, JAMES.   1633/34.

The Trivmph of Peace. A Masque, presented by the Foure Honourable Houses, or Innes of Court. Before the King and Queenes Majesties, in the Banquetting-house at White Hall, February the third, 1633. Invented and Written, By James Shirley, of Grayes Inne, Gent. Primum hunc Arethusa mihi— London, Printed by Iohn Norton, for William Cooke, and are to be sold at his Shop, neere Furnivals-Inne-gate, in Holborne. 1633.

From the copy belonging to the late Robert Hoe, Esq.

SHIRLEY, JAMES.   1635.

The Traytor. A Tragedie, vvritten by Iames Shirley. Acted By her Majesties Servants. London: Printed for William Cooke, and are to be sold at his Shop at Furnivals Inne-gate in Holborne. 1635.

From the copy belonging to the late Robert Hoe, Esq.

SHIRLEY, JAMES.   1637.

The Lady of Pleasvre. A Comedie, As it was Acted by her Majesties Servants, at the private House in Drury Lane. Written by James Shirly. London, Printed by Tho. Cotes, for Andrew Crooke, and William Cooke. 1637.

From the copy belonging to the late Robert Hoe, Esq.

SHIRLEY, JAMES. 1637.

Hide Parke a comedie, As it was presented by her Majesties Servants, at the private house in Drury Lane. Written by James Shirly. London, Printed by Tho. Cotes, for Andrew Crooke, and William Cooke. 1637.

From the copy belonging to the late Robert Hoe, Esq.

SHIRLEY, JAMES. 1637.

The Yovng Admirall. As it was presented By her Majesties Servants, at the private house in Drury Lane. Written by James Shirly. London, Printed by Tho. Cotes, for Andrew Crooke, and William Cooke. 1637.

From the copy belonging to the author of the present study, identical, as to title-page, with the copy belonging to the late Robert Hoe, Esq.

SHIRLEY, JAMES. 1637.

The Example. As it vvas presented by her Majesties Servants At the private House in Drury-Lane. Written by Iames Shirly. London. Printed by Iohn Norton, for Andrew Crooke, and William Cooke. 1637.

From the copy belonging to the late Robert Hoe, Esq.

SHIRLEY, JAMES. 1637.

The Gamester. As it vvas presented by her Majesties Servants At the private House in Drury-Lane. Written By Iames Shirly. London. Printed by Iohn Norton, for Andrew Crooke, and William Cooke. 1637.

From the copy belonging to the late Robert Hoe, Esq.

SHIRLEY, JAMES. 1637.

The Schoole of Complement. As it vvas acted by her Majesties

Servants at the Private house in Drury Lane.—Hæc placuit semel.
By I. S. London. Printed By I. H. for Francis Constable, and
are to be sold at his shop under Saint Martins Church neere Ludgate. 1637.

The second edition. From the copy belonging to the late Robert Hoe,
Esq.

SHIRLEY, JAMES. 1637.

The Gratefvll Servant. A Comedie. As it was lately presented
with good applause in the private House in Drury-Lane. By her
Majesties Servants. Written by James Shirley Gent.—Usque ego
postera Crescam laude recens. London: Printed by I. Okes for
William Leake, and are to be sold at his shop in Chancery-lane
neere the Roules. 1637.

The second edition. From the copy belonging to the late Robert Hoe,
Esq.

SHIRLEY, JAMES. 1638.

The Royall Master; As it was Acted in the new Theater in
Dublin: and Before the Right Honorable the Lord Deputie of
Ireland, in the Castle. Written by Iames Shirley.—Fas extera
quærere regna. Printed by T. Cotes, and are to be sold by Thomas
Allot and Edmond Crooke, neare the Castle in Dublin. 1638.

The Irish issue of the first edition. From the copy belonging to the late
Robert Hoe, Esq.

SHIRLEY, JAMES. 1638.

The Royall Master; As it was Acted in the new Theater in
Dublin: and Before the Right Honorable the Lord Deputie of
Ireland, in the Castle. Written by Iames Shirley—Fas extera
quærere regna. London, Printed by T. Cotes, and are to be sold
by Iohn Crooke, and Richard Serger, at the Grayhound in Pauls
Church-yard. 1638.

The English issue of the first edition. From the copy belonging to the
late Robert Hoe, Esq.

SHIRLEY, JAMES.   1638.

The Dvkes Mistris, As it vvas presented by her Majesties Servants, At the private House in Drury-Lane. Written by Iames Shirly. London, Printed by John Norton, for William Cooke, 1638.

From the copy belonging to the late Robert Hoe, Esq.

SHIRLEY, JAMES.   1639.

The Ball: a Comedy; As it vvas presented by her Majesties Servants, at the private House in Drury Lane. Written by George Chapman, and James Shirly. London, Printed by Tho. Cotes, for Andrew Crooke, and William Cooke. 1639.

From the copy in the British Museum: 643. d. 2.

SHIRLEY, JAMES (and CHAPMAN, GEORGE).   1639.

The Tragedie of Chabot Admirall of France: As it vvas presented by her Majesties Servants, at the private House in Drury Lane. Written by George Chapman, and James Shirly. London, Printed by The Cotes, for Andrew Crooke, and William Cooke. 1639.

From the facsimile title-page in Lehman's edition, 1906.

SHIRLEY, JAMES.   1639.

The Maides Revenge. A Tragedy. As it hath beene Acted with good Applause at the private house in Drury Lane, by her Majesties Servants. Written by Iames Shirley Gent. London. Printed by T. C. for William Cooke, and are to be sold at his shop at Furnivalls Inne Gate in Holbourne. 1639.

From the copy belonging to the late Robert Hoe, Esq.

SHIRLEY, JAMES.   1640.

The Hvmorovs Covrtier. A Comedy, As it hath been presented with good applause at the private house in Drury-Lane. Written by Iames Shirley Gent. London. Printed by T. C. for William

Cooke, and are to be sold by James Becket, in the Inner Temple.
1640.

From the copy belonging to the late Robert Hoe, Esq.

SHIRLEY, JAMES.   1640.

Loves Crveltie. A Tragedy, As it was presented by her Maj-
esties Servants, at the private House in Drury Lane. Written by
James Shirley Gent. London, Printed by Tho. Cotes, for Andrew
Crooke. 1640.

From the copy belonging to the late Robert Hoe, Esq.

SHIRLEY, JAMES.   1640.

A Pastorall called the Arcadia. Acted by her Majesties Ser-
vants at the Phœnix in Drury Lane. Written by Iames Shirly
Gent. London, Printed by I. D. for Iohn Williams, and F.
Eglesfeild and are to be sould at the signe of the Crane in Pauls
Church-yard. 1640.

From the copy belonging to the late Robert Hoe, Esq.

SHIRLEY, JAMES.   1640.

The Opportvnitie a comedy, As it was presented by her Maj-
esties Servants; at the private House in Drury Lane. Written by
Iames Shirley. London. Printed by Thomas Cotes for Andrew
Crooke, and Will. Cooke, and are to be sold at the Signe of the
Greene Dragon in Pauls Church-yard. 1640.

From the copy belonging to the author of the present study, identical,
as to title-page, with the copy belonging to the late Robert Hoe, Esq.

SHIRLEY, JAMES.   [1640.]

The Opportvnitie a comedy, As it was presented by her Maj-
esties Servants, at the private House in Drury Lane. Written by
Iames Shirley. London. Printed by Thomas Cotes for Andrew
Crooke, and are to be sold at the Signe of the Greene Dragon in
Pauls Church-yard. [n.d.]

From the copy belonging to the late Robert Hoe, Esq. Described in
his *Catalogue of Early English Books,* iv, 161, as "The sheets of the 1640
edition reissued, with the imprint alone altered. Collation: The same as
the first edition."

SHIRLEY, JAMES.   1640.

The Coronation   a comedy. As it was presented by her Majesties Servants at the private House in Drury Lane. Written by
John Fletcher. Gent. London, Printed by Tho. Cotes, for Andrew Crooke, and William Cooke, and are to be sold at the signe
of the Greene Dragon, in Pauls Church-yard. 1640.

From the copy belonging to the late Robert Hoe, Esq.
The publication of this play with Fletcher's name upon the title-page,
was made during Shirley's absence in Ireland. That it is Shirley's, however, there can be no doubt: it was licensed as Shirley's February 6,
1634/5; and it was publicly reclaimed by Shirley in "A Catalogue of the
Authors Poems already Printed," appended to *The Cardinal*, 1652 (in *Six
New Playes*, 1653), in the following words: "*The Coronation.* Falsely
ascribed to Jo. Fletcher."

SHIRLEY, JAMES.   1640.

St. Patrick for Ireland. The first Part. Written by James
Shirley. London, Printed by J. Raworth, for R. Whitaker. 1640.
From the copy belonging to the late Robert Hoe, Esq.

SHIRLEY, JAMES.   1640.

The Constant Maid. A Comedy. Written by James Shirley.
London, Printed by J. Raworth, for R. Whitaker. 1640.
From the copy belonging to the late Robert Hoe, Esq.

SHIRLEY, JAMES, reviser.   1640.

The Night Walker or the Little Theife. A Comedy, As it was
presented by her Majesties Servants, at the Private House in
Drury Lane. Written by John Fletcher. Gent. London, Printed
by Tho. Cotes, for Andrew Crooke, and William Cooke. 1640.

From the copy in the British Museum: 644. e. 3.
A play of Fletcher's revised by Shirley.

SHIRLEY, JAMES.   1646.

Poems &c. By James Shirley. Sine aliquâ dementiâ nullus
Phœbus. London, Printed for Humphrey Moseley, and are to be

sold at his shop at the signe of the Princes Armes in St. Pauls
Church-yard. 1646.

From the copy belonging to the late Robert Hoe, Esq.
The frontispiece is the same engraving of Shirley that again appears
in *Six New Playes,* 1653, a portrait marked "W. Marshall sculpsit, 1646."
Further on, some one has inserted in this copy the portrait of Shirley
marked: "Iacobus Shirlaeus," "G. Phenik pinx.," "R. Gaywood fecit,
1658." After the first 80 pages, the numbering begins anew with the
following title-page:

Narcissus, or, The Self-Lover. By James Shirley. Hæc olim—
London, Printed for Humphrey Moseley, and are to be sold at
his shop at the signe of the Princes Armes in St. Pauls Church-
yard. MDCXLVI.

Of this part, the page-numbers run, 1–46, and then 147–159. Beginning p. 35, are "Prologues and Epilogues; written to severall Playes Presented in this Kingdom, and elsewhere." Then, with new pagination,
follows:

The Trivmph of Beavtie. As it was personated by some young
Gentlemen, for whom it was intended, at a private Recreation.
By James Shirley. London, Printed for Humphrey Mosely, and
are to be sold at his shop, at the Signe of the Princes Armes In St.
Pauls Churchyard. MDCXLVI.

SHIRLEY, JAMES.   1647.

To the Reader.

An address prefixed to:

Comedies and Tragedies Written by Francis Beavmont And
Iohn Fletcher Gentlemen. Never printed before, And now pub-
lished by the Authours Originall Copies. Si quid habent veri
Vatum præsagia, vivam. London, Printed for Humphrey Robin-
son, at the three Pidgeons, and for Humphrey Moseley at the
Princes Armes in St Pauls Church-yard. 1647.

From the copy belonging to Ernest Dressel North, Esq.

SHIRLEY, JAMES.   1649.

Via ad Latinam Linguam Complanata. The Way made plain

[409]

to the Latine Tongue. The Rules composed in English and Latine Verse: For the greater Delight and Benefit of Learners. By James Shirley. Avia Pieridum peragro loca. Lucret. London, Printed by R. W. for John Stephenson, at the signe of the Sun on Ludgate-Hill. 1649.

From the copy belonging to the late Robert Hoe, Esq.

SHIRLEY, JAMES.   1653.

Six New Playes, Viz. The Brothers. Sisters. Doubtfull Heir. Imposture. Cardinall. Court Secret. The Five first were acted at the Private House in Black Fryers with great Applause. The last was never Acted. All Written by James Shirley. Never printed before. London, Printed for Humphrey Robinson at the Three Pigeons, and Humphrey Moseley at the Prince's Armes in St. Paul's Curch-yard, 1653.

From the copy belonging to the author of the present study, identical, as to title-pages, with the copy belonging to the late Robert Hoe, Esq.

Facing the joint title-page, as frontispiece, is an engraving of Shirley (identical with that previously prefixed to the *Poems*) signed "W. Marshall sculpsit, 1646." The title-pages of the several plays are as follows:

The Brothers, A Comedie, As It was Acted at the private House in Black Fryers. Written By James Shirley. Never Printed before. London, Printed for Humphrey Robinson at the Three Pigeons, and Humphrey Moseley at the Prince Armes in St. Paul's Church-yard. 1652.

The Sisters, A Comedie, As It was acted at the private House in Black Fryers, Written By James Shirley. Never Printed before. London, Printed for Humphrey Robinson at the Three Pigeons, and Humphrey Moseley at the Prince's Arms in St. Paul's Church-yard. 1652.

The Doubtful Heir. A Tragi-comedie, As It was Acted at the private House in Black Friers, Written By James Shirley. Never Printed before. London, Printed for Humphrey Robinson at the three Pigeons, and Humphrey Moseley at the Prince's Arms in St. Paul's Church-yard. 1652.

The Impostvre A Tragi-Comedie, As It was Acted at the private House in Black Fryers. Written By James Shirley. Never Printed before. London, Printed for Humphrey Robinson at the Three Pigeons, and Humphrey Moseley at the Prince's Armes in St. Paul's Curch-yard. 1652.

The Cardinal, A Tragedie, As It was acted at the private House in Black Fryers, Written By James Shirley. Not Printed before. London, Printed for Humphrey Robinson at the Three Pigeons, and Humphrey Moseley at the Prince's Arms in St. Paul's Church-yard. 1652.

The Court Secret, A Tragi-Comedy: Never Acted, But prepared for the Scene at Black-Friers. Written By James Shirley. Never printed before. London, Printed for Humphrey Robinson at the three Pigeons, and for Humphrey Moseley at the Prince's Armes in Saint Paul's Church-yard. 1653.

At the end of *The Cardinal* is appended a "Catalogue of the Authors Poems already Printed," which I have quoted in a note in Chapter V. In Mr. Hoe's copy, there was appended to *The Court Secret* a list of books for sale by Humphrey Moseley, containing evidence, which I have quoted in my second chapter, as to the identity of *The Brothers* of 1652.

SHIRLEY, JAMES. 1653.

Cvpid and Death. A Masque. As it was Presented before his Excellencie, The Embassadour of Portugal, Upon the 26. of March, 1653. Written by J. S. London: Printed according to the Authors own Copy, by T. W. for J. Crook, & J. Baker, at the Sign of the Ship in St. Pauls Church-Yard, 1653.

From the copy in the British Museum: 644. c. 64.

SHIRLEY, JAMES. 1655.

The Gentleman of Venice A Tragi-Comedie Presented at the Private house in Salisbury Court by her Majesties Servants. Written by James Shirley. London, Printed for Humphrey Moseley and are to be sold at his Shop at the Princes Armes in St. Pauls Church-yard. 1655.

From the copy belonging to the author of the present study, identical, as to title-page, with the copy belonging to the late Robert Hoe, Esq.

SHIRLEY, JAMES.   1655.

The Polititian, A Tragedy, Presented at Salisbury Court By Her Majesties Servants; Written By James Shirley. London, Printed for Humphrey Moseley and are to be sold at his Shop at the Princes Armes in St. Pauls Church-yard. 1655.

From the copy belonging to the author of the present study, identical, as to title-page, with the copy belonging to the late Robert Hoe, Esq.

SHIRLEY, JAMES.   1656.

The Rudiments of Grammar. The Rules Composed in English Verse, For The greater Benefit and delight of young Beginners. By James Shirley. Vtile dulci. London, Printed by J. Macock for R. Lownds, and are to be sold at his shop at the white Lyon in Paul's Church-yard, 1656.

From the copy in the British Museum: E. 1704. (2).

SHIRLEY, JAMES.   1659.

Honoria and Mammon. Written by James Shirly Gent. Scene Metropolis, or New-Troy. Whereunto is added the Contention of Ajax and Ulisses, for the Armour of Achilles. As it was represented by young Gentlemen of quality at a private entertainment of some Persons of Honour. London, Printed for John Crook, and are to be sold at his shop at the signe of the Ship in S. Pauls Churchyard, 1659.

The foregoing transcript is from one of the copies belonging to the late Robert Hoe, Esq., in whose library were three copies, one of which, bound with *The Triumph of Beauty,* appears to lack the joint title-page. The division title-pages are as follows:

Honoria and Mammon. Written by James Shirley. [Three lines in Latin.] London, Printed by T. W. for John Crook, at the sign of the ship in S. Pauls Church-yard. [n.d.]

The Contention of Ajax and Ulysses, for the Armor of Achilles. As It was nobly represented by young Gentlemen of quality, at a private Entertainment of some persons of Honour. Written By James Shirley. London, Printed for John Crook, at the sign of the ship in S. Pauls Church-yard. [n.d.]

SHIRLEY, JAMES.   1659.

Cupid and Death. A Private Entertainment, represented with Scenes & Musick, Vocall & Instrumental. Written by J. S. London, Printed for John Crooke and John Playford, and are to be sold at their Shops in St. Paul's Church-yard and in the Inner Temple. 1659.

From the copy in the British Museum: 644. c. 66.

SHIRLEY, JAMES.   1660.

Manductio: or, A leading of Children by the Hand Through the Principles of Grammar. The second Edition, Enlarged. By Ja: Shirley. Perveniri ad summum nisi ex principiis non potest. London, Printed for Richard Lowndes, at the White Lion in S. Pauls Church-yard. 1660.

From the copy in the British Museum: E. 1931 (2).

SHIRLEY, JAMES.   1660.

The Wedding. As it was lately Acted by her Majesties Servants, at the Phœnix in Drury Lane. Written by James Shirley, Gent. Horat.—Multaq; pars mei Vitabit Libitinam— London. Printed for William Leake, and are to be sold at the Crowne in Fleet-Street, between the two Temple Gates, 1660.

From the copy in the British Museum: 644. c. 68.

SHIRLEY, JAMES.   1660[?].

The Grateful Servant. A Comedy. As it was Presented with good Applause in the private House in Drury-Lane. By Her Majesties Servants. Written by James Shirley, Gent. London,

[413]

Printed for William Leake, at the Crown in Fleetstreet, between the two Temple Gates. [n.d.]

1660? From the copy in the British Museum: 644. c. 38.

SHIRLEY, JAMES. 1661.

Love will finde out the Way. An Excellent Comedy. By T. B. As it was Acted with great Applause, by Her Majesties Servants, at the Phœnix in Drury Lane. London: Printed by Ja: Cottrel, for Samuel Speed, at the Signe of the Printing-Press in St. Paul's Church-yard. 1661.

From the copy belonging to the late Robert Hoe, Esq.
This is Shirley's *Constant Maid,* 1640, with a new title, and a false ascription as to authorship. See the edition of 1667, below.

SHIRLEY, JAMES. 1667.

The Constant Maid: or, Love will finde out the Way. A Comedy. By J. S. As it is now Acted at the new Play-house called The Nursery, in Hatton-Garden. London: Printed by Ja: Cotterel, for Samuel Speed, at the signe of the Rainbow between the two Temple-gates. 1667.

From the copy in the British Museum: 644. c. 70.

SHIRLEY, JAMES. 1667.

Love Tricks, or, the School of Complements; As it is now Acted by His Royal Highnesse The Duke of York's Servants At the Theatre in Little Lincolns-Inne Fields. By J. S. Licens'd May 24, 1667. Roger L'Estrange. London, Printed by R. T. and sold by Thomas Dring Junior, at the White-Lion near Chancery Lane in Fleetstreet, 1667.

From the copy in the British Museum: 644. c. 71.

SHIRLEY, JAMES. 1692.

The Traytor. A Tragedy: With Alterations, Amendments, and Additions. As it is now Acted at the Theatre Royal, by their Majesties Servants. Written by Mr. Rivers. London, Printed for

Richard Parker at the Royal Exchange, and Sam. Briscoe in Covent Garden, over against Wills Coffee-House.   MDCXCII.

From the copy in the Library of Columbia University, 823 Sh. 6 X;
identical, as to title-page, with the copy in the British Museum, 643. d. 65.

For the claims of Mr. Rivers, the Jesuit, consult the preface of this
edition, and the passage quoted in this Bibliography under "Gentleman's
Journal," 1692.

SHIRLEY, JAMES, revised by JOHNSON.   1712.

The Wife's Relief: or, The Husband's Cure. A Comedy. As
it is Acted at the Theatre-Royal in Drury-Lane, By Her Majesty's
Servants. Written by Mr. Cha. Johnson.— Perjurum fuit in Ma-
ritum Splendide Mendax. London: Printed for Jacob Tonson,
at Shakespear's Head over-against Catherine-street in the Strand.
1712.

From the copy in the Library of Columbia University, B 824 J 62.

This is a revision of Shirley's *The Gamester,* 1637. Cf. Garrick's revision, *The Gamesters,* 1758.

SHIRLEY, JAMES.   1744.

The Gamester. A Comedy. By Mr. James Shirley.
Being pp. 97–178 in Dodsley's
A Select Collection of Old Plays. Volume the Ninth. Lon-
don: . . . M.DCC.XLIV.

SHIRLEY, JAMES.   1744.

The Bird in a Cage. A Comedy. By Mr. James Shirley.
Being pp. 179–252 in Dodsley's
A Select Collection of Old Plays. Volume the Ninth. Lon-
don: . . . M.DCC.XLIV.

SHIRLEY, JAMES.   1744.

Love Will find out the Way. An Excellent Comedy. By T. B.
Being pp. 95–170 in Dodsley's
A Select Collection of Old Plays. Volume the Twelfth. Lon-
don: . . . M.DCC.XLIV.

S., J. (Not JAMES SHIRLEY.)   1744.
    Andromana: or, The Merchant's Wife. A Tragedy. By J. S.
    Being pp. 171–241 in Dodsley's
    A Select Collection of Old Plays. Volume the Eleventh. Lon-
don: . . . M.DCC.XLIV.

SHIRLEY, JAMES.   1750.
    St. Patrick for Ireland. A Tragi-Comedy. First Acted By His
Majesty's Company of Comedians in the Year 1639. Written by
James Shirley, Esq; To which is prefix'd, An Account of the
Author, and his Works: And an Abstract of The Life of St. Pat-
rick: Collected from the best Historians. Dublin: Printed, and
Sold by the Editor W. R. Chetwood, in the Four-court-marshal-
sea; Messrs. G. and A. Ewing, P. Wilson, and H. Hawker, in
Dame-street; G. Faulkner, and A. Long, in Essex-street; J. Hoey,
in Skinner-row; and J. Esdall, on Cork-hill, Booksellers.
MDCCL.
    From the copy in the British Museum: 11775. b. 61.

SHIRLEY, JAMES.   1751.
    St. Patrick for Ireland. A Tragi-Comedy. First Acted By
His Majesty's Company of Comedians, in the Year 1639. Written by James Shirley, Esq; To which is prefix'd, An Account of
the Author, and his Works: And an Abstract of The Life of St.
Patrick, Collected from the best Historians. Dublin printed: London re-printed; . . . M.DCC.LI. (Price Six-pence.)
    From the copy in the British Museum: 1346. b. 3.

SHIRLEY, JAMES.   1754.
    The Arcadia a Pastoral. Written by James Shirley And acted
at the Phœnix in Drury-Lane, in the Year 1640: Founded on the
same Story with the New Tragedy, call'd Philoclea, Now acting
at the Theatre Royal in Covent-Garden.—Arcades Ambo, Et can-
tare Pares. London: Printed and sold by W. Reeve, in Fleet-
Street. M.DCC.LIV. (Price One Shilling.)
    From the copy in the British Museum: 1346. d. 17.

SHIRLEY, JAMES, revised by GARRICK. 1758.

The Gamesters: A Comedy alter'd from Shirley. As it is perform'd by His Majesty's servants at the Theatre-Royal in Drury-Lane. London: Printed for J. and R. Tonson, in the Strand. MDCCLVIII. (Price One Shilling.)

The play is prefaced with the following "Advertisement":

"In the year 1711, Mr. Charles Johnson alter'd *The Gamester,* written originally by Shirley, into a Comedy which he call'd *The Wife's Relief, or The Husband's Cure.* In this play he retain'd Shirley's underplot of Leonora, Violante, and Beaumont, which has no necessary dependence upon the principal action, and has therefore been generally censur'd as impertinent; nor has it, separately consider'd, any excellence to attone for that defect. The editor of *The Gamesters,* as it is now a second time alter'd from Shirley, will not presume to offer any objections to the alterations and additions which Mr. Johnson has been pleas'd to make. It will be sufficient for him to inform the reader that he has nothing in common with Johnson but what both he and Johnson have in common with Shirley. The characters of Barnacle, and the Nephew, which were before unconnected with the principal action, are now interwoven with it: what alterations and additions have been now made, will be better known by a comparison of this play with the original, and are, with great deference, submitted to the candor of the public."

SHIRLEY, JAMES. 1780.

The Bird in a Cage.

Being pp. 191–297 in Dodsley's

A Select Collection of Old Plays. . . .The Second Edition, . . . Volume VIII. London, . . . MDCCLXXX.

SHIRLEY, JAMES. 1780.

The Gamester.

Being pp. 1–108 in Dodsley's

A Select Collection of Old Plays. . . . The Second Edition, . . . Volume IX. London, . . . MDCCLXXX.

S., J. (Not JAMES SHIRLEY.) 1780.

Andromana.

Being pp. 1–77 in Dodsley's

A Select Collection of Old Plays. . . . The Second Edition, . . . Volume XI. London, . . . MDCCLXXX.

SHIRLEY, JAMES, revised by GARRICK.   1792.

The Gamesters. A Comedy as altered from Shirley and C. Johnson. Adapted for Theatrical Representation, as performed at the Theatres-Royal, Drury-Lane and Covent Garden . . . London: . . . John Bell . . . M DCC XCII.

In:

Bell's British Theatre . . . Vol. VI. . . .

SHIRLEY, JAMES.   1793.

The Royal Master, A Comedy. Written by James Shirley, Gentleman.—Fas extra queære regna. London: Printed 1638, Re-printed 1793, by T. Wilkins, Aldermanbury.

From the copy in the British Museum: 11777. cc. 2(2).

SHIRLEY, JAMES.   1793.

The Maid's Revenge. A Tragedy. Written by James Shirley, Gentleman. London. Printed 1639, Re-Printed 1793, by T. Wilkins, Aldermanbury.

From the copy in the British Museum: 11777. cc. 2(1).

SHIRLEY, JAMES, revised by SHEIL, R. L.   1819.

Evadne; or, The Statue: A Tragedy, in Five Acts: As performed at the Theatre Royal, Covent-Garden. By Richard Sheil, Esq. Second Edition. London . . . 1819.

"The Author has employed a part of the fable of Shirley's *Traytor,* in the construction of his plot. In that tragedy, a kinsman and favorite of the Duke of Florence contrives to excite in him a dishonourable passion for the sister of a Florentine nobleman, as the means of procuring the murder of the Duke by the hand of the injured brother, and thus opening the way for his own elevation to the throne. To that extent only, the plot of this tragedy is derived from Shirley. The incidents, situations, distribution, characters, and language, (such as they are), the Author hopes he may be pardoned for observing, are his own." (Preface, a 2.)

SHIRLEY, JAMES.   1833.

The Dramatic Works and Poems of James Shirley, now first collected; with notes by the late William Gifford, Esq., and additional notes, and some account of Shirley and his writings, by the

[418]

Rev. Alexander Dyce. In six volumes. Vol. I. Containing Some
Account of Shirley and His Writings. Commendatory Verses on
Shirley. Love Tricks, or the School of Complement. The Maid's
Revenge. The Brothers. The Witty Fair One. The Wedding.
London: John Murray, Albemarle Street, MD CCC XXXIII.

. . . Vol. II. Containing: The Grateful Servant. The Traitor. Love's Cruelty. Love in a Maze. The Bird in a Cage.
Hyde Park. . . .

. . . Vol. III. Containing: The Ball. The Young Admiral.
The Gamester. The Example. The Opportunity. The Coronation. . . .

. . . Vol. IV. Containing: The Lady of Pleasure. The Royal
Master. The Duke's Mistress. The Doubtful Heir. St. Patrick
for Ireland. The Constant Maid. The Humorous Courtier. . . .

. . . Vol. V. Containing: The Gentleman of Venice. The
Politician. The Imposture. The Cardinal. The Sisters. The
Court Secret. . . .

. . . Vol. VI. Containing: Honoria and Mammon. Chabot,
Admiral of France. The Arcadia. The Triumph of Peace. A
Contention for Honour and Riches. The Triumph of Beauty.
Cupid and Death. The Contention of Ajax and Ulysses, &c.
Poems. . . .

This is the only complete collection of the plays and poems of Shirley.
For reviews, see under *The American Quarterly Review* and *The
Quarterly Review.*

SHIRLEY, JAMES.   1872.

The Traitor.

Being pp. 505–528 in:

The Works of the British Dramatists . . . [Edited] by John
S. Keltie . . . Edinburgh . . . 1872.

SHIRLEY, JAMES.   1872.

The Brothers.

Being pp. 528–549 in:

The Works of the British Dramatists . . . [Edited] By John
S. Keltie . . . Edinburgh . . . 1872.

JAMES SHIRLEY, DRAMATIST

SHIRLEY, JAMES.   1888[?].

The Mermaid Series. James Shirley. With an Introduction
by Edmund Gosse, M.A., Clark Lecturer at Trinity College,
Cambridge. "I lie and dream of your full Mermaid wine."—
Beaumont. London: T. Fisher Unwin. New York: Charles
Scribner's Sons. [n.d.]

Contents: James Shirley. *The Witty Fair One. The Traitor. Hyde
Park. The Lady of Pleasure. The Cardinal. The Triumph of Peace.*
For comment on the Introduction, see under "Gosse, Edmund."

SHIRLEY, JAMES, (and CHAPMAN, GEORGE).   1906.

Publications of the University of Pennsylvania. Series in Philology and Literature. Volume X. The Tragedie of Chabot
Admirall of France. Written by George Chapman and James
Shirley. Reprinted from the Quarto of 1639. Edited with an
Introduction and Notes by Ezra Lehman, Sometime Harrison Fellow in English, University of Pennsylvania. Published for the University, Philadelphia, 1906. The John C. Winston Co., Publication Agents, Philadelphia, Pa.

SHIRLEY, JAMES: (and CHAPMAN, GEORGE.)   1910.

The Tragedy of Chabot, Admiral of France.
Being pp. 273–337 in:
The Plays and Poems of George Chapman. The Tragedies.
Edited with introductions and notes by Thomas Marc Parrott,
Ph.D., Professor of English Literature at Princeton University.
London: George Routledge & Sons, Limited. New York: E. P.
Dutton & Co. [1910].

SHIRLEY, JAMES.   1911.

The Lady of Pleasure.
Being pp. 800–829 in:
The Chief Elizabethan Dramatists excluding Shakespeare. Se-
lected plays . . . edited . . . by William Allan Neilson, Ph.D.,
Professor of English, Harvard University. Boston and New York
. . . 1911.

SHIRLEY, JAMES.   1911.

The Cardinal.

Being pp. 830–853 in:

The Chief Elizabethan Dramatists excluding Shakespeare. Selected Plays . . . edited . . . by William Allan Neilson, Ph.D.,
Professor of English, Harvard University. Boston and New York
. . . 1911.

SHIRLEY, JAMES.   1911.

Der königliche Meister (The Royal Master). Schauspiel in
fünf Akten von James Shirley. (1596–1666.) Übersetzt von J.
Schipper. . . .

Being pp. 363–445 in:

James Shirley, sein Leben und seine Werke. Nebst einer Übersetzung seines Dramas "The Royal Master," von J. Schipper. . . .
Wien und Leipzig: Wilhelm Braumüller . . . 1911.

For annotation, see under "Schipper, J."

SHIRLEY, JAMES.   1914.

James Shirley. The Royal Master. Edited with Critical Essay
and Notes by Sir Adolphus William Ward, Litt.D., F.B.A.,
Master of Peterhouse, Cambridge.

Being pp. 545–652 in:

Representative English Comedies . . . [edited by] . . .
Charles Mills Gayley . . . Volume III. . . . New York, . . .
1914.

Part II

WORKS CONTAINING REFERENCES TO SHIRLEY, ARRANGED ALPHABETICALLY BY AUTHORS

American Quarterly Review.

An anonymous review entitled:

The Dramatic Works and Poems of James Shirley . . . by the late William Gifford . . . and . . . the Rev. Alexander Dyce.

Being pp. 103–166 in:

The American Quarterly Review. Vol. XVI. September & December, 1834. Philadelphia: Key and Biddle, 23 Minor Street. T. K. Collins & Co., Printers. 1834.

This review is rarely more than a pleasing summary of the plays, elaborated with extensive extracts. The reviewer displays little knowledge of dramatic art, or of the history of the English drama, or of the social conditions which Shirley's comedies of manners were intended to depict. Of *The Cardinal*, indeed, he gives (pp. 158–165) a fairly discriminating critique; but, for the most part, he confines his critical discussions to a commendation of the poetry and a condemnation of the immorality of the plays of Shirley. Of the condemnation, the following extract is typical:

"*The Maid's Revenge* . . . is reprehensible, in a high degree, for its extravagance and grossness; and some surprise is naturally felt on perusing it, that a *Reverend* personage should have been the instrument of ushering it into public notice. This remark, indeed, may be extended to the editorship of the whole. Few, if any, of the pieces contained in these volumes, are such as may be considered to be perfectly in keeping with the clerical gown." (p. 104.)

Apology for the Believers in the Shakspeare-Papers, An. (Anon.)

See Chalmers, George.

BIBLIOGRAPHY: PART II

ARBER, EDWARD.

For An English Garner, . . . 1897, *containing* Three to One, *see under* PEEKE, RICHARD.

For A Transcript of the Registers of the Company of Stationers, . . . Edited by Edward Arber . . . 1877, *see under* STATIONERS' REGISTER.

BAKER, D. E.

Biographia Dramatica; or a Companion to the Playhouse . . . Originally compiled, to the year 1764, by David Erskine Baker. Continued thence . . . by Isaac Reed, F.A.S. and . . . Stephen Jones. In three volumes. Vol. I.—Part II. London, . . . 1812.

The sketch of James Shirley, pp. 666–668, is, for the most part, plagiarized from Wood. A few touches come from Phillips, Farmer, and others. It offers little that is original except its errors.

BANCROFT, THOMAS.

Two Bookes of Epigrammes and Epitaphs. Dedicated to the two top-branches of Gentry: Sir Charles Shirley, Baronet, and William Davenport, Esquire. Written By Thomas Bancroft. London: Printed by I. Okes, for Matthew Walbancke, and are to be sold at his shop in Grayes-Inne-gate. 1639.

From the copy in the British Museum: 1077. b. 15.

BROOKE, J. M. S., and HALLEN, A. W. C.

For The Transcript of the Registers of . . . S. Mary Woolchurch . . . , *see under* ST. MARY WOOLCHURCH.

BRYDGES, S. E.

Censura Literaria. Containing titles, abstracts, and opinions of old English books, with original disquisitions, articles of biography, and other literary antiquities. By Samuel Egerton Brydges, Esq. Volume II. London: . . . 1806.

Volume II, p. 382, presents an alleged transcript of the title-page of the lost *Eccho, or the Infortunate Lovers*, 1618. The entry reads:
"Art. 26. Echo, or the Infortunate Lovers, a poem, by James Sherley,

[423]

Cant. in Art. Bacc. Lond. 1618. 8vo. Primum hunc Arethusa, mihi concede laborem.

"From a Ms. note to Astle's copy of Wood's *Athenæ*."

See also Volume VI, pages 1 and 25. Cf. edition of 1815, II, 381–387.

BULLEN, A. H.

A Collection of Old English Plays. In Four Volumes. Edited by A. H. Bullen. Vol. II. Privately printed by Wyman & Sons, Great Queen Street, Lincoln's-Inn Fields, London, 1883.

In Volume II, pp. 1–99, Bullen reprints the old play of *Dicke of Devonshire*, which Fleay has since attempted to identify with Shirley's lost play, *The Brothers* of 1626.

In the same volume, p. 315 *et. seq.*, Bullen attempts to prove that the play which he reprints under the title *Captain Underwit* is by Shirley. The play is really *The Country Captain* by William Cavendish, Duke of Newcastle. See Schelling, *Elizabethan Drama*, II, 283–284.

CAMBRIDGE HISTORY OF ENGLISH LITERATURE.

For the half-chapter on Shirley, see NEILSON, W. A.

CAMPBELL, T.

Specimens of the British Poets; with biographical and critical notices, and an essay on English Poetry. By Thomas Campbell. In seven volumes. Vol. I. Essay on English Poetry. London: John Murray, Albemarle-Street, 1819.

In Volume I, pp. 225–232, Campbell gives cordial but, on the whole, discriminating praise to Shirley, illustrated with four pages of extracts from his works.

In Volume IV, pp. 1–62, he gives a brief notice of Shirley and long extracts from *The Cardinal, The Royal Master, The Grateful Servant, The Doubtful Heir, The Lady of Pleasure*, and *Chabot*.

CHALMERS, GEORGE. (ANON.)

An Apology for the Believers in the Shakspeare-Papers, which were exhibited in Norfolk-Street. . . . London: . . . 1797.

Note *v*, pp. 513–514, is the Lord Chamberlain's letter of June 10, 1637, "from a MS. book in his office."

Note *w*, pp. 515–516, is the list of plays belonging to the Cockpit, August 10, 1639.

CHAMBERS, E. K.

Plays of the King's Men in 1641, by E. K. Chambers.
Being pp. 364–369 in:
Collections Parts IV & V. The Malone Society. 1911.

A letter from the Earl of Essex, Lord Chamberlain, to the Stationers' Company forbidding the publication of *The Doubtful Heir, The Imposture, The Brothers,* and other plays belonging to the King's Men, August 7, 1641.

CHETWOOD, W. R.

A General History of the Stage; (More Particularly the Irish Theater) . . . by W. R. Chetwood . . . Dublin: . . . M DCC XLIX.

Pages 51–52 present a brief account of John Ogilby's theater in Warberg Street, Dublin, 1635–1641.

CIBBER, THEOPHILUS.

The Lives of the Poets of Great Britain and Ireland. Compiled from ample Materials scattered in a Variety of Books, and especially from the MS. Notes of the late ingenious Mr. Coxeter and others, collected for this Design by Mr. Cibber and other hands. Vol. II. London: Printed for R. Griffiths, at the Dunciad in St. Paul's Church-Yard. MD CC LIII.

This work, according to opinions now accepted, was the labor not of Theophilus Cibber but, chiefly, of one Robert Shiels. Mr. Cibber's contribution was merely his notoriety (he was then in jail) and perhaps some slight revision. The account of Shirley, Volume II, pp. 26–32, is a delightfully imaginative paraphrase of that by Wood.

CLUTTERBUCK, ROBERT.

The History and Antiquities of the County of Hertford; compiled from the best printed Authors and Original Records preserved in public repositories and private collections. . . . By Robert Clutterbuck, of Watford, Esq., F.S.A. Volume the First. London: . . . 1815.

In Volume I, p. 48, Clutterbuck gives some account of the Edward the Sixth Grammar School at St. Albans and, in a foot-note, a list of the schoolmasters in which appears for the year 1623 the name of James Sherley. In the same volume, p. 83 *et seq.*, Clutterbuck gives a biographical sketch of Shirley, plagiarized from Wood.

COLLIER, J. P.

The History of English Dramatic Poetry to the Time of Shakespeare: and Annals of the Stage to the Restoration. By J. Payne Collier, Esq., F.S.A. Volume the second. London: . . . MDCCCXXXI.

The "Annals of the Stage," which constitute pp. 1–119 of Volume II, include extracts from Herbert's office-book and other interesting documents. Among these are to be noted: an extract from the diary of Sir Humphrey Mildmay, II, 70, note; a letter of the Lord Chamberlain of June 10, 1637, II, 83–84, note; the Cockpit list of Aug. 10, 1639, II, 92, note; and the appointment of Davenant to the management of the Cockpit in place of W. Beeston, II, 101, note.

DIBDIN, CHARLES, the elder.

A Complete History of the Stage, written by Mr. Dibdin. The players cannot keep counsel; they'll tell all. Vol. IV. London. Printed for the author and sold by him at his warehouse, Leicester Place, Leicester Square. [n.d.]

This work is assigned by the *Dictionary of National Biography*, xv, 5, to the year 1795. The British Museum catalogue dates it "[1800]."

Dibdin's nine pages upon Shirley, Volume IV, pp. 38–47, are devoted to brief comment, usually unfavorable, upon the several plays. He thinks that "tragedy was not the forte of Shirley" (IV, 40), and remarks of *The Doubtful Heir* and *The Impostor* [sic] that "you always pity him for making Fletcher his model" (IV, 44–45).

DICKE OF DEVONSHIRE.

See BULLEN, A. H.

DICTIONARY OF NATIONAL BIOGRAPHY (*DNB.*).

See WARD, A. W.

DODSLEY, ROBERT.   1744.

A Select Collection of Old Plays. Volume the First. London: Printed for R. Dodsley in Pall-Mall. M.DCC.XLIV.

This, the first edition of Dodsley's *Old Plays,* published in twelve volumes, contains the following plays by Shirley or ascribed to ˙Shirley: *The Gamester* (IX, 97–178); *The Bird in a Cage* (IX, 179–252); *Andromana: or, The Merchant's Wife. A Tragedy. By J. S.* (XI, 171–241); *Love Will find out the Way. An Excellent Comedy. By T. B.* (XII, 95–170; from the edition of 1661). It contains also *A Dialogue on Plays and Players* (XI, i–xxxvii) by James Wright.

DODSLEY, ROBERT.   1780.

A Select Collection of Old Plays. In Twelve Volumes. The Second Edition, corrected and collated with the Old Copies. With Notes Critical and Explanatory. Volume VIII. London, . . . MDCCLXXX.

Volume VIII, pp. 191–297, reprints Shirley's *The Bird in a Cage,* with a sketch of Shirley based on Wood prefixed, and a reprint of the title-page of 1633 appended.

Volume IX, pp. 1–108, reprints Shirley's *The Gamester,* with a transcript of the title-page of 1637 appended.

Volume XI, pp. 1–77, reprints *Andromana,* by J. S., with a transcript of the title-page of 1660 appended.

Volume XII, pp. 337–363, reprints James Wright's *Historia Histrionica.*

DODSLEY, ROBERT.   1825.

A Select Collection of Old Plays. In twelve volumes. Vol. I. A New Edition: with additional notes and corrections, by the late Isaac Reed, Octavius Gilchrist, and the editor [J. Payne Collier]. London. . . . M DCCC XXV.

From this edition, all plays by Shirley were omitted in the expectation of the early appearance of Gifford's *Shirley.* The edition retains, however, Wright's *Historia Histrionica,* in Vol. I, pp. cxxxix–clxix.

DODSLEY, ROBERT.   1876.

A Select Collection of Old English Plays. Originally published by Robert Dodsley in the year 1744. Fourth Edition, now first chronologically arranged, revised and enlarged with the notes of all the commentators, and new notes by W. Carew Hazlitt. Volume the fifteenth. London: . . . 1876.

This edition of 1876 omits all plays by Shirley—unless we so classify *Andromana: or the Merchant's Wife. . . . By J. S.* It contains, however (XV, 399–431), a reprint of James Wright's *Historia Histrionica,* 1699 (q.v.).

DOWNES, JOHN.

Roscius Anglicanus, or an historical review of the stage from 1660 to 1706. By John Downes. A fac-simile reprint of the rare original of 1708. With an historical preface by Joseph Knight. London. . . . 1886.

As Downes explains in his preface, his official connection with the theatrical companies of the Restoration and the access that he had to the records of the several theaters, make his account of the stage from 1660 to 1706 particularly valuable. Four passages that refer to plays by Shirley, I quote at length:

"The Company [his Majesty's Company of Comedians] being thus Compleat, they open'd the New Theatre in Drury-Lane, on Thursday in Easter Week, being the 8th Day of April 1663, with *The Humorous Lieutenant* [p. 3]. . . . These being their Principal Old Stock Plays, yet in this Interval from the Day they begun, there were divers others Acted, . . . *The Opportunity, The Example,* . . . *The Cardinal,* [p. 8] . . . *The Traytor,* . . . These being Old Plays, were Acted but now and then; yet, being well Perform'd, were very Satisfactory to the Town" [p. 9].

"Next follows the Plays Writ by the then Modern Poets, . . . [p. 9] yet they Acted divers others . . . as . . . *Love in a Maze"* [p. 15].

"After this [in 1666] the Company [of Sir William Davenant, in Lincoln's Inn Fields] Reviv'd Three Comedies of Mr. Sherly's, viz. *The Grateful Servant, The Witty Fair One, The School of Complements.* . . . These Plays being perfectly well Perform'd; especially Dulcino the Grateful Servant, being Acted by Mrs. Long; and the first time she appear'd in Man's Habit, prov'd as Beneficial to the Company, as several succeeding new Plays" [p. 27].

"Upon the 9th of April, 1705, Captain Vantbrugg open'd his new Theatre in the Hay-Market. . . . The first Play Acted there, was *The Gamester"* [p. 48].

DRYDEN, JOHN.

The Globe Edition. The Poetical Works of John Dryden. Edited with a memoir, revised text, and notes, by W. D. Christie, M.A., of Trinity College, Cambridge. . . . London. 1908.

In *MacFlecknoe,* 1682, Dryden (Globe edition, p. 144, lines 29–32) makes Flecknoe say to Shadwell:

> Heywood and Shirley were but types of thee,
> Thou last great prophet of tautology.
> Even I, a dunce of more renown than they,
> Was sent before but to prepare thy way.

And at the coronation of Shadwell (p. 146, lines 98–103),

> No Persian carpets spread the imperial way,
> But scattered limbs of mangled poets lay;

> From dusty shops neglected authors come,
> Martyrs of pies. . . .
> Much Heywood, Shirley, Ogleby there lay,
> But loads of Shadwell almost choked the way.

DYCE, ALEXANDER.

Some Account of Shirley and his Writings.

Being pp. iii–lxvi in:

The Dramatic Works and Poems of James Shirley, now first collected; with notes by the late William Gifford, Esq., and additional notes, and Some Account of Shirley and his Writings, by the Rev. Alexander Dyce. In Six Volumes. Vol. I. . . . London: . . . MD CCC XXXIII.

This account by Dyce, based upon the sketch by Wood, Malone's extracts from Herbert's office-book, the works of Shirley, and such miscellaneous sources as the register of Merchant Taylors' School and the burial records of St. Giles in the Fields, is still, after eighty years, a surprisingly accurate and complete statement of the little that we know of Shirley's life.

DYCE, ALEXANDER; and GIFFORD, WILLIAM.

For reviews of their edition of The Dramatic Works and Poems of James Shirley . . . 1833, *see*.

AMERICAN QUARTERLY REVIEW.

QUARTERLY REVIEW.

ENGLISH STAGE, SOME ACCOUNT OF THE. (ANON.)

See GENEST, REV. JOHN.

FARMER, RICHARD.

An Essay on the Learning of Shakespeare: addressed to Joseph Cradock, Esq; By Richard Farmer, M.A., Fellow of Emmanuel-College, Cambridge, and of The Society of Antiquaries, London. Cambridge: Printed by J. Archdeacon, Printer to the University; For W. Thurlbourn & J. Woodyer, in Cambridge; and Sold by J. Beecroft, in Pater-noster-Row; J. Dodsley, in Pall-Mall; and T. Cadell in the Strand, London. M.DCC.LXVII.

From the copy in the British Museum: 641: e. 27(5).
To a passage in this Essay, Dyce and Ward attribute the revival of

[429]

Shirley's reputation as a dramatist. See Dyce in *Works,* I, xi, and Ward in *DNB.,* LII, 129, and in *English Dramatic Literature,* III, 95. Farmer wrote: "Shirley is spoken of with contempt in *MacFlecknoe;* but his imagination is sometimes fine to an extraordinary degree." And then he quoted from *The Brothers* the exquisite description of Jacinta at vespers.

FARMER, RICHARD.

Essay on the Learning of Shakspeare addressed to Joseph Cradock, Esq. By Richard Farmer, D.D., Master of Emmanuel College, Cambridge, and Principal Librarian of that University. London: . . . 1821.

In this edition, the reference to Shirley is on pp. 37–38.

FLEAY, F. G.

Annals of the Careers of James and Henry Shirley.
Being pages 405–414 in:
Anglia. Zeitschrift für Englische Philologie. Herausgegeben von Richard Paul Wülker. Mit einem kritischen Anzeiger. Herausgegeben von Moritz Trautmann. VIII Band. Halle a. S. Max Niemeyer. 1885.

This is an important but unreliable contribution to the biography of Shirley. Among the typographical errors, I note the following:
Page 406, line 17: The date when *Love Tricks* was entered in the Stationers' Register should be 1630/31, not 1630 unless marked "Old Style."
Page 406, line 20: The date when *The Duke* was licensed should be May 17, not May 7.
Page 407, line 14: The date when *The Bird in a Cage* was entered should be March 19, not March 10.
Page 408, line 47: The date when *The Ball* and *Chabot* were entered should be October 24, not December 24.
Page 409, line 7: The date when *The Humorous Courtier* was entered should be July 29, not July 20.
Page 409, line 17: The date when *Looke to the Ladie* was entered should be March 11, not March 10.
Page 412, line 20: The date when *St. Patrick* was entered should be April 28, not October 28.
Page 412, passim: "Williams and Egglestone" should read "Williams and Egglesfeild."

FLEAY, F. G.

A Biographical Chronicle of the English Drama. 1559–1642.

BIBLIOGRAPHY: PART II

By Frederick Gard Fleay, M.A., author of "The Life and Work of Shakespeare," "A Chronicle History of the London Stage, 1559–1642," Etc. In two volumes. Volume II. London. . . . 1891. . . .

Pages 233–247 are devoted to James Shirley. The account is valuable; but its value is much lessened by numerous misprints, among which I note the following:

Page 233, line 28: The date on which *The Gamester* was entered in the Stationers' Register should be November 15, not October 18.

Page 234, line 15: The date on which *The Humorous Courtier* was entered should be July 29, not July 20.

Page 237, line 18: The date on which *The Duke* was licensed should be May 17, not May 7.

Page 246, line 5: The date of *The Doubtful Heir* is, of course, 1652, not 1552.

FORSYTHE, ROBERT STANLEY.

The Relations of Shirley's Plays to the Elizabethan Drama. By Robert Stanley Forsythe, Ph.D., Sometime University Scholar and University Fellow in English, Columbia University. New York. Columbia University Press. 1914. . . .

A most scholarly contribution.

GENEST, REV. JOHN (ANON.).

Some Account of the English Stage, from the Restoration in 1660 to 1830. In ten volumes. . . . Vol. IX. Bath . . . 1832.

To the student of Shirley, this work is valuable not so much for its abstracts of the plots of Shirley's plays as for its record of Shirleian revivals. See especially, IX, 541–563; but also, I, 78–79; I, 339–341; I, 350–351; II, 30–31; II, 491–493; III, 142–144; VI, 399–400.

Genest worked from first-hand sources, the play-bills and the records of the theaters. His *Account,* in the words of Joseph Knight (*DNB.,* XXI, 119), is "a work of great labour and research, which forms the basis of most exact knowledge concerning the stage. Few books of reference are equally trustworthy, the constant investigation to which it has been subjected having brought to light few errors and none of grave importance."

GENTLEMAN'S JOURNAL.

The Gentleman's Journal: or the Monthly Miscellany. By Way of Letter To a Gentleman in the Country. Consisting of

News, History, Philosophy, Poetry, Musick, Translations, &c. April, 1692. Plus multo tibi debiturus hic est, Quam debet Domino suo libellus. Licensed, April 13th, 1692. R. Midgley. London, Printed for Rich. Parker; and are to be Sold by Rich. Baldwin, near the Oxford Arms in Warwick Lane. 1692.

From the copy in the British Museum: P. P. 5255.
On p. 21 occurs the following passage:
"*The Traytor,* an old Tragedy, hath not only been revived the last Month, but also been reprinted with Alterations and Amendments: It was supposed to be Shirly's, but he only usher'd it in to the Stage; The Author of it was one Mr. Rivers, a Jesuite, who wrote it in his Confinement in Newgate, where he died. It hath always been esteemed a very good Play, by the best Judges of Dramatick Writing."

GENTLEMAN'S MAGAZINE.

See SMITH, G. BARNETT.

GIFFORD, WILLIAM; and DYCE, ALEXANDER.

For reviews of their edition of The Dramatic Works and Poems of James Shirley . . . 1833, *see:*

AMERICAN QUARTERLY REVIEW.

QUARTERLY REVIEW.

GLÖDE, O.

Review of:

P. Nissen: James Shirley. . . . 1901.

Being pp. 392–394 in:

Englische Studien. Organ für englische philologie . . . Herausgegeben von Johannes Hoops. . . . 34 band. Leipzig. . . . 1904.

GOSSE, EDMUND.

James Shirley.

Being pp. vii–xxx in:

The Mermaid Series. James Shirley, with an introduction by Edmund Gosse, M.A., Clark Lecturer at Trinity College, Cambridge. "I lie and dream of your full Mermaid wine."—Beaumont. London . . . New York . . . [n.d.]

Gosse's Introduction is the customary sketch, biographical and critical:

a pleasing little article, but marred by a willingness to accept as facts the suppositions of any previous writer. To the errors of his predecessors, Gosse adds a few of his own, as when he speaks of *The Brothers* as a tragedy, and places *The Bird in a Cage* before *Hyde Park* and *The Ball,* forgetful that the date he has given for the former, 1632, is Old Style, and should read January 21, 1632/3.

HERBERT, SIR HENRY, MASTER OF THE REVELS.

See MALONE, EDMOND.

HISTORIA HISTRIONICA. (ANON.)

See WRIGHT, JAMES.

HOE, ROBERT.

Catalogue of Books by English Authors who lived before the year 1700, forming a part of the Library of Robert Hoe. Volume IV. Printed in New York, April 1904. Sold by George H. Richmond.

Pages 151–172 of this catalogue give transcripts of the entire title-pages of the original quartos and folios of the plays of Shirley, of which Mr. Hoe had an almost complete collection. I have compared these transcripts with those which I myself made from the plays in Mr. Hoe's library and from the ten that I possess, and have found but one typographical error. on page 170, line 1, the date of *A Contention for Honour and Riches* should read "1633" not "1653."

HOE, ROBERT.

Catalogue of the Library of Robert Hoe of New York . . . Part I—L to Z. To be sold by auction beginning on Monday, May 1, 1911, by the Anderson Auction Company, . . . New York. . . .

The Shirley items (pp. 513–519) fetched, according to the "Priced List" subsequently issued, the following prices:

3023.	The Wedding, 1629	$305.00
3024.	The Grateful Servant, 1630	180.00
3025.	The School of Complement, 1631	190.00
3026.	Changes: or, Love in a Maze, 1632 . . .	145.00
3027.	The Bird in a Cage, 1633	175.00
3028.	A Contention for Honour and Riches, 1633 .	105.00
3029.	The Triumph of Peace, 1633, 2d issue . .	90.00
3030.	The Witty Fair One, 1633	185.00

3031.	The Traitor, 1635	$150.00
3032.	The Example, 1637	150.00
3033.	The Gamester, 1637	105.00
3034.	Hyde Park, 1637	160.00
3035.	The Lady of Pleasure, 1637	105.00
3036.	The Young Admiral, 1637	80.00
3037.	The Duke's Mistress, 1638	200.00
3038.	The Royal Master, 1638, Irish issue . . .	265.00
3039.	The Royal Master, 1638, London issue . .	55.00
3040.	The Maid's Revenge, 1639	160.00
3041.	The Constant Maid, 1640	55.00
3042.	The Coronation, 1640	180.00
3043.	The Humorous Courtier, 1640	70.00
3044.	Love's Cruelty, 1640	115.00
3045.	The Opportunity, 1640	85.00
3046.	The Arcadia, 1640	200.00
3047.	St. Patrick for Ireland, 1640	205.00
3048.	Six New Plays, 1653	135.00
3049.	Poems, 1646	155.00
3050.	Via ad Latinam Linguam Complanata, 1649 .	75.00
3051.	The Cardinal, 1652	250.00
3052.	The Doubtful Heir, 1652	25.00
3053.	The Gentleman of Venice, 1655	220.00
3054.	The Politician, 1655	80.00
3055.	Honoria and Mammon; The Contention of Ajax and Ulysses, 1659	105.00
3056.	The Triumph of Beauty, 1646; Honoria and Mammon, 1659; The Contention of Ajax and Ulysses, n.d.	140.00
3057.	Andromana, by J. S., 1660	100.00
3058.	Love will find out the Way, by T. B., 1661 .	50.00
3059.	The Opportunity, n.d. (sheets of 1640, with new imprint)	75.00
3060.	Dramatic Works, 1833	95.00

HOE, ROBERT.

Catalogue of the Library of Robert Hoe of New York . . . Part II—L to Z. To be sold by auction beginning on Monday, January 15, 1912, by the Anderson Auction Company, . . . New York. . . .

The Shirley items (p. 488) fetched, according to the "Priced List" subsequently issued, the following amounts:

3068.	The Wedding, 1633 (2d edition)	$25.00
3069.	The Grateful Servant, 1637 (2d edition) . .	30.00
3070.	The School of Complement, 1637 (2d edition).	10.00

3071. The Doubtful Heir, 1652 . . . . $35.00
3072. Six New Plays, 1653 . . . . 50.00
3073. Honoria and Mammon; The Contention of
      Ajax and Ulysses, 1659 . . . . . . 4.00

HOWARD, J. J.

See VISITATION OF LONDON.

HUNTER, JOSEPH.

Chorus Vatum Anglicanorum. Collections concerning the Poets and Verse-Writers of the English Nation. By Joseph Hunter, F. S. A. 1845. Volume III.

Pages 417–422 present an ill-digested but extensive body of material, biographical, genealogical, and bibliographical, concerning James and Henry Shirley.

HUTTON, W. H.

University of Oxford. College Histories. S. John Baptist College, by William Holden Hutton, B.D., Fellow, Tutor, and Precentor, and formerly Librarian, of S. John Baptist College; Examining Chaplain to the Lord Bishop of Ely. London. . . . 1898.

Hutton's references (pp. 92–93) to Shirley's possible connection with the college are based largely upon Wood; but he makes an interesting reference to a manuscript book of the reign of Charles I, by a St. John's man, Abraham Wright: "In a MS. book of his are some shrewd comments on the literature of his day, on the plays of Ben Jonson, Beaumont and Fletcher, on the S. John's man Shirley, and on Shakspere, with short shrewd comments on the plays" (p. 90).

KINGSLEY, CHARLES.

Plays and Puritans.

Being pp. 3–79 in:

Plays and Puritans and other Historical Essays. By Charles Kingsley. London: . . . 1885. . . .

Otherwise entitled:

The Works of Charles Kingsley. Volume XVI. Plays and Puritans. London. . . . 1885.

On pp. 53–58, Kingsley discusses Shirley's *The Gamester* as an example of the immorality of the seventeenth-century drama.

[435]

KRAPP, G. P.

The Legend of Saint Patrick's Purgatory: its later literary history. A dissertation . . . Johns Hopkins University . . . By George Philip Krapp. . . . Baltimore, . . . 1900.

In note 2, p. vi, Krapp is "inclined to think" that Shirley's intended subject for the promised second part of *St. Patrick for Ireland* was St. Patrick's Purgatory.

LAMB, CHARLES.

Specimens of English Dramatic Poets, who lived about the time of Shakspeare. With notes. By Charles Lamb. London: . . . 1808.

Lamb quotes at length from *Chabot* (pp. 453–459), *The Maid's Revenge* (pp. 459–469), *The Politician* (pp. 470–472), *The Brothers* (pp. 473–480), and *The Lady of Pleasure* (pp. 481–484). His critical comment (p. 459) is as follows:

"Shirley claims a place amongst the worthies of this period, not so much for any transcendent genius in himself, as that he was the last of a great race, all of whom spoke nearly the same language, and had a set of moral feelings and notions in common. A new language and quite a new turn of tragic and comic interest came in with the Restoration."

LANGBAINE, GERARD, THE YOUNGER.

An Account of the English Dramatick Poets. Or, Some Observations and Remarks On the Lives and Writings, of all those that have Publish'd either Comedies, Tragedies, Tragi-Comedies, Pastorals, Masques, Interludes, Farces, or Opera's in the English Tongue. By Gerard Langbaine. Oxford, Printed by L. L. for George West, and Henry Clements. An. Dom. 1691.

From the copy in the British Museum: 011795. ee. 1.

Langbaine's account of Shirley (pp. 474–485) shows little influence of Dryden or of Oldham. On the contrary, he opens with praise of Shirley that is, at least in part, an echo of Edward Phillips, 1675: "James Shirley . . . One of such Incomparable parts that he was the Chief of the Second-rate Poets: and by some has been thought even equal to Fletcher himself." Langbaine goes on to say, of Shirley's plays: "Of these I have seen four since my Remembrance, two of which were acted at the King's House; and the other two presented at the Duke's Theatre, in Little Lincolns-Inn Fields: viz. *Court Secret, Chances* [sic], *Grateful Servant, School of Compliments* [sic]." He gives a paragraph to each of Shirley's plays; and concludes his account by quoting with approval four lines by Hall to "the surviving Honour and Ornament of the English Scene:

> "Yet this I dare assert, when Men have nam'd
> Johnson (the Nation's Laureat,) the fam'd
> Beaumont, and Fletcher, he, that cannot see
> Shirley, the fourth, must forfeit his best Eye."

LANGBAINE, GERARD, THE YOUNGER, revised by CHARLES GILDON.

The Lives and Characters of the English Dramatick Poets. Also An Exact Account of all the Plays that were ever yet Printed in the English Tongue; their Double Titles, the Places where Acted, the Dates when Printed, and the Persons to whom Dedicated; with Remarks and Observations on most of the said Plays. First begun by Mr. Langbain, improv'd and continued down to this Time, by a Careful Hand. London: . . . 1699.

Pages 131–134 are a revision and condensation of the sketch in Langbaine's *Account* of 1691. Significant is the change of tone:
"James Shirley . . . was once of Grays-Inn, and Servant to the King, and a Poet esteemed in the Days of Charles the First. Mr. Langbain gives him no small Praise, and indeed he does to most of the indifferent Poets, so that shou'd a Stranger to our Poets read him, they wou'd make an odd Collection of our English Writers, for they wou'd be sure to take Heywood, Shirley, &c, and leave Dryden, &c." (p. 131.)

LAWRENCE, W. J.

The Elizabethan Playhouse and Other Studies by W. J. Lawrence. Illustrated. Shakespeare Head Press. Stratford-upon-Avon. MCMXII.

For the staging of *The Doubtful Heir* and *The Triumph of Peace*, see pp. 53, 100–103.

LEHMAN, EZRA.

The Tragedies of Chapman derived from French Historical Material.

Being pp. 5–37 in:

Publications of the University of Pennsylvania. Series in Philology and Literature. Volume X. The Tragedie of Chabot,

Admirall of France. Written by George Chapman and James Shirley. Reprinted from the Quarto of 1639. Edited with an Introduction and Notes by Ezra Lehman, sometime Harrison Fellow in English, University of Pennsylvania. Published for the University. Philadelphia, 1906. . . .

Pages 24–28 excellently summarize the evidence concerning the collaboration of Chapman and Shirley in *Chabot*.

MALONE, EDMOND.

History of the English Stage.
In Volume I, Part II of:
The Plays and Poems of William Shakspeare, in ten volumes; . . . to which are added . . . an historical account of the English stage; . . . by Edmond Malone. . . . London; . . . MD CC XC.

For the student of Shirley, Malone's *History* is especially important for its summaries and extracts from the lost office-book of Sir Henry Herbert, Master of the Revels.

MALONE, EDMOND.

An Enlarged History of the Stage.
In:
The Plays and Poems of William Shakspeare with the corrections and illustrations of various commentators: comprehending a Life of the Poet and an Enlarged History of the Stage, by the late Edmond Malone. With a new glossarial index. . . . Vol. III. London: . . . 1821.

This edition, like that of 1790, contains Malone's extracts from the no longer extant office-book of Sir Henry Herbert, Master of the Revels. For Shirley, see especially III, 231–242. For the Lord Chamberlain's letter to the Stationers' Company, June 10, 1637, see pp. 160–161, note. For the Cockpit list of August 10, 1639, see pp. 159–160, note. For post-Restoration revivals of Shirley, see pp. 272-276. In the list of plays by Shirley licensed by Sir Henry Herbert, one misprint occurs: the date of the licensing of *The Gentleman of Venice* should be 1639, not 1629. That the error in this edition is typographical appears both from the fact that the date appears correctly in Malone's edition of 1790 and from the fact that, in a list chronologically arranged, this "1629" stands between "1638" and "1640."

BIBLIOGRAPHY: PART II

MERCHANT TAYLORS' SCHOOL.

MS. Register.

The book is without title-page; but upon p. 1 appears the heading: "The Names of all those who have been Chief Masters of Merchant Taylors School in the Parish of Laurence Pountney, London, wch began Anno Domini 1561, Elisabethæ R. 3̃io, with the time of their Entrance upon and Continuance in the place"; and upon p. 2 appears the heading: "The Register of the Schooles Probation."

References to Shirley appear in the tables for December 11, 1608; March 11, September 11, and December 11, 1609; March 11, September 11, and December 11, 1610; March 11, September 11, and December 11, 1611; and March 11, 1612. The pages whence references were taken for this monograph were all in a good state of preservation, the writing good and clear, and all figures distinctly made. Unfortunately several gaps occur throughout, owing to missing pages.

MOULTON, C. W.

The Library of Literary Criticism of English and American Authors. Volume II. 1639–1729. Edited by Charles Wells Moulton assisted by a corps of able contributors. The Moulton Publishing Company. Buffalo, New York. 1901.

The biographical and critical account of Shirley, pp. 189–193, is an extensive but undiscriminating compilation from some twenty "authorities."

MURRAY, J. T.

English Dramatic Companies, 1558–1642. By John Tucker Murray, M.A. Sometime Edward William Hooper Fellow of Harvard University. Volume I. London Companies, 1558–1642. London: . . . 1910.

This work includes excellent accounts of the three companies with which Shirley was successively connected: the Queen's men of the Phœnix in Drury Lane, the later company of the same name at Salisbury Court, and the King's men of the Black Friars and Globe theaters.

NATION, THE.

An anonymous and untitled paragraph recording a performance of Shirley's *The Opportunity* at the University of Illinois, June 1, 1906.

On page 491 of:

The Nation. A Weekly Journal devoted to Politics, Literature,

Science & Art. Volume LXXXII, from January 1, 1906, to June 30, 1906. New York. New York Evening Post Company. 1906.

The paragraph is as follows:

"A performance of James Shirley's *The Opportunity,* the first, it is believed, since the seventeenth century, was given by the members of the Alethenai and Philomathean Literary Societies of the University of Illinois on Friday evening, June 1. The stage, writes a correspondent, which was built on the south campus, was enclosed at the back and sides with green cloth, with trees showing above. The different scenes were indicated by appropriate properties, brought in and off by young men in crimson velvet doublets; and most of the entrances and exits were made from the sides. To atone for the absence of scenery, which was hardly felt, the costumes were markedly handsome. The text used was about three quarters the length of the original, cuts being required both by the change of taste and by the time element. The play combines romantic intrigue, based upon mistaken identity, with splendid low comedy; and, in spite of its many conventionalities, it scored a complete success. The plot was unfolded with absolute clearness, even to those unfamiliar with the story. The acting was fully up to the standard set by the performance of *Friar Bacon* last year."

NEILSON, W. A.

Ford and Shirley. By W. A. Neilson, M.A. (Edinburgh), Ph.D. (Harvard), Professor of English in Harvard University.

Being Chapter VIII in:

The Cambridge History of English Literature. Edited by A. W. Ward, Litt.D., F.B.A., Master of Peterhouse, and A.R. Waller, M.A., Peterhouse. Volume VI. The Drama to 1642. Part II. New York: G. P. Putnam's Sons. Cambridge, England: University Press. 1910.

Neilson's contribution is a readable and scholarly account of Shirley's life and works.

NEILSON, W. A.

The Chief Elizabethan Dramatists excluding Shakespeare. Selected Plays . . . edited . . . by William Allan Neilson, Ph.D., Professor of English, Harvard University. Boston and New York . . . 1911.

Contents (for Shirley): *The Lady of Pleasure,* pp. 800–829; *The Car-*

dinal, pp. 830–853; Notes on these plays, p. 860; Bibliography of Shirley (erroneously including Gärtner's study of *John* Shirley), p. 867; Biographical sketch, p. 874.

Nissen, P.

James Shirley. Ein Beitrag zur englischen Litteraturgeschichte. Von Oberlehrer Dr. P. Nissen.

Being pp. 1–26 in:

Realschule in Eilbeck zu Hamburg. Bericht über das Schuljahr 1900–01. . . . Hamburg, 1901. . . . Progr. Nr. 804.

This study, which was intended as a biographical introduction to a more extensive work, is, on the whole, the most scholarly life of Shirley that has yet appeared. I heartily second the words of Glöde (*Englische Studien,* xxxiv, 394): "To the continuation of Nissen's study, which is to give a review of Shirley's dramatic works, and to be devoted to the consideration of individual plays, and especially to the relation of the poet to his sources, we look forward with interest."

Nissen, P.

For a review of his James Shirley, *see* Glöde, O.

Oldham, John.

The Works of Mr. John Oldham, Together with his Remains. London. Printed for H. Hindmarsh, at the Golden Ball in Cornhil, MDCXCVIII.

In Book III, p. 163, in a poem entitled "A Satyr. The Person of Spencer is brought in, Dissuading the Author from the Study of Poetry, and shewing how little it is esteem'd and encourag'd in this present Age," occur the following lines:

> "How many Poems writ in ancient time,
> Which thy Fore-fathers had in great esteem,
> Which in the crowded Shops bore any rate,
> And sold like News-Books, and Affairs of State,
> Have grown contemptible, and slighter since,
> As *Pordage, Fleckno,* or the *British Prince?*
>
> .   .   .   .
>
> And so may'st thou perchance pass up and down,
> And please a while th' admiring Court and Town,
> Who after shalt in *Duck-lane* Shops be thrown,
> To mould with *Silvester* and *Shirley* there,
> And truck for pots of Ale next *Stourbridg*-Fair."

PAGE, WILLIAM.

The Victoria History of the County of Hertfordshire edited by William Page, F.S.A. Volume Two. London. Archibald Constable and Company Limited. 1908.

In the section on "Schools," contributed by A. F. Leach, M.A., F.S.A., a brief reference to Shirley's head-mastership at St. Albans appears on p. 63.

PARROTT, T. M.

The Tragedy of Chabot: Introduction.

Being pp. 631–637 in:

The Plays and Poems of George Chapman. The Tragedies. Edited with introductions and notes by Thomas Marc Parrott, Ph.D., Professor of English Literature at Princeton University. London: George Routledge & Sons, Limited. New York: E. P. Dutton & Co. [1910].

A scholarly discussion of Chapman's sources and of Shirley's revision.

PEEKE, RICHARD.

Three to One. Being an English-Spanish combat performed by a Western Gentleman of Tavistock in Devonshire, with an English quarterstaff, against three Spaniards [at once] with rapiers and poniards; at Sherries [Xeres] in Spain, the 15th day of November 1625: in the presence of Dukes, Condes, Marquises, and other great Dons of Spain; being the Council of War. The author of this book, and the actor in this encounter; R[ichard] Peeke. Printed at London for I. T. and are to be sold at his shop.

Being pp. 621–643 in:

An English Garner. Ingatherings from our History and Literature, by Edward Arber, F.S.A. . . . Volume I. . . . MD CCC XCVII.

This pamphlet is the source of the anonymous play published by Bullen as *Dicke of Devonshire,* which Fleay accounts Shirley's lost play *The Brothers* of 1626.

PEPYS, SAMUEL.

The Diary of Samuel Pepys . . . transcribed by the late Rev.

Mynors Bright, M.A., . . . edited . . . by Henry B. Wheatley,
F.S.A. . . . London . . . 1893 . . .

Nine volumes, 1893–1899.
Pepys speaks of attending the following plays by Shirley: October 10,
1661, *The Traitor* (II, 112); October 2, 1662, *The Cardinal* (II, 329);
August 18, 1664, *The Court Secret* (IV, 206–207); August 5, 1667, *Love
Tricks, or The School of Complements* (VII, 54); December 30, 1667,
Love's Cruelty (VII, 239–240); July 11, 1668, *Hyde Park* (VIII, 60). Pepys
speaks also of attending, on May 21, 1662, *The French Dancing Mistress*,
which some editors have sought to identify with the play mentioned by
Herbert as *A Dancing Master*, December 10, 1661 (Malone's *Shakspere*,
1821, III, 275), and with Shirley's *The Ball*, which, in the list appended
to *The Cardinal*, 1652, bears the double title, *The Ball, or French Dancing
Master*.

PHILLIPS, EDWARD.

Theatrum Poetarum, or A Compleat Collection of the Poets,
Especially the most Eminent, of all Ages. By Edward Phillips
. . . London . . . M.DC.LXXV.

"James Shirly, a just pretender to more than the meanest place among
the English poets, but most especially for dramatic Poesy, in which he
hath written both very much; and for the most part with that felicity that
by some he is accounted little inferior to Fletcher himself" (p. 80).

PLAYS, A SELECT COLLECTION OF OLD. (ANON.)

See DODSLEY, ROBERT.

PRYNNE, WILLIAM.

Histrio-Mastix. The Players Scovrge, or, Actors Tragædie,
Divided into Two Parts. Wherein it is largely evidenced, by
divers Arguments, by the concurring Authorities and Resolutions
of sundry texts of Scripture; of the whole Primitive Church, both
under the Law and Gospell; of 55 Synodes and Councels; of 71
Fathers and Christian Writers, before the yeare of our Lord 1200;
of above 150 foraigne and domestique Protestant and Popish Authors, since; of 40 Heathen Philosophers, Historians, Poets; of
many Heathen, many Christian Nations, Republiques, Emperors,
Princes, Magistrates; of sundry Apostolicall, Canonicall, Imperiall

JAMES SHIRLEY, DRAMATIST

Constitutions; and of our owne English Statutes, Magistrates, Vniversities, Writers, Preachers:

That popular Stage-playes (the very Pompes of the Divell which we renounce in Baptisme, if we beleeve the Fathers) are sinfull, heathenish, lewde, ungodly Spectacles, and most pernicious Corruptions; condemned in all ages, as intolerable Mischiefes to Churches, to Republickes, to the manners, mindes and soules of men. And that the Profession of Play-poets, of Stage players; together with the penning, acting, and frequenting of Stage-playes, are unlawfull, infamous and misbeseeming Christians. All pretences to the contrary are here likewise fully answered; and the unlawfulnes of acting, of beholding Academicall Enterludes, briefly discussed; besides sundry other particulars concerning Dancing, Dicing, Health-drinking, &c. of which the Table will inform you.

By William Prynne, an Vtter-Barrester of Lincolnes Inne.

. . . .

London, Printed by E. A. and W. I. for Michael Sparke, and are to be sold at the Blue Bible, in Greene Arbour, in little Old Bayly, 1633.

From the title-page of the copy belonging to the library of Union Theological Seminary. The passages concerning Women actors are pp. 162, 214–215, 1002, 1003, and the index entry; concerning Henry Shirley, p. 553.

QUARTERLY REVIEW.

An anonymous review entitled:

The Dramatic Works and Poems of James Shirley . . . by the late William Gifford . . . and . . . the Rev. Alexander Dyce . . . London, 1832 [*sic*].

Being pp. 1–29 in:

The Quarterly Review. Vol. XLIX. Published in April & July, 1833. London: John Murray, Albemarle Street. 1833.

This review is a spirited and able notice of the life and writings of James Shirley as presented in the Gifford and Dyce edition of 1833. The reviewer gives us first a picture of Shirley's times and a summary of his life; then, after some general critical considerations, he discusses in turn the work of Shirley in tragedy, in romantic tragicomedy, and in comedy of manners; and illustrates his discussion with extensive extracts from *The Traitor, The Cardinal, The Brothers,* and *The Lady of Pleasure.* He concludes with commendation of the labors of Dyce and Gifford.

RISTINE, F. H.

English Tragicomedy, Its Origin and History. By Frank Humphrey Ristine, Ph.D. New York. The Columbia University Press. 1910.

Ristine's discussion of Shirley, pp. 135–139, is an acceptable account of Shirley's tragicomedies. See also pp. xiii, 124, 140, 150, 155, and 184.

RIVERS'S alleged authorship of *The Traitor.*
 See:
 SHIRLEY, JAMES: THE TRAYTOR, 1692.
 GENTLEMAN'S JOURNAL, 1692.

ROBINSON, C. J.

A Register of the Scholars admitted to Merchant Taylors' School, from A.D. 1562 to 1874, compiled . . . by the Rev. Charles J. Robinson, M.A., . . . 1882.

The references to Shirley (Vol. I, p. 60, and note) are of little value.

S., J.

Andromana: or the Merchant's Wife. The scæne, Iberia. By J. S. London, Printed for John Bellinger, and are to be sold at his shop in Cliffords-Inn-lane in Fleet-street, 1660.

Ascribed to Shirley merely because of the initials.
For reprints, see the several editions of Dodsley's *Old Plays.*

ST. GEORGE, SIR HENRY, KT., RICHMOND HERALD, ETC.
 See VISITATION OF LONDON.

ST. GILES, CRIPPLEGATE.

The Register Booke. Belonging to the Parish Church of S. Giles without Cripplegate in London, of all the Christenings,

[445]

Burials, Weddings, beginning the first day of March, 1606, in the
fift yeare of our most gracious Soveraigne Lord, King James. &c.

[1624/5]

"Christnings in February.—
"Mathias sonne of Mr. James Shurley gentleman —   26"

ST. GILES IN THE FIELDS.

St. Giles in Ye Fields.   1638–68.

"October 1666. . . .
"29 { Mr. James Sherley
    { Mris. Frances Sherley his wife"

ST. MARY WOOLCHURCH.

Register.

"1596. . . .
"James the sonne of James Sharlie was baptized the seventh of September."

ST. MARY WOOLCHURCH.

The Transcript of the Registers of the United Parishes of S.
Mary Woolnoth and S. Mary Woolchurch Haw, in the City of
London, from their Commencement 1538 to 1760 . . . By J. M.
S. Brooke, M.A., F.R.G.S., . . . and A. W. C. Hallen, M.A.,
F.S.A., . . . London: . . . 1886. . . .

For data for a genealogy of "James, son of James Sharlie," see pp.
lviii, 300, 301, 302, 308, 310, 311, 312, 313, 347, 370, 371, 372, 378, 379, 383,
384, and 388.

SCHELLING, F. E.

Elizabethan Drama, 1558–1642. A History of the Drama in
England from the Accession of Queen Elizabeth to the Closing
of the Theaters, to which is prefixed a Résumé of the Earlier
Drama from its Beginnings. By Felix E. Schelling, Professor in
the University of Pennsylvania. Two volumes. Volume Two.
Boston and New York: Houghton, Mifflin & Company. 1908.

Pages 284–297 in Volume II are an acceptable critique of Shirley's
realistic plays; pages 312–326 are an equally acceptable account of his
romantic plays. Schelling's brief discussion of Shirleian bibliography is

to be found chiefly on page 534. It is remarkable chiefly for one error—an error which it has successfully passed onward to *The Cambridge History of English Literature*. Henceforth let bibliographers take notice that O. Gärtner's *Shirley, sein Leben und Werken,* Halle Diss., 1904, refers not to James Shirley, but to John (1366?–1456).

SCHIPPER, J.

James Shirley, sein Leben und seine Werke. Nebst einer Übersetzung seines Dramas "The Royal Master," von J. Schipper. Mit einem auf dem in der Bodleiana zu Oxford Befindlichen Porträt Shirleys Beruhenden Bilde des Dichters. Wien und Leipzig. Wilhelm Braumüller. . . . 1911.

As a popular introduction to his translation of *The Royal Master,* Schipper's three hundred and sixty-one pages on the life and works of Shirley must be accounted excellent. As a contribution, however, to Shirleian scholarship or to Shirleian criticism, the book is disappointing.

The half-tone picture of Shirley which forms the frontispiece is a reproduction not of the Oxford portrait but of the Lupton engraving of 1833. Witness the suggestion of a pillar at the left, the absence of the bay-wreath, and the black mustache.

SELECT COLLECTION OF OLD PLAYS, A. (ANON.)

See DODSLEY, ROBERT.

SHEIL, RICHARD L.

See SHIRLEY, JAMES, REVISED, 1819.

SHIELS, ROBERT.

See CIBBER, T.

SHIRLEY, E. P. (ANON.)

Stemmata Shirleiana; or the Annals of the Shirley Family, Lords of Nether Etindon in the County of Warwick, and of Shirley in the County of Derby. . . . Privately Printed . . . Westminster. MDCCCXLI.

First edition. See p. 92 and *passim.*

SHIRLEY, E. P. (ANON.)

Stemmata Shirleiana; or the Annals of the Shirley Family, Lords of Nether Etindon in the County of Warwick, and of Shirley in the County of Derby. . . . Second edition, Corrected and Enlarged. . . . Westminster, MDCCCLXXIII.

See pp. 119, 269–271, 339, and *passim*.

SHIRLEY, E. P.

Who was Henry Shirley, the Author of *The Martyr'd Soldier? Being pp. 26–27 in:*

Notes and Queries: a Medium of Inter-Communication for Literary Men, Artists, Antiquaries, Genealogists, Etc. . . . Volume Twelfth. July–December, 1855. London: . . . 1855.

A valuable contribution.

SHIRLEY, E. P.

The Noble and Gentle Men of England; or notes touching the Arms and Descents of the ancient knightly and gentle houses of England. . . . By Evelyn Philip Shirley, Esq., M.A., F.S.A. . . . Westminster: . . . Second Edition, Corrected. 1860.

For a drawing of the arms of Shirley of Eatington, see p. 254; for the blazon, "Paly of six, or and azure, a quarter ermine," see p. 255.

SHIRLEY, JAMES.

For Shirley's will, formerly at Doctors' Commons, see SOMERSET HOUSE, PREROGATIVE COURT OF CANTERBURY, *Mico,* folio 170.

SMITH, G. BARNETT.

Shirley.

Being pp. 584–610 in:

The Gentleman's Magazine. Volume CCXLVI. January to June, 1880. . . . Edited by Sylvanus Urban, Gentleman. London. . . . 1880.

This is a graceful essay, biographical and critical: briefer than Swinburne's, more appreciative of Shirley's merits, and yet more discriminating. It concludes:

"The truth is that too much has been made of the charge that Shirley

is but the follower and close imitator of his immediate predecessors. We
do not see why his laurels in tragedy should be regarded as being filched
from Webster, or his laurels in comedy from Fletcher. Had he written
precisely contemporaneously with them, his fame would now have been
greater. He suffered by comparison with those who had already enrap-
tured the world by their dazzling lustre, and he was charged with having
lit the flame of his own genius at their shrine. Literary judgments have
been subject to revision from the earliest ages of the world until now;
and it may be that with a future generation the dramatic talents of Shirley will stand much higher than they do at present. His fine lyrical
faculty is already universally acknowledged, whereas for upwards of a
century it met with little recognition; and his position in the realm of
dramatic art may yet come to be equally assured. He is no unworthy
companion of the men who filled with noble music 'the spacious times of
great Elizabeth' " (p. 610).

SOME ACCOUNT OF THE ENGLISH STAGE. (ANON.)

See GENEST, REV. JOHN.

STAGE, ENGLISH, SOME ACCOUNT OF THE. (ANON.)

See GENEST, REV. JOHN.

STATIONERS' REGISTER.

A Transcript of the Registers of the Company of Stationers of
London; 1554–1640 A.D. Volume IV. . . . Edited by Edward
Arber. . . . Privately printed. London. 1 May, 1877.

See III, 286; and IV, 125, 195, 215, 238, 262, 265, 267, 287, 303, 355, 369,
373, 385, 415, 437, 438, 447, 465, 472, 475, and 482.

STEMMATA SHIRLEIANA. (ANON.)

See SHIRLEY, E. P.

STIEFEL, A. L.

Die Nachahmung spanischer Komödien in England unter den
ersten Stuarts. Von A. L. Stiefel.

Being pp. 193–220 in:

Romanische Forschungen. Organ für Romanische Sprachen
und Mittellatein Herausgegeben von Karl Vollmöller. V Band.
. . . 1890.

This article is devoted chiefly to a detailed comparison between Shirley's *The Opportunity* and Tirso de Molina's *El Castigo del Penséque.* It asserts, moreover, but does not attempt to prove, that Shirley's *The Young Admiral* is based upon Lope de Vega's *Don Lope de Cardona.*

STIEFEL, A. L.

Die Nachahmung spanischer Komödien in England unter den ersten Stuarts. III.

Being pp. 309–350 in:

Archiv für das Studium der neueren Sprachen und Literaturen . . . CXIX . . . 1907.

This, a continuation of the foregoing article, is a detailed examination of the relation between Shirley's *The Young Admiral* and Lope de Vega's *Don Lope de Cardona.*

SWINBURNE, A. C.

Essay on the Poetical and Dramatic Works of George Chapman.

In:

The Works of George Chapman: Poems and Minor Translations. With an introduction by Algernon Charles Swinburne. London: . . . 1875.

For Swinburne's opinion as to the authorship of *Chabot,* see p. xxxii.

SWINBURNE, A. C.

James Shirley.

Being pp. 461–478 in:

The Fortnightly Review. Edited by Frank Harris. Vol. XLVII. New Series. January 1 to June 1, 1890. (Vol. LIII. Old Series.) London: . . . 1890. . . .

Despite the justice of its concluding estimate of Shirley, and the high acceptability of portions here and there, this essay by Swinburne, considered as a whole, is deeply disappointing. The status of Shirleian criticism in the year 1890 and the distinguished ability of Swinburne as a critic of poetry and drama, both justified the expectation that this essay would be a notable contribution to the subject. But such is not the case. Indeed, to sum up my impressions of Swinburne's essay upon Shirley, I can but use the words that Swinburne himself applied to Shirley's works: the several passages into which his essay might be separated, "fall naturally into three categories or classes: those in the first class are very good,

[450]

those in the second class are very fair, those in the third class are very poor" (p. 478). Those passages that deal with *The Traitor* and *The Example* "belong beyond all question to the first class"; those that deal with certain of the realistic comedies "stand high in the second"; of the remaining passages, a majority belong, beyond all question, to the third. In short, one must say of Swinburne's essay as he says of Shirley's plays: "A considerable section . . . is taken up by such vapid and colorless sketches, such mere shadows or phantoms of invertebrate and bloodless fancy, as leave no trace behind on the memory but a sense of tedious vanity and unprofitable promptitude of apparently copious but actually sterile invention. . . . They never . . . sink below a certain modest level of passable craftsmanship and humble merit; but they never rise into palpable distinction or cohere into substantial form. . . . You read them, and feel next day as if you had read nothing" (p. 461).

From the more acceptable portions of the essay, I have quoted at length in my chapters on *The Traitor* and *The Example*. Here, however, in view of the supposed importance of Swinburne's contribution, I must not leave unnoted three defects.

In the first place, Swinburne's knowledge of the plays he criticizes is often inaccurate and superficial. In an article nearly eleven thousand words in length, he dismisses twelve plays with an average of six and one fourth lines apiece. Among these, he grants to *The Royal Master,* one of the most delightful of the comedies, but forty-two words, and to *The Duke's Mistress,* twenty-five. Even *The Cardinal,* which Shirley deemed his greatest play, and to which most critics give at least the second place, Swinburne dismisses with a perfunctory quarter-page—one hundred and forty four words. If Swinburne's criticisms were illuminating, we could forgive their brevity; but they are not. They have, despite their dogmatism, the tone of one who has not studied but skimmed, of the reader he himself describes, "who spends *an hour or so*" (p. 475) in the perusal of a five-act play, of the reviewer who must bolt thirty-three plays in quick succession, without time for mastication or digestion. This haste is evident not only in his superficial treatment of what he deems (not always justly) the less important plays, but even in those that he attempts to treat most thoroughly. In his criticism of *The Traitor,* for example, his careless reading of the opening scene leads him into a radical misconception of Shirley's motivation. Of the character of Cosmo, he remarks: "The unreal unselfishness of unnatural devotion and the sentimental vehemence of moral paradox, which mark the decline of English tragedy from the level of Shakespeare's more immediate followers, are flagrant in the folly of such a conception as this of a lover who insists on resigning his mistress against her will to a friend already betrothed or pledged in honor to another woman" (p. 467). Now the fact is, that unselfishness and devotion and sentimental vehemence are precisely the qualities most conspicuously lacking in the character of Shirley's Cosmo in the scene discussed. If ever a man was actuated by cowardly and coldly selfish policy, that man was Cosmo. He saw, behind the manœuvering

[451]

of his friend Pisano and Pisano's servant, the controlling hand of the powerful and dangerous Lorenzo, and he executed an instantaneous retreat. "There is an engine levell'd at my fate," he says, "and I must arm" (*The Traitor*, I, i; *Works*, II, 104). For this reason—not from devotion to his friend—did Cosmo surrender his betrothed. Such is Swinburne's knowledge of what he accounts (p. 467) "the one play which gives its author a place among the tragic poets of Shakespeare's age and country"! If a critic is thus superficial where he aims to do his best, what is he at his worst?

This discussion of Swinburne's superficial and inaccurate knowledge of the plays of Shirley, leads directly to the second count in our indictment: that his style is often neither specific nor becoming. For lack of facts, he indulges in opprobrious generalizations; having no case, he abuses the opposing counsel. He talks of "the idiotic monstrosity of speculative impudence" (p. 473); of "the most injudicious and ineffectual perversity or debility of devotion" (p. 475); of plays that are "anæmic and invertebrate" (p. 462); of another play that is "anæmic and invertebrate" (p. 471); of fancy that is "invertebrate and bloodless" (p. 461); of "invertebrate versification" (p. 475); of a "feebly preposterous and impotently imitative abortion" (pp. 462–463); and of a "preposterous and irritating inanity of impotent invention" (p. 463).

Third and lastly, Swinburne's indifference to accuracy of fact leads him repeatedly into errors of statement and of inference. I do not now refer to his unqualified ascription of *The Country Captain* to our dramatist, although here, at least, Swinburne would rush in where scholars fear to tread. I refer rather to matters in which accuracy and certainty might have been had almost for the asking. For example, any appropriate reference-books would have told him that Charles I came to the throne in March, 1625, and that Shirley's *The Grateful Servant* was licensed November 3, 1629, full four years later; yet Swinburne asserts that "Charles I had been six months on the throne when this comedy was licensed" (p. 466). Again, in his discussion of Shirley's comedy *The Ball*, Swinburne at once sneers at the ladies and their lovers as being "lamentably shadowy and shapeless" (p. 470), misquotes Shirley's own reference to his having been "bribed to a modest expression of their antic gambols" (p. 471), and scoffs at the correctness of Shirley's explanation (p. 471). Yet he had but to turn to the oft-quoted extract from Herbert's office-book to find a full and official record of the censoring of this play (Malone's *Shakspere*, 1821, III, 231–232), a record which not only proves the essential truth of Shirley's statement but accounts for the shadowiness and shapelessness of Shirley's lords and ladies in *The Ball*.

In these three respects, then—in a frequent superficiality of acquaintance with the plays discussed, in a tendency to substitute adjectives for specific facts, and in a seeming indifference to accuracy in matters of exact scholarship—Swinburne's essay is not all that we could wish. Happy were he, could we say of his position among Shirley's critics as he says of the place of James Shirley among English poets: "The place of Swinburne among the critics of Shirley 'is naturally unpretentious and modest: it is indisputably authentic and secure' " (p. 478).

THORNDIKE, A. H.

Tragedy. By Ashley H. Thorndike, Professor of English in Columbia University. Author of "The Influence of Beaumont and Fletcher on Shakspere." Boston and New York . . . [1908].

Pages 229–234 constitute a brief but acceptable account of Shirley's tragedies. See also pp. 199, 235, 237, 238, 240, 251, 252, 255, 256, 282, 344.

TIERNEY, M. A.

The History and Antiquities of the Castle and Town of Arundel; including the Biography of its Earls, from the Conquest to the Present Time. By the Rev. M. A. Tierney, F.S.A., Chaplain to his Grace the Duke of Norfolk. Vol. I. London: . . . 1834.

In Volume I, on p. 67, note (*a*) reads as follows:

"Sir Ed. Bishop was the second Baronet of that name, of Parham, in Sussex. In the 'Weekly account of certain special passages, &c. from Wednesday, Jan. 3, to the 10th of the same, 1644,' he is said to be the person 'who some yeares since embrued his wilful hands in the blood of Master Henry Sherley, kinsman to Mr. James Sherley, the Playwright, and who did excel him in that faculty.' "

TUPPER, JAMES W.

The Relation of the Heroic Play to the Romances of Beaumont and Fletcher.

Being pp. 584–621 in:

Publications of the Modern Language Association of America . . . Vol. XX. New Series, Vol. XIII. . . . Baltimore. 1905.

This article makes no mention of the plays of Shirley; but it clears the way for a study of the relation of Shirley's dramatic romances to the heroic drama of the Restoration.

VEGA CARPIO, LOPE DE.

Comedia Famosa de Don Lope de Cardona.

In:

Decima Parte de las Comedias de Lope de Vega Carpio, familiar del santo oficio: sacadas de sus originales. Dirigidas por el mismo al Exemo Sr Marques de Santa Cruz, Capitan general de la Esquadro de España. Madrid: año 1620.

In the Ticknor Collection, Boston Public Library: **D:148.3, Vol. x. This play is the source of a portion of Shirley's romantic comedy *The Young Admiral*. Stiefel quotes an edition of 1618.

VISITATION OF LONDON.

The Publications of the Harleian Society. Established A.D. MD CCC LXIX. Volume XVII. For the year MD CCC LXXXIII. The Visitation of London, Anno Domini 1633, 1634, and 1635. Made by Sr. Henry St. George, Kt., Richmond Herald, and Deputy and Marshal to Sr. Richard St. George, Kt., Clarencieux King of Arms. Volume II. Edited by Joseph Jackson Howard, LL.D., F.S.A. London: 1883.

The pedigrees and arms of James Shirley, goldsmith, of London, and of his brother John, pp. 235–236, appear to forbid the assumption that James Shirley the dramatist was a member of their family.

WARD, A. W.

James Shirley.
Being pp. 126–133 in:
Dictionary of National Biography. Edited by Sidney Lee. Vol. LII. Shearman—Smirke. New York . . . London . . . 1897.

Although sometimes overpositive concerning matters still uncertain, this article must be accounted a scholarly summary of the facts of Shirley's life. Unfortunately, however, it is marred by no less than thirteen typographical errors.

Page 126, second column, line 35: The date of *St. Albans* should be "14 Feb. 1639/40," not "1639."

Page 126, second column, line 38: The date of the baptism of Mathias Shirley should be "26 Feb. 1624/5," not "1624."

Page 126, second column, line 48: The date of *Love Tricks* should be "10 Feb. 1624/5," not "4 Feb. 1625/6."

Page 128, first column, line 10: The date of *The Traitor* should be "1635," not "1638."

Page 128, first column, line 46: Read "the hitherto unprinted dramas by Beaumont and Fletcher," not "ten hitherto unprinted dramas."

Page 130, second column, line 28: The statement that *The Wedding* was "licensed 9 Feb. 1626" and the reference to Fleay as authority on the point, are incorrect in several ways. The date is a misprint, occasioned by a repetition of the date of *The Maid's Revenge*, above: no record of the licensing of *The Wedding* has been preserved. Fleay's hypothesis concerns not the licensing but the acting of *The Wedding;* and the date he gives is not "9 Feb." but May 31.

Page 131, first column, line 39: The date of *The Arcadia* should be "1640," not "1614."

Page 132, first column, line 34: The initials should be "T. B.," not "J. B."

Page 132, second column, line 10: The date on which *The Doubtful Heir* was printed as one of *Six New Playes* should not be "1654." The date on the title-page of *The Doubtful Heir* is "1652"; that on the joint title-page of *Six New Playes* is "1653."

Page 132, second column, line 34: The date of *The Duke* should be "17 May," not "7 May."

Page 133, first column, line 44: The date of *The Beauties* should be "1633," not "1643."

Page 133, first column, line 48: For *"Looke to the Ladies"* read, *"Looke to the Ladie."*

Page 133, second column, line 21: For "T. G. Fleay" read "F. G. Fleay."

WARD, A. W.

A History of English Dramatic Literature to the Death of Queen Anne. By Adolphus William Ward, Litt.D., Hon. LL.D. . . . New and Revised Edition. Vol. III. London . . . New York . . . 1899. . . .

The account of Shirley's plays, III, 89–125, is, for the most part, excellent. Ward's chief weakness, perhaps, results from his ignorance of the work of Stiefel concerning Shirley's debt to Spanish sources. A few misprints, copied from Ward's article in the *Dictionary of National Biography,* occur.

WARD, A. W.

James Shirley. The Royal Master. Edited with Critical Essay and Notes by Sir Adolphus William Ward, Litt.D., F.B.A., Master of Peterhouse, Cambridge.

Being pp. 545–652 in:

Representative English Comedies . . . [edited by] . . . Charles Mills Gayley . . . Volume III. . . . New York, . . . 1914.

The Critical Essay occupies pp. 547–562.

JAMES SHIRLEY, DRAMATIST

WHITELOCKE, BULSTRODE. (ANON.)

Memorials of the English Affairs: or an historical account of what passed from the beginning of the reign of King Charles the First to King Charles the Second his happy Restauration . . . London. . . . MDCLXXXII.

Pages 18–21 give an elaborate account of the presentation of Shirley's *Triumph of Peace* by the Inns of Court, but make no direct mention of the dramatist.

WILSON, H. B.

The History of Merchant Taylors' School, from its foundation to the present time. In two parts. I. Of its founders, patrons, benefactors, and masters. II. Of its principal scholars. By the Rev. H. B. Wilson, B.D., Second Under Master . . . London: 1812. . . .

The second volume (1814) contains the best of Wood and Whitelocke, but no record of Shirley's life at the school. See Volume II, pp. 672–675, 693, 710, 741, 779, 792–794.

WINSTANLEY, WILLIAM.

The Lives of the most famous English Poets, or the honour of Parnassus; in a brief essay of the works and writings of above two hundred of them, from the time of K. William the Conqueror to the reign of his present majesty King James II. . . . Written by William Winstanley, author of the English Worthies. . . . London, . . . 1687.

The notice of Shirley, pp. 138–139, is but a paraphrase of that by Edward Phillips, 1675.

WOOD, ANTHONY À.

Athenæ Oxonienses. An Exact History of all the Writers and Bishops who have had their Education in the most ancient and famous University of Oxford, from the Fifteenth Year of King Henry the Seventh, Dom. 1500, to the End of the Year 1690. Representing the Birth, Fortune, Preferment, and Death of all those Authors and Prelates, the great Accidents of their Lives, and

the Fate and Character of their Writings. To which are added
the Fasti or Annals, of the said University. The Second Volume,
Compleating the whole Work.—Antiquam exquirite Matrem.
Virgil. London: Printed for Tho. Bennet at the Half-Moon in
S. Pauls Churchyard, MDCXCII.

Wood's account of Shirley, pp. 260–262, is the earliest biographical
sketch of him that we possess. Subsequent biographers have been content
to cite Wood as an authority, forgetful of the fact that the *Athenæ* appeared in 1691, almost half a century after the closing of the theaters,
and a full quarter-century after Shirley's death. On one point, the age
of the dramatist at his death, we have documentary grounds for believing
Wood to be in error. That he has made no other errors is scarcely
probable.

The first volume is dated 1691.

WOOD, ANTHONY À.

Athenæ Oxonienses. An Exact History of all the Writers and
Bishops who have had their education in the University of Oxford.
To which are added the Fasti, or annals of the said University.
By Anthony à Wood, M.A., of Merton College. A new edition
with additions, and a continuation by Philip Bliss, fellow of St.
John's College. Vol. III. . . . London: . . . 1817.

In this edition the account of Shirley appears in Vol. III, pp. 737–744.

WOOD, ANTHONY À.

The Life of Anthony à Wood, from the Year 1632 to 1672,
written by himself, and published by Mr. Thomas Hearne. Now
continued to the time of his death from authentic materials. The
whole illustrated with notes and the addition of several curious
original papers never before printed. Oxford, . . . M DCC
LXXII. . . .

Contained in:

The Lives of those eminent antiquaries John Leland, Thomas
Hearne, and Anthony à Wood; with an authentick account of their
respective writings and publications, from Original Papers. In
which are occasionally inserted memoirs relating to many eminent
persons and various parts of Literature. Also several engravings

of antiquity never before published.   In two volumes.   Vol. II.
Oxford: . . . M DCC LXXII.

This detailed chronicle of the life of Wood, written by the antiquarian
himself, contributes nothing to warrant a belief that he was personally
acquainted with James Shirley.

WRIGHT, JAMES. (ANON.)

A Dialogue on Plays and Players.
Being pp. i–xxxvii in Dodsley's
A Select Collection of Old Plays.   Volume the Eleventh.   Lon-
don: Printed for R. Dodsley in Pall-Mall.   M.DCC.XLIV.

This *Dialogue* is the *Historia Histrionica.*

WRIGHT, JAMES. (ANON.)

Historia Histrionica.
Being pp. 337–363 in Dodsley's
A Select Collection of Old Plays. . . . The Second Edition,
. . . Volume XII.   London, . . . MDCCLXXX.

WRIGHT, JAMES. (ANON.)

Historia Histrionica.
Being pp. cxxxix–clxix in Dodsley's
A Select Collection of Old Plays. . . . Vol. I.   A New Edi-
tion: . . . London. . . . MDCCCXXV.

WRIGHT, JAMES. (ANON.)

Historia Histrionica.   An Historical Account of the English
Stage; showing the Ancient Uses, Improvement, and Perfection
of Dramatic Representations, in this Nation.   In a Dialogue of
Plays and Players.—Olim meminisse juvabit.   London.   Printed
by G. Croom, for William Haws, at the Rose in Ludgate-Street.
1699. 8°.

Being pp. 399–431 in:
A Select Collection of Old English Plays.   Originally published by Robert Dodsley in the year 1744.   Fourth Edition, now

first chronologically arranged, revised, and enlarged with the notes of all the commentators, and new notes by W. Carew Hazlitt. Volume the Fifteenth. London: . . . 1876.

The principal references to Shirley's plays occur in the following passage, pp. 404–405:

"Hart and Clun were bred up boys at the Blackfriars, and acted women's parts. Hart was Robinson's boy or apprentice; he acted the Duchess in the tragedy of *The Cardinal,* which was the first part that gave him reputation. Cartwright and Wintershal belonged to the Private House in Salisbury Court; Burt was a boy, first under Shank at the Blackfriars, then under Beeston at the Cockpit; and Mohun and Shatterel were in the same condition with him at the last place. There Burt used to play the principal women's parts, in particular Clariana, in *Love's Cruelty;* and at the same time Mohun acted Bellamente, which part he retained after the Restoration."

See also the reference to *The Wedding,* p. 405.

INDEX

[461]

INDEX

INDEX

INDEX

INDEX

[465]

INDEX

Paulina (in *The Sisters*), 363-365, 385
Peeke, Richard, 63, 64, 66, 423, 442
Peele, George, 173
Pembroke and Montgomery, Philip, Earl of; Lord Chamberlain, 125-126, 129, 424, 426, 438
Pepys, Samuel, 155, 156, 157, 161, 229, 442
Phenik, G., 11, 151, 161, 409
Philaster, 169, 180, 242, 274
Phillips, Edward, 5, 397, 423, 436, 443
Philoclea, 416
Phœnix, The (The Cockpit; the Private House in Drury Lane), 41, 42, 43, 44, 57, 71, 75, 84, 95, 96, 99, 100, 101, 105, 106, 123, 127, 128, 130, 152, 385, 401, 402, 403, 404, 405, 406, 407, 408, 413, 414, 426, 459
Pike. See Peeke
Piperollo (in *The Sisters*), 365-371, 392
Plague in London, 92-93, 111, 120, 127, 131
Playford, J., 413
Playhouse, The Elizabethan. See Lawrence, W. J.
Plays and Puritans. See Kingsley
Plays, A Select Collection of Old. See Dodsley
Plays of the King's Men in 1641. See Chambers
Plot, Sir Solitary (in *The Example*), 258-259, 393
Plan of this monograph, 6, 7, 382
Poems, 137, **138-140**, 145, 153, 161, 408, 419, 434
Poets, English, The Lives of the most famous. See Winstanley
Politician, The, **47-54**, 66, 104, 128, 129, 130, 132, 144, 146, **147**, 161, 289, 292, 305, **307-312**, 313, 314, 319, 320, 381, 390, 396, **412**, 419, 434, 436
Politique Father, The, 46, **47-62**, **108**, 132, 142, 147, 169, 242, 289, 292, 320, 321, **336-342**, 362, 379, 387, 389, 392. See *The Brothers* of 1652.
Polonius, 170
Private House in Drury Lane. See Phœnix
Private House in Salisbury Court. See Salisbury Court
Protectorate, 3
Prynne, William, 4, 72, **76-79**, 245, 443
Publication, Right of, 125-126
Publications of the Modern Language Association. See Tupper
Pumicestone (in *The Example*), 258, 393

QUARREL with the Queen's men, Shirley's alleged, 109, **122-131**, 133, 385

Quarterly Review, The, 419, 429, 432, 444
Queen's men. See Servants, Her Majesty's

RAWBONE (in *The Wedding*), 179, 180, 392
Red Bull actors, 154
Register Booke, The, Belonging to the Parish Church of S. Giles without Cripplegate. See St. Giles, Cripplegate
Register of Merchant Taylors' School, MS. See Merchant Taylors' School
Register of the Scholars admitted to Merchant Taylors' School, A. See Robinson
[Register of] St. Giles in ye Fields. 1638-68. See St. Giles in the Fields
Register of St. Mary Woolchurch. See St. Mary Woolchurch
Registers of . . . S. Mary Woolnoth and S. Mary Woolchurch Haw, Transcript of the. See St. Mary Woolchurch
Relation of the Heroic Play to the Romances of Beaumont and Fletcher, The. See Tupper
Relations of Shirley's Plays to the Elizabethan Drama, The. See Forsythe
Representative English Comedies. See Gayley
Restoration, The, 3, 153 154, 222, 277, 280, 307, 379, 383
Revels, Company of his Majesty's, 41, 44, 51, 57, 127, 130, 402
Revels, Master of. See Herbert, Sir Henry
Revenge of Bussy D'Ambois, The. See Chapman
Ristine, F. H., 445
Rivers, Mr., 414-415, 432, 445
Robinson, C. J., 445
Robinson, Humphrey, 143, 144, 409, 410, 411
Romances of Beaumont and Fletcher, The Relation of the Heroic Play to the. See Tupper
Romanische Forschungen. See Stiefel
Romantic Comedy, 5, **169**, 182, 184, 191, 242, 247, 254, 262, 263, 275, 288, 292, 303, 330, 361, 362, 371, 379, 381, 388, 391, 393, **394-395**
Romantic Tragedy, 5, 108, **169**, 170, 182, 184, 198, 201, 220, 222, 254, 274, 280, 287, 292, 307, 312, 344, 379, 381, 383, 388, 391, 393, **395-396**
Rome, Church of, 31, 32, 33, 66-67, 68
Romeo and Juliet, 169
Rosania (The Doubtful Heir), 50, 54, 60, 118, 124, 132, 142, 289

INDEX

[469]

INDEX

INDEX